PSYCHOLOGICAL DEVELOPMENT FROM INFANCY:
Image to Intention

CROSSCURRENTS IN CONTEMPORARY PSYCHOLOGY

A series of volumes edited by Marc H. Bornstein
Princeton University

1979 PSYCHOLOGICAL DEVELOPMENT FROM INFANCY:
Image to Intention
BORNSTEIN AND KESSEN

PSYCHOLOGICAL DEVELOPMENT FROM INFANCY:
Image to Intention

Edited by

MARC H. BORNSTEIN
PRINCETON UNIVERSITY

WILLIAM KESSEN
YALE UNIVERSITY

 LAWRENCE ERLBAUM ASSOCIATES, PUBLISHERS
1979   Hillsdale, New Jersey

DISTRIBUTED BY THE HALSTED PRESS DIVISION OF
JOHN WILEY & SONS
New York   Toronto   London   Sydney

Lawrence Erlbaum Associates, Inc., Publishers
62 Maria Drive
Hillsdale, New Jersey 07642

Distributed solely by Halsted Press Division
John Wiley & Sons, Inc., New York

Library of Congress Cataloging in Publication Data

Main entry under title:

Psychological development from infancy.

   (Crosscurrents in contemporary psychology)
   Includes bibliographies and indexes.
   1. Infant psychology.   2. Developmental
psychology.   I. Bornstein, Marc H.   II. Kessen,
William.   III. Series.   [DNLM: 1. Child development.
2. Child psychology.   3. Human development.
WS105.3 P9743]
BF723.16P78   155.4   78-27566
ISBN 0-470-26603-1

155.4
Bok
pp

62241

Printed in the United States of America

Series Prologue

CROSSCURRENTS IN CONTEMPORARY PSYCHOLOGY

Psychology is today an increasingly diversified, sophisticated, pluralistic, and specialized discipline. Research investigators venture beyond the confines of their narrow subdiscipline only rarely; typically to do so requires a seemingly heroic effort. Nonetheless, regardless of specialty, psychologists frequently encounter similar problems, ask similar questions, and share similar concerns. Yet there are far too few forums for the expression or investigation of common supradisciplinary problems, questions, or concerns. The series *Crosscurrents in Contemporary Psychology* is intended to serve as such a forum.

The principal aim of this series is to provide integrated perspectives on supradisciplinary issues in psychology and therefore to countervail the growing tendency toward specialization. The contributions to this series are calculated to explore issues that cross psychological subdisciplines. Each volume will take a different perspective or level of analysis and will concern itself with a different specific intra-disciplinary theme. Each volume will interrelate psychological subdisciplines and a variety of disciplines outside psychology.

Because of the nature and intent of this series, its contributing authors come from the broad spectrum of psychologists and social scientists. Indeed, contributions from anthropology to zoology are appropriate. Typically, however, the authors are noted authorities actively contributing to the contemporary psychological literature.

Although each volume in the series is self-contained, comprehensive, and valuable of itself to the discipline, the series of books as a group endeavors to bring new or shared perspectives to bear on a wide variety of topics in psychological thought and research. As a consequence of this structure and the flexibility and scope it provides, books in the series *Crosscurrents in Contemporary Psychology* will appeal, individually or as a group, to psychologists with diverse interests.

Crosscurrents in Contemporary Psychology is a series whose stated intent is to explore a broader range of supradisciplinary issues in psychology. In its concern with larger problems, the series is devoted to a growth of interest in the interconnectedness of research, method, and theory in psychological study.

Marc H. Bornstein
Editor

Contributors to This Volume

Marc H. Bornstein, *Department of Psychology, Princeton University, Princeton, New Jersey 08540*

David Elkind, *Eliot Pierson Department of Child Study, Tufts University, Medford, Massachusetts 02155*

Joseph F. Fagan, III, *Department of Psychology, Case Western Reserve University, Cleveland, Ohio 44106*

Eleanor J. Gibson, *Department of Psychology, Cornell University, Ithaca, New York 14853*

Adrienne E. Harris, *Department of Psychology, Rutgers University, Newark, New Jersey 07102*

Jerome Kagan, *Department of Psychology and Social Relations, Harvard University, Cambridge, Massachusetts 02138*

William Kessen, *Department of Psychology, Yale University, New Haven, Connecticut 06520*

Claire B. Kopp, *Department of Pediatrics, University of California School of Medicine, Los Angeles, California 90024*

Jean Matter Mandler, *Department of Psychology, University of California at San Diego, La Jolla, California 92093*

Robert B. McCall, *Boys Town Center for the Study of Youth Development, Boys Town, Nebraska 68010*

Paul Mussen, *Institute of Human Development, University of California at Berkeley, Berkeley, California 94720*

Katherine Nelson, *Graduate Center, City University of New York, New York, New York 10031*

Hanuš Papoušek, *Entwicklungspsychobiologie, Max-Plank-Institute für Psychiatrie, 8-München-40, West Germany*

Herbert L. Pick, Jr., *Center for Research in Human Learning, University of Minnesota, Minneapolis, Minnesota 55455*

John J. Rieser, *Department of Psychology, George Peabody College, Nashville, Tennessee 37203*

Arnold J. Sameroff, *Institute for the Study of Developmental Disabilities, University of Illinois at Chicago Circle, Chicago, Illinois 60680*

H. Rudolph Schaffer, *Department of Psychology, University of Strathclyde, Glasgow, Scotland G1 1RD, United Kingdom*

Albert Yonas, *Center for Research in Human Learning, University of Minnesota, Minneapolis, Minnesota 55455*

Contents

PART II: COGNITIVE DEVELOPMENT

Preface

As one reads or surveys the literature in developmental psychology, two themes consistently reappear. First, infancy is held to be a unique period of human development. In many respects, infants have been segregated practically and experimentally from the psychological study of the life span, and the sociology of infancy studies has left the scientific study of infants somewhat secluded. Nevertheless, a second, seemingly contradictory theme exists in theories of development. Many commentators assert that higher order, mature behaviors assume or reflect or continue lower order behaviors found in infancy. Both positions are unarguable, and both are more than implicit in developmental thought. Yet to a certain degree these two positions have not been properly reconciled. Just how are infancy and later development interrelated?

The original impetus for this book derived from our observation of the paradox of uniqueness and continuity. We came to believe that it would be useful for the field of developmental studies if a group of active and prominent investigators addressed the issue of development from infancy. In adopting the theme *Psychological Development from Infancy,* we hoped that the contributors to this book would address the nodal question of what precursors to later cognitive and social development may be identified in early infancy.

Because of historical precedent (or accident), the task we assigned was obviously not easy to meet. Nevertheless, our contributors responded estimably and the result is, we believe, a fortunate advance for developmental thought. We take this opportunity to thank them formally for their efforts and to thank E.J. Gibson of Cornell University, J. Mandler of the University of

California, San Diego, and P. Mussen of the Institute of Human Development at the University of California, Berkeley, who agreed to read and assess in printed commentary the contributions to this book. We believe that these commentary sections enrich the original contributions by providing readers with the interpretations and assessments of other distinguished scholars.

The contributions to this collection are organized along traditional lines in developmental psychology, distinguishing among perceptual, motor, cognitive, language, and social development. Obviously and correctly, our contributors did not feel constrained by our arbitrary divisions, and there is, as a consequence, considerable spillage of interest and topics among the chapters. The commentators reflect this pluralism as well.

Several audiences will find this book of interest. Because it represents recent, inclusive, and substantive statements by prominent investigators in developmental psychology, it meets the needs of specialists in the several areas of psychological development. As a whole it also meets the needs of a variety of advanced students and research investigators in psychology who are interested in the origins and ontogeny of behavior. Finally, the topics covered explore motor, perceptual, cognitive, language, and social development from empirical as well as theoretical vantages. We believe, therefore, that this book will be read profitably by students as well as by our professional colleagues.

Several good workers aided in the preparation of this volume. We especially thank Sondra Guideman, Rose Fioravanti, Julie Grabel, Beverly Hoffmann, Sharon Olsen, Arlene Rakower, Liz Novins, and Carol Smith for their good humor and patient assistance in the production of the book.

Marc H. Bornstein
William Kessen

For our parents

PSYCHOLOGICAL DEVELOPMENT FROM INFANCY:
Image to Intention

1 Introduction

William Kessen
Yale University

Not so long ago, we had occasion to celebrate the centenary of developmental psychology, an anniversary marked by the publication of Charles Darwin's notes on son Doddy in *Mind.* The event was noteworthy for several reasons, but, for those of us who try to make sense of early human mind, Darwin's biographical sketch claims our current attention primarily for two reasons. In the first place, we have lived so long with the idea of continuous development, both in its phylogenetic and its ontogenetic forms, that it is difficult for us to reclaim the revolutionary character of Darwin's proposals about the lives of children. Second, there are signs in contemporary communities that the hundredth birthday of evolutionary ontogenesis may also mark its decline, even its imminent demise. Should we maintain our commitment to the notion of continuous connected human development from infancy to adulthood?

It is worth remembering how the scientific study of children was twinned at its birth with the larger developmental principle that all life derives from its past and grows toward its future. Spencer, who had the bad luck to publish his *Principles of Psychology* just four years before the appearance of *The Origin of Species,* pushed the application of evolutionary principles to psychology as hard as he could and, along the way, he proposed the apparently eternal succession of reflex, instinct, memory, reason, feeling, and will. Yet even Spencer did not make the ontogenetic leap. For him, the hierarchical order of "the growth of intelligence" was a *phylogenetic* succession. As he said (1899):

1

> ... high intelligence ... lies latent in the brain of the infant. ... Thus it happens that faculties ... which scarcely exist in some inferior human races, become congenital in superior ones. Thus it happens that out of savages unable to count up to the number of their fingers, and speaking a language containing only nouns and verbs, arise at length our Newtons and Shakspeares [p. 471].

For Spencer, as for all other evolutionists of his time, the only hope for ontogenetic change was in waiting for the tedious flow of phylogenetic change. The developmental revolution was to come in the recognition that Newton and Shakespeare were epigenetically available even in the savage Papuan.

In the last 20 years of the nineteenth century, the ontogenetic principle burst into life. Preyer, Taine, Hall, and Chamberlain were but the most audible proclaimers of the new doctrine—ascribed to Haekel but in the very air—*ontogeny recapitulates phylogeny*. In the life of the child could be seen the life of the race and, happy biconditional, in the life of the race could be seen the life of the child. The feverish recognition of the applicability of the developmental principle to the growth of the child produced a literature of enthusiasm that can best be compared with William Jennings Bryan's speeches on the virtue of silver.

But there was a way to go yet. The child as a reflection of the species is a static and, as it turned out, not a richly productive theoretical advance. It was left to James Mark Baldwin and Sigmund Freud to take the liberating next step—the step to epigenesis. Yes, they said in their very different ways, there are analogies (perhaps even homologies) between the growth of the mind and the growth of the species, but they are not *analogies of content* (Spencer's reflex to Spencer's will); they are *analogies of construction*. Each higher level of functioning does not lie latent in the baby, awaiting its scheduled call. Rather, each developmental moment is a moment of creation, an ever-recurring exchange between what the child's mind is and what his experience asks of him. Baldwin (1895) made the contrast between antique doctrines and the new vision:

> The old argument was this, — ... consciousness reveals certain great ideas as simple and original. ... If you do not find them in the child-mind, then you must read them into it.
>
> The genetic idea reverses all this. Instead of a fixed substance, we have the conception of a growing, developing activity. ... Are there principles in the adult consciousness which do not appear in the child consciousness; then the adult consciousness must, if possible, be interpreted by *principles* present in the child consciousness; and when this is not possible, the *conditions* under which these later principles take their rise and get the development must still be adequately explored [p. 2f.; italics mine].

Development can be understood only as a continuous interplay of principles and conditions, the dance of ontogenetic adaptation.

The ontogenetic principle — regularity of progression — and the more demanding epigenetic principle—continuous adaptation—have been adhered to, give a little, take a little, for the last 100 years of child study. To be sure, the range of variation within the general adherence has been wide — Freud and Gesell and Piaget and Skinner all claim the sensible epigenetic middle ground. Now, the new dialecticians have rediscovered Baldwin, and the skeptical historian of developmental psychology may wonder whether many prized ideas in our study of children have not been sidesteps in evasion of the implications of an epigenetic analysis. Whatever our theoretical predisposition, most of us prefer conceptions of the child that do not require constant revision. The literature is not crowded with specific testable propositions about how the child's mind at a particular moment in his life is transformed by his environment or his experience to a new level of functioning.

The editors' sense that concrete proposals for the working of epigenetic change are rare and their recognition of the recent tendency, noted earlier, to be dubious about the developmental principle altogether led to the book that lies before you. In its most general form, the question we asked of our developmental colleagues was: Can we illustrate, in theory and data, the development of the child from one specifiable period of his life to another? In its narrower form, the question reads: Can we show, specifically and rigorously, how the infant becomes the noninfant?

Let us say briefly why we chose infancy as the testing ground for the more general question.

No one can speak wisely about all of development; some scissions must be made in the 70-year strand in order to avoid vacuous speculation. Readers of textbooks and of scholarly treatises as well are familiar with our favorite lines of division — between preschool and school, between adolescence and adulthood, between maturity and senility. The most common cutting point, and the only one that runs back to antiquity and that has never left modern expositions of development, is the line between the infant and the noninfant. The segregation of talkers from nontalkers—to pick the most persistent definition of the boundary—has profound cultural roots in dress, games, caretaking, expectations of responsibility, and ascriptions of competence, but the boundary has more academic marks. The methods that are used to study the behavior of the littlest people do not often overlap the methods used to study *what are purported to be the same conceptual issues* in older children. The theories used by those of us who look at babies and those who look at, say, the preschool child are different in central propositions as well as in parameters. Even the marks of mind that we observe—the basic "responses" of legendary consequence— shift markedly when we go from newborns to yearlings to 2-year-olds. There is not room here to explore many of the implications of the infant–noninfant wall that developmental psychology faces, but several summary notes will help get you ready for the chapters of the present book. Some developmental psychologists have effectively denied the boundary by concentrating their attention on processes assumed to be general. The most widely held such functional position has been maintained by the researchers committed to a learning analysis of behavioral change over age. Some developmental psychologists have recognized the wall between infants and noninfants and have called on a paired proposition—the existence of stages and the operation of general theoretical principles — to handle the boundary. Psychoanalytic theorists and Piaget are chiefs here; again, the skeptical observer sees more theoretical and empirical work going on within stages than between them. Some developmental psychologists seize on concepts of continuation (temperament, IQ, social class) to pierce the wall in the ballistic assumption that there are underlying (a favorite word for all of us) regularities in personal traits. Finally, there is a new return to the oldest idea of all — that infancy is not momentously connected with the rest of the developmental course but represents a biological continuation of pregnancy, which may be interesting in its own right but need not deter us in the study of later changes with age.

The last-noted position, the indifference proposition, is rare enough to emphasize another major characteristic of the segregation between infants and noninfants. In spite of our faltering attempts to get over the wall, there had been little doubt until recently that the events of the first months of life are of far-reaching consequence for later development. Perhaps the single shared ideological commitment of learning theorists, psychoanalysts, Piagetians, Wenerians, and maturationalists has been the belief in the high significance of the early months and years of life. Personalities are shaped, basic knowledge is acquired, directions are set. In sometimes lunatic fashion, mothers are urged to perform early-days rituals of caregiving, and frights are raised about the consequence of insufficient early support to intellectual growth, all in the name of infancy's uniquely formative and defining place in life.

Thus, the editors saw a potentially productive paradox. Developmentalists study infants and noninfants in different ways, we talk about them in different ways, we have grave trouble connecting them up. Yet we persist in the rarely examined conviction that what happens to infants is a determinant of all later development. The transition from nontalker to talker seemed ideally suited to put our attention precisely on the problem of developmental transitions, their theory, and their data.

The book that follows on our introduction is made up of 11 original chapters and three commentaries on those chapters. We invited essays from 13 investigators who have worked with and thought about both infants and older children. We asked them to take some particular topic of interest to them and to attempt to make their way over, through, or around the boundary that segregates infants from noninfants. As you will see, they have carried out their assignment with uniform high intelligence and good spirit. We leave to our commentators and to our readers to judge with what success.

Amid the fine variety of the chapters you are about to read, there are some recurrent themes. First among them, naturally enough in light of our assignment, is the issue of *continuity.* Not always addressed directly, the question of getting from infant to noninfant with a coherent set of ideas is constantly present. Several other persistencies lie under the major one. *Liberation from the response* appears throughout; whether the exemplary case is drawn from perception or action, language or thought, the critical move from the conceptual importance of the visible response to the importance of the mental act that must be inferred is usual. In a happy controversial phrase from one of our authors, mind begins to control muscle. Closely tied to the peculiar reduction of the response are the problems of *context* and *decentration.* No attempt to understand perception or language (and perception and language are models for the rest of developmental study) can conscientiously ignore the troubling puzzle of how young children parcel out their experience into categories of figure and ground, of important and less important, of same and different. The development of a textured organized surrounding, in which some things go with some other things and some things matter more than other things, is a heart issue of this book. When the editors first talked about the book, we wanted to call it *From Image to Intention* in order to emphasize our conviction that *one* of the defining problems of the development from infancy to noninfancy was the coming on of plans, the child's shift from species-general solutions of presented problems to particular solutions, from solutions based on the here-and-now to solutions based on memory, symbol, and reasoning. The title was canned, but the issue remains. How does the young child move toward that less automatic, less quick, and less uniform treatment of a problem he faces that marks the transition from image to intention?

Continuity, response-to-thought, context, and image-to-intention are everywhere concerns of the book's authors. However, the best contribution of these chapters almost certainly is not in solving fundamental and general psychological questions that we can hardly put into words but rather in wrestling, specifically and concretely, with the "principles" and "conditions" that carry the child from birth to conversation.

REFERENCES

Baldwin, J. M. *Mental development in the child and the race.* New York: Macmillan, 1895.
Spencer, H. *The principles of psychology.* New York: Appleton, 1899.

PERCEPTUAL AND MOTOR DEVELOPMENT

2 Perspectives on Infant Motor System Development

Claire B. Kopp
University of California at Los Angeles

INTRODUCTION

Movement is so fundamental to human existence that performance of countless acts scarcely intrudes upon consciousness. Yet one has only to see a single individual struggling with "nonbidding" limbs in executing otherwise routine tasks to appreciate the personal significance of motor behaviors. They are means to communication, exploration, tension release, skill, self-care, mastery, and work. Furthermore, empirical studies suggest that movement contributes to learning, perception, attention, memory, problem solving, motivation, and socialization. Movement has an ubiquitous character.

Because of this and sometimes despite it, the study of movement, its origins, controls, functions, and influences, has fascinated researchers for years. Although not without controversy, historic analyses of human motor research show trends often paralleling interests evident in other areas of psychological investigation. For example, studies of adult motor performance have shifted from a product orientation to examination of links between information processing and motor performance (Irion, 1966; Pew, 1974; Stelmach, 1976). As is seen later, a similar shift from product to process has characterized research on infant motor development.

The study of acquisition of voluntary movement, only one domain of a much larger research field, has been of particular interest to developmentalists. At the very least, to scientist as well as layman, awesome transformations of infant motor patterns take place—from first rudimentary forms, to endlessly practiced transitional structures, to mature configurations skillfully executed. But beyond fascination, there is theory. Increasingly, developmentalists have thought about the significance of movement and ascribed to it a singular role in development. Infant motor acts are, after all, striking characteristics of the first two years of life and represent a common means by which the very young convey their abilities and feelings. Eventually, infant movement became the *sine qua non* of cognitive and social development. Only in the last decade or so has this view been questioned.

REFLECTIONS

To gain some perspective on ideas that governed much of our earlier thinking, it is useful to review in a summary way former periods of theory and research. This review is selective and arbitrary. For example, for organizational purposes four phases of research have been delineated, covering the period from the turn of the century to the present time. Although several common threads link the phases, one of the most striking concerns the emphasis and interest developmentalists placed on the age period of motor acquisition. Thus, almost all the ensuing discussion relates to the first year of life.

The first phase, spanning several decades (through the 1940s), was the "cataloging" period when details concerning the ontogeny of prehension and postural control were assiduously collected (Bayley, 1935; Castner, 1932; Gesell, 1929a; Gesell & Thompson, 1934; Halverson, 1931; Hetzer & Wolf, 1928; McGraw, 1935, 1943; Shirley, 1931). This was the necessary descriptive period in the first stage of scientific inquiry.

During this period, gathering descriptions appeared to be of greater interest than investigation of issues, although there were a few notable exceptions. Among them, for example, was Dennis's (1941) study of developmental rates of prehension, locomotion, and social responses of twins reared under restrictive conditions. Dennis, following Gesell's (1929a, 1929b) maturational bias, hypothesized a greater intrinsic influence on development than would be observed consequent to specific experiential conditions. Although he anticipated few differences in rates of change between his twins and infants reared in more usual home situations, his results only partially confirmed his expectations. The twins evidenced considerable delay on developmental items that involved social responses or practice. In contrast to Dennis, Watson and his associates (Jones, 1926; Watson & Watson, 1921) approached the study of motor behaviors from the vantage point of a behaviorist. As such, they attempted to teach prehension to very young infants; Watson's results were disappointingly negative.

The major conceptual theme emerging from this period inextricably linked infant motor development to growth of the mind. Baldly stated, without activity there could be no infant intellect — the beginnings of prehension represented the growth of mind (Gesell, 1929a). Not only was Gesell one of the foremost proponents of this view; he also proposed that rate of prehensile change reflected growth of mind. Thus, the belief spread that motor acts — particularly those involving hands — were necessary preconditions to mentality and that motor precocity was advantageous. Virtually no one at the time questioned this motor-mental bond (see an earlier review by Wellman, 1931); what caused controversy was the issue of rate with respect to its consequences (Bayley, 1935; McGraw, 1935). Neither Bayley's nor McGraw's data supported Gesell's contention, but their findings were ignored for many years.

Gesell, a prodigious, gifted writer, was fascinated by Darwin, evolution, studies of infancy in other species, and anthropology. He often paralleled human ontogeny with evolution. As early as 1929, Gesell (1929a) wrote that the mechanisms of evolution and individual growth had much in common but differed mainly in relation to time. "What evolution achieves in ages, the infant in his growth accomplishes in brief moments [p. 374]." Yet, Gesell continued, the infant grows and adapts in a manner comparable to the evolutionary process.

Later Gesell (1952) elaborated his evolutionary theme by noting, "In the race and in the child alike the contrivance and use of tools are closely correlated with the genesis of practical reasoning...[p. 55]." Writing in almost lyrical style, he compared (1948) infant prehensile approach movements to primitive scooping tools, repetitive banging to paleolithic stones used for splintering other stones, and pulling, pushing, and probing activities observed toward the end of the human infant's first year to possibly "retracing in a condensed manner maneuvers by which the race falteringly and accumulatively mastered the elementary physics of its environment [p. 90]."

Many of these ideas were totally alien to developmentalists of the period. Not until recently, with research from our own and other fields, have some of these views received a forum and subsequent endorsement. Nonetheless, it is a curious fact that, although Gesell's biologic, evolutionary, and maturational tenets were out of phase with and largely unacceptable to mainstream psychology, his linking motor function with growth of mind was sanctioned. The implications were profound for, to professional and parent, imperfect or late acquisition of infant motor skills spelled impairment of development or poor intellectual capability.

A second period of research (from 1960 through the early 1970s), coincident with American psychology's acceptance of Piaget's developmental theory, heralded renewed attention to infant motor acts. A conceptual unity existed between the first and second periods because Piaget (1952, 1954) highlighted sensorimotor activity as *the* basis of early and later intelligence. From the very first editions of his writings on infants to a recent theoretical chapter, he has consistently stated the necessity for infants to act upon their world in order "to know" (Piaget, 1936, 1970). Though articulated differently from Gesell's maturational theory, Piaget's mental-motor point of view was clear and was embraced by many. Inadvertently, Piagetian theory also contributed to an emphasis on *rates of change* because some developmentalists, interpreting Piaget, placed heavy emphasis on the environmental side of Piaget's organism–experience equation. Thus, experiences were favored that could foster motor precocities.

On an empirical level, the second research phase vastly differed from the preceding one. Theory, heretofore largely neglected, was used extensively to formulate research questions. For example, the classic study of White, Castle, and Held (1964) concerning the role of varied experiences on the sequence and rate of visually directed reaching, was both a test and replication of Piaget's theory and ad hoc observations. So too were the sensorimotor series designed to measure prehensile sequences (Corman & Escalona, 1969; Uzgiris & Hunt, 1966).

In this second research phase, motor behaviors were explored for their role as mediating mechanisms, not solely for description. Thus, Bruner (1968, 1970, 1973) examined prehensile skills for their instrumental value in infant play and problem solving, and Bower (1974) utilized observations of reach and grasp as a means to study early perceptual discriminations. Developmental processes were beginning to assume a role as important as developmental products.

During the 1960s the entire nature of infant research underwent rapid change with the introduction of new measurement techniques and subsequent evaluation of infant attention, discrimination, and memory. As the implications of this research began to be appreciated, questions arose about the motor-mental bond. The issue centered on abilities of motorically immature infants to learn by using auditory and visual mechanisms. Kagan (1971) was among the first to argue that these new data could not be ignored. His point of view received added support from studies of infants who had restricted motor usage. Décarie's (1969) dramatic evidence proved that infants with missing portions of limbs could develop object permanence even though object interactions were limited, and Kopp and Shaperman (1973), following a child born without any limbs, observed that even in these circumstances sensorimotor and psychometric intelligence evolved. Ever so slowly, the edifice erected on the foundation of motor-mental structure began to show cracks.

Somewhat paralleling the time span of the second research phase, a third phase appeared with an orientation derived from ethology and comparative psychology (Hess, 1970; Lorenz, 1965; Tinbergen, 1951). With an emphasis on observation and description, it appeared at first glance that ethologically based studies of infant behavior were similar to the "catalogs" generated earlier. However, this was only partially true, for on a conceptual level the approaches showed differences. In ethology, descriptions are not seen as endpoints; they are used to study genetically programmed units of behavior (smiling, crying, reaching and grasping) for their adaptive functions and as a means to delineate types of motor acts used in nonverbal communication systems (Blurton-Jones, 1972). However, on another level, ethologically oriented researchers bear resemblance to catalogers of the first phase — many disclaim the role of theory in research. With the exception of Bowlby (1969, 1973), Ainsworth (1973), and a few others, much ethological research is atheoretical by choice (Blurton-Jones, 1972). Finally, it should be noted that ethologically oriented research has been biased toward study of infant motor acts in the *service* of social interactions. Included in this category is research on smiling as well as prehension and locomotion (Ainsworth & Bell, 1970; Ainsworth & Wittig, 1969; Ambrose, 1961; Blurton-Jones & Leach, 1972; Freedman, 1964, 1974; Richards & Bernal, 1972).

In earlier phases, a central issue of dispute turned on the motor concomitants of intellectual growth; with ethologically based research, controversy arose rather in the context of social development. At the nub of the controversy was the role of infant motor acts in the development of infant-caregiver attachment. Ainsworth's (1967) seminal work in Uganda and her subsequent laboratory research relied heavily on proximity-seeking behavior of infants, whether by prehension or locomotion, as an index of attachment. As use of her experimental paradigm spread, questions were raised about insufficient emphasis on visual and vocal interactions (Ferguson, 1971; Walters & Parke, 1965). It is probably not coincidental that recent ethologically oriented studies show increased use of these measures of attachment.

Finally, a fourth phase of interest is beginning to appear. However, it is too recent to determine its direction or definition. There is a group of researchers exploring the relationship between vision and prehension. For example, the role of visual input and feedback on reaching and grasping behaviors is being examined (Field, 1976, 1977; Lasky, 1977; McDonnell, 1975). Another group of researchers has debated the concordance and integration of visual manipulative behaviors (Rubenstein, 1974; Ruff, 1976; Schaffer, 1975). The study of individual differences in prehensile acts also has received some attention (Kopp, 1974). It is far too early to state what will emanate from this phase. However, it is interesting to notice that again the focal point of interest relates to abilities that begin to emerge early in the first year.

In this brief overview, trends and issues that have dominated thinking and research in motor system development have been presented. Historically, three main themes emerge: (1) Increasingly, developmentalists have turned to theory to guide research on infant motor acts, (2) a shift has occurred from studying movement solely as product to studying movement as mediating mechanism, and (3) conceptual and research emphasis has been attached to motor changes that occur early in the first year of life. This last point brings us to the next section in which the theme of the remainder of the chapter will unfold.

AN EXPANDED VIEW

An intriguing aspect of research concerning infant motor development relates to the scientific community's preoccupation with immature forms of prehension and locomotion. Granted, substantial theoretical issues have been addressed by research, but consider the additional questions that could be posed if attention were directed to the older infant. A fundamental question should involve an inquiry into the various ways children use self-controlled prehensile and locomotor activities to facilitate or impede their own cognitive and social growth. Surely, such studies would yield meaningful implications for short- and long-term individual differences. Yet research on the infant motor system, reflecting a one-age-period interest, invariably denies significance to mediating influences of motor behaviors observed past eight or ten months of life. Therefore, succeeding portions of this chapter are devoted to a broadening of perspectives. The focus is on the entire age range of infancy—from early months through the second year.

Before proceeding, it is useful to present the framework that has guided much of this line of thinking. The influence of Piaget, Flavell, and Bruner will be apparent. Furthermore, my concern for expanding age periods of inquiry stems from a belief that in the second year of life the infant begins to obtain knowledge that *one has about one's own movement.* With functionally mature prehension and locomotion *guided* by cognition, the child begins to be aware that it is the self, not others, that controls one's actions, and that movements can be planned and directed to many activities in the service of many needs. In essence, mind begins to control muscle with consequent expansion in the ways that movement is employed as means to chosen ends. This self-generating data base stems from the profound cognitive leaps made earlier and includes awareness of means–ends relationships, object permanence, refined sensory differentiation, improved recognition memory, and so forth.

In contrast, the younger infant has far fewer *means* and understands far less than the older infant. During the period of acquisition of motor behaviors, cognition is at a primitive level. In large measure, the infant knows little of why and what is done, and the motor system bound by biological constraints reflects largely the operation of unplanned survival and adaptive mechanisms. The developing prehensile and locomotor system can be used in only limited ways for limited activities.

With this orientation serving as a background, the remainder of the chapter is focused as follows: First, on the basis of several strands of thinking and empirical evidence, data are presented to show minimal flexibility in form and function of motor acts during the genesis of new behaviors (the ontogenesis period). These findings indicate that immature forms of voluntarily controlled prehension and locomotion are constrained in their ranges of application; thus, infants reveal far more similarities than variations. Although one consistent individual difference — rate of change — has been observed during ontogenesis, additional findings demonstrate this has limited developmental significance.

Subsequently, the chapter focus shifts to the time span when prehension and locomotion become functionally mature. Signs indicate increased flexibility of motor behavior and changing potentials for long-term environmental influences. Next, contributions of locomotion to self-awareness and of prehension to intellectual development are discussed. In these areas one is forced to speculate because empirical data are sparse. Last, the chapter ends with a few comments aimed at redirecting our thinking in the area of motor development.

THE PERIOD OF ONTOGENESIS

In this section, I adopt the thesis that basically unalterable motor behaviors lead to predictable object and social interactions during a major portion of the first year of life. Both behavior and sequence probably are mediated by genetic preadaptions. If this thesis has validity, then we may expect the following: (1) A species–general sensory–motor repertoire should be observed in all but the most damaged of infants, essentially independent of environmental circumstances. (2) The specific behaviors that are observed should reflect a characteristic sameness; that is, abilities should be used in more or less the same way for basically similar types of interactions. (3) Major individual differences should be observed only under special conditions of organism insult. In subsequent discussion, data pertaining to these points will be examined. However, before turning to research, current thinking on biological influences should be summarized.

Biological Influences

A view of infancy that is increasingly gaining acceptance is that human beings are born with genetic preadaptions for early social interactions, sensorimotor knowledge, attainment of motor skills, and communication systems (Ainsworth, Bell, & Stayton, 1974; Bowlby, 1969; Bruner, 1970, 1973; Emde, Gaensbauer, & Harmon, 1976; Hinde, 1974; Piaget, 1952, 1954; Scarr–Salapatek, 1976). It is suggested that the appearance as well as early functional change of specific sensorimotor behaviors — attention, habituation, postural control, prehension, vocal signals, affective expressions, and object permanence among others — are mediated by biologically based structures. The developmental rationale underlying such mechanisms may be numerous, but a crucial one is that of survival. Many sensorimotor behaviors are potent influences that draw caregivers into interaction with helpless infants (Bell, 1974; Bowlby, 1969; Scarr–Salapatek, 1976).

The sensorimotor repertoire is also an adaptive mechanism, providing infants with means for early learning, with abilities to detect the familiar in contrast to the novel, with capabilities to develop affiliative interactions with persons other than caregivers, and in general, with abilities to bring organization into their world of experiences (Bowlby, 1969; Bruner, 1972; Scarr–Salapatek, 1976). A nonselective endowment of adaptive systems implies that the young of all human groups and societies have ongoing potential for growth.

Questions invariably arise regarding the length of time biological factors mediate sensorimotor behaviors and the specific role of experiences. There is growing consensus that genetic preadaptations are operative throughout a considerable portion of the first year of life, contributing to the appearance of new forms of behavior and fostering change in those previously emerged (Emde et al., 1976; Wohlwill, 1973). Of course, admitting a relatively long biological influence does not denigrate the role of the environment. The environment activates change (Flavell, 1972), provides the "materials and opportunities" for learning (Scarr–Salapatek, 1976), influences motivation to engage in activities, and promotes some early developmental precocities (Zelazo, Zelazo, & Kolb, 1972).

Genetic preadaptations underlying postnatal sequences of reflexive and voluntary motor behaviors can be inferred from neurophysiological and anatomical studies of animal and human infants (Bergstrom, 1969; Conel, 1941; Purpura, Shafer, Housepion, & Noback, 1964; Skogland, 1960). Moreover, findings indicate that certain structural changes in subcortical and cortical processes logically can be linked to types of motor activity and patterns of activation (Bergstrom, 1969; McGraw, 1943). For example, various forms of postnatal brain maturation parallel behavioral transitions, starting from random, poorly controlled movements to those of later periods that are ordered with respect to temporal and spatial dimensions. The latter specifically infers activation of cortical inhibitory centers. To date, no findings have emerged to contradict inferred links between maturing brain organization and motor functions.

Normal and Atypical Motor Development

Motor sequences, linked as they are to biological underpinnings, has been documented with respect to locomotion by Shirley (1931) and Gesell and

Amatruda (1941) and to prehension by Bruner (1970), Castner (1932), Halverson (1931), Piaget (1952), Uzgiris (1967), and White et al. (1964). It is unnecessary to recapitulate specific observations except to comment that locomotion involves emergent control of head, trunk, and limbs for head raising, body turning, prewalking progression, and upright locomotion and that manipulation entails progressive control of arm, forearm, wrist, hand, fingers, and thumb for sequences of bi- and unimanual reaching, grasping, transfering, and releasing.

Concentrating momentarily on normal infants, findings show little variability in the organization or function of initial forms of nonreflexive prehensile and locomotor behaviors (acts that are self-induced, in contrast to those elicited solely by reflex activation). Consider, for example, data and observations collected by means of developmental examinations such as those of Bayley (1969) or Gesell (Gesell & Amatruda, 1941), which contain catalogs of expected responses. These tests are used worldwide (see Werner, 1972), but no researcher has reported individual or group differences in purely motoric control items (e.g., swiping, reaching, rolling, or crawling) or those that represent attention (e.g. memory, exploration, alertness, or social differentiation), except those in rate of development or frequency of use of particular behaviors (Bayley, 1949; Dennis, 1941; Konner, 1976; McGraw, 1935; Phatak, 1970; Pikler, 1968; Werner, 1972). No modification of motor functions or of any early sensorimotor behaviors can be found, despite vastly differing caregiver practices or even early specialized training (Konner, 1976; McGraw, 1935; Zelazo et al., 1972).

What factors constrain infant function? Bruner (1970), in a series of studies on prehensile functions, described some limitations. At four to five months, reaching, though activated and often leading to successful grasping, lacks autoregulation in organization and patterning. Once initiated, these early forms of prehensile activities must be carried to an endpoint or terminated midway; corrections *en route* are beyond capability. Moreover, each new emergent component of prehension requires extraordinary attentional demands. Although by six to eight months modulated reaching and grasping can be incorporated into several ways of approaching objects, there is still little differentiated use of objects (Uzgiris, 1967, 1976) and little appreciation that self is distinguished from object (Piaget, 1952). However, infants freed of some attentional demands of prehension start to focus on object features (Bruner, 1970).

In summary, during the period of ontogenesis prehensile acts are constrained by difficulties in correction of acts, limitations in spatiotemporal patterning, inability to plan, and attentional demands (Bruner, 1970). It is hardly surprising that functions can be directed solely to objects of determinate size, shape, and number (Halverson, 1931).

Although the research discussed in the foregoing paragraphs has been limited to normal infants, it can be inferred that many of these findings have implications for infants who have suffered biological insult or who have been exposed to deleterious caregiving. With respect to the former, researchers have observed that the same motor repertoire is used for essentially similar types of object and social interactions under conditions of visual, auditory, and even neuromuscular handicap (Décarie, 1969; Eibl-Eibesfeldt, 1975; Fraiberg, 1971; Kopp & Shaperman, 1973). Of course, in a few instances of central nervous system dysfunctions (e.g., athetosis, spasticity, or blindness), distortions of major expression may occur, and programmatic interventions may be necessary to facilitate function (Fraiberg, 1971).

Among other findings yielding similarity of function are those obtained from studies of infants born with Down's syndrome. Typically, these children have a multiplicity of physiological, neuromuscular, and intellectual problems. By school age, their intelligence quotients are two or more standard deviations below the average range. However, during ontogenesis, the appearance, function, and effects of their motor repertoire essentially duplicate those of normal infants, albeit changes occur more slowly. Although Down's syndrome infants are frequently hypotonic and slow to move and have limited ranges of affective expressiveness, they eventually achieve most of the prehensile and locomotor milestones found on developmental examinations (Carr, 1975; Dicks-Mireaux, 1972), despite the fact that they are limited in certain kinds of explorations. Likewise, other research demonstrates many analogues in motorically mediated affective responses of young normal and Down's syndrome infants, although a delay in genesis of new behaviors and a constricted variety of acts were also noted (Cicchetti & Mans, 1976; Cicchetti & Sroufe, 1976).

Other examples of atypical infants could be cited, but the point seems clear: Even when there is marked impairment, when learning is limited, and when the opportunity to engage actively in interactions is restricted, the form and function of motor acts as measured by developmental examination data correspond to those of intact infants. During early infancy, the most striking individual and group differences relate to rates of developmental change.

Similar conclusions are reached about the abilities of infants reared under less-than-optimal conditions. All too often, unfortunately, comprehensive deprivation leads to apathetic, bland, developmentally delayed infants who show low investment in objects and have meager response repertoires (Barrera-Moncada, 1963; Provence & Lipton, 1962). Nonetheless, examination of observational reports and developmental data forces us to conclude that postural and manipulative acts mirror those of children reared under more positive circumstances (Collard, 1971; Provence & Lipton, 1962). Movements may be uncoordinated and poorly modulated, but even deprived infants reach for a caregiver and occasionally hold a toy (Provence & Lipton, 1962).

It was once thought that the immature motor system was highly flexible. Indeed, "plasticity" was the term used by White and Held (1966) to describe variations in visual–motor development that occurred as the result of several different kinds of planned enrichments of institution-reared infants. If by plasticity these authors meant that they found differences in amounts of distributed attention, time of onset of components of reaching, and amount of hand regard, there can be no disagreement. However, White's data, as well as that of others, show that the basic structural and functional organization of motor behavior is relatively immutable to change, so that plasticity should not be construed to mean "capable of being (easily) molded."

Without belaboring the point of genetic preadaptations and species generality, we note that no study has demonstrated that the *fundamental motor acts* of early infancy are changed by insult to the organism or by atypicality of rearing conditions. However, integrity of the organism and opportunities provided by the environment may impose constraints on rate of development and quality of response. In addition, motivation may be affected. Nonetheless, all available data speak to a species-general repertoire of behaviors during the period of ontogenesis.

Given that developmentalists may agree on the foregoing points, there still may be disagreement about the significance of variations in timing or in rates of developmental change. Rate of change during ontogenesis is the focus of the next section.

Individual Differences During Ontogenesis

From the first days of life, individual differences are observed. Some infants are more expressive, intense, or alert than others, and within the normal developmental range some will show a fast pace of developmental change in motor skills. Are these variations in rate significant?

As a prelude to answering this question, it is useful to discuss briefly motor precocities. In the first year of life, locomotor and prehensile precocities are not uncommon. Found among infants worldwide, they may stem from caregiving practices, special training, or genetic factors (Geber & Dean, 1957; Konner, 1976; McGraw, 1935; Rebelsky, 1972; Super, 1976; Werner, 1972; Zelazo et al., 1972). The developmental literature accords precocities a special role, ascribing to "advanced" prehensile and locomotor abilities a means by which *early* cognitive and social abilities may be achieved. This perspective, seemingly ignoring powerful evidence of infant learning without motor concomitants, derives in part from the emphasis placed on manipulative acts by Bruner (1970), Gesell (1952), and Piaget (1952, 1954, 1970). Nonetheless, examination of data shows that within the normal range, precocious or delayed development of motor skills offers at best only temporary advantages or disadvantages. These data are explored in the following paragraphs.

A construct useful for understanding implications of variation in rates of developmental change is Blank's (1964) "focal motor hypothesis." Briefly restated, the hypothesis encompasses the following points. At the time when a developmental skill is newly emerging (i.e., the focal period), there is wide variation of abilities; some infants have acquired the skill whereas others show only tentative beginnings. During the focal period, precocities and delays are highly related to overall developmental status, because many of the behaviors that are measured are *functions of the emergent skill.* For example, an infant who shows precocious development of manipulative abilities may apply hand skills to a greater variety of objects than does an infant whose manipulative skills are not well refined. Last, Blank suggests that when a skill becomes part of the general behavioral repertoire, individual variation is markedly reduced.

Data that corroborate the focal motor hypothesis and attest to its usefulness are available. With respect to prehension, Blank (1964) validated her own construct with an investigation of the relationships among developmental test scores, level of prehensile skills, and quality of manipulative play in infants 20 to 28, 39 to 46, and 71 to 73 weeks old. Seeking a focal period in the development of hand skills, she utilized a detailed measurement system of play that included specifications of frequencies, time counts, variation of acts, and spontaneity parameters. These were analyzed with respect to different levels of Griffiths' (1954) developmental test scores, which in turn were analyzed in relation to eye–hand and other subscale scores.

It was only at the youngest age periods that Blank observed the most advanced forms of play among infants whose developmental quotients were in the upper ranges of group abilities. It was also in this period that the highest correlations were obtained between eye–hand subscale scores and overall scores ($r = 0.93$). At later age periods, manipulative play generally was not significantly related to developmental quotients. These data suggest that a focal period of hand skills occurs at about five to six months of age. Therefore, precocities and delays in prehensile skills and their associated effects on function are most apparent at that time.

It is not surprising that other researchers also obtain moderate to high correlations between fine motor skills and cognitive-social abilities of 6-month-old infants (e.g., Yarrow, Rubenstein, & Pedersen, 1975). Yet, extending the focal motor construct, one has to question whether this relationship would have been maintained. Unfortunately, these researchers did not include other age periods.

Turning to locomotor skills, other kinds of evidence can be used to infer indirectly a focal period, which, as might be expected, occurs towards the latter part of the first year. For example, in correlational studies, Bayley (1935) examined prewalking progression (e.g., crawling and creeping) with developmental mental and motor sigma scores at 4 to 6, 10 to 12, 18 to 24, and 33 to 36 months. Her data showed that the highest correlations, signifying greatest variability, were obtained for mental age scores ($r = 0.42$) at the 10-to 12-month period, the usual age of creeping and beginning upright locomotion. Bayley found that correlations in the first age period (4 to 6 months) were 0.32 and in the latter periods only 0.20 and 0.16.

In light of these trends, it is not surprising to find that long-term developmental studies demonstrate even more powerfully the attenuated effects of rates of change. With respect to childhood intellectual abilities, early gross motor precocities or delays lose virtually all their impact (Bayley, 1935, 1949; McGraw, 1935). There is, however, some clinical evidence that suggests that very early gross motor precocities may be *deleterious* for some cognitive functions. High energy levels and early locomotion may promote object inattention and blurring of cue distinctiveness during infancy (Heider, 1966).

Developmental findings on prehension are generally consistent with empirical data on locomotion (McCall, Hogarty, & Hurlburt, 1972; Nelson & Richards, 1939; Shirley, 1933). McCall's longitudinal data are particularly interesting because he obtained a 6-month psychomotor trend that had a low, though significant, relationship with a 24-month developmental profile. It did not, however, relate to later intellectual performance. The 6-month trend incorporated visually guided manipulative acts and gross and fine motor behaviors, including reaching, grasping, banging, and playing with objects — acts interpreted as embodying perceptual contingencies. Although sample, methodology, and data analyses of McCall et al. (1972) differ from those of Blank (1964), his data provide additional support for a focal period of prehension.

Given these findings, one is forced to conclude that individual differences in rates of change of *immature* motor skills have an evanescent quality. As Bayley (1933) wrote many years ago, "Superiority in one function does not insure superiority in the subsequent development of more complex functions ... [p. 81]."

Summary and Comments

Two points have been made in this section. First, during the period of ontogenesis, basic motor competencies are probably mapped by genetic preadaptations. Thus, emergent behaviors have a species-general quality. They are observed in almost all infants and across almost all rearing conditions and are applied in similar ways, irrespective of infant and culture. Second, differences in rates of developmental change in motor abilities are unrelated to long-term development. There is only a brief period when individual differences in motor skills are highly correlated with overall developmental capabilities.

Our understanding of the nature of early infancy has theoretical and practical significance because upon it depends the intensity of our efforts to single out infancy as being more crucial to development and more worthy of study than later periods. The purpose of this section was not to deny significant change roles to early life but to show that its function is universal and fundamental. Perhaps the first phase of infancy is even less momentous than we thought.

However, it is appropriate to ask if any of the conclusions reached in this review conform to theory. In the main, findings presented as evidence for species-typical behaviors of young infants are congruent with the views of Piaget (1952, 1954, 1971), Gesell (1929a, 1952), and Bruner (1970). Although each theorist articulated different maturational-environmental biases and emphasis, each one inferred a commonalty to early infant behaviors. Moreover, all posited a biological basis that contributes to a relatively undeviating emergent pattern of motor acts, as expressed by Piaget in the context of hierarchal development of prehension with invariant sequences, by Gesell in discussions of maturationally programmed growth gradients present even in instances of atypicality, and by Bruner with comments on genetically derived programs fostering regulation of movement with consequent freeing of attentional demands.

In general, developmental theorists have been less concerned with individual differences than with generic characteristics of infants. Nonetheless, Gesell did devote attention to this issue for, in his role as practitioner, he was called upon to determine suitability of infants for adoptive placement (1929a). However, beyond that responsibility, Gesell was intrigued by variations in rates of development and documented numerous atypical cases (Gesell, 1929a; Gesell & Amatruda, 1941). He, more than any other theorist, accorded infant precocities an important long-term role. Notwithstanding, developmental findings generated over four decades attest to the unstable features of infant motor precocities or delays.

Finally, the previously cited data base can be used too as partial negation of motor-mental linkages espoused by theorists and commonly repeated in professional and lay literature. Although no one would want to deny the importance of movement, even if its significance were only to aid in reduction of tension, there is no evidence at present that actually defines motor concomitants of cognitive growth. It is likely that continued search for these presumed linkages during early infancy will be fruitless. However, investigation of older aged infants may show that some motor functions have a lasting influence on aspects of cognitive and social development. We explore this supposition in the next section of this chapter. Turning to the older infant, the period associated with functional maturation is explored. Promising areas for future research are presented.

FUNCTIONAL MATURATION

Developmental Implications

Functional maturation of prehension (e.g., reaching, grasping, and releasing) and upright locomotion (e.g., standing and independent walking) almost immediately spell adaptability and increase of self-generated options. Freed of many attentional demands required of early forms of motor acts, older infants turn their energies to objects, consequences of acts, and environs. Opportunely, they are aided by the somewhat parallel maturation of prehension and locomotion which offers efficiency and latitude in mechanisms that can be used to gather information and initiate social interactions.

Little benefit would accrue to the child if change in motor skills were not bracketed by concomitant growth in cognitive abilities. Otherwise, children would be incapable of directing the uses of motor functions, and almost all control would have to stem from external sources. Consider how perilous it would be for our species if early locomotion were totally devoid of intent!

Fortunately, impressive cognitive growth occurs toward the end of the first year and the beginning of the second (Kagan, 1977; McCall, this volume; Piaget, 1952, 1954; Uzgiris, 1967). Even though thought at this age represents a fraction of its ultimate level and motor skills barely characterize the exquisite precision they ultimately are capable of, the emergence of a cognitively based motor control system represents a fundamental achievement of the second year of life.

Unfortunately, virtually nothing is known of the processes involved in this early cognitive-motor regulatory mechanism. Intuitively, though, it would appear to have commonalties with forms of self-regulation revealed by behaviors of preschool children, which often incude ability to delay, awareness of rules and prohibitions, strategies, and short-term planning. Typically, self-control has been associated with Luria's (1961, 1969) theory of verbal regulation of behavior, although empirical tests of the theory have met with only partial success (Wozniak, 1972).

Nonetheless, Flavell (1977), using Luria as background, proposed a broader interpretation of self-regulation than that provided solely by verbal communications. Not surprisingly, Flavell suggested that a growing repertoire of cognitive processes directs self-control, probably with forms of multiple strategies, mental sets, planning, diversionary tactics, and the like.

Extending Flavell's thesis to a younger age period, it seems reasonable to infer that primitive types of strategies and planning motivate the young child's functional activities. Consider play, for example. There is ample documentation of discernment in object interactions, with attention devoted to shapes, apertures, components, and even socially approved functions.

Moreover, children combine objects in meaningful ways and closely imitate behaviors of others (McCall, 1975; Uzgiris, 1976). Additional examples can be cited, but it is evident that some form of self-regulation guides the young child's functionally mature motor system. Parenthetically, it is suggested that growth of regulatory processes is fostered by caregiver practices and social conditions.

Of all the impressive changes that accrue from functional maturation and cognitive control, no others may be as meaningful to a very young child as those that represent *increases in options*. By this, I refer to an individual ability to select and use preferential modes — visual, auditory, motor, or vocal — singly or in combination, to sample varied aspects of the environment. In effect, functional maturation of motor abilities provides another option, under one's own control, for paths to increasing competence.

The ensuing sections focus on selective use of motor mechanisms as contributors to self-awareness and enhancement of attention. Although discussion centers on locomotion as fostering autonomy and on manipulation as fostering attention, it is emphasized that these are not the only pathways to the respective achievements.

Self-awareness and Upright Locomotion

One of the most interesting conceptualizations of self-development has been proposed by Mahler and her associates (Mahler, Pine, & Bergman, 1975), who discussed relative contributions of cognitive skills, caregiver–child relationships, and emergent locomotor abilities to autonomous functions. In the following paragraphs a brief recapitulation of Mahler's perspectives is offered, followed by a summary of her interpretations of locomotion apropos selfhood.

For Mahler, the psychological birth of the infant incorporates processes of *separation–individuation* that eventually lead to a sense of individual identity. Complementary processes, separation involves the child's "emergence from a symbiotic fusion with the mother," whereas individuation consists of the infant's taking on individualized characteristics. In order for these processes to occur, the child must differentiate self from mother, establish a bond with her, and ultimately develop autonomous ego functions with her support.

These requirements are met during four phases of separation–individuation that generally occur between 4 and 36 months of age. The first subphase involves differentiation of self from caregiver, which may be typified a month or so later, with scanning comparisons of mother and other.

A second subphase, consisting of two parts, emerges when the infant develops independent locomotion. Mahler refers to the initial part as the "early practicing period," consisting of crawling and creeping; the second, called the "practicing period proper," is characterized by independent, upright locomotion. Skills involving locomotion are dominant forms of activity during this period.

A third subphase, occurring about the middle of the second year, includes another spurt in cognitive abilities and a renewed recognition of a "need" for maternal emotional support. The relative imperviousness to maternal presence that Mahler suggests characterizes the second subphase is replaced by concerns regarding caregiver whereabouts, desire "to share," and incipient forms of anxieties regarding separation. Separation anxiety reaches a peak several months later. The dependence–independence ambivalences so often noted during this period are manifested by the child's attempts to use mother as an extension of self—for example, the child will draw mother into a task.

Finally, the fourth subphase, emerging at about 2½ years, involves the child's achievement of individuality and attainment of affective object constancy. The latter signifies to Mahler that the child has developed a stable image or representation of mother that can transcend temporary discomforts. As a result, separations can be tolerated more successfully than in the previous subphase.

Although Mahler's conceptualizations have not been empirically validated, isolated studies support aspects of her observations. For example, Rheingold, Hay, and West (1976) found sharing to be a common behavioral pattern in the second year. Wenar (1976) noted that children between 12 and 20 months demonstrated locomotor acts in pursuit of effectance, and White and Watts (1973) documented the relatively small percentage of time that children between 1 and 2 years and their caregivers engaged in direct interactions.

It was noted previously that Mahler incorporated several developmental systems into the foundation of selfhood; not the least of these is locomotion. Mahler and her associates suggested that walking brings to children some totally novel experiences. Included among these are new planes of visual awareness, expanded spatial locales for exploration, and increased awareness of body functioning. Behaviors requiring higher levels of mastery emerge, many of them centered around the uses of locomotion. One result appears to be an "intoxication" with self faculties, particularly those involving locomotion (Mahler et al., 1975). The practice and mastery of these faculties become recurrent behavioral patterns between 12 and 18 months.

Mahler's interpretations are in agreement with those of others. For example, positive affect, signifying pleasure in doing and accomplishment, has been recorded in conjunction with locomotor activities (Ames, 1949; Freud & Burlingham, 1944; Mittlemann, 1954). Ames recorded the number and types of stimuli that elicited smiles in samples of children at several ages. At 18 months, more than half of the total number of smiles derived from the child's own activities, and of these more than three-quarters stemmed from gross motor behaviors. Mittlemann's (1954) anecdotal descriptions of toddlers' activities also recount numerous instances of positive affect in association with locomotion.

It is possible to infer a few very specific contributions that locomotion, in concert with cognitive skills, makes to self-awareness. Intentional physical distancing from caregivers may promote autonomy, intentional approaches to others may lead to increased cognizance of one's own control systems, and locomotor-based imitative acts may foster awareness of socially accepted practices. In essence, locomotion can be a potent means for the child to test reality (Mahler et al., 1975).

Assume, though, that because of caregiving practices, developmental delay, or biological insult, locomotor contributions to self-awareness are necessarily limited. What are the alternatives? Investment in language, fine motor skills, or social interactions surely must be channels to competence and burgeoning self-awareness. A case in point is a normal child observed from the time she was 13 months of age until she was 6 years old. From early in her life her parents noted precocious language skills, whereas gross motor abilities invariably lagged behind age expectations. In the second year of life, the child, ambulating clumsily though adequately, never showed interest in locomotor abilities, which was in contrast to her obvious pleasure with her verbal productions. She repeatedly practiced linguistic skills, repeating old words and phrases, trying out new words, combining new and old. With the vehicle of language, the child gave every indication of growing self-awareness, competence, and ability to interact with others on her own terms.

Additional evidence, derived from observations of young children constrained by physical impairments, attests to similar use of alternative options as mechanisms to promote development of selfhood. An example is derived from study of a child born without limbs; his cognitive development was previously reported by Kopp and Shaperman (1973). During the second year of life, this boy was extremely irritable and sickly. Although he had the cognitive capacity to guide behavioral planning, the most he was physically capable of doing was rolling along the floor, occasionally pushing an object with his buttocks or perhaps holding a small object between chin and shoulder. Surely, distancing and reality testing (Mahler et al., 1975) had to be limited, as was his ability to engage in "effectance" behaviors (White, 1959). Throughout the extraordinarily demanding period of the second year of life, reports indicate that the child's caregivers remained supportive, providing him with the opportunities to perform those few activities he could accomplish. In addition, it appeared that his gradually increasing capability to use functional language allowed him to elicit additional social interactions. Perhaps even more importantly, language provided a means by which he could ask others to act as his proxy on his environment. Thus, indirectly he achieved autonomy. Later on, with successful fitting of prostheses and provision of an electrically driven wheelchair, the child gained more access to environmental control.

Our notes, taken when the child was 3, 4, and 5 years of age, showed a child with a well-integrated ego. He spoke of himself, his capabilities, and his limitations; he used peers, siblings, and caregivers as sources of help when appropriate. He manifested autonomy in his struggles to achieve in situations where he thought he could. In essence, selfhood, probably hampered initially because of physical incapacities, moved forward.

Both of the foregoing examples indicate that sensitive caregiving plays a vital role in facilitating use of motoric and nonmotoric paths to self-awareness, a point consistently stressed by Mahler and her associates (1975). Although it would be useful to have empirical documentation of the parameters of caregiver support as well as other contributing factors (i.e., locomotion, language, and so forth), such data are not available.

Although the preceding discussion focused on locomotion vis-a-vis self-awareness, it is important to remember that many young children derive great pleasure from movement, sometimes movement solely for the sake of moving. This is, after all, a manifestation of effectance behavior (White, 1959). Although children differ considerably in the amount of movement they produce and seem to need, there are indications that too many restrictions promote frustration. Clarke–Stewart's (1973) longitudinal observations of parent–child interactions contain documentation of this nature. One of her groups of caregivers was loving, but restrictive, and rather concerned with providing physical care. In turn, the children between 1 and 2 years of age were irritable, unhappy, relatively nonvocal and inactive, and physically attached to their mothers. They were less competent at this age than at earlier periods. One could infer that it was not only locomotion that was limited but growing selfhood, autonomy, and even later cognitive growth. It might prove instructive to explore the ways a child adapts when deemphasis or restrictions on specialized sets of emerging skills are forced by social situations or caregiver styles.

In summary, locomotive skills of infants in the second year of life have been discussed in relation to growing selfhood, autonomy, and cognitive growth. The discussion, however, has been largely inferential since direct evidence is sparse. Conceptually and empirically it would be useful to examine further how and under what circumstances locomotion contributes to cognitive and social abilities.

Fostering Attention by Manipulation of Objects

The ability to attend selectively to salient features of the environment, an ongoing requisite for learning and adaptation, is evident from the first days of life (Salapatek, 1975). Yet attention in early months is constrained. It lacks cognitively based recognition and meaning and is highly dependent on intrinsic mechanisms controlling arousal, extrinsic influences of caregiver style, and regulation of the immediate environment.

It is apparent that older infants and toddlers circumvent some of these limitations, although the mechanisms are not fully documented. In all probability, young children are aided by growth of cognitive processes, including development of new strategies and more efficient means of attending (Flavell, 1977; Pick, Frankel, & Hess, 1975). Undoubtedly, attention is also fostered by children's experiencing autonomous control of movement. Independent locomotion affords access to the environment less subject to another's control, and prehension begins to function as an instrumental aid.

The following discussion centers on the role of manipulation in fostering learning, specifically attention, in very young children. Since empirical data are scarce, my comments are nonspecific and speculative. To establish a framework, the section begins with historical and conceptual perspectives.

The conviction that learning is expedited by doing is hardly novel. It has roots in several early works, for example Dewey's (1916) philosophy, Montessori's (1912) programmatic efforts, and Kohler's (1925) studies of problem-solving. Indeed, Montessori was so convinced of the advantages of *doing* that she developed numerous materials for young children to manipulate and use in play. It was thought that, by attending to stimulus dimensions, the child would learn shape, mass, weight, length, and so forth.

In addition, interpretations of developmental theories suggested that there were advantages to manipulative acts of preschool and school-aged children. However, the ideational tie that theorists established between motor and mental abilities appeared to be looser for children than for infants. For example, an elucidation of Piaget suggests that an optimal way of learning is to *start* with manipulative activities (Flavell, 1963). By analogy, a reading of Bruner (Bruner, Olver, & Greenfield, 1966) indicates that manipulation is one among several means of achieving cognitive growth.

In the developmental literature, there tends to be a general endorsement of manipulative acts as aids to learning. However, analysis of the limited amount of research that is available suggests that laboratory conditions can be manipulated to provide instances where manipulation had beneficial effects on performance and a few where it was a detriment (Goodnow, 1971).

Goodnow (1969, 1971; Minichiello & Goodnow, 1969; Weiner & Goodnow, 1970) directly addressed the issue of young children's manipulative actions vis-à-vis their cognitive skills. Her findings demonstrated that manipulation is one of several effective ways by which attention to stimulus dimensions may be facilitated. In one study, Weiner and Goodnow (1970) observed that memory for objects of four 5-year-old children was fostered either by manipulation or solely by visual regard when the object was encased in an eye-catching plastic dome. In effect, each condition directed children to task characteristics. In another study, Minichiello and Goodnow (1969) promoted conservation in 5-year-olds who had been given the opportunity to construct a task that involved filling two beakers with objects in the containers on a one-to-one basis. Goodnow interpreted the one-to-one activity as an attention-getting device that reminded the children of the equality of the units they were handling. These two studies clearly demonstrate that motor acts of preschoolers foster attention and lead to differential sampling of stimulus properties.

I suggest that this small set of findings can be extended to a consideration of motor functions of younger children. It is logical to assume that instrumental prehensile acts may be an important way to increase the likelihood of attention to salient dimensions of the environment. Consider that the young child, particularly between 1 and 2 years of age, can be confronted by many new, and possibly competing, attractions. Not the least of these may be the child's own emerging abilities. Earlier it was noticed that new forms of cognitive, linguistic, and motor skills appear during this period. That children become preoccupied with mastery of these new achievements also is documented. It is possible that children who engage in numerous forms of locomotor and verbal effectance behaviors unwittingly bombard themselves with self-generated stimuli. Under these circumstances, it may be difficult for the child to take in visually sufficient dimensions of objects that are found within the immediate environment. Therefore, manipulation of playthings could be a potent mechanism by which the child's attention is drawn to features and characteristics. If these speculations have any validity, one would suspect that an important contributing variable is caregiver behavior. Those parents who find sensitive ways to engineer their children's environments can directly facilitate attention.

Although the foregoing data are too limited to discuss their long-range implications, it is not unreasonable to suggest that inattention of children, often described in the early school years, must have antecedents. Research on factors facilitating and inhibiting attention of children between 12 and 24 months is warranted.

In summary, this section reviews theory and data regarding the role of manipulation in fostering general and specific skills of young children. The data were extended to a consideration of attributes of children in the second year of life who might use manipulative activities specifically to direct their attention to object features. Much of this review has been supposition and will remain so until research is generated.

COMMENTS

The underlying theme for this chapter has been motor function. Explicitly and implicitly, questions have been raised concerning the availability, type, and age periods of motor functions.

It is obvious from the data presented that it is less difficult to focus on younger infants than older ones. Bountiful material exists regarding the former, whereas a scant handful is available for the latter.

Apparently, the period of genesis of motor behaviors has had, and continues to maintain, a fascination for developmentalists. One can find absorbing theoretical discussions—not only those of Piaget, which are familiar to many, but in the lesser known, early writings of Gesell. In addition, one finds a data base that is extremely extensive and varied. It ranges from the classic catalogs of prehension, to descriptions of swaddled infants, to beautifully documented studies of neuromuscular maturation, to twin training. Then, one can turn to more recent research and find reexamination of issues and use of clever techniques. Still, the emphasis is on the young infant.

If quantity is any criterion, then it is reasonable to conclude that an extraordinary preoccupation exists with this age period. It is almost as if the early age and its associated functions were considered end points of development. However, in all likelihood, this is not the meaning that we wish to convey.

Nonetheless, the unbalanced perspective found in the literature should motivate attempts to discuss differences inherent in an immature and mature motor system and to suggest implications of motor behaviors for children in the second year of life. Moreover, it is impressive to see the sheer delight children manifest by having at their disposal self-directed manipulation and locomotion; probably this, too, has ramifications for the development of other behaviors.

If in time future research interest is generated apropos motor functions in older infants, it seems important that it maintain a realistic perspective. In light of our current understanding, it would be foolhardy to imbue the motor system with an influence that goes beyond that which is justified. Motor behaviors need to be considered as one of many of the child's resources. Motor functions should be examined as a channel to social, cognitive, and emotional growth, not as entities in and of themselves.

ACKNOWLEDGMENT

The writing of this chapter was supported in part by grant Maternal and Child Health Services #r-060396-01-0 and contract #300-77-0306 from Bureau for the Education of the Handicapped.

REFERENCES

Ainsworth, M. D. S. The development of infant-mother attachment. In B. M. Caldwell & H. N. Ricciuti (Eds.), *Review of child development research.* Chicago, Ill.: The University of Chicago Press, 1973.
Ainsworth, M. D. S. *Infancy in Uganda: Infant care and the growth of love.* Baltimore, Md.: Johns Hopkins University Press, 1967.

Ainsworth, M. D. S., & Bell, S. M. Attachment, exploration and separation: Illustrated by the behavior of one-year-olds in a strange situation. *Child Development,* 1970, *41,* 49–67.

Ainsworth, M. D. S., Bell, S. M., & Stayton, D. J. Infant–mother attachment and social development: "Socialization" as a product of reciprocal responsiveness to signals. In M. P. M. Richards (Ed.), *The integration of a child into a social world.* London: Cambridge University Press, 1974.

Ainsworth, M. D. S., & Wittig, B. A. Attachment and exploratory behavior of one-year-olds in a strange situation. In B. M. Foss (Ed.), *Determinants of infant behavior* (Vol. 4). London: Methuen, 1969.

Ambrose, J. A. The development of the smiling response in early infancy. In B. M. Foss (Ed.), *Determinants of infant behavior* (Vol. 1). London: Methuen, 1961.

Ames, L. B. Development of interpersonal smiling responses in the preschool years. *Journal of Genetic Psychology,* 1949, *74,* 273–291.

Barrera-Moncada, G. *Estudios sobre alteraciones del crecimiento y del desarrollo psicológico del sindrome pluricarencial (Kwashiorkor).* Caracas: Edetora Grafos, 1963.

Bayley, N. Mental growth during the first three years: A developmental study of 61 children by repeated tests. *Genetic Psychology Monographs,* 1933, *14,* 1–92.

Bayley, N. The development of motor abilities during the first three years. *Monographs of the Society for Research in Child Development,* 1935, *1,* 1–26.

Bayley, N. Consistency and variability in the growth of intelligence from birth to eighteen years. *Journal of Genetic Psychology,* 1949, *75,* 165–196.

Bayley, N. *Manual for the Bayley scales of infant development.* New York: Psychological Corporation, 1969.

Bell, R. Q. Contributions of human infants to caregiving and social interaction. In M. Lewis and L. A. Rosenblum (Eds.), *The effect of the infant on its caregiver.* New York: Wiley, 1974.

Bergstrom, R. M. Electrical parameters of the brain during ontogeny. In R. J. Robinson (Ed.), *Brain and early behavior.* London: Academic Press, 1969.

Blank, M. A focal periods hypothesis in sensorimotor development. *Child Development,* 1964, *35,* 817–829.

Blurton–Jones, N. *Ethological studies of child behavior.* London: Cambridge University Press, 1972.

Blurton-Jones, N., & Leach, G.M. Behavior of children and their mothers at separation and greeting. In N. Blurton-Jones (Ed.), *Ethological studies of child behavior.* Cambridge: Cambridge University Press, 1972.

Bower, T. G. R. *Development in infancy.* San Francisco: Freeman, 1974.

Bowlby, J. *Attachment and loss: Attachment* (Vol. 1). New York: Basic Books, 1969.

Bowlby, J. *Attachment and loss: Separation, anxiety and anger* (Vol. 2). New York: Basic Books, 1973.

Bruner, J. S. *Processes of cognitive growth: Infancy.* Worcester, Mass.: Clark University Press, 1968.

Bruner, J. S. The growth and structure of skill. In K. J. Connolly (Ed.), *Mechanisms of motor skill development.* New York: Academic Press, 1970.

Bruner, J. S. The nature and uses of immaturity. *American Psychologist,* 1972, *27,* 1–22.

Bruner, J. S. Organization of early skilled action. *Child Development,* 1973, *44,* 1–11.

Bruner, J. S., Olver, R. R., & Greenfield, P. M. *Studies in cognitive growth.* New York: Wiley, 1966.

Carr, J. *Young children with Down's syndrome: Their development, upbringing and effect on their families.* London: Butterworth, 1975.

Castner, B. M. The development of fine prehension in infancy. *Genetic Psychology Monographs,* 1932, *12,* 105–191.

Cicchetti, D., & Mans, L. *Down's syndrome and normal infants' responses to impending collision.* Paper presented at the meetings of the American Psychological Association, Washington, D.C., September, 1976.

Cicchetti, D., & Sroufe, L. A. The emotional development of the infant with Down's syndrome. *Child Development,* 1976, *47,* 920–929.

Clarke–Stewart, K. A. Interactions between mothers and their young children: Characteristics and consequences. *Monographs of the Society for Research in Child Development,* 1973, *38,* (6–7, Serial No. 153).

Collard, R. R. Exploratory and play behaviors of infants reared in an institution and in lower- and middle-class homes. *Child Development,* 1971, *42,* 1003–1015.

Conel, J. L. *The postnatal development of the human cerebral cortex* (Vol. 2). Cambridge, Mass.: Harvard University Press, 1941.

Corman, H., & Escalona, S. Stages of sensorimotor development: A replication study. *Merrill-Palmer Quarterly,* 1969, *15,* 351–361.

Décarie, T. G. A study of the mental and emotional development of the thalidomide child. In B. M. Foss (Ed.), *Determinants of infant behavior* (Vol. 4). London: Methuen, 1969.

Dennis, W. Infant development under conditions of restricted practice and of minimum social stimulation. *Genetic Psychology Monographs,* 1941, *23,* 143–189.

Dewey, J. *Democracy and education: An introduction to the philosophy of education.* New York: McMillan, 1916.

Dicks–Mireaux, M. J. Mental development of infants with Down's syndrome. *American Journal of Mental Deficiency,* 1972, *77,* 26–32.

Eibl–Eibesfeldt, I. *Ethology: The biology of behavior.* New York: Holt, Rinehart & Winston, 1975.

Emde, R. N., Gaensbauer, T. J., & Harmon, R. J. Emotional expression in infancy: A biobehavioral study. *Psychological Issues,* 1976 (Whole No. 37).

Ferguson, L. R. Origins of social development in infancy. *Merrill–Palmer Quarterly,* 1971, *17,* 120–137.

Field, J. The adjustment of reaching behavior to object distance in early infancy. *Child Development,* 1976, *47,* 304–308.

Field, J. Coordination of vision and prehension in young infants. *Child Development,* 1977, *48,* 97–103.

Flavell, J. H. *The developmental psychology of Jean Piaget.* Princeton, N. J.: Van Nostrand, 1963.

Flavell, J. H. An analysis of cognitive-developmental sequences. *Genetic Psychology Monographs,* 1972, *86,* 279–350.

Flavell, J. H. *Cognitive development.* Englewood Cliffs, N. J.: Prentice–Hall, 1977.

Fraiberg, S. Intervention in infancy: A program for blind infants. *Journal of American Academy of Child Psychiatry,* 1971, *10,* 381–405.

Freedman, D. G. Smiling in blind infants and the issue of innate vs. acquired. *Journal of Child Psychology and Psychiatry,* 1964, *5,* 171–184.

Freedman, D. G. *Human infancy: An evolutionary perspective.* New York: Halsted Press, 1974.

Freud, A., & Burlingham, D. T. *Infants without families.* New York: International Universities Press, 1944.

Geber, M., & Dean, R. F. A. Gesell tests on African childen. *Pediatrics,* 1957, *20,* 1055–1065.

Gesell, A. *Infancy and human growth.* New York: McMillan, 1929. (a)

Gesell, A. Maturation and infant behavior pattern. *Psychological Review,* 1929, *36,* 307–319. (b)

Gesell, A. *Studies in child development.* New York: Harper, 1948.

Gesell, A. *Infant development: The embryology of early human behavior.* New York: Harper: 1952.

Gesell, A., & Amatruda, C. S. *Developmental diagnosis.* New York: Hoeber, 1941.

Gesell, A., & Thompson, H. *Infant behavior: Its genesis and growth.* New York: McGraw-Hill, 1934.

Goodnow, J. J. Effects of active handling illustrated by uses for objects. *Child Development,* 1969, *40,* 201–212.

Goodnow, J. J. The role of modalities in perceptual and cognitive development. In J. P. Hill (Ed.), *Minnesota Symposia on Child Psychology* (Vol. 5). Minneapolis: University of Minnesota Press, 1971.

Griffiths, R. *The abilities of babies: A study in mental measurement.* New York: McGraw-Hill, 1954.

Halverson, H. M. An experimental study of prehension in infants by means of systematic cinema records. *Genetics Psychology Monographs,* 1931, *10,* 107–286.

Heider, G. M. Vulnerability in infants and young children: A pilot study. *Genetic Psychology Monographs,* 1966, *73,* 1–216.

Hess, R. D. Ethology and developmental psychology. In P. H. Mussen (Ed.), *Carmichael's manual of psychology.* New York: Wiley, 1970.

Hetzer, H., & Wolf, K. Eine testserie fur das erste lebensjahr. *Zeitschrift fur Psychologie,* 1928, *107,* 62–104.

Hinde, R. A. *Biological bases of human social behavior.* New York: McGraw-Hill, 1974.

Irion, A.L. A brief history of research on the acquisition of skill. In E. A. Bilodeau (Ed.), *Acquisition of skill.* New York: Academic Press, 1966.

Jones, M. C. The development of early behavior patterns in young children. *Pedagogical Seminary,* 1926, *33,* 537–585.

Kagan, J. *Change and continuity in infancy.* New York: Wiley, 1971.

Kagan, J. *The growth of memory and the fears of infancy.* Paper presented at the biennial meeting of the Society for Research in Child Development, New Orleans, March 1977.

Kohler, W. *The mentality of apes.* New York: Harcourt Brace, 1925.

Konner, M. J. Maternal care, infant behavior and development among the !Kung. In R. B. Lee & I. DeVore (Eds.), *Kalahari Hunter-gatherers: Studies of the !Kung San and their neighbors.* Cambridge, Mass.: Harvard University Press, 1976.

Kopp, C. B. Fine motor behaviors of infants. *Developmental Medicine and Child Neurology,* 1974, *16,* 629–636.

Kopp, C. B., & Shaperman, J. Cognitive development in the absence of object manipulation during infancy. *Developmental Psychology,* 1973, *9,* 430.

Lasky, R. E. The effect of visual feedback of the hand on the reaching and retrieval behavior of young infants. *Child Development,* 1977, *48,* 112–117.

Lorenz, K. Z. *Evolution and modification of behavior.* Chicago, Ill.: University of Chicago Press, 1965.

Luria, A. R. *The role of speech in the regulation of normal and abnormal behavior.* London: Pergamon Press, 1961.

Luria, A. R. Speech development and the formation of mental processes. In M. Cole & I. Maltzman (Eds.), *A handbook of contemporary Soviet psychology.* New York: Basic Books, 1969.

Mahler, M. S., Pine, F., & Bergman, A. *The psychological birth of the human infant.* New York: Basic Books, 1975.

McCall, R. B. *Imitation in infancy.* Paper presented at biennial meeting of the Society for Research in Child Development, Denver, March 1975.

McCall, R. B., Hogarty, P. S., & Hurlburt, N. Transitions in infant sensorimotor development and the prediction of childhood IQ. *American Psychologist,* 1972, *27,* 728–748.

McDonnell, P. M. The development of visually guided reaching. *Perception and Psychophysics,* 1975, *18,* 181–185.

McGraw, M. *Growth: A study of Johnny and Jimmy.* New York: Appleton Century, 1935.

McGraw, M. *The neuromuscular maturation of the human infant.* New York: Columbia University Press, 1943.

Minichiello, M. D., & Goodnow, J. J. Effect of an "action cue" in conservation of amount. *Psychonomic Science,* 1969, *16,* 200–201.

Mittlemann, B. Motility in infants, children, and adults: Patterning and psycho-dynamics. *Psychoanalytic Study of the Child,* 1954, *9,* 142–177.

Montessori, M. *The Montessori method.* New York: F. A. Stokes, 1912.

Nelson, V. L., & Richards, T. W. Studies in mental development III. Performance of twelve months old children on the Gesell Schedule and its predictive value for mental status at two and three years. *Journal of Genetic Psychology,* 1939, *54,* 181–191.

Pew, R. W. Human perceptual-motor performance. In B. H. Kantowitz (Ed.), *Human information processing: Tutorials in performance and cognition.* Hillsdale, N. J.: Lawrence Erlbaum Associates, 1974.

Phatak, P. Motor growth patterns of Indian babies and some related factors. *Indian Pediatrics,* 1970, *7,* 619–624.

Piaget, J. *La naissance de l'intelligence chez l'enfant.* Neuchatel: Delachaux et Niestlé, 1936

Piaget, J. *The origins of intelligence in children.* New York: International Universities Press, 1952.

Piaget, J. *The construction of reality in the child.* New York: Basic Books, 1954.

Piaget, J. Piaget's theory. In P. H. Mussen (Ed.), *Carmichael's manual of child psychology.* New York: Wiley, 1970.

Piaget, J. *Biology and knowledge: An essay on the relations between organic regulations and cognitive processes.* Edinburgh: Edinburgh University Press, 1971.

Pick, A. D., Frankel, D. G., & Hess, U. L. Children's attention: The development of selectivity. In E. M. Hetherington (Ed.), *Review of child development research* (Vol. 5). Chicago, Ill.: University of Chicago Press, 1975.

Pikler, E. Some contributions to the study of the gross motor development of children. *Journal of Genetic Psychology,* 1968, *113,* 27–39.

Provence, S., & Lipton, R. C. *Infants in institutions.* New York: International Universities Press, 1962.

Purpura, D. P., Shafer, R. J., Housepion, E. M., & Noback, C. R. Comparative ontogenesis of structure–function relations in cerebral and cerebellar cortex. *Progress in Brain Research,* 1964, *4,* 187–218.

Rebelsky, F. G. First discussant's comments: Cross-cultural studies of mother–infant interaction—description and consequence. *Human Development,* 1972, *15,* 128–130.

Rheingold, H. L., Hay, D. F., & West, M. H. Sharing in the second year of life. *Child Development,* 1976, *47,* 1148–1158.

Richards, M. P. M., & Bernal, J. F. An observational study of mother–infant interaction. In N. Blurton-Jones (Ed.), *Ethological studies of child behaviour.* London: Cambridge University Press, 1972.

Rubenstein, J. L. A concordance of visual and manipulative responsiveness to novel and familiar stimuli in six-month-old infants. *Child Development,* 1974, *45,* 194–195.

Ruff, H. A. the coordination of manipulation and visual fixation: A response to Schaffer (1975). *Child Development,* 1976, *47,* 868–871.

Salapatek, P. Pattern perception in early infancy. In L. B. Cohen & P. Salapatek (Eds.), *Infant perception: From sensation to cognition* (Vol. 1). New York: Academic Press, 1975.

Scarr–Salapatek, S. An evolutionary perspective on infant intelligence: Species patterns and individual variations. In M. Lewis (Ed.), *The origins of intelligence: Infancy and early childhood.* New York: Plenum, 1976.

Schaffer, H. R. Concordance of visual and manipulative responses to novel and familiar stimuli: A reply to Rubenstein (1974). *Child Development,* 1975, *46,* 290–291.

Shirley, M. M. *The first two years: A study of twenty-five babies I. Postural and locomotor development.* Minneapolis: University of Minnesota Press, 1931.

Shirley, M. M. *The first two years: A study of twenty-five babies II. Intellectual development.* Minneapolis: University of Minnesota Press, 1933.

Skoglund, S. The activity of muscle receptors in the kitten. *Acta Physiologica Scandinavica,* 1960, *50,* 203–221.

Stelmach, G. E. *Motor control: Issues and trends.* New York: Academic Press, 1976.

Super, C. Environmental effects on motor development: The case of "African Infant Precocity." *Developmental Medicine and Child Neurology,* 1976, *18,* 561–567.

Tinbergen, N. *The study of instinct.* London: Oxford University Press, 1951.

Uzgiris, I. C. Ordinality in the development of schemes for relating to objects. In J. Hellmuth (Ed.), *The exceptional infant I. The normal infant.* Seattle, Wash.: Special Child Publications, 1967.

Uzgiris, I. C. Organization of sensorimotor intelligence. In M. Lewis (Ed.), *Origins of intelligence: Infancy and early childhood.* New York: Plenum, 1976.

Uzgiris, I. C., & Hunt, J. McV. *An instrument for assessing infant psychological development.* Mimeographed paper, Psychological Development Laboratory, Urbana, University of Illinois, 1966.

Walters, R. H., & Parke, R. R. The role of the distance receptors in the development of social responsiveness. In L. Lipsitt & C. Spiker (Eds.), *Advances in child development and behavior* (Vol. 2). New York: Academic Press, 1965.

Watson, J. B., & Watson, R. R. Studies in infant psychology. *Scientific Monthly,* 1921, *13,* 493–515.

Weiner, B., & Goodnow, J. J. Motor activity: Effects on memory. *Developmental Psychology,* 1970, *2,* 448.

Wellman, B. L. Physical growth and motor development and their relation to mental development in children. In C. Murchison (Ed.), *A handbook of child psychology.* Worcester, Mass.: Clark University Press, 1931.

Wenar, C. Executive competence in toddlers: A prospective, observational study. *Genetic Psychology Monographs,* 1976, *93,* 189–285.

Werner, E. E. Infants around the world: Cross-cultural studies of psychomotor development from birth to two years. *Journal of Cross-cultural Psychology,* 1972, *3,* 111–134.

White, B. A., & Watts, J. C. *Experience and environment: Major influences on the development of the young child* (Vol. 1). Englewood Cliffs, N. J.: Prentice-Hall, 1973.

White, B. L., Castle, P., & Held, R. Observations on the development of visually directed reaching. *Child Development,* 1964, *35,* 349–364.

White, B. L., & Held, R. Plasticity and sensorimotor development in the human infant. In J. F. Rosenblith & W. Allinsmith (Eds.), *The causes of behavior: Readings in child development and educational psychology.* Boston: Allyn and Bacon, 1966.

White, R. W. Motivation reconsidered: The concept of competence. *Psychological Review,* 1959, *66,* 297–333.

Wohlwill, J. F. *The study of behavioral development.* New York: Academic Press, 1973.

Wozniak, R. H. Verbal regulation of motor behavior: Soviet research and non-Soviet replications. *Human Development,* 1972, *15,* 13–57.

Yarrow, L. J., Rubenstein, J. L., & Pedersen, F. A. *Infant and environment: Early cognitive and motivational development.* Washington, D.C.: Hemisphere, 1975.

Zelazo, P., Zelazo, N., & Kolb, S. "Walking" in the newborn. *Science,* 1972, *176,* 314–315.

3

Perceptual Development: Stability and Change in Feature Perception

Marc H. Bornstein
Princeton University

> *The nervous system is not a neutral medium on which learning imposes any form of organization whatever. On the contrary, it has definite predilections for certain forms of organization and imposes these upon the sensory impulses which reach it.*
> —K. S. Lashley (1949, p. 35)

INTRODUCTION

This chapter is concerned with feature perception, which is one type of qualitative information processing, and with stability and change in feature perception at different periods in human development. The discussion first focuses on the mechanisms of discrimination that are characteristic of sensory capacity and that give rise to feature perception. Examples from mature perception are reviewed, and the existence of feature perception in human infants is documented. Second, infrahuman parallels and biological bases of feature perception are examined. Third, to explain variation in feature perception among adult human populations, the role of experience in perceptual development is discussed. Last, the several functions and advantages of feature perception in infancy and maturity are enumerated and detailed.

Two themes appear and reappear in the discussion of perceptual development. One theme returns to the nativist–empiricist question. Psychologists are interested in both genetic and experiential contributions to behavior, and developmental psychologists particularly have concerned themselves with the issue of nature and nurture. Of the several subfields in development, perception more than any other has played at center stage in the nativist–empiricist debate. This chapter compares perception in infancy, before much experience, and in maturity, after extensive experience. The second theme focuses on the distinction between qualitative and quantitative perceptual discriminations. A psychophysical analysis is offered that explains the role of this distinction in feature perception.

PERCEPTUAL FEATURES

The environment consists of several classes of energy, energy constantly in flux. Energy is the source of sensation, and change in energy provides information for perception. Each of the human senses has adapted to extract specific types of information from the ambient flux of physical energy. For example, the gustatory and olfactory systems are sensitive to chemical energy but not to electromagnetic radiation. Sensory systems also respond to different regions within an energy domain. Thus, some electromagnetic radiation (light) provides effective stimulation for the visual system; another type of electromagnetic radiation (infra-red) provokes thermal sensations. Finally, the characteristics of sensory discriminability vary across stimulus domains. That is, within some physical dimensions the ability to perceive change in energy is relatively constant or monotonic while within others that ability is varying or nonmonotonic. This psychophysical relation is key to the definition of perceptual features.

As energy varies quantitatively and continuously along physical dimensions, changes in the resulting percept register quantitatively. For example, discriminability of pitch and brightness, the psychological correlates of frequency and luminance, is relatively uniform across their respective stimulus continua. Along some dimensions, however, equal changes in physical energy do not always give rise to equivalent or uniform changes in psychological perception. In some regions of these physical continua, discrimination is fine. In other regions, it is poor, though rarely absent. Poverty of discrimination is reflected in the perception of similarity between nearby stimuli; that is, generalizations are the reciprocal of poor discrimination. For example, phonemes and hues represent psychological generalizations to change across poorly discriminated regions of the voice-onset time and wavelength dimensions, and acuity of discrimination is reflected in more abrupt transitions between phonemes and between hues. Thus, the voice-onset time and wavelength dimensions vary both quantitatively *and* qualitatively.

The reciprocal relation between discrimination and generalization has been termed by behaviorists *the inverse hypothesis*. Although Pavlov (1926/1927) originally conceived this relation to depend on irradiation of central nervous system excitation, neo-Pavlovians (e.g., Hull, 1943) and others have suggested that the inverse relationship is, rather, based on experience or measurement error. This chapter supports the position that, in the cases under review at least, the origin of the inverse relationship may be shifted from behavior theory back to psychophysiology (but *not* to an origin in spatial position, as assumed by Pavlov). The data for this position derive from infant and infrahuman studies that call into question a wholly experiential explanation.

In summary, discrimination capacity may be constant or may vary depending on the physical domain. Where discriminability is poor, generalization results. These generalizations across changes in energy I call *perceptual features.* When measured under optimal spatiotemporal conditions, discriminability of such domains may be good but is still nonmonotonic. When measurement is nonoptimal, for example if it is temporally successive or if absolute judgments are elicited, discriminability suffers and generalizations broaden. Absolute identifications typically provoke the *categorization* of poorly discriminated stimuli. Perceptual features in this way relate to categories. This is a new use of the term perceptual feature, as Gibson discusses in her Commentary.

Figure 3.1 shows the plan of this chapter. Discrimination and perceptual features at two stages of *development,* infancy and maturity, are examined in two exemplary modalities—audition and vision. Within each modality,

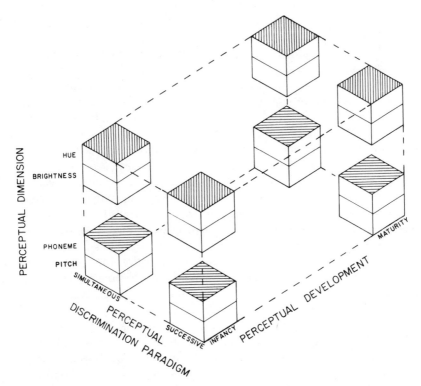

FIG. 3.1. Schematic plan of this chapter.

two perceptual *dimensions* have been selected to exemplify discriminations that are monotonic or nonmonotonic, perceptions that are solely quantitative or those that are quantitative *and* qualitative. These dimensions are brightness and hue perception in vision. In audition, they are pitch and phonemic perception. Finally, the relation of perceptual dimensions to the measurement *paradigm* (simultaneous or successive) is examined. The chapter details arguments on each of these points.

MATURE FEATURE PERCEPTION

Audition: Discriminations of Pitch and of Phonemes

Sinusoidal vibration is a fundamental stimulus in audition, and frequency is the count of sinusoidal stimulus vibrations. The psychological correlate of frequency is pitch. The mature auditory system can be sensitive to frequencies in the range of 20 to 20,000 Hz. Like other dimensions of physical energy, the frequency spectrum is continuous. Among a host of variables (Boring, 1940), two principally influence discrimination of frequency (Δf). The first is the frequency of the standard, or referent, and the second is the technique by which the quantity Δf is obtained.

As to the frequency of the standard, Figure 3.2a shows that in the speech region of the frequency spectrum (between approximately 20 and 4000 Hz) Δf is relatively constant, $\Delta f \leq$ 8 Hz depending on the intensity level. As the frequency of the standard is increased above 4000 Hz, however, Δf increases. Thus, pitch discrimination is monotonic and consistently acute across the most salient part of this physical dimension (Shower & Biddulph, 1931; Thurlow, 1971). Second, measurement procedures, both simultaneous and successive, influence the degree of pitch discrimination. Simultaneous soundings of pure tones present to discrimination distracting difficulties such as beats (Perrott & Nelson, 1969). When standard and comparison frequencies are not simultaneously present, judgments of tonal similarity and difference necessarily involve memory (Wickelgren, 1969). Consequently, frequency discrimination is less acute (e.g., Bachem, 1954; Harris, 1952; Massaro, 1971). However, under either condition, discriminability is roughly symmetrical around a given standard (Harris, 1948; Massaro, 1970; Wickelgren, 1969). Thus, the discrimination function for tonal frequencies that are important in everyday life exemplifies a relationship in which continuous physical change engenders quantitative and relatively monotonic changes in perception.

Like pitch, other psychological domains in audition are perceived to vary monotonically with physical change. For example, Fry, Abramson, Eimas, and Liberman (1962) found that listeners distinguished intraphonemic differences and perceived the changes in steady-state vowels from /I/ to / ɛ / to /æ/ to occur in continuous and nearly equal steps.

AUDITION

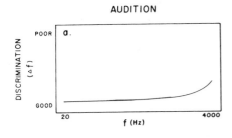

a.

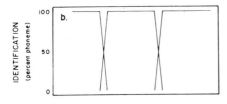

b.

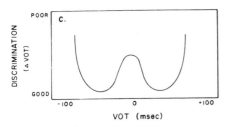

c.

VOT (msec)

FIG. 3.2. Psychological discriminability and perceptual features in audition. a. Frequency discrimination (in Hz) as a function of frequency (20 to 4000 Hz). Across this region of the frequency spectrum, pitch discrimination varies minimally and is generally quite acute. b. Phoneme identification (in percentages) as a function of the voice onset time difference (in msec) between the first and second formants. These functions reflect categorical perception of phonemes—here, for example, of (left to right) prevoiced, voiced, and voiceless consonant initial stops. c. Discrimination of VOT as a function of the difference in voice onset time between formants (−100 to +100 msec VOT). Across this region of the VOT continuum, discriminability varies nonmonotonically between good and poor. Notice that the abscissae for panels b and c are the same. Identification and discrimination of VOT are related. Where discriminability is poor, identification approaches categorical, and where discriminability is acute, perceptual variation between categories is manifest.

In contrast to the perceptual monotonicity of frequency discrimination, acoustic voicing is perceived to change in an oscillating or nonmonotonic fashion with physical change. Where discrimination is poor, voicing features appear; and, labeling studies show that voicing is in turn identified categorically (Liberman, Cooper, Shankweiler, & Studdert-Kennedy, 1967). Voicing thus exemplifies an acoustic dimension reflective of the inverse relationship between discrimination and generalization. Let us examine how.

Voicing yields a particularly salient cue along which some phonemes (the meaningful sounds in a language) are produced and differentiated (Lisker & Abramson, 1964, 1970; Slis, 1970). Distinctions of voicing are cued by temporal relationships among formants or bands of energy in the speech spectrum, and the displacement among formants is denoted in terms of their relative voice-onset time (VOT). This voicing cue represents very nearly a panlinguistic phonetic contrast. In cross-language research, Lisker and Abramson (1964) found that phonetic distinctions in 11 different languages are not arbitrarily distributed, although intuitively one knows that the differences among languages should be constrained only by anatomical limits on production. Rather, two specific values along the VOT continuum seem to serve as points of transition that partition that continuum into three phonetic categories: prevoiced, voiced, or voiceless. Initial-position stop consonants in English (the bilabials, /b/ and /p/, for example) exemplify these varations in production. The onset of the first formant relative to the second and third formants distinguishes the voiced (first) from the voiceless (second) member of this cognate pair.

Production and perception are related (Lisker & Abramson, 1970). The two right-hand identification functions in Figure 3.2b show that if the first formant leads the second, begins simultaneously with the second, or trails the onset of the second by as much as 25 msec, English speakers tend to hear and identify the sound stimulus in one way, as a /b/. If, however, the first formant follows the onset and transition of the second formant by more than 35 msec, English speakers tend to identify the sound in another way, as a /p/ (Lisker & Abramson, 1970). According to cross-language research, transitions between a pre-voiced and a voiced category and a voiced and a voiceless category lie approximately between -45 and -35 msec and between $+25$ and $+35$ msec VOT, respectively. As Figure 3.2b shows, phonetic categories for bilabial stops typically extend below -45 msec, between -35 and $+25$ msec, and beyond $+35$ msec VOT.

Identification functions for other voicing contrasts (at the alveolars, /d/ and /t/, and at the velars, /g/ and /k/) follow a similar format. Psychological correspondences to change along still other physical continua in speech also show such categorical identifications. For example, Mattingly, Liberman, Syrdal, and Halwes (1971) found that changes in the transition of the second formant will cue categorical contrasts in place of articulation (/b/ $-$ /d/ $-$ /g/ and /p/ $-$ /t/ $-$ /k/), and Miyawaki, Strange, Verbrugge, Liberman, Jenkins, and Fujimura (1975) found that, among English speakers, starting frequencies of the third formant transition will cue a categorical contrast of the liquids (/r/ $-$ /l/).

Discrimination of VOT (among these other dimensions) is, as expected, reciprocally related to identification (see Figure 3.2c). Typically, listeners discriminate sounds selected from different phonetic categories but cannot discriminate nearly so well sounds selected from the same phonetic category (Eimas, 1963; Liberman et al., 1967; Lisker & Abramson, 1964, 1970). As a comparison between panels b and c in Figure 3.2 shows, discrimination is poor but not absent within a psychological category.

Initially, psycholinguists had claimed that categorical judgments were unique to speech and that discrimination within categories was nonexistant (e.g., Eimas, 1963; Liberman et al., 1967; Liberman, Harris, Hoffman, & Griffith, 1957; Lisker & Abramson, 1970; Stevens & House, 1972). Several investigators, including Barclay (1970), Pisoni (Pisoni & Lazarus, 1974;

Pisoni & Tash, 1974), and Hanson (1977), have now clearly demonstrated intraphonemic discriminability. Others, moreover, have shown that the test methods that result in nonmonotonic discrimination with speech stimuli do so with select nonspeech sounds (Cutting & Rosner, 1974; Cutting, Rosner, & Foard, 1976; Locke & Keller, 1973; Miller, Wier, Pastore, Kelly, & Dooling, 1976). Thus, categorical perception is not unique to speech, and there is within-category discriminability.

In summary, two acoustic dimensions—frequency and VOT—engender modes of discrimination that differ fundamentally. Frequency discrimination is relatively monotonic and constant. Discrimination of VOT is a nonmonotonic function of physical change. Poor discrimination of VOT suggests feature perception, and absolute judgments of VOT result in categorical identifications.

Vision: Discriminations of Brightness and of Hue

The spectrum of illumination potentially available to adult human beings is enormously broad. Man's visual sensitivity extends over a range of approximately 10,000,000,000 to 1. Brightness is a fundamental sensation in visual perception, and the resolution of differences in luminance provides an important basis for the ability to detect objects in the visual environment. The present discussion focuses on photopic vision which, like the speech register to audition, is particularly salient to vision.

The quality of luminance discrimination (ΔL) depends on a series of physical factors that includes length of adaptation to the reference illumination, size and duration of exposure of the comparison illumination, and the degree of contrast between the two. Most directly, however, the absolute level of reference illumination determines absolute discriminability. Over the more than six log-unit range of photopic vision, between threshold (0.003 cd/m²) and the upper limit of visual tolerance (5000 cd/m²), human ability to discriminate minimal differences in illumination is extraordinarily sensitive (see Figure 3.3a). It is nearly a constant proportion, approximately 1 to 2%, of the level of reference illumination. Fine brightness discrimination data are a product of studies that have used contrast arrangements, that is, simultaneous discrimination of luminance (e.g., König & Brodhun, 1889; Steinhardt, 1936). The detection of difference in luminance without contrast, however, is simply less acute than the detection of spatial contrast. Thus, the threshold for simple luminance discrimination in a successive task is about 8 to 10% (Herrick, 1956; Holway & Hurvich, 1938; Keller, 1941). Here, also, the ratio remains approximately constant. In short, luminance discriminability is acute, and brightness discrimination can be viewed as being part of a general model of constant psychological discrimination of a continuous physical variable.

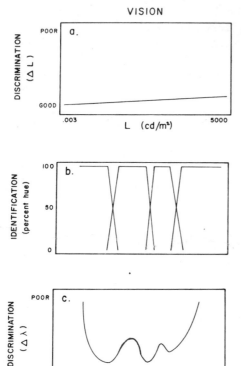

VISION

FIG. 3.3. Psychological discriminability and perceptual features in vision. a. Luminance discrimination (in cd/m²) as a function of luminance (0.003 to 5000 cd/m²). Across this region of the luminance spectrum, brightness discrimination varies minimally and is generally quite acute. b. Hue identification (in percentages) as a function of wavelength (in nm). These functions reflect categorical perception of hues — here, for example, of (left to right) blue, green, yellow, and red. c. Wavelength discrimination ($\Delta\lambda$) as a function of wavelength (400 to 700 nm). Across this region of the electromagnetic spectrum, wavelength discriminability varies nonmonotonically between good and poor. Notice that the abscissae for panels b and c are the same. Identification and discrimination of wavelength are related: Where discriminability is poor, identification approaches categorical, and where discriminability is acute, perceptual variation between categories is manifest.

Hue represents a second principal psychological dimension of visual sensation. Objects in the visual environment are identifiable and immediately distinguishable by qualitative differences among hues. The physical stimulus associated with the perception of hue is wavelength. Although physical variation between wavelengths is continuous, human discrimination of wavelength is contrastingly variable. Wavelength discriminability correlates strongly with qualitative distinctions inherent in the identification of hue. I first discuss identification of hue and next, discrimination of wavelength.

Newton (1671–1672) was among the first to identify the apparent perceptual discontinuities evident in the continuous spectrum. In the fifth proposition of his "New Theory about Light and Colors," Newton identified two sorts of colors — one the "Original or primary colours," the other "Intermediate gradations" between the simple hues. Following Newton, the results of several identification studies that have used methods as diverse as color naming (Beare, 1963), color scaling (Boyton & Gordon, 1965), and the estimation of chromatic similarity (Ekman, 1963) have reconfirmed that under normal foveal viewing conditions the wavelength spectrum is perceived as being a qualitative array of hues. Figure 3.3b shows that from its short- to long-wave end, four principal or unitary hues have commonly been identified: blue, green, yellow, and red. Physically, these hues differ from one another by wavelength only; psychologically and qualitatively they are unique (Berlin & Kay, 1969; Bornstein, 1973, 1975a; Dimmick & Hubbard, 1939a, 1939b). This identification pattern is so prominent that even taking into consideration the other dimensions of color—brightness and saturation —all chromatic experiences can be identified adequately using four basic hues (Sternheim & Boynton, 1966). These four hues are theoretically fundamental (Hering, 1878/1964).

Wavelength discrimination ($\Delta\lambda$) defines the capacity of the visual system to differentiate chromatic stimuli when both brightnesss and saturation differences are absent. The fineness of wavelength discrimination depends on several physical factors that include stimulus luminance and size, surround luminance and chromaticity, locus on the retina, and the state of adaptation of the eye, in addition to the method of measurement (W. D. Wright, 1947). Highly influential among these variables is the reference wavelength. Normally, wavelength discrimination functions are derived from simultaneous, side-by-side comparisons of steady-state luminous fields. Figure 3.3c shows that under such circumstances discrimination is quite fine. In the middle of the visible spectrum (495 nm $< \lambda <$ 610 nm), $\Delta\lambda$ fluctuates around a value of approximately 3 to 7 nm; at the extremes of the spectrum ($\lambda <$ 495 nm and $\lambda >$ 610 nm) discrimination approaches infinity for all visual intents and purposes. Discrimination is particularly good around 495 nm, 565 nm, and 610 nm. Thus, wavelength discrimination is nonmonotonic, and its fluctuating nature provokes qualitative perceptual changes. Both color-naming identification (Beare, 1963) and hue generalization functions (Boyton & Gordon, 1965) reflect high points in $\Delta\lambda$, or regions of poor discrimination, whereas in general the slopes between basic color names reflect regions of more acute discrimination. Adults certainly discriminate physical variation within perceptual categories of hue, but, as with voicing categories, discrimination within hues is less acute than discrimination between hues.

In summary, the nonmonotonic character of visual discrimination of wavelength is reflected in the perception of qualitative variation along the wavelength dimension. Intercategory transitions are nearly isomorphic with $\Delta\lambda$ minima. Thus, perception of hue (generalization) is inversely related to wavelength discriminability, a basic observation that has been consistently supported in the work of Ekman (1963), Graham, Turner, and Hurst (1973), Jacobs and Gaylord (1967), Smith (1971), and A. A. Wright (1972).

Summary

Psychophysical data indicate that, in audition and vision, dimensions of sensation exist along which the perception of change is more or less constant. Discrimination of frequency and luminance is constant, whereas VOT and wavelength engender nonconstant discrimination even when measured under optimal spatiotemporal conditions. For VOT and wavelength, peaks and troughs in discriminability correspond with plateaus and boundaries of identification functions. Discriminative nonmonotonicity in this way sets the occasion for the perception of qualitative differences that I have called perceptual features.

Two caveats qualify these intramodal and intermodal comparisons. First, pitch discrimination involves the detection of difference between simple stimuli, whereas phoneme discrimination involves the detection of difference between complex stimuli. Likewise, the analogy drawn between audition and speech on the one hand and vision and color on the other is not exact. Categories of hue reflect change along a single, unitary dimension: wavelength. Phonemic categories entail changes among several distinctive features, including voicing, aspiration, and articulatory force. Nevertheless, Lisker and Abramson (1964) and Liberman et al. (1967) have suggested that these distinctive features derive from a single articulatory variable, namely VOT. The chromatic continuum and the speech continuum are, in this regard, as analogous as modality differences allow. Furthermore, in all cases context variables may influence discriminability; this discussion has proceeded as though discriminability were measured independent of context.

IMMATURE FEATURE PERCEPTION: INNATE KNOWLEDGE?

Where once psychologists (James, 1890) were prone to characterize the infant's perceptual world as a "blooming, buzzing confusion [p. 488]," contemporary developmental investigators find instead discerning responses to complex visual and auditory displays. The belief that infants may be congenitally able to analyze or otherwise to process external information in selective, organized ways flowed from early investigations into newborn looking patterns (see, for example, Kessen, 1967). Current research into infant speech and color perception has given this view new impetus. In this section, I review infant sensory and perceptual functions previously examined in adults. These functions include frequency discrimination and speech categorization as well as luminance discrimination and hue categorization. A close look at infantile perception reveals foundations of and parallels with mature behavior.

Only very few studies of pitch and brightness discrimination in infants exist, and virtually none of these has attempted to test whether discrimination of frequency or luminance is constant or nonconstant. These studies have traditionally sought to assess discriminative capacity. Although they do not provide data that speak directly to the quantitative-qualitative distinction, they suggest that discriminations are adultlike and therefore probably monotonic in character. Likewise, early indications from research in the areas of speech and hue indicate that infants, like adults, discriminate change of VOT and wavelength nonmonotonically. Such discriminations appear to result in perceptual features for the infant as they do for the adult.

Audition: Discriminations of Pitch and of Phonemes

Young infants discriminate reasonably well among pure tone stimuli that differ in frequency. This observation is supported by studies that have attended to physical variables such as intensity level, to behavioral state, and especially to response methodology (e.g., Bartoshuk, 1962; Bridger, 1961; Bronshtein & Petrova, 1952/1967; Kasatkin & Levikova, 1935; Weir, 1976; Wormith, Pankhurst, & Moffitt, 1975). For example, Wormith et al. (1975) rewarded infants with auditory feedback — the sound of a pure 200-Hz tone—for high-amplitude sucking. Following habituation, 1-month-old infants discriminated change to a 500-Hz tone (minimum intensity = 45 dB). Likewise, 6-week-old infants showed increased cardiac orienting to an 1100-Hz tone following habituation to a 1900 Hz-tone, or vice versa (Leavitt, Brown, Morse, & Graham, 1976, Experiment 3). Using similar procedures, Bridger (1961) had earlier found a differential threshold of 50 Hz. Typically, studies of auditory discrimination involve successive test procedures. Thus, although some investigators (e.g., Trehub, 1973) have failed to extract good tonal discrimination from infants, Wormith et al. and Leavitt et al. have succeeded by rendering rewarding stimuli available continously. Their procedures more closely approximate a simultaneous discrimination situation, which has been demonstrated to favor increased discriminative acumen in adults.

Because no complete psychophysical study of frequency discrimination in the human infant has yet been conducted, it is premature to say whether infantile discriminability is constant across the frequency spectrum. Indeed, it may never be possible in infant auditory research to match the fineness of adult psychophysical discriminations—at 40 dB SPL adults discriminate approximately 79 steps between 200 Hz and 500 Hz (Stevens & Davis, 1938, Figure 63). However, the cochlea is anatomically mature prenatally (Hecox, 1975), and the Bridger, Wormith, and Leavitt studies previously cited suggest that, once decision criteria, state, sensitivity, and methodology are well controlled, infants will discriminate among bands of quite narrow frequency. Following this line of reasoning, Weir (1976) recently applied signal-detection analysis to the pitch discrimination data of Hutt, Hutt, Lenard, Bernuth, and Muntjewerff (1968) and found that newborn infants manifest highly acute sensitivity to frequency change.

Frequency discrimination is a basic characteristic of auditory perception and is crucial to the detection and analysis of complex environmental sounds, including speech. That the human infant is, like the adult, frequency-bound (Eisenberg, 1976)—in the sense that he is more sensitive to audible frequencies less than 4000 Hz—is significant because these frequencies carry the most important information about human speech (Thurlow, 1971). Not surprisingly, the infant, like the adult, is provided with more than rudimentary equipment for the analysis of speech. Several recent studies of infantile sensitivity to speech sounds show that the infant's discriminability is in many ways adult-like. For example, 8-week-old babies, like adults, show good (continuous) vowel discrimination. Specifically, Swoboda, Morse, and Leavitt (1976) found that psychological change along a continuum of spectrally similar vowels from /i/ to /I/ was monotonic with physical change for infants as it is for adults.

With the research of Lisker and Abramson (1964, 1970) and others on categorical speech perception in mind, Eimas (1975b, 1975c) and his associates (Eimas, Siqueland, Jusczyk, & Vigorito, 1971) proposed that a phenomenon so ubiquitous and important as phonetic perception might appear early in life. Specifically, Eimas et al. (1971) sought to discover whether preverbal human infants would perceive equal acoustic changes along the VOT continuum in a way that paralleled adult phonetic perception. They tested infants' perception of the adult phonetic boundary located at approximately + 25 msec. Discriminative sensitivity in two groups of 4-month-old infants was studied using the high-amplitude sucking procedure with pairs of stimuli that differed by identical 20-msec differences in VOT. The two experimental groups thus examined the "categorical" hypothesis in that they experienced physical changes of equal magnitude but presumed psychological changes of unequal magnitude. One group first heard and habituated to an acoustic stimulus that corresponded to the adult phoneme /b/ (20-msec delay between onset of first and second formants), which was later switched (across the boundary) to the adult /p/ (40-msec delay). A second group first habituated to one /b/ (20-msec lead), then heard a second /b/ (simultaneous onset). A third group experienced no change. In this way, the first group tested between-category discriminability, the second group tested within-category discriminability, and the third group served as a control (see Figure 3.2b). The results showed clear between-category but no within-category discriminacion; infants did not distinguish within a phoneme but will distinguish phonemic contrasts such as the bilabial /b/ – /p/. These findings were later replicated with both synthetic and natural speech stimuli and extended to other voicing contrasts (for example, the alveolar /d/ – /t/ by Trehub and Rabinovitch, 1972, and Eimas, 1975c). They were also extended to place of articulation contrasts (for example, /d/ – /g/ by Moffitt, 1971, Morse, 1972, Eimas, 1974, and Miller and Morse, 1976), to the liquid contrast /r/ – /l/ (by Eimas, 1975b), and to other speech contrasts (see Eilers & Minifie, 1975; Leavitt et al., 1976; Trehub, 1976). Although results like these do not imply that infants process acoustic variations as being invested with meaning, the ability of infants to distinguish contrastive phoneme pairs and their failure to distinguish allophonic variation suggest that the mechanisms underlying future "speech" perception may well be innate.

Two further considerations fill out the infant–adult comparison. First, the technique used by Eimas et al. (1971) is a successive discrimination task; it is a rather insensitive psychophysical measure. Under better conditions, infants may be capable of distinguishing certain intra-phonemic contrasts (cf. pages 42-43). Therefore, in the available studies, infant perceptual acumen may be diminshed simply because of the time error (e.g., Leavitt et al., 1976). Nevertheless, these studies clearly indicate asymmetry in perceptual discrimination of VOT by infants. Second, as in adults, infant categorical discrimination is not unique to speech sounds. The same investigators who showed that adults perceive change among selected nonspeech, musical sounds categorically (Cutting & Rosner, 1974; Cutting et al., 1976) have also found that 2-month-old infants discriminate the same nonspeech stimuli nonmonotonically (Jusczyk, Rosner, Cutting, Foard, & Smith, 1977). Whatever the mechanism underlying "categorical" perception, its operating characteristic seems to be ontogenetically stable; discriminations that are not monotonic with physical change in maturity are not monotonic in infancy either.

The results from such research with infants speak for themselves in evidence of a nativist view of perceptual features in audition. Because perceptual features in this view reflect the influence of nature to a greater degree than that of nurture, psychophysical and neurophysiological analyses of the perceptual behavior of infrahuman species who share the same or an analogous biological makeup as man should reveal similar predispositions toward perceptual features. Additionally, studies of infantile discriminability in different cultural settings should reveal patterns of sensitivity that are uniform among infants. Later in this chapter I review comparative and cross-cultural investigations on these points. First, however, parallel examples of monotonic and nonmonotonic *visual* discriminations of brightness and of hue in infancy are discussed.

Vision: Discriminations of Brightness and of Hue

Young infants' gross motility (Smith, 1936), pupillary diameter (Sherman, Sherman, & Flory, 1936), and visual preference (Hershenson, 1964) all change in response to variations in ambient illumination. These reactions suggest that infants discriminate luminance very early in life. Just how well they do is surprising.

Recently, Peeples and Teller (1975) measured brightness discrimination in

2-month-old infants by using a pattern-preference technique. In their study, the infant was exposed to two homogeneous white photopic fields, and his attention was observed to change toward one field when it contained a white bar that differed from the background by as little as 5%. Consequently, by 2 months and under conditions of brightness contrast, infants discriminate small luminance increments or decrements. These infant data are comparable with those of the adult: Recall (pages 43-44) that in contrast detection, adults can discriminate a 1% difference in luminance. Because they tested along the luminance continuum and at several values that represented equal changes from the background luminance, Peeples and Teller (1975) were able to show that discrimination of luminance in infants is approximately constant with change in intensity.

Simultaneous discrimination in infancy, as in maturity, is much more acute than is detection of difference in luminance without contrast (successive discrimination). Indeed, Kessen and Bornstein (1978) found that 4-month-old infants were equally insensitive to a doubling or halving of luminance when stimuli were presented in temporal succession. This insensitivity is considerably greater than that of the adult (see pages 43-44) and probably reflects interference and decay of brightness information in infant memory.

Thus, although there may be some rapid development in brightness perception during the first 2 months of life (Doris, Casper, & Poresky, 1967; Doris & Cooper, 1966), these rudimentary measures suggest that by the end of that time brightness discrimination approaches mature acumen. These studies suggest additionally that, under the appropriate methodological circumstances, young children can discriminate small constant differences in luminance and that their luminance discriminability characteristic is monotonic.

Is infant discrimination of hue monotonic or nonmonotonic against wavelength change? Bornstein (1978a) has collected pertinent but preliminary data on simultaneous wavelength discrimination in an infant. The observations suggest that discriminability is nonmonotonic. In Bornstein's study, one 5-month-old habituated to a single (reference) wavelength that appeared in two spatially separate positions simultaneously. Following the infant's habituation to the pair, light in one position was randomly varied 5, 10, or 15 nm longer than the reference wavelength, whereas the reference light was maintained in the other position. In different sessions the reference wavelength was selected from one of five spectral loci: two minima and three maxima on the adult wavelength discrimination function (see Fig. 3.3c). When the reference wavelength was 490 nm or 560 nm, $\Delta\lambda$ minima and loci of good discriminability, the infant doubled his looking to very small wavelength changes. However, when the reference was 450 nm, 520 nm, or 630 nm, $\Delta\lambda$ maxima and loci of poor discriminability, large changes were generally insufficient to elicit a similar amount of dishabituation or discrimination. These preliminary results suggest that under conditions of simultaneous stimulus presentation, infant discriminability is not monotonic with wavelength change. Because by 3 months of age infants probably possess color-normal, trichromatic vision (Bornstein, 1976a), the data additionally suggest that such discriminability is a property of the sensory capacity of the organism.

Studies of successive discrimination of wavelength in infants are more extensive, and they provide the opportunity for detailed investigation of hue change. These data show that babies approximately 4 months of age actually partition the physical spectrum into qualitative categories that resemble adult partitioning and that, like adults, infants see inter-category boundaries at minima on the wavelength discrimination function. Bornstein, Kessen, and Weiskopf (1976) used an attention–habituation paradigm with monochromatic spectral lights to assess wavelength discriminability in 4-month-old infants. Babies looked at selected spectral stimuli repeatedly until their visual attention waned. The stimuli were selected from the four basic adult hue categories—blue, green, yellow, and red. Following habituation, babies were shown a series of test wavelengths that included the original light and two new lights. For several groups, one of the new lights was selected from the same adult hue category, and the other was selected from a different adult hue category. For other groups, the original and new lights were selected from the same hue. Wavelength selection in the tests adhered to the design of a categorical paradigm: For all groups, the new wavelengths were chosen to be equal physical distances from the original. Infants' discrimination across three inter-hue boundaries, near minima on the discriminability function, 495 nm, 565 nm, and 610 nm, and at the spectral extremes, blue (430 to 495 nm) and red (610 to 660 nm), were tested in this way. Analyses of the infants' visual attention to the different colors presented during the test phase indicated that on the whole infants distinguished and hence categorized wavelengths very much the way adults do. That is, babies discriminated four qualitatively distinct spectral hues: "blue" (approximately 430 to 480 nm), "green" (approximately 510 to 560 nm), "yellow" (approximately 570 to 600 nm), and "red" (approximately 620 to 680 nm).

Commonly, psychologists (Beare, 1963; Graham, 1965), psycholinguists (Brown & Lenneberg, 1954; Kopp & Lane, 1968), and anthropologists (Carroll, 1966; Ray, 1952, 1953; Whorf, 1952) have maintained that hue categorization reflects arbitrarily derived discriminations and develops from differential training in childhood. Any regularity associated with hue categorization would, in their view, reflect common (cultural or linguistic) training. As the foregoing suggests, however, hue perception is closely allied to the capacity for wavelength discrimination. Hue categorization, therefore, must be innate or mature quite soon after birth.

Summary

The data that are available indicate that in infancy, as in maturity, discrimination of energy change is continuous and approximately constant for the dimensions of frequency and luminance. Energy changes along the physical dimensions of VOT and wavelength, however, engender variable discrimination, the psychological correlates of which are perceptual features. Generalizations within poorly discriminated regions of the VOT spectrum result in phonemes, and generalizations within poorly discriminated regions of the wavelength spectrum result in hues. Regions of acute discriminability along these two continua represent points of transition among perceptual features.

This argument and the infant data that support it are built explicitly on the biological nature of discriminability. To wit, perceptual features reflect nonmonotonicity in the operating characteristics of certain sensory systems vis-à-vis particular physical continua. In this sense, sensory system sensibilities may provide infants with a kind of innate knowledge. To support the supposition that these data reflect the existence and operation of perceptual processes that are rooted in sensory system function, two additional lines of evidence need to be marshaled. First, cross-cultural infant research would help to corroborate the pan-human existence of perceptual features. If infants from language communities in which Indo-European phonemic distinctions are not present discriminate similar phonetic changes, it would argue that such threshold discontinuities know no cultural qualifications. Likewise, infants from language communities that partition the physical spectrum differently should nevertheless show uniform categories of hue. Second, infrahuman research would help to corroborate the universal biological basis of perceptual features. If other mammalian species that possess sensory systems akin to those of the human being — in audition, monkey or chinchilla and in vision, monkey or chimpanzee — process acoustic variation of VOT or chromatic variation of wavelength in non-monotonic or qualitative modes, such discriminations will be shown not to be uniquely human but reflective of shared sensory physiology. It is to the latter animal studies that we briefly turn first.

THE BIOLOGY OF PERCEPTUAL FEATURES

Perceptual Features of "Speech" in Infrahuman Organisms

Since it was first suggested that the categorical perception of phonemes constituted evidence for the uniquely human status of speech (Abramson & Lisker, 1970; Eimas, 1975c; Liberman et al., 1967; Lisker & Abramson, 1964, 1970), that status has been challenged in several ways. Not the least interesting has been the attempt to demonstrate "speech" perception in organisms other than man. In practice, two animals with auditory systems similar to the human have engaged the attention of behavioral investigators. They are the monkey and the chinchilla.

Three "speech" discrimination studies were conducted with monkeys. Morse and Snowdon (1975), Waters and Wilson (1976), and Sinnott, Beecher, Moody, and Stebbins (1976) all asked whether primates, specifically rhesus monkeys (*Macaca*), would discriminate phonetic categories of speech using behavioral measures. Waters and Wilson (1976) found that monkeys would bisect the VOT continuum into two categories of stops, placing the boundary at approximately + 30 msec VOT, the value that divides voiced from voiceless stops in many human languages (Lisker & Abramson, 1970). Previously, Morse and Snowdon (1975) had found that monkeys, like human beings, categorize formant onset differences that specifically delimit place of articulation. Morse and Snowdon used the cardiac (EKG) component of orienting to index discriminability. In their study, between-category differences were differentiated better than within-category differences. [Later, Miller and Morse (1976) found that human infants tested in the same way would discriminate between- but not within-category changes for the place cues.] Last, in a study that used sensitive signal detection procedures, Sinnott et al. (1976) compared human and monkey behavioral discriminations of place. Two of their results are significant. First, they found that human beings were more sensitive than monkeys to intra-phonemic stimulus differences. Second, they found expectedly that inter-phonemic discriminations magnified for both monkeys and human beings as the judgment was transposed over time.

Together, these data suggest that nonmonotonic discriminability of formant relations may be a characteristic of the sensory apparatus and initally have only little to do with linguistic experience. Other comparative data support this conclusion. Kuhl and Miller (1975, 1976) compared stop contrast perception behaviorally in groups of chinchillas (*Chinchilla laniger*) and adult human beings. The rodent chinchilla is a second mammal with an auditory capacity known to be similar to that of man. Kuhl and Miller found that these animals discriminated phonetic boundaries between labial, alveolar, and velar cognates at VOT values highly similar to the values typically produced by English-speaking adults. Moreover, for both chinchillas and human beings, the boundary shifts with place of articulation. Thus actual place of articulation is salient. Finally, Kuhl argues that chinchillas discriminate between stimuli that fall into two phonetic categories better than they discriminate between stimuli that fall in the same category.

Adult human beings may process "speech" tokens in a unique way, as conditioned by a history of language exposure. However, voicing and place-of-articulation distinctions used in natural language are clearly and qualitatively differentiated by infrahuman mammals (who are not predisposed to develop language), as they are by man. We can conclude from these studies that categorical or feature perception of sounds does not represent a uniquely human mode of processing. Rather, the animal data strongly support the view that naturally occurring distinctive oppositions are cued by a noncontinuous psychoacoustic processing of VOT.

Perceptual Features of "Hue" in Infrahuman Organisms

Color vision is present in several different diurnal species, including teleosts, sauropsidians, and primates. Wherever perceptual features of hue have been sought — in bee, pigeon, monkey, and chimpanzee, as in man — they have been found. The sensory psychophysical analysis that applied in audition to phonemes appears to hold in vision for hues as well. In general, infrahuman hue data are more complete than infrahuman speech data.

Various studies of color vision in bee, pigeon, monkey, and chimpanzee reveal the systematic relationship between perceptual features of hue and wavelength discriminability. As a part of his behavioral experiments on communication and sensory capacities in honey bees (*Apis mellifera*), Frisch (1950) demonstrated that bees could discriminate colors from a series of achromatic stimuli that differed in lightness from white to black (i.e., that bees possess color vision) and that bees would "confuse" certain ranges of wavelengths but not others (i.e., that bees categorize certain wavelengths as being similar and dissimilar from others). Frisch's experiments and those of Kühn (1927) were behavioral. The results of their studies show four categories of hue for the bee: 300 to 400 nm, 400 to 490 nm, 490 to 500 nm, and 500 to 600 nm. Naturally, honey bee generalizations across wavelengths (categorizations) reflect the organism's ability to discriminate among wavelengths; Helversen (1972) measured wavelength discrimination in the honey bee and showed two minima, near 400 nm and 500 nm, wavelengths that mark hue transitions in the bee. Discriminability seems to be relatively poor elsewhere in the bee spectrum. Pigeons (*Columba livia*) that have in another context been shown to possess color vision (see Blough, 1957, and A. A. Wright, 1972) also see categories of hue in the spectrum. A. A. Wright and Cumming (1971), employing behavioral procedures, found that birds typically grouped certain wavelengths together as being qualitatively similar, distinguishing these from other groupings. The main results of their experiments show three hue categories for the pigeon: 450 to 540 nm, 540 to 590 nm, and 590 to 650 nm. Again, pigeon hues reflect the pigeon's wavelength discriminability. Using signal detection techniques, A. A. Wright (1972) measured wavelength discrimination in the pigeon and found two minima, as might be expected, at 540 nm and 590 nm. Pigeon discriminability is poor elsewhere in its spectrum. Finally, there is good evidence that two species of rhesus monkey (*Macaca fascicularis* and *M. mulatta*) perceive hue categorically. Sandell, Gross, and Bornstein (1979) have found unequal generalization in extinction with animals trained on one wavelength and tested with different wavelengths that were selected to be equally distant in physical terms from the training wavelength but to be unequally distant psychologically. Following the categorical paradigm, some test wavelengths fell within the hue of the training wavelength; the others fell across a (presumed) boundary between adjacent hues. The color vision of both species of monkey is by most psychophysical tests (including wavelength discrimination) identical with that of man (De Valois & De Valois, 1975). Expectedly, the chimpanzee (*Pan*) also sees four basic hues in the spectrum, analogous to the human blue, green, yellow, and red (Essock, 1977).

One important set of neurological mechanisms that may subserve hue discriminability among primates has been identified. De Valois (see De Valois & De Valois, 1975, for a review) has recorded from individual neurons in the lateral geniculate nuclei (LGN) of the Macaque monkey (*Macaca irus*), which has also demonstrated behaviorally a color vision identical with that of color-normal (trichromatic) man. Through electrophysiological research, De Valois identified statistically four classes of neural cells that are selectively sensitive to the blue-, green-, yellow-, and red-appearing ranges of the spectrum, respectively. The activity and discriminative characteristic of these cell types point to a foundation for hue categorization: De Valois, Abramov, and Mead (1967) have shown that the primate $\Delta\lambda$ function is adequately predicted by the discrimination capacities of the four chromatic-sensitive cell types taken together. Having isolated an individual type, De Valois et al. (1967) found that each discriminated wavelength change differentially and that the envelope of maximal sensitivity of the four types together matched the wavelength discrimination function that the monkeys produced behaviorally. Similar neurological mechanisms have not yet been unearthed in the visual system of either the bee or pigeon.

The data reviewed here suggest that in various species perceptual discriminability is not monotonic with wavelength change and that discriminative poverty coexists with perceptual features of hue in a logical and compelling reciprocal relationship. The animal data confirm that, in this reciprocal relationship, visual discriminative capacity that is given biologically underwrites the tendency toward perceptual categorization.

Summary

Discriminative discontinuities that have their basis in sensory function play a prominent role in perceptual and cognitive processes, especially those involving recognition of speech and hue. Two principal demonstrations of this view may be found in research conducted among adults and human infants. A second line of evidence derives from research on infrahuman organisms.

Certain changes in the perceptual environment seem to trigger specific sensory discriminations in all animals that share a similar sensory apparatus, and several different species have evolved similar biological bases for the detection and rapid processing of particular, salient kinds of information. Both neurophysiologists and behaviorists have engaged in research aimed at identifying the mechanisms in lower species whose properties and characteristics suggest that they are devoted to the perception of speech features or to color. The position outlined in this chapter, then, is not unlike others in the animal behavior literature. I have attempted here to provide human examples of these perceptual phenomena. The animal research helps particularly to disambiguate biological predispositions from selective experience and training in a manner impossible even with young children. Categories of phonemes and of hues have been identified in organisms that share man's biology but not his experience. These results confirm the importance of biological predisposition to feature perception.

EXPERIENCE AND PERCEPTUAL DEVELOPMENT

If perceptual features reflect operating characteristics of the sensory systems and are innate, what role does experience play in their development? In this section I review the possible roles of selection and instruction in the development of feature perception. Selection implies that the organism is endowed to perceive features from birth and that those features that obtain an adequate amount of stimulation persist in development. Instruction implies that the environment influences the development of feature perception. Selection and instruction are discussed here in the context of three kinds of experience —anomalous, general, and specific. In the final section of this chapter, the biological and psychological significance of features in perception and cognition are assessed.

Experience and the Development of Perceptual Features

Several questions naturally arise concerning the ontogenetic course of feature perception. First, what kinds of experience are requisite for the ontogeny of perceptual features? Although the biology of sensory systems may provide sufficient foundation for the initial existence of perceptual features, perception necessitates some general experience to ensure operation. Are perceptual features universal? Surely, if feature perception reflects sensory system function, perceptual features must exist wherever biological homoplasies do. Third, do perceptual features naturally follow any specific ontogenetic course? To what particular factors is developmental change attributable? Perception and the structure of perceptual features seem to change during ontogeny, and the direction of that change is predictable.

Finally, to what degree are perceptual features plastic with respect to selective experience? Clearly, experience may foster, transact with, or override the genetic endowment of the organism. Which outcome occurs will obviously be a function of the type of experience and the extent to which perceptual features (and their anatomical bases) are plastic. Perceptual development may be influenced by various kinds of experience. For those discontinuous perceptual features with which we have been concerned thus far—phonemes and hues—adequate experimental data exist to enable us to examine the influence of these different types of experience against the baseline that infants provide.

What kinds of experience are necessary to the ontogeny of perceptual features? Sensory systems need environmental stimulation of some sort to grow and to respond to. However, developing organisms may encounter three sorts of anomalous environments: one that fails to provide any adequate stimulation, one that fails to provide stimulation relevant to a particular sensory system or perceptual domain, or one that fails to provide stimulation for which a particular perceptual feature is tuned. Let us define *anomalous perceptual experience,* then, as being formative exposure to environments in which the organism may develop without any perceptual experience, without any relevant perceptual experience, or without any specific perceptual experience.

Silent- and dark-rearing studies could begin to answer questions about the influence or necessity of general auditory or visual experience to the development of perceptual features. Ordinarily, however, such rearing conditions so mar the anatomical, cognitive, and social fabrics of the organism as to render it next to worthless as an object of experimentation. Nevertheless, hue studies with dark-reared monkeys have been conducted, and their results suggest that hue discrimination, probably present at birth, is generally resilient to deprivation of visual experience. Boothe, Teller, and Sackett (1975), for example, deprived an infant pigtail monkey (*Macaca nemestrina*) of light for its first 3 months and subsequently found that it could discriminate all wavelengths from white—that is, that it still possessed color vision. We already know the nature of the normal or experienced trichromat's perceptual features of hue, but Ganz and Riesen (1962) have provided more systematic data on the light-deprived trichromat's hue perception. They reared four monkeys in darkness for 10 weeks and subsequently tested wavelength generalization in these four and a control group reared under normal lighting conditions. Whereas the experienced group produced steep generalization gradients from the first day of testing, the naive animals first showed flat functions that progressively steepened over 7 days of testing. With only a little experience, then, the deprived group produced "normal" data.

Von Senden (1932/1960) and Gregory and Wallace (1963) studied hue perception in human beings who had also been deprived of light during their early development. Their data further suggest that perceptual features of hue are resilient to light deprivation. According to these reports, chromatic discriminations were among the first systematic visual functions to appear following removal of congenital cataracts in adulthood.

We can conclude that perceptual features of hue are probably resilient to deprivation from infancy. Infrahuman organisms differentially sensitive to VOT have not (yet) been reared from birth in environments devoid of acoustic stimulation. Hence, it is impossible to say whether perceptual features or the neurological mechanisms that subserve them would atrophy under conditions of silent rearing or show resilience similar to perceptual features of hue. Moreover, silent rearing, like dark rearing or light deprivation, would be expected to result in animals with unwanted but unavoidable anatomical, cognitive, and social abnormalities. Therefore, there are not many appropriate auditory deprivation data. What data are available come from studies of institutionalized infants (Trehub, cited in Doty, 1974) and children with congenital sensorineural hearing loss (Bennett & Ling, 1973). These studies are of only questionable relevance. However, both studies suggest that features of speech are resilient to early deprivation. Additional research on the influence of auditory deprivation is necessary.

In summary, the vision and auditory literatures are weak on the question of experiential deprivation and feature perception. Nevertheless, visual studies suggest that perceptual features of hue are resilient to sensory deprivation, and auditory studies seem to corroborate that conclusion. Later we shall see that features of color and speech that are present in infancy but that remain unused through early ontogeny are still available in maturity. This fact again indicates the resilience of perceptual features to selective deprivation.

The first question, "What kinds of experience are necessary to the ontogeny of perceptual features?" may then be answered tentatively in the following way. Barring anatomical degeneration or other extraneous disruption of function, perceptual features of both hue and speech that are "wired in" at birth are fairly resilient to early experiential deprivation. According to Ganz and Riesen (1962), "Generalization in some cases simply follows automatically from the physiological properties of the receptor system involved and does not require previous experience [p. 97]." Obviously, however, feature perception takes place in relation to specific environmental stimulation, and some relevant experience at some time is therefore necessary for its expression. Deprivations that are relevant or specific to a particular perceptual domain will influence particular perceptual features and are discussed in subsequent sections.

Do perceptual features naturally follow any specific ontogenetic course? If so, to what factors may developmental changes be attributable?   In the view of classical (James, 1890; Miller & Dollard, 1941; Werner, 1948) and modern developmental theorists alike (e.g., E. J. Gibson, 1969; Witkin, Dyk, Faterson, Goodenough, & Karp, 1962), perceptual abilities sharpen in ontogeny, and this specificity is a universal process where the organism is exposed to a range of experience. Let us define *general perceptual experience* as being exposure to an environment in which the organism develops with a variety of experiences, at least some of which may be relevant or appropriate for feature perception. Perceptual information in such an environment is neither attenuated nor tailored, there being no specific bias to heighten or alter particular perceptions. Will feature perception sharpen in this kind of environment?

Rubel and Rosenthal (1975) recently provided a particularly clear model of ontogenetic specificity under conditions of general experience, demonstrating development along a perceptually continuous dimension. After habituating an orienting response in chicks (*Gallus domesticus*) to a tone of a single frequency, they tested generalization at surrounding frequencies. The experiment was performed on the day of hatching, when the chicks were 3 to 4 days old, and when they were 9 to 10 days old. One-day-old chicks displayed reliably flatter generalization gradients than did either of the older groups, which did not differ. Rubel and Rosenthal (1975) argued that early in normal development and in the context of general experience—chicks in this study were "incubated and reared communally in order to provide a wide range of auditory experience [p. 296]"—response capacities differentiate and perceptual coding processes sharpen.

Perceptual sharpening also occurs in the development of both speech and color identifications. The differentiation of perceptual features follows a qualitatively different course from that of perception along psychologically continuous dimensions. Zlatin and Koenigsknecht (1975), for example, studied VOT identification for labial, alveolar, and velar stop cognates in children 2 and 6 years of age and in adults. They ascertained the crossover points (in VOT), and they measured the widths of the boundaries between phoneme categories by assessing the distance (in msec) between symmetric points on adjacent phoneme identification functions. Although multiple comparisons were made, the three age groups did not basically differ in positioning crossover points. However, 2-year-olds showed significantly wider inter-category boundaries than did the 6-year-olds and adults, who did not differ. This study confirmed Wolf (1973), who had earlier found that boundary points for labial and alveolar stops did not differ between 5½ and 7½ years in any systematic way but that younger children tended to identify phonemes less reliably (as evidenced by their wider inter-category widths) than did the older children. Furthermore, Wolf (1973) noted that children discriminated among phonemes less accurately than did adults.

Hue categorization can be characterized by similar developmental phenomena. Although there is universal agreement about the positions of color foci (Berlin & Kay, 1969; Bornstein, 1973; Harkness, 1973; Mervis,

Catlin, & Rosch, 1975), even in infancy (Bornstein, 1975b), there is considerably less agreement culturally (Berlin & Kay, 1969) or ontogenetically about color boundaries (Mervis et al., 1975). Mervis et al. (1975) studied color naming at 5½ years and in adults. They found that, although locations of focal colors did not change between their youngest and oldest observers, judgments of both foci and boundaries of color categories engendered decreasing variance with age. The variance around color boundaries was reliably greater at every age than was the variance surrounding focal colors. Expectedly, the amount of judged overlap between adjacent colors decreased developmentally. Elsewhere, Gaines and Little (1975) confirmed that hue discriminability is inversely related to age.

The kind of boundary-width analysis Zlatin and Koenigsknecht (1975) applied to child VOT identifications could also be applied to categorical judgments of hue or color naming in young children and adults. My own unpublished observations show that color naming is disorganized among 2-year-olds but that the boundaries between color-naming functions narrow between 3 and 4 years. In a color-naming study cited earlier, Boynton and Gordon (1965) asked three young-adult observers to identify monochromatic lights. A boundary-width analysis of these data shows no differences between Boyton and Gordon's 12-year-old and two 20-year-old observers. To summarize, in color identification as in phoneme identification some normative developmental specificity seems to occur between infancy and puberty to sharpen boundary widths between categories. After puberty, this development seems to reach an asymptote.

With a wide range of *general* experience, therefore, perceptual differentiation is canalized, and response specificity seems to prevail in development. This finding exemplifies a long tradition within developmental and perceptual theory. Explanations for this type of ontogenetic change differ, however. Perhaps (least interestingly) differentiation reflects the methodology or a lack of experimenter control over behavior. Investigators of both speech and hue perception typically employ successive-discrimination paradigms that are particularly open to perceptual or judgmental error from infants and young children. These methods fail to assess sensory function per se. Hence, data generated under such experimental conditions may be less sensitive than canalization analyses demand. Second, perhaps perceptual differentiation reflects the development or maturation of the anatomical or sensory apparatus after infancy. The infant is clearly not the same person as the adult who lacks experience: The fact that infants have legs does not mean that they can walk. Third, differentiation may more parsimoniously reflect the development of selective attention with age. In studies of sensory discrimination, children would tend unavoidably to be subject to attentional distraction or to invoke labeling processes. For example, Mervis et al. (1975) found variance in both focal- and boundary-color judgments to be inversely related to age. Indeed, in studying ontogenetic changes in selective attention, Mednick and Lehtinen (1957) suggested that a difference between immature and mature reactivity may be unrelated to the psychological or physical differences among stimuli but may be related, rather, to higher error rates in children.

A fourth and perceptually reasonable explanation is that exposure to specific and reinforcing experience in a particular environment causes boundaries between perceptual categories to sharpen. Let us define *specific perceptual experience* as being exposure to an environment in which the organism develops with experiences that foster or selectively reinforce certain perceptual features over others. One might argue that Zlatin and Koenigsknecht's (1975) result reflects perceptual experience with the phonemes that children actually say and hear. An informal test of this hypothesis can be found in Kuhl and Miller (1976), who compared boundary widths for labial, alveolar, and velar stops in chinchillas and in human beings. Although both mammals may have had a broad range of general auditory experience, the human being displayed narrower boundary widths than did the chinchillas, which suggests that specific human experience with the language influenced the development of discriminative ability. A difficulty, of course, with this interpretation as it stands is the fact that error variance—humans may be better observers than chinchillas—can never be eliminated as a factor.

The psychological problem in general is to disentangle the influences of maturation from specific experience and the influences of methodological artifacts or attention from sensory differences. One method that might help to separate maturational processes from the influence of experience is perceptual deprivation (if the problems associated with anatomical degeneration can be avoided). As suggested at the outset, no deprivation studies on organisms sensitive to VOT or hue have been conducted in a manner that might indicate the relative contributions of canalized maturation and specific experience. However, Kerr and Rubel (1977) have extended their studies on maturation of perceptual coding to conditions of auditory deprivation. They plugged the ears of prehatchling chick embryos, thus attenuating input 40 dB until they tested the chicks 3 to 4 days after hatching. Three-day-old deprived chicks produced generalization gradients that were flat like 1-day-old chicks and unlike experienced 3-day-old chicks. Therefore, brief, early generalized experience seems to play a critical role in perceptual sharpening.

Techniques that might help to separate methodological and attentional artifacts from sensory development include signal detection procedures. Such studies remain to be conducted, however.

Despite idiosyncrasies regarding the origins of perception and the mechanisms of perceptual change, most developmental theories agree that specificity, tuning, and differentiation best characterize perceptual development. However, two aspects of the development of perceptual features point to important exceptions to this general rule. First, as boundaries between categories narrow, the categories themselves broaden. This aspect of the ontogenetic change is shown in Figure 3.4. Thus, over the course of development a larger number of stimuli are categorized and consequently "confused." Normally, according to Gibson and Gibson (1955) increased perceptual precision is synonymous with reduced generalization: "A stimulus item starts out by being indistinguishable from a whole class of items in the stimulus universe tested, and ends by being distinguishable from all of them [p. 38]." However, in feature perception (as assessed by forced-choice identification), adults seem to accept wider within-category variation than do children, a result that reinforces the notion that all aspects of perceptual development need not adhere to the same principles (e.g., Hershenson, 1971).

A second exception to the general rule of differentiation can be found in perceptual feature development. Certain perceptual features are apparently distinguished in infancy but not in maturity. When unused, perceptual distinctions blur, and stimuli seem to become subsumed by neighboring perceptual features. This generalization phenomenon is discussed later.

In summary, the two questions posed on page 58 may be answered in the following way. The boundaries between perceptual features of both color and speech sharpen during the course of development; the feature plateaus themselves broaden. These universal ontogenetic shifts may be attributable to variance in methodology, to change in sensory capacity, to growth of selective attention, or to the positive influence of specific experience. The relative contributions of these various sources of change are open to study.

Are perceptual features universal? To what degree are perceptual features plastic, and is their development subject to the effects of selective experience? Feature perception characterizes the organization of one type of perceptual information processing in young human infants as well as in mature animals, a finding that strongly suggests that some perceptual features are "wired in." Yet cultural and linguistic forces are known to exploit or reinforce features differently. Thus, adults with differing *specific* experiences differ in their perception of features. Two questions arise, then, in a consideration of the influence of specific experience on feature perception. Are perceptual features common even among infants reared in varying experiential contexts? How malleable are perceptual features in development? The fact that different language and ecological communities construct different auditory and visual environments creates a kind of natural experiment in which to examine, first, the universality of feature perception and, second, the plasticity of perceptual features.

Specific perceptual experience includes selective deprivation or enrichment, and defining specific experience presupposes a knowledge of exactly which perceptual features are wired in. First, we must calculate the endowment. The results of the studies of speech perception reviewed earlier show

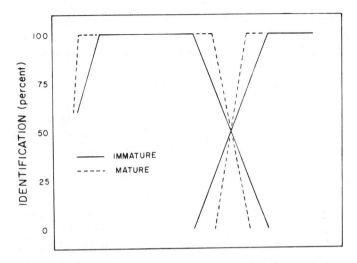

FIG. 3.4. Change in the structure of a perceptual feature and boundary with a change in developmental status. Notice that the category plateau broadens in normal development and that the boundary between adjacent categories narrows.

that American infants are prone to make phonemic distinctions important in English. Eimas (1975c; Cutting & Eimas, 1975) has also found that American babies discriminate between bilabial phones on either side of a −50 msec VOT boundary. This prevoiced-voiced boundary is common to many languages (e.g., Thai) but not to English. Likewise, 10-week-old Canadian infants from English-speaking families discriminate the French and Polish oral-nasal contrast, /pã/ vs. /pa/, and the Czech strident contrast, /za/ vs. /řa/, to the same degree they do the English /p/ − /b/ contrast (Trehub, 1976). However, neither American (Eimas, 1975c) nor Guatemalan infants from monolingual Spanish families (Lasky, Syrdal-Lasky, & Klein, 1975) discriminate an adult Spanish labial boundary.

These results describe three cells of a 2 X 2 developmental matrix. One matrix side is distinguished by the presence or absence of a perceptual feature in infancy, and the other is distinguished by its presence or absence in maturity. Infant features may be present in adults; infant features may not be present in adults; and adult features may not be present in infants. (Quite obviously, though less interestingly, features may be present neither in infants nor in adults.) If available data are placed in these cells, they indicate that infants naturally discriminate many more distinctions than may actually be used in their immediate language community. They suggest, first, that all babies might naturally distinguish a regular series of VOT, place of articulation, or other contrasts. Second, they suggest that adult perception is not necessarily congruent with infant perception.

Two recent cross-cultural studies provide a detailed examination of infants' perceptions of phonetic contrasts in language communities in which phonemic contrasts differ from those that are extant in infants. In one study, Lasky et al. (1975) investigated discrimination of VOTs among infants from Spanish monolingual families living in Guatemala. In Spanish, the principal voicing distinction exists between approximately − 10 and + 10 msec VOT, near the simultaneous onset of the first and higher formants (Abramson & Lisker, 1973; Williams, 1977). Lasky et al. used habituation and change in infants' heart rate to detect discrimination, and they found that Guatemalan 4- to 6-month-olds did not respond differentially to a change from − 20 to + 20 msec VOT, surrounding the Spanish stop boundary, but did discriminate values of + 20 and + 60 msec VOT, on opposite sides of the English initial stop boundary, and values of − 60 and − 20 msec VOT, surrounding a prevoiced boundary in Thai. In a second, similar series of experiments, Streeter (1976a, 1976b) examined phonemic distinctions among infant and adult Kikuyu. African adults who speak Kikuyu, a Bantu language native to Kenya, do not contrast the English bilabials /b/ − /p/ (at + 30 msec VOT). Rather, Kikuyu has only one labial stop, a prevoiced /b/ whose average VOT is − 64 msec (Streeter, 1976b). Streeter (1976a) tested 2-month-old Kikuyu infants using the sucking-habituation technique, and she found that they discriminated a difference between + 10 and + 40 msec VOT (the "English" stop) but not a difference between + 50 and + 80 msec VOT.

First, these studies help to establish what may be a universal baseline for feature perception in infancy. American, Spanish, and Kikuyu infants alike seem to discriminate one phonetic boundary between approximately + 25 and + 35 msec VOT and a second boundary between − 30 and − 50 msec. The latter boundary is found in Kikuyu but not in English or Spanish; the former boundary is found in English but not in Spanish or Kikuyu. Neither American nor Spanish infants, however, display a Spanish labial boundary around 0 msec VOT. Thus, together, the results suggest that infants are innately predisposed to perceive one phonetic boundary around − 40 msec VOT and another around + 30 msec VOT. The results of these cross-cultural studies suggest that infants naturally distinguish three phonetic tokens along the VOT continuum, and the infant results correspond strikingly with phonetic production and perception that is widespread among adults (Abramson & Lisker, 1970; Lisker & Abramson, 1970). See also pages 41-43 and Figure 3.2b. Additionally, the French nasal, Czech strident, and English liquid contrasts exemplify other phonetic distinctions that may be universal among human infants.

Second, these studies provide appropriate conditions under which to examine the influence of specific experience on perceptual development. They indicate that native perceptual features are subject to experiential modification—addition or deletion—early in life. All logical possibilities have been demonstrated. Kikuyu babies distinguish prevoiced stops (− 30 and 0 msec VOT) that do not seem to be universal among infants but to which they in particular are frequently exposed (Streeter, 1976a). Streeter's study, then, exemplifies the case of early addition to a universal baseline. Adult Japanese produce and perceive the liquids /r/ and /l/ interchangeably (Goto, 1971; Miyawaki et al., 1975), but speakers of English take advantage of physical distinctions between liquids to categorize a phonemic contrast. Eimas (1975b) has shown that this categorical distinction is present in American 2-to 3-month-old infants as well. Thus, barring infantile racial differences, Japanese children fail to capitalize on a potential discrimination. Finally, Guatemalan specific experience combines both tendencies: Between infancy and maturity Spanish speakers lose both a prevoiced-voiced contrast and a voiced-voiceless contrast but learn to distinguish a voiced-voiceless contrast (at simultaneous VOT) that they did not distinguish as infants.

Inasmuch as features can be added to an endowed repertoire, it must be that initial discriminative capacity does not constrain the organism. Thus, if phonemic perception were strictly digital and categorical, it would not be possible to discriminate between or to develop tokens of VOT within categories. Clearly, the nonmonotonic nature of VOT discriminability allows for the development of new perceptual distinctions.

An important question that arises over such additions asks whether a new boundary is a wholly new discrimination or simply a modulation of what is essentially a universal boundary. Voicing perception among bilinguals provides a tentative answer because it seems to be mutually influenced by characteristics of the two languages they know. Caramazza, Yeni-Komshian, Zurif, and Carbone (1973) found that unilingual Canadian French uniformly discriminate short VOT crossover points for bilabial, alveolar, and velar initial stops and that unilingual Canadian English uniformly discriminate long VOT crossovers. The crossovers for Canadian French-English bilinguals, however, fall consistently at intermediate positions, and their compromise status strongly evidences malleability of perception.

Studies in the Spanish language address this question as well. English unilinguals show a single peak in discrimination of VOT at approximately $+25$ to $+30$ msec, where the boundary between adjacent phonemic categories in English occurs. Spanish unilingual discrimination is, constrastingly, bimodal; adult Spanish monolinguals evidence a primary discrimination maximum between -10 and 0 msec VOT, where their two phonemic categories cross, and a secondary discrimination maximum at approximately $+30$ msec VOT, which is in the middle of the Spanish voiceless category (Williams, 1977). As suggested earlier (see Figure 3.2b), the secondary discrimination maximum is the typical site of infant and cross-language boundaries. The Spanish language seems to have modulated away from the original site, whereas the Spanish ear still retains discriminative acumen at the natural boundary.

As the Spanish case suggests, discriminative abilities enjoyed in infancy but not used during ontogeny are attenuated but not irretrievably lost.

Thus, adult Japanese have difficulty distinguishing the English /r/ and /l/ in the same way that English-speaking adults experience difficulty with the Czech /z/ and /ř/. Like other within-category contrasts, neither discrimination is unresolvable. Likewise, adult Kikuyu can discriminate the English labial voiced-voiceless (/b/ – /p/) contrast (which they do not use) but not as well as their own prevoiced /b/ (Streeter, 1976b). The persistence of these abilities, even in the absence of relevant experience, probably reflects their basis in the natural psychoacoustic properties of the auditory system. Consequently, lack of specific experience does not easily erode biologically rooted perceptual capacities. Perhaps general experience with the wide range of sounds produced in the natural environment is sufficient to maintain feature sensitivity that is native.

Similar instances of the universality of perceptual features and their plasticity may be found in the realm of hue perception. Surveying the linguistic organization of color, Berlin and Kay (1969) first observed that nomenclature systems for colors varied in different cultures but that nomenclature referents for color were standardized and uniform across cultures. Later Hays, Margolis, Naroll, and Perkins (1972) amplified on the salience of particular color name categories, and Bornstein (1973) provided evidence that universals in color naming were supported by physiological referents.

In hue perception as in phoneme perception, adult status must relate to an initial infant baseline. The developmental data on color perception are not as complete in this respect as are the data on speech perception, and several questions parallel to the phoneme studies remain to be answered. For example, do infants in different cultures partition the spectrum into perceptual features of hue as do American infants? Based on the relationship between discriminability and categorization, it is reasonable to expect that they do.

A second general question addresses the notion of developmental change in hue perception. Tracy (1970) observed that ducklings reared in monochromatic light (589 nm), trained to respond to 589 nm, and later tested with a series of surrounding wavelengths gave steep or peaked generalization functions that resembled those of ducklings reared in heterogeneous white light. Tracy's result implies that rearing with specific perceptual experience (deprivation) does not alter innate discriminations.

In the human experimental literature, experientially specific monochromatic rearing conditions are nonexistent. However, a second kind of specific experience thought to be directly related to the nature of perceptual features of hue is linguistic specificity. Philosophers, psychologists, anthropologists, and linguists have often suggested that language, through cultural learning, influences perception (for summaries and critiques, see Berlin & Kay, 1969, Bornstein, 1975a, or Segall, Campbell, & Herskovits, 1966). The Whorfian dictum reads that if the language the child learns partitions the wavelength spectrum into particular categories, the child will learn to see it partitioned so. One important deduction of this hypothesis is that wavelength discriminability might then vary with linguisitic environment (Kopp & Lane, 1968).

Kopp and Lane (1968) provided one of the few seemingly direct tests of the Whorfian hypothesis. They first extracted color-naming data, and then, using the ABX procedure to assess discrimination, they tested hue discriminability among the Tzoltzil. The Tzoltzil gave drastically different wavelength-discriminability and color-naming functions from those of English speakers. Based on the well-founded observation that hue discriminability is best at the boundaries of color-naming categories but increasingly poor toward the centers of these categories, Kopp and Lane (1968) argued that their Tzoltzil data on hue discriminability and color naming supported the Whorfian hypothesis. That is, these researchers maintained that hue discrimination does not reflect sensory capacity but rather, linguistic environment. They concluded that "hue discriminability functions may vary systematically from one language community to the next to the extent that color categories in different languages partition the hue continuum differently [p. 62]." Curiously, however, Kopp and Lane's position tends to diminish the significance of structural uniformity of the human visual system, and it tends to subvert electrophysiological evidence (De Valois & De Valois, 1975) that demonstrates clear involvement of LGN cell activity in wavelength discriminability. Further analysis suggests that Kopp and Lane's methodological procedures are suspect. In their ABX paradigm, the discriminability of X from A or B is supposed to depend on the subject's sensitivity, but the paradigm does not tap sensory discriminability purely, because neither A nor B is present when X is. Thus, the observer cannot see A, B, and X together to discriminate among them. Rather, in the ABX procedure, the observer is left to discriminate X from his own memory codes of A and B. Such a code would probably be semantic and, especially in this case, make use of color terminology. Thus, the ABX test is a strict variant of color naming, and one would expect the hue discriminability functions so derived to match color-naming functions appropriately. Kopp and Lane's (1968) study fails, then, to test the influences of specific cultural experience on the development of feature perception.

Together the Bornstein et al. (1976) infant data and the Berlin and Kay (1969) cross-cultural data suggest that color-designation universals are ontogenetically stable. What about the addition and deletion of perceptual features of hue? Obviously, new color-naming distinctions may be added to the hue categories present in infancy (Chapanis, 1965), and this creative phenomenon taps the analogue nature of wavelength discriminability. The vast array of human color names supports this point. Are infantile distinctions lost if they are not used? Probably not. The paucity of developmental hue data notwithstanding, results of the monochromatic-rearing studies combined with the "hard-wired" nature of discriminability (Kikuyu adults continue to be able to discriminate the "English" phoneme although they do not use or hear it themselves) suggest in general that native perceptual discriminations tend not to be lost with disuse, although they may weaken.

In summary, the third set of questions as asked on page 62 may be tentatively answered in the following way. Psychological tokens or perceptual features along different physical continua are shared by members of different cultures. The same sets of basic tokens exist in human infants and, long before extensive experience, involve the perceptual analysis of acoustic or visual variation in a psychophysical mode. Feature perception is ontogenetically canalized, and its pancultural validity biases the newborn system in the direction of mature perceptual analysis. Feature perception is adaptive, moreover, and during ontogeny it is subject to tempered modification, through addition or attrition, but under somewhat rigid constraints.

Summary

In discussions of the origins of perception and of perceptual development, several questions persist. First, what is the state of the organism at birth, or with minimal experience? Second, what range of experience is prerequisite for normal development? Third, does perceptual development follow a canalized ontogenetic path? Fourth, is perception plastic, that is, to what degree can it be influenced by selective experience? Finally, to what extent are the processes that are associated with perceptual development universal? Studies of feature perception address each question. Since features are natural and based in sensory function, they are probably present at birth to the degree that the sensory apparatus is developed at birth. The universality of particular features among infants reared in cultural environments in which those features are not shared by adults further supports this conclusion. Categories of perceptual features broaden, and the boundaries between adjacent features sharpen with maturation and experience, although the relative contributions of these twin influences to perceptual development are difficult to assess at present. Furthermore, various deprivation data suggest that only a very little general or specific experience is necessary to maintain perceptual features that are natural. Additionally, the analogue nature of discriminability permits new perceptual features to be added onto the native repertoire. Finally, specific experience with some speech contrasts seems to facilitate the perception of other naturally discriminable contrasts. This conclusion suggests that general experience is important to the development of the perceptual system as a whole.

Theories of perceptual development vary in the degree to which they ascribe the origins and ontogenetic course of change in perceptual abilities to nature or nurture. Almost certainly, however, perceptual development between infancy and maturity involves some complex transaction of these influences. Much of this transaction remains to be explored, and we have only suggestive answers to a variety of fundamental questions. What is the time course of the acquisition of a new perceptual feature? Are new features solely conditioned by context and environment? Are new features limited other than by sensory discriminability? Are later specific experiences of value to native distinctions disused since infancy?

Longitudinal and cross-cultural studies of development will provide answers to some of these questions. For example, Eilers and her associates (Eilers & Minifie, 1975; Eilers, Wilson, & Moore, 1976) examined the acquisition of one phonemic contrast microscopically. Using the sucking-habituation technique, Eilers and Minifie (1975) found that 1- to 4-month-old infants failed to discriminate the fricative contrast /s/ − /z/. In a follow-up study, Eilers et al. (1976) used a conditioned head-turning paradigm to test 6-to 8-month-olds on the same distinction. Those infants and older babies (12 to 14 months) both resolved an /s/ − /z/ distinction. Perhaps the younger babies were incapable of the distinction, or perhaps the sucking technique employed with younger infants was too insensitive to expose true discriminative capacity. Although the latter explanation is possible, Eilers et al. (1976) also found that both 1- to 4-month-old suckers and 6- to 8-month-old headturners were incapable of the fricative discrimination /f/ − /θ/.

In a cross-cultural study, Streeter and Landauer (1976) observed Kikuyu children learning English as a second language. They did this cross-sectionally with children aged 7½, 10, 13, and 15 years. Two important findings emerged. First, the youngest children who had no exposure to English could discriminate a prevoiced labial common to Kikuyu as well as a voiced-voiceless labial distinction found in English and other languages (Lisker & Abramson, 1970). Thus, the Kikuyu perceptual feature available to adults but not to infants developed after 7½ years of specific experience. Second, the oldest children who had more exposure to English were much better at (English) voiced-voiceless discriminations than were the younger children. These results suggest that specific experience, too, can operate to sharpen discriminations that are naturally distinctive. How well would the age mates of the oldest children discriminate English contrasts in which they were unschooled? Streeter (1976b) suggests that they would be poor.

Similar questions extend to the perceptual discriminability of naturally continuous dimensions; they, too, necessarily reflect the influence of specific experience. Galizio and Baron (1976), for example, showed that label training would increase distinctiveness among tones (Miller & Dollard, 1941). Special training may influence categorization, too. For example, Locke and Keller (1973) observed that only trained musicians would categorize the components of triadic chords, Siegel and Siegel (1977) found that experienced musicians only have acquired categories of tonal variation, and Cuddy (1968, 1970) showed that the identification of frequency (absolute pitch) is a learned ability. Nevertheless, there are no stable boundaries between sine waves of different frequencies, and discriminability is essentially monotonic even when labels are artificially applied to different frequencies (Kopp & Livermore, 1973). These cognitive phenomena apply to speech in addition to nonspeech auditory domains: Although English and Swedish speakers show similar discriminability of rounded vowels (/i/ – /y/ – /ʉ/), these vowels are phonemic and identified in a categorical manner only in Swedish (Stevens, Liberman, Studdert-Kennedy, & Öhman, 1969).

In their origin and ontogeny, perceptual features exemplify many of the characteristics that perceptual theorists have employed to describe, analyze, and explain perceptual development. Perhaps because they represent unique possibilities for exploring further the relations between the organism and experience, they will engage the attention of additional animal and cross-cultural developmental research.

MEANING, FUNCTION, AND SIGNIFICANCE OF PERCEPTUAL FEATURES

In the nineteenth-century radical empiricist view, man's knowledge about the world was believed to come through his senses. The senses, as we know, are organs of pain and pleasure, but they are as well particularly important devices for the reception and analysis of information available in the environment. Vision and audition, especially, provide man with higher level, "cognitive" information. One example of such sensory information is feature perception. Feature perception provides a basic mechanism for refinement, coding, and further analysis of otherwise unorganized perceptual information available at the sensory surface. In this final section, the meaning, function, and significance of perceptual features are briefly assessed. Perceptual features of the type herein described seem to operate on several levels, each of which has real perceptual and cognitive consequences for the immature and the mature organism. These consequences include (1) perceptual contrast and clarity, (2) encoding, processing, and recognition of information, and (3) learning, cognition, and rule induction.

Perceptual Contrast and Clarity

At the lowest level, nonmonotonic discriminability of energy change produces perceptual contrast and opposition. Contrasts automatically segment the flux of energy into (usable) chunks of information (Miller, 1956). Oppositions clarify and, therefore, they afford distinct sources of information. Since differential discriminability represents an initial stage of perception, it results in the early availability of perceptual contrast and clarity.

By partitioning environmental flux in a regular way, perceptual features provide various kinds of information. Selected from a small subset, perceptual contrasts are, in Garner's terms (1962), good patterns, stable, and subject to quick organization. Discontinuous structures are the easiest to perceive (Sokal, 1974) and for this reason may have been exploited by different modalities. Hue, for example, is principal in visual detection and discrimination, and the photocontrasts based on qualities of hue, it has been argued (e.g., McFarland & Munz, 1975; Walls, 1942), are responsible for the evolution of chromatic vision. Second, because of their holistic quality, features may emerge (as figure from ground) out of the general perceptual noise in which they are embedded. Third, in that perceptual features rest on distinctive discriminations, they serve, to distinguish ranges of sensory stimulation from one another, as, for example, speech cues from other sounds. Perceptual features thus help to place particular kinds of information in context.

The "categorical" quality of feature perception—wherein psychological discriminability is reduced over a given range of energy change—serves importantly to enhance perceptual clarity. Both the organism and the stimulus environment constantly change, and the categorical aspect of feature perception permits perceptual stability or invariance to emerge. In essence, information quality is maintained in the face of natural variation. The functional importance of such a mechanism to communication can hardly be overestimated. In human speech, for example, acoustic invariance is never the case, and it is clearly beneficial to ignore acoustic variations of context or speaker that are irrelevant. Similarly, in photopic vision, hue qualities remain largely constant over relatively wide changes in context or illumination (Boynton & Gordon, 1965). The fact that encoding of perceptual features is accomplished so early in the hierarchy of information analysis by the nervous system strongly promotes the notion that such features are important and show fidelity to the stimulus source.

Encoding, Processing, and Recognition of Information

An immediate asset of discontinuous discriminability associated with features is perceptual invariance, and the reduction of variance facilitates information encoding. Perceptual features reduce to manageable codes larger amounts of information that might otherwise overload processing capacity. In this sense, categorization renders energy variation comprehensible. As Bruner, Goodnow, and Austin (1956) observed, "Virtually all cognitive activity involves and is dependent upon categorization [p. 246]." Even though 7,500,000 colors are discriminable (Nickerson & Newhall, 1943), they comfortably reduce to a handful of qualitative differences. (Because the perceptual system is basically analogue, it can still take advantage of sharper discriminations.) The fact that infrahuman organisms and human infants alike discriminate in this way indicates that they possess the great potential for immediate encoding. Perceptual features facilitate incipient analyses of information by providing natural categories into which nonmeaningful variations in stimulation might be clustered or encoded.

Categorization speeds encoding time, especially when the categories are immediately available. McGuirk and Hebert (1973) studied latency patterns in category judgments and found "that the further away from a category boundary a given stimulus falls, the more rapid the response to that stimulus value [p. 458]." Furthermore, Ingling (1972) showed that identification of individual stimuli by physical features was unnecessary when more-encompassing categories are available during visual search, and Garner (1966) showed that perceptual dimensions marked by high discriminability, such as features, encourage rapid classification and sorting. Finally, Monroe and Bornstein (1978) have ascertained that identifying a color center is faster than boundary classification even when the two are equally available. Certainly, immediate categorizations yield the most information with the least cognitive effort (Cutting et al., 1976)—indeed, a single sampling provides sufficient information. Additionally, features or perceptual categories ease mental manipulation (Sokal, 1974) by providing a psychological basis for rapid perceptual decision making.

Encoding further realizes an economy of memory and facilitates recognition. It is well known that efficacious storage and retrieval both operate in terms of entities or chunks of information not unlike the features discussed here (Miller, 1956). Additionally, recognition processes depend on discriminability and are advanced, as the Gestaltists knew, when there is clear structural organization (Saul & Osgood, 1954; Wiseman & Neisser, 1974). Like a template, coding processes such as those involved in feature perception engage immediate stimulus recognition. The categorical nature of perceptual features sets the occasion for false recognitions, however. Among infants, for example, inappropriate recognition occurs for different physical instances (wavelengths) of the same feature (hue) (Bornstein, 1976b). Similarly, among children errors in phonemic memory are largely explainable in terms of a perceptual feature-encoding analysis (Eimas, 1975a).

Learning, Cognition, and Rule Induction

Since Hume and Mill, many philosophers and psychologists have argued that learning proceeds by the association of events. None has denied, however, the essential role of sensation in the development of associations. The kind of perceptual features that have been described here clearly best fit the idea behind such sensations. In contrast to purely quantitative sensations, qualitative changes convey more information because they abstract and segment relevant aspects of the environment. Until the identification of perceptual features, learning theorists (e.g., Miller & Dollard, 1941) could only point to the necessity of labels to mediate phenomenal contrasts; perceptual features provide similar contrasts prior to linguistic development or tuition.

Those sensations that are discriminable and organized into perceptual features potentiate their own use as cognitive cues. Because they are discriminable, they engage attention, are perceived as dominant, and are likely to be preferred. These processes, in turn, engender futher differentiation, promote salience, and facilitate problem solving (Fernandez, 1976; Suchman & Trabasso, 1966; Trabasso, Stave, & Eichberg, 1969). Moreover, the perception of invariance reduces uncertainty and is itself rewarding.

Perceptual features provide initial guidance to the emergence of rules of communication and of rudimentary cognitive behavior. For example, the categorical nature of features implies that some perception of abstract similarity is built in. It is likely, then, that those dimensions that are salient or qualitative in the sense described here may proceed earliest in cognitive development. "Prototypes" act as selected representatives of perceptual categories (Reed, 1972) and of features. The attention that they engage serves as a filter for perception, action, and memory. Thus, focal hues (exemplars of hue features) hold babies' attention longest (Bornstein, 1975b, 1978b), are learned fastest by children and have names attached to them most easily (Heider, 1971, 1972; Rosch, 1973), are remembered better (Bornstein, 1978a; Heider, 1971), and are initially preferred in children's classification and sorting (Bornstein, 1978a). They also remain salient in adulthood (e.g., Bornstein, 1975c; Hays et al., 1972).

The perceptual invariance associated with features of hue and speech may serve yet another cognitive function. In that they tolerate input variation, features are constancies of a sort, acting on information change in a many-to-one fashion. Thus, perceptual features resemble simple visual and auditory concepts (Bornstein, 1978a). Significantly for developmental theory, Piaget (1952/1963) and Elkind (Chapter 9, this volume) both have observed that the conservation of discontinuous quantities (beads) precedes the conservation of continuous quantities (liquids). Discontinuous elements such as features are perceptually separate and do not provide the impediment to operational thinking that continuous dimensions do.

The connected stages between sensory coding and the ontogeny of logic are summarized quite elegantly by Barlow (1974). One can see, he writes,

a continuity between the formation of sensory messages from physical stimuli, the rearrangement of these messages to make our sensations and perceptions, the formation of concepts about these perceptions, the attachment of words to concepts and percepts, and the modifications to the meanings of words by inductive inference [p. 132].

Summary

It is widely accepted that categorization is a ubiquitous cognitive process. In categorization, nonidentical stimuli are treated as being functionally similar and are distinguished from other classes of stimuli. Categorization therefore includes abstraction of select properties and filtering of irrelevancies. Clearly, such classificatory propensities increase survival value by improving efficiency of information processing.

Here I suggest that categorization has its roots in infant sensation and perception, that these earliest categorizations are nonarbitrary, and that they serve several variegated functions. Perceptual features organize the world. They partition dimensions of sensation into stable units and provide critical information about those dimensions. Perceptual features are encoded, processed, and recognized with facility. Moreover, they provide a key basis for elementary learning. Finally and more speculatively, the stimulus equivalences that are perceptual features may form *Anlagen* for mature conceptual behavior and the treatment of transformations or variations of other stimulus sets.

ACKNOWLEDGMENTS

Preparation of this chapter was partially supported by grants from the Spencer Foundation and the National Institutes of Mental Health. I wish to thank Helen G. Bornstein, James E. Cutting, Daly Enstrom, Carol S. Furchner, Charles G. Gross, Ronald A. Kinchla, and Anthony A. Wright for comments on earlier drafts and Kay D. Patterson, Julia Sandell, and Carol Smith for assistance in preparing the manuscript.

REFERENCES

Abramson, A. S., & Lisker, L. Discriminability along the voicing continuum: Cross-language tests. In *Proceedings of the Sixth International Congress of Phonetic Sciences, Prague, 1967.* Prague: Academia, 1970.

Abramson, A. S., & Lisker, L. Voice-timing perception in Spanish word–initial stops. *Journal of Phonetics,* 1973, *1,* 1–8.

Bachem, A. Time factors in relative and absolute pitch determination. *Journal of the Acoustical Society of America,* 1954, *26,* 751–753.

Barclay, J. R. Noncategorical perception of a voiced stop consonant. *Proceedings of 78th Annual Convention of the American Psychological Association,* 1970, *5,* 9–10.

Barlow, H. B. Inductive inference, coding, perception, and language. *Perception,* 1974, *3,* 123–134.

Bartoshuk, A. K. Human neonatal cardiac acceleration to sound: Habituation and dishabituation. *Perceptual and Motor Skills,* 1962, *15,* 15–27.

Beare, A. C. Color-name as a function of wave-length. *American Journal of Psychology,* 1963, *76,* 248–256.

Bennett, C. W., & Ling, D. Discrimination of the voiced-voiceless distinction by severely hearing-impaired children. *Journal of Auditory Research,* 1973, *13,* 271–279.

Berlin, B., & Kay, P. *Basic color terms: Their universality and evolution.* Berkely: University of California Press, 1969.

Blough, D. S. Spectral sensitivity in the pigeon. *Journal of the Optical Society of America,* 1957, *47,* 827-833.

Boothe, R., Teller, D. Y., & Sackett, G. P. Trichromacy in normally reared and light-deprived infant monkeys. *Vision Research,* 1975, *15,* 1187-1191.

Boring, E. G. The size of the differential limen for pitch. *American Journal of Psychology,* 1940, *53,* 450-455.

Bornstein, M. H. Color vision and color naming: A psychophysiological hypothesis of cultural difference. *Psychological Bulletin,* 1973, *80,* 257-285.

Bornstein, M. H. The influence of visual perception on culture. *American Anthropologist,* 1975, *77,* 774-798.(a)

Bornstein, M. H. Qualities of color vision in infancy. *Journal of Experimental Child Psychology,* 1975, *19,* 401-419.(b)

Bornstein, M. H. On light and the aesthetics of color: Lumia kinetic art. *Leonardo,* 1975, *8,* 203-212.(c)

Bornstein, M. H. Infants are trichromats. *Journal of Experimental Child Psychology,* 1976, *21,* 425-445.(a)

Bornstein, M. H. Infants' recognition memory for hue. *Developmental Psychology,* 1976, *12,* 185-191.(b)

Bornstein, M. H. Chromatic vision in infancy. In H. W. Reese & L. P. Lipsitt (Eds.), *Advances in child development and behavior* (Vol. 12). New York: Academic Press, 1978. (a)

Bornstein, M. H. Visual behavior of the young human infant: Relationships between chromatic and spatial perception and the activity of underlying brain mechanisms. *Journal of Experimental Child Psychology,* 1978, *26,* 174-196. (b)

Bornstein, M. H., Kessen, W., & Weiskopf, S. Color vision and hue categorization in young human infants. *Journal of Experimental Psychology: Human Perception and Performance,* 1976, *2,* 115-129.

Boynton, R. M., & Gordon, J. Bezold-Brücke hue shift measured by color-naming technique. *Journal of the Optical Society of America,* 1965, *55,* 78-86.

Bridger, W. H. Sensory habituation and discrimination in the human neonate. *American Journal of Psychiatry,* 1961, *117,* 991-996.

Bronshtein, A. I., & Petrova, E. P. The auditory analyzer in young infants. In Y. Brackbill & G. G. Thompson (Eds.), *Behavior in infancy and early childhood.* New York: Free Press, 1967. (Originally published, 1952.)

Brown, R. W., & Lenneberg, E. H. A study in language and cognition. *Journal of Abnormal and Social Psychology,* 1954, *49,* 454-462.

Bruner, J. S., Goodnow, J. J., & Austin, G. A. *A study of thinking.* New York: Wiley, 1956.

Caramazza, A., Yeni-Komshian, G. H., Zurif, E. B., & Carbone, E. The acquisition of a new phonological contrast: The case of stop consonants in French-English bilinguals. *Journal of the Acoustical Society of America,* 1973, *54,* 421-428.

Carroll, J. B. (Ed.), *Language, thought, & reality: Selected writings of Benjamin Lee Whorf.* Cambridge, Mass: MIT Press, 1966.

Chapanis, A. Color names for a color space. *American Scientist,* 1965, *53,* 327-346.

Cuddy, L. L. Practice effects in the absolute judgment of pitch. *Journal of the Acoustical Society of America,* 1968, *43,* 1069-1076.

Cuddy, L. L. Training the absolute identification of pitch. *Perception & Psychophysics,* 1970, *8,* 265-269.

Cutting, J. E., & Eimas, P. D. Phonetic feature analyzers and the processing of speech in infants. In J. F. Kavanagh & J. E. Cutting (Eds.), *The role of speech in language.* Cambridge, Mass: MIT Press, 1975.

Cutting, J. E., & Rosner, B. S. Categories and boundaries in speech and music. *Perception & Psychophysics,* 1974, *16,* 564–570.

Cutting, J. E., Rosner, B. S., & Foard, C. F. Perceptual categories for musiclike sounds: Implications for theories of speech perception. *Quarterly Journal of Experimental Psychology,* 1976, *28,* 361–378.

De Valois, R. L., Abramov, I., & Mead, W. R. Single cell analysis of wavelength discrimination at the lateral geniculate nucleus in the macaque. *Journal of Neurophysiology,* 1967, *30,* 415–433.

De Valois, R. L., & De Valois, K. K. Neural coding of color. In E. C. Carterette & M. P. Friedman (Eds.), *Handbook of perception* (Vol. 5). New York: Academic Press, 1975.

Dimmick, F. L., & Hubbard, M. R. The spectral location of psychologically unique yellow, green, and blue. *American Journal of Psychology,* 1939, *52,* 242–254.(a)

Dimmick, F. L., & Hubbard, M. R. The spectral components of psychologically unique red. *American Journal of Psychology,* 1939, *52,* 348–353.(b)

Doris, J., Casper, M., & Poresky, R. Differential brightness thresholds in infancy. *Journal of Experimental Child Psychology,* 1967, *5,* 522–535.

Doris, J., & Cooper, L. Brightness discrimination in infancy. *Journal of Experimental Child Psychology,* 1966, *3,* 31–39.

Doty, D. Infant speech perception. *Human Development,* 1974, *17,* 74–80.

Eilers, R. E. Context-sensitive perception of naturally produced stop and fricative consonants by infants. *Journal of the Acoustical Society of America,* 1977, *61,* 1321–1336.

Eilers, R. E., & Minifie, F. Fricative discrimination in early infancy. *Journal of Speech and Hearing Research,* 1975, *18,* 158–167.

Eilers, R. E., Wilson, W. R., & Moore, J. M. Developmental changes in speech discrimination in 3-, 6-, and 12-month-old infants. (Unpublished manuscript, 1976, cited in Eilers, 1977.)

Eimas, P. D. The relation between identification and discrimination along speech and nonspeech continua. *Language and Speech,* 1963, *6,* 206–217.

Eimas, P. D. Auditory and linguistic processing of cues for place of articulation by infants. *Perception & Psychophysics,* 1974, *16,* 513–521.

Eimas, P. D. Distinctive feature codes in the short-term memory of children. *Journal of Experimental Child Psychology,* 1975, *19,* 241–251. (a)

Eimas, P. D. Auditory and phonetic coding of the cues for speech: Discrimination of the [r-l] distinction by young infants. *Perception & Psychophysics,* 1975, *18,* 341–347. (b)

Eimas, P. D. Speech perception in early infancy. In L. B. Cohen & P. Salapatek (Eds.), *Infant perception: From sensation to cognition* (Vol. 2). New York: Academic Press, 1975. (c)

Eimas, P. D., Siqueland, E. R., Jusczyk, P., & Vigorito, J. Speech perception in infants. *Science,* 1971, *171,* 303–306.

Eisenberg, R. B. *Auditory competence in early life.* Baltimore, Md: University Park Press, 1976.

Ekman, G. Contributions to the psychophysics of color vision. *Studium Generale,* 1963, *16,* 54–64.

Essock, S. M. Color perception and color classification. In D. M. Rumbaugh (Ed.), *Language learning by a chimpanzee: The LANA project.* New York: Academic Press, 1977.

Fernandez, D. Dimensional dominance and stimulus discriminability. *Journal of Experimental Child Psychology,* 1976, *21,* 175–189.

Frisch, K. *Bees: Their vision, chemical senses, and language.* Ithaca, N. Y.: Cornell University Press, 1950.

Fry, D. B., Abramson, A. S., Eimas, P. D., & Liberman, A. M. The identification and discrimination of synthetic vowels. *Language & Speech,* 1962, *5,* 171–189.

Gaines, R., & Little, A. C. Developmental color perception. *Journal of Experimental Child Psychology,* 1975, *20,* 465–486.

Galizio, M., & Baron, A. Label training and auditory generalization. *Learning and Motivation,* 1976, *7,* 591–602.

Ganz, L., & Riesen, A. H. Stimulus generalization to hue in the dark-reared macaque. *Journal of Comparative and Physiological Psychology,* 1962, *55,* 92–99.

Garner, W. R. *Uncertainty and structure as psychological concepts.* New York: Wiley, 1962.

Garner, W. R. To perceive is to know. *American Psychologist,* 1966, *21,* 11–19.

Gibson, E. J. *Principles of perceptual learning and development.* New York: Appleton-Century-Crofts, 1969.

Gibson, J. J., & Gibson, E. J. Perceptual learning: Differentiation or enrichment? *Psychological Review,* 1955, *62,* 32–41.

Goto, H. Auditory perception by normal Japanese adults of the sounds "L" and "R." *Neuropsychologia,* 1971, *9,* 317–323.

Graham, B. V., Turner, M. E., & Hurst, D. C. Derivation of wavelength discrimination from color naming. *Journal of the Optical Society of America,* 1973, *63,* 109–111.

Graham, C. H. Discriminations that depend on wavelength. In C. H. Graham (Ed.), *Vision and visual perception.* New York: Wiley, 1965.

Gregory, R. L., & Wallace, J. G. Recovery from early blindness: A case study. *Experimental Psychology Society Monograph,* 1963, Whole No. 2.

Hanson, V. L. Within-category discriminations in speech perception. *Perception & Psychophysics,* 1977, *21,* 423–430.

Harkness, S. Universal aspects of learning color codes: A study in two cultures. *Ethos,* 1973, *1,* 175–200.

Harris, J. D. Pitch discrimination under masking. *American Journal of Psychology,* 1948, *61,* 194–204.

Harris, J. D. Pitch discrimination. *Journal of the Acoustical Society of America,* 1952, *24,* 750–755.

Hays, D. G., Margolis, E., Naroll, R., & Perkins, D. R. Color term salience. *American Anthropologist,* 1972, *74,* 1107–1121.

Hecox, K. Electrophysiological correlates of human auditory development. In L. B. Cohen & P. Salapatek (Eds.), *Infant perception: From sensation to cognition* (Vol. 2). New York: Academic Press, 1975.

Heider, E. R. "Focal" color areas and the development of color names. *Developmental Psychology,* 1971, *4,* 447–455.

Heider, E. R. Universals in color memory and naming. *Journal of Experimental Psychology,* 1972, *93,* 10–20.

Helversen, O. von. Zür spektralen Unterschiedsempfindlichkeit der Honigbiene. *Journal of Comparative Physiology,* 1972, *80,* 439–472.

Hering, E. *[Outlines of a theory of the light sense]* (L. M. Hurvich and D. Jameson, trans.). Cambridge, Mass: Harvard University Press, 1964. (Originally published, 1878.)

Herrick, R. M. Foveal luminance discrimination as a function of the duration of the decrement or increment in luminance. *Journal of Comparative and Physiological Psychology,* 1956, *49,* 437–443.

Hershenson, M. Visual discrimination in the human newborn. *Journal of Comparative and Physiological Psychology,* 1964, *58,* 270–276.

Hershenson, M. The development of visual perceptual systems. In H. Moltz (Ed.), *The ontogeny of vertebrate behavior.* New York: Academic Press, 1971.

Holway, A. H., & Hurvich, L. M. Visual differential sensitivity and retinal area. *American Journal of Psychology,* 1938, *51,* 687–694.

Hull, C. L. *Principles of behavior.* New York: Appleton, 1943.

Hutt, S. J., Hutt, C., Lenard, H. G., von Bernuth, H., & Muntjewerff, W. Auditory responsivity in the human neonate. *Nature,* 1968, *218,* 888–890.

Ingling, N. W. Categorization: A mechanism for rapid information processing. *Journal of Experimental Psychology*, 1972, *94*, 239-243.

Jacobs, G. H., & Gaylord, H. A. Effects of chromatic adaptation on color naming. *Vision Research*, 1967, *7*, 645-653.

James, W. *The principles of psychology*. New York: Henry Holt, 1890.

Jusczyk, P. W., Rosner, B. S., Cutting, J. E., Foard, C. F., & Smith, L. B. Categorical perception of nonspeech sounds by 2-month-old infants. *Perception & Psychophysics*, 1977, *21*, 50-54.

Kasatkin, N. I., & Levikova, A. M. On the development of early conditioned reflexes and differentiations of auditory stimuli in infants. *Journal of Experimental Psychology*, 1935, *18*, 1-19.

Keller, M. The relation between the critical duration and intensity in brightness discrimination. *Journal of Experimental Psychology*, 1941, *28*, 407-418.

Kerr, L. M., & Rubel, E. W. *Effects of auditory deprivation on perceptual sharpening in the chicken*. Paper presented at the meeting of the Animal Behavior Society, 1977.

Kessen, W. Sucking and looking: Two organized congenital patterns of behavior in the human newborn. In H. W. Stevenson, E. H. Hess, & H. L. Rheingold (Eds.), *Early behavior: Comparative and developmental approaches*. New York: Wiley, 1967.

Kessen, W., & Bornstein, M. H. Discriminability of brightness change for infants. *Journal of Experimental Child Psychology*, 1978, *25*, 526-530.

König, A., & Brodhun, E. Experimentelle untersuchungen ueber die psychophysische fundamentalformel in Bezug auf den Gesichtssinn. Sitzungsber. *Preuss Akademie Wissenschaft*. 1889. *27*. 641-644.

Kopp, J., & Lane, H. Hue discrimination related to linguistic habits. *Psychonomic Science*, 1968, *11*, 61-62.

Kopp, J., & Livermore, J. Differential discriminability or response bias? A signal detection analysis of categorical perception. *Journal of Experimental Psychology*, 1973, *101*, 179-182.

Kuhl, P. K., & Miller, J. D. Speech perception by the chinchilla: Voiced-voiceless distinction in alveolar plosive consonants. *Science*, 1975, *190*, 69-72.

Kuhl, P. K., & Miller, J. D. Speech perception by the chinchilla: Identification functions for synthetic VOT stimuli. *Journal of the Acoustical Society of America*, 1976, *60*, 581\.

Kühn, A. Uber den Farbensinn der Bienen. *Zeitschrift fur vergleichende Physiologie*, 1927, *5*, 762-800.

Lashley, K. S. Persistent problems in the evolution of mind. *Quarterly Review of Biology*, 1949, *24*, 28-42.

Lashley, K. S., & Wade, M. The Pavlovian theory of generalization. *Psychological Review*, 1946, *53*, 72-87.

Lasky, R. E., Syrdal-Lasky, A., & Klein, R. E. VOT discrimination by four to six and a half month old infants from Spanish environments. *Journal of Experimental Child Psychology*, 1975, *20*, 215-225.

Leavitt, L. A., Brown, J. W., Morse, P. A. & Graham, F. K. Cardiac orienting and auditory discrimination in 6-week-old infants. *Developmental Psychology*, 1976, *12*, 514-523.

Liberman, A. M., Cooper, F. S., Shankweiler, D. P., & Studdert-Kennedy, M. Perception of the speech code. *Psychological Review*, 1967, *74*, 431-461.

Liberman, A. M., Harris, K. S., Hoffman, H. S., & Griffith, B. C. The discrimination of speech sounds within and across phoneme boundaries. *Journal of Experimental Psychology*, 1957, *54*, 350-368.

Lisker, L., & Abramson, A. S. A cross-language study of voicing in initial stops: Acoustical measurements. *Word*, 1964, *20*, 384-422.

Lisker, L., & Abramson, A. S. The voicing dimension: Some experiments in comparative phonetics. In *Proceedings of the Sixth International Congress of Phonetic Sciences, Prague, 1967*. Prague: Academia, 1970.

Locke, S., & Keller, L. Categorical perception in a non-linguistic mode. *Cortex,* 1973, *9,* 355–369.

McFarland, W. N., & Munz, F. W. Part III: The evolution of photopic visual pigments in fishes. *Vision Research,* 1975, *15,* 1071–1080.

McGuirk, F. O., & Hebert, J. A. Latency patterns in category judgments. *Bulletin of the Psychonomic Society,* 1973, *1,* 457–459.

Massaro, D. W. Retroactive interference in short-term recognition memory for pitch. *Journal of Experimental Psychology,* 1970, *83,* 32–39.

Massaro, D. W. Effect of masking tone duration on perceptual auditory images. *Journal of Experimental Psychology,* 1971, *87,* 146–148.

Mattingly, I. G., Liberman, A. M., Syrdal, A. K., & Halwes, T. Discrimination in speech and nonspeech modes. *Cognitive Psychology,* 1971, *2,* 131–157.

Mednick, S. A., & Lehtinen, L. E. Stimulus generalization as a function of age in children. *Journal of Experimental Psychology,* 1957, *53,* 180–183.

Mervis, C. B., Catlin, J., & Rosch, E. Development of the structure of color categories. *Developmental Psychology,* 1975, *11,* 54–60.

Miller, C. L., & Morse, P. A. The "heart" of categorical speech discrimination in young infants. *Journal of Speech and Hearing Research,* 1976, *19,* 578–589.

Miller, G. A. The magical number seven plus or minus two: Some limits on our capacity for processing information. *Psychological Review,* 1956, *63,* 81–97.

Miller, J. D., Wier, C. C., Pastore, R. E., Kelly, W. J., & Dooling, R. J. Discrimination and labeling of noise–buzz sequences with varying noise–lead times: An example of categorical perception. *Journal of the Acoustical Society of America,* 1976, *60,* 410–417.

Miller, N. E., & Dollard, J. *Social learning and imitation.* New Haven: Yale University Press, 1941.

Miyawaki, K., Strange, W., Verbrugge, R., Liberman, A. M., Jenkins, J. J., & Fujimura, O. An effect of linguistic experience: The discrimination of [r] and [l] by native speakers of Japanese and English. *Perception & Psychophysics,* 1975, *18,* 331–340.

Moffitt, A. R. Consonant cue perception by twenty- to twenty-four-week-old infants. *Child Development,* 1971, *42,* 717–731.

Monroe, M. D., & Bornstein, M. H. *Time to categorize chromatic information: Effects of psychological structure.* Unpublished manuscript, Princeton University, 1978.

Morse, P. A. The discrimination of speech and nonspeech stimuli in early infancy. *Journal of Experimental Child Psychology,* 1972, *14,* 477–492.

Morse, P. A., & Snowdon, C. T. An investigation of categorical speech discrimination by rhesus monkeys. *Perception & Psychophysics,* 1975, *17,* 9–16.

Newton, I. New theory about light and colors. *Philosophical Transactions of the Royal Society,* 1671–1672, *80,* 3075–3087.

Nickerson, D., & Newhall, S. M. A psychological color solid. *Journal of the Optical Society of America,* 1943, *33,* 419–422.

Pavlov, I. P. *[Conditioned reflexes: An investigation of the physiological activity of the cerebral cortex]* (G. V. Anrep, trans.). London: Oxford University Press, 1927. (Originally published, 1926.)

Peeples, D. R., & Teller, D. Y. Color vision and brightness discrimination in two-month-old human infants. *Science,* 1975, *189,* 1102–1103.

Perrott, D. R., & Nelson, M. A. Limits for the detection of binaural beats. *Journal of the Acoustical Society of America,* 1969, *46,* 1477–1481.

Piaget, J. *[The origins of intelligence in children]* (M. Cook, trans.). New York: Norton, 1963. (Originally published, 1952.)

Pisoni, D. B., & Lazarus, J. H. Categorical and noncategorical modes of speech perception along the voicing continuum. *Journal of the Acoustical Society of America,* 1974, *55,* 328–333.

Pisoni, D. B., & Tash, J. Reaction times to comparisons within and across phonetic categories. *Perception & Psychophysics,* 1974, *15,* 285–290.

Ray, V. F. Techniques and problems in the study of human color perception. *Southwestern Journal of Anthropology,* 1952, *8,* 251–259.

Ray, V. F. Human color perception and behavioral response. *Transactions of the New York Academy of Sciences,* 1953, *16,* 98–104.

Reed, S. K. Pattern recognition and categorization. *Cognitive Psychology,* 1972, *3,* 382–407.

Rosch, E. H. Natural categories. *Cognitive Psychology,* 1973, *4,* 328–350.

Rubel, E. W., & Rosenthal, M. H. The ontogeny of auditory frequency generalization in the chicken. *Journal of Experimental Psychology: Animal Behavior Processes,* 1975, *1,* 287–297.

Sandell, J., Gross, C. G., & Bornstein, M. H. Color categories in Macaques. *Journal of Comparative and Physiological Psychology,* 1979, in press.

Saul, E. V., & Osgood, C. E. Perceptual organization of materials as a factor influencing ease of learning and degree of retention. *Journal of Experimental Psychology,* 1954, *4,* 372–379.

Segall, M. H., Campbell, D. T., & Herskovitz, M. J. *The influence of culture on visual perception.* Indianapolis: Bobbs–Merrill, 1966.

Senden, M. von *[Space and sight: The perception of space and shape in the congenitally blind before and after operation]* (P. Heath, trans.). London: Methuen, 1960. (Originally published, 1932.)

Sherman, M., Sherman, I., & Flory, C. D. Infant behavior. *Comparative Psychology Monographs,* 1936, *12 (4,* Whole No. 79).

Shower, E. G., & Biddulph, R. Differential pitch sensitivity of the ear. *Journal of the Acoustical Society of America,* 1931, *3,* 275–287.

Siegel, J. A., & Siegel, W. Categorical perception of tonal intervals: Musicians can't tell *sharp* from *flat. Perception & Psychophysics,* 1977, *21,* 399–407.

Sinnott, J. M., Beecher, M. D., Moody, D. B., & Stebbins, W. C. Speech sound discrimination by monkeys and humans. *Journal of the Acoustical Society of America,* 1976, *60,* 687–695.

Slis, I. H. Articulatory measurements on voiced, voiceless, and nasal consonants: A test of a model. *Phonetica,* 1970, *24,* 193–210.

Smith, D. P. Derivation of wavelength discrimination from colour-naming data. *Vision Research,* 1971, *11,* 739–742.

Smith, J. M. The relative brightness values for three hues for newborn infants. *University of Iowa Studies of Child Welfare,* 1936, *12,* 91–140.

Sokal, R. R. Classification: Purposes, principles, progress, prospects. *Science,* 1974, *185,* 1115–1123.

Steinhardt, J. Intensity discrimination in the human eye. I. *Journal of General Physiology,* 1936, *20,* 185–209.

Sternheim, C. E., & Boynton, R. M. Uniqueness of perceived hues investigated with a continuous judgmental technique. *Journal of Experimental Psychology,* 1966, *72,* 770–776.

Stevens, K. N., & House, A. S. Speech perception. In J. V. Tobias (Ed.), *Foundations of modern auditory theory.* New York: Academic Press, 1972.

Stevens, K. N., Liberman, A. M., Studdert-Kennedy, M., & Öhman, S. E. G. Crosslanguage study of vowel perception. *Language and Speech,* 1969, *12,* 1–23.

Stevens, S. S., & Davis, H. *Hearing: Its psychology and physiology.* New York: Wiley, 1938.

Streeter, L. A. Language perception of two-month-old infants shows effects of both innate mechanism and experience. *Nature,* 1976, *259,* 39–41.(a)

Streeter, L. A. Kikuyu labial and apical stop discrimination. *Journal of Phonetics,* 1976, *4,* 43–49.(b)

Streeter, L. A., & Landauer, T. K. Effects of learning English as a second language on the acquisition of a new phonemic contrast. *Journal of the Acoustical Society of America,* 1976, *59,* 448-451.

Suchman, R. G., & Trabasso, T. Color and form preference in young children. *Journal of Experimental Child Psychology,* 1966, *3,* 177-187.

Swoboda, P. J., Morse, P. A., & Leavitt, L. A. Continuous vowel discrimination in normal and at risk infants. *Child Development,* 1976, *47,* 459-465.

Thurlow, W. R. Audition. In J. W. Kling & L. A. Riggs (Eds.), *Woodworth & Schlosberg's experimental psychology.* New York: Holt, Rinehart & Winston, 1971.

Trabasso, T., Stave, M., & Eichberg, R. Attribute preference and discrimination shifts in young children. *Journal of Experimental Child Psychology,* 1969, *8,* 195-209.

Tracy, W. K. Wavelength generalization and preference in monochromatically reared ducklings. *Journal of the Experimental Analysis of Behavior,* 1970, *13,* 163-178.

Trehub, S. E. Infants' sensitivity to vowel and tonal contrasts. *Developmental Psychology,* 1973, *9,* 91-96.

Trehub, S. E. The discrimination of foreign speech contrasts by infants and adults. *Child Development,* 1976, *47,* 466-472.

Trehub, S. E., & Rabinovitch, M. S. Auditory-linguistic sensitivity in early infancy. *Developmental Psychology,* 1972, *6,* 74-77.

Walls, G. L. *The vertebrate eye and its adaptive radiation.* Bloomfield Hills, Mich. Cranbrook Institute of Science, 1942.

Waters, R. S., & Wilson, W. A. Speech perception by rhesus monkeys: The voicing distinction in synthesized labial and velar stop consonants. *Perception & Psychophysics,* 1976, *19,* 285-289.

Weir, C. Auditory frequency sensitivity in the neonate: A signal detection analysis. *Journal of Experimental Child Psychology,* 1976, *21,* 219-225.

Werner, H. *Comparative psychology of mental development.* New York: Follett, 1948.

Whorf, B. L. *Collected papers on metalinguistics.* Washington, D. C.: Foreign Service Institute, 1952.

Wickelgren, W. A. Associative strength theory of recognition memory for pitch. *Journal of Mathematical Psychology,* 1969, *6,* 13-61.

Williams, L. The perception of stop consonant voicing by Spanish-English bilinguals. *Perception & Psychophysics,* 1977, *21,* 289-297.

Wiseman, S., & Neisser, U. Perceptual organization as a determinant of visual recognition memory. *American Journal of Psychology,* 1974, *87,* 675-681.

Witkin, H. A., Dyk, R. B., Faterson, H. F., Goodenough, D. R., & Karp, S. A. *Psychological differentiation.* New York: Wiley, 1962.

Wolf, C. G. The perception of stop consonants by children. *Journal of Experimental Child Psychology,* 1973, *16,* 318-331.

Wormith, S. J., Pankhurst, D., & Moffitt, A. R. Frequency discrimination by young infants. *Child Development,* 1975, *46,* 272-275.

Wright, A. A. Psychometric and psychophysical hue discrimination functions for the pigeon. *Vision Research,* 1972, *12,* 1447-1464.

Wright, A. A., & Cumming, W. W. Color-naming functions for the pigeon. *Journal of the Experimental Analysis of Behavior,* 1971, *15,* 7-17.

Wright, W. D. *Researches on normal and defective colour vision.* St. Louis: C. V. Mosby, 1947.

Zlatin, M. A., & Koenigsknecht, R. A. Development of the voicing contrast: Perception of stop consonants. *Journal of Speech and Hearing Research,* 1975, *18,* 541-553.

4 The Origins of Facial Pattern Recognition

Joseph F. Fagan, III
Case Western Reserve University

INTRODUCTION

The aim of this chapter is to describe the origins of facial recognition. The focus is on the infant's ability to discriminate among and to recognize representations of faces during the first 7 months of life. Prior to a survey of the principal findings, a basic measure of infant visual perception is noted: the tendency of the infant to devote more fixation to some stimuli than to others. One such naturally occurring preference is more attention to a novel than to a previously seen target. The summary of results begins with illustrations of how visual preferences and novelty preferences in particular have yielded information on the infant's ability to discriminate among and to recognize faces. I then review data on some of the individual difference and stimulus parameters that control infants' recognition of faces. Instances in which infants give evidence of having abstracted particular invariant characteristics of faces then occupy our attention. The survey concludes with a demonstration of specific techniques that facilitate face recognition. Two themes recur throughout the review. One is that most, if not all, of the phenomena associated with the infant's recognition of faces are also associated with the infant's recognition of nonsocial, abstract patterns. The other is that many of the essential characteristics of facial recognition found in adulthood are to be found in infancy. The implications of such trends along with those raised by the various findings on infant facial recognition are considered more fully in a concluding discussion section.

The present survey of facial recognition is not exhaustive. No attempt has been made to include all the work on adult recognition of faces, a topic summarized in a paper by Ellis (1975). Neither has there been any concern here with the infant's affective responses to faces (e.g., "stranger anxiety") or with the early development of personality as inferred from the infant's social recognition ability. Such issues have been treated comprehensively by Lewis and Brooks (1975).

OPERATIONAL DEFINITIONS

Fantz (1956) developed "visual interest" as a test of the infant's discriminative ability. He recorded the activity of the infant's eyes, his assumption being that if infants consistently gaze at some stimuli more often than at others, they must be able to differentiate among them. Differential visual fixation operationally defines discrimination and is obtained when, for example, one of a pair of targets elicits significantly more than 50% of infants' fixation. Most of the studies reviewed here were based on a paired-comparison test of recognition memory in which the infant was first exposed to a target for a certain study period and then presented with the recently exposed and a novel target simultaneously. On the recognition test pairing, infants typically devoted the greater part of their visual fixation to the novel target, indicating both discrimination and recognition.

DIFFERENTIATION AT FIVE TO SEVEN MONTHS

In the present section we see that 5- to 7-month infants are quite capable of making subtle distinctions among abstract patterns and among photographs of faces. Although I do not dwell on conditions limiting the infant's pattern recognition ability—such considerations have been left for a later section—I do note certain restrictions on face recognition set by inter-item similarity and by face pose. The robust nature of infant memory is emphasized by demonstrations of long-term retention and resistance to interference for recognition of abstract patterns and for face recognition.

Abstract Patterns

By five months, the infant is quite capable of making distinctions among highly similar abstract patterns on a recognition test. Moreover, memory for abstract patterns lasts for appreciable periods of time and is not liable to disruption by interference. A summary of previous demonstrations of infants' discriminations among abstract patterns as evidenced either by naturally ocurring preferences for certain patterns or by differential fixation to novel stimuli on recognition tests is provided in Fantz, Fagan, and Miranda (1975, see especially pp. 274–276). Specific examples of the

5-month-old infant's ability to differentiate among patterns composed of different arrangements of the same linear elements (e.g., a checkerboard versus a bullseye arrangement of small squares) are in studies by Fagan (1973, 1974). In a recent unpublished experiment, a sample of 64 infants from 21 to 23 weeks of age served as subjects in an attempt to explore some of the limits imposed by inter-item discriminability on the 5-month-old infant's capacity for differentiating abstract patterns. The patterns employed are presented in Figure 4.1, which has four separate illustrations. Each illustration pictures different collections of abstract patterns. As we proceed through the chapter, each of these four illustrations in Figure 4.1 will be noted. For our present purposes, we focus on the top left illustration, which lists eight targets, four pairings of patterns composed of arrangements of small diamonds. Specifically, a number of abstract black and white patterns was created by successively displacing two, four, six, or eight out of 24 elements of an overall diamond-shaped pattern. This series of targets, to the adult eye, varies from a regular, symmetrical, large diamond to essentially a random arrangement of small diamonds. The infant was shown a particular pattern paired with itself for a 60-second study period followed by a pairing of the previously exposed target with another pattern for two, 5-second

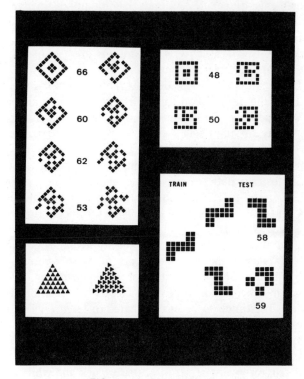

FIG. 4.1.   Abstract figures.

recognition test pairings. The pairings shown in Figure 4.1, each consisting of one level of displacement of the overall diamond form paired with another (intact with two, two with four, four with six, and six with eight displaced elements), served as recognition tasks for four groups of 16 infants each. The 64 infants averaged 28.8 seconds of fixation during the study period. The percentages of total fixation paid to the novel target on test for each of the four groups are noted in Figure 4.1. The infants who discriminated the intact diamond from the diamond with two displaced elements showed a reliable preference for novelty, as did the group given the patterns with two and four displaced elements, and so did the infants shown diamonds with four and six displaced elements. Only those infants presented with diamonds that had six and eight elements displaced failed to give evidence of discrimination and recognition. There is no simple way to describe the differences between these particular pairings of patterns composed of small diamonds to explain why discrimination was shown for three of the pairings and was not in evidence for the other pairing. The chief stimulus factor that seems to be implicated is the departure from a compact, regular, symmetrical form represented by the diamond (and, to some extent, by the patterns with two and four displaced elements) to the essentially random arrangements of small diamonds having no distinctive or obvious general configuration, as represented by the patterns with six or eight elements displaced. Whatever the explanation, one clear implication of the results of this study is that 22-week-old infants are capable of quite subtle discriminations among abstract patterns.

Studies by Fagan (1970, 1973) demonstrate the infant's ability to retain for long periods the information gained from exposure to abstract patterns. Fagan (1970, Experiment II) obtained 2-hour delayed novelty preferences on pairings of widely varying black and white abstract patterns from 5-month-old infants. Some indirect support was also provided for the existence of retention over days (Fagan, 1970, Experiment I). A direct test of long-term memory for abstract patterns was made in an initial experiment in the Fagan (1973) study. Specifically, observations were made of immediate and delayed (24 and 48 hours) recognition memory for pairs of abstract black and white targets varying either multidimensionally (e.g., form and length of contour, number of elements, etc.) or only in patterning (different arrangements of black squares) on the part of 5- to 6-month-old infants. Infants 5 to 6 months of age proved capable of recognizing, after as long as 2 days, which member a pair of abstract targets had been previously exposed, even when the stimuli to be discriminated differed only in arrangement of the same pattern elements. The fact that the infant's memory for abstract patterns is not easily disrupted was demonstrated in a study by Fagan (1971) in which both immediate and delayed recognition tests were made for each of three "novelty problems" (sets of abstract black and white patterns varying multidimensionally) administered during a single testing session. Infants demonstrated more attention to novel targets, on both immediate and delayed recognition tests for each problem. The degree of differential fixation to novel targets exhibited no decline from immediate to delayed testing and was not altered by the serial order the problem occupied during testing, indicating no evidence for disruption of memory due to proactive or retroactive interference.

Faces

As with abstract patterns, by at least 5 months, infants can make subtle discriminations among achromatic face photographs, recognizing, for example, a man's face when it is paired with the face of a woman. Examples of the face photographs differentiated one from another by 5-month-old infants are illustrated in the middle row of Figure 4.2. These stimuli were employed in a series of studies (Fagan, 1972, 1973, 1974, 1977) in which 22-week-old infants exhibited reliable preferences for whichever target served as the novel member of a pair of faces. Independent confirmation of the 5-month-old infant's ability to differentiate paired novel and previously exposed face photographs is provided in a study by Cornell (1974), who presented faces of men and women, and by Miranda and Fantz (1974), who used a woman's and a baby's face as discriminanda.

Given the 5-month-old infant's facility in discriminating among quite different faces (e.g., woman from baby), a recent experiment (Fagan, 1976, Experiment I) examined the 7-month-old infant's ability to make rather fine discriminations among photographs of adult male faces. Pairs of faces judged by adults as being more or less similar were employed to discover if the infant would find certain faces more difficult to discriminate than others. The faces, illustrated in Figure 4.3, were slightly modified versions of four men from a set of 255 male faces shown to adults in a study by Goldstein, Harmon, and Lesk (1971). The judges in the Goldstein et al. experiment had selected the men in the first and second rows of Figure 4.3 as being the least similar pair of faces and the men shown in the third and fourth rows as being the most similar pair from all possible pairings of the 255 men. As an additional feature of the Fagan (1976) experiment, infants were required to differentiate between two men shown in full-face, three-quarter, or profile views. The question was whether the features peculiar to some poses would facilitate the infant's discrimination among faces. As one can see from the percentage to novelty (% N) scores listed under each face pairing in Figure 4.3, the faces judged as being highly discriminable by adults were easily differentiated by the 7-month-old infants. High and reliable preferences for novelty were shown regardless of the pose, that is, the means given under the three pairings of men in the top two rows were greater than a chance level of 50%. Infants had some difficulty, however, with faces judged as being of low discriminability. Only performance on the

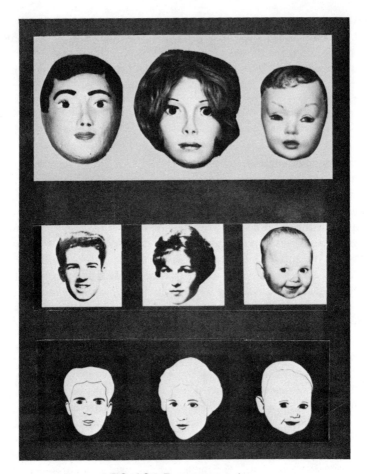

FIG. 4.2.   Face representations.

three-quarter poses was at a level with that for faces of high discriminability, although the mean of 56% for the low discriminability, full-face photos was itself reliable. In short, data from 7-month-olds indicate that some of the features that adults use in discriminating among faces may be quite basic, with infants' "judgments" of discriminability following a similar course. In addition, infants seem to find three-quarter poses more informative than full faces or profiles when discriminations between highly similar faces are called for. The latter conclusion receives additional support from a recent unpublished study in which samples of 22-week-old infants were required to differentiate, on a recognition test, between the very dissimilar men pictured in the top two rows of Figure 4.3 when the pairings were presented in either the full-face, the three-quarter, or the profile views. Testing procedures were identical to those used for the 7-month-old infants in the Fagan (1976) study. The interesting finding from the tests at 22 weeks was that reliable novelty preferences were found only when the three-quarter poses of the two men were shown. A low and unreliable preference resulted from the full-face pairing, and clearly chance performance was evident with profile poses for the 18 subjects given that task. In other words, the 5-month-old infants were not as facile in discriminating among the highly dissimilar male faces as were the 7-month-olds. However, comparing the 5-month performance on dissimilar faces with the seven-month performance on highly similar men, the pattern of results relative to ease of discrimination as a function of face pose was the same across ages.

Some understanding as to why infants find it easier to discriminate among men in a three-quarter pose than among the same men in full-face or profile views can be gained by examining the manner in which mens' faces were judged as being more or less similar by the adult raters in the Goldstein et al. study. The Goldstein et al. judges found 21 features to be most useful in discriminating among and in identifying male faces. Of most

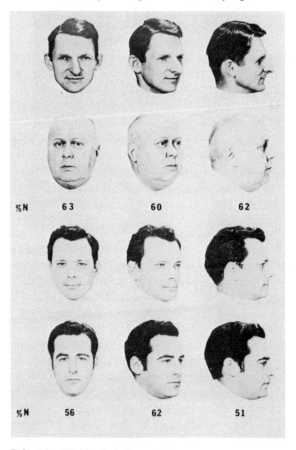

FIG. 4.3.   Highly dissimilar and highly similar pairs of faces.

importance for our purposes is the fact that some of those 21 features are either not present in or are difficult to judge from a full-face view (e.g., chin or forehead profile and ear length). Similarly, some of the 21 features are not visible in profile (e.g., separation between the eyes and mouth width). None of the 21 features, however, is not present in a three-quarter view. In other words, a three-quarter view of a face, it would seem, is more informative for face discrimination or identification than a full-face or a profile pose — more informative in the sense that the three-quarter view contains more distinctive features than do the other poses. Thus, it is not surprising that infants, who agree with adult judges that certain pairs of faces are more discriminable than are others, also agree with adults that a three-quarter pose is more informative for discrimination than a full-face or a profile view.

Regardless of the speculation as to why infants find men's faces more discriminable in a three-quarter pose, one clear implication of such a result is that infants appear to be capable of discriminating one pose of a man from another. A direct test of whether 7-month-old infants could differentiate between two poses of the same man was made in a second experiment in the Fagan (1976) study. The design included recognition tests involving discriminations of full-face from three-quarter, full-face from profile, and three-quarter from profile poses. To achieve generality, such tests were made for each of the two men pictured in the first and second rows of Figure 4.3. Each discrimination of one pose from another was easily performed with reliable mean values of 62.5% to the novel target for full-face paired with three-quarter views, a mean of 68.4% on tests of full-face distinguished from profile, and 60.9% when three-quarter and profile views were to be distinguished. In summary, recognizing whether a man was previously seen in one pose or another appears to be a relatively simple task for the 7-month-old infant.

Thus far we have seen that the 5- to 7-month-old infant is capable, on recognition testing, of making some rather subtle discriminations among face photographs. We now ask if such recognition is robust. Specifically, does the infant's memory for a face photograph last for any appreciable period of time and, if it is lasting, is it easily subjected to disruption? Such questions were posed in a series of experiments (Fagan, 1973) designed to explore delayed recognition on the order of hours, days, and weeks for a variety of discriminations on the part of 5- to 6-month-old infants. The general procedure of the Fagan (1973) study was to expose the infant for 2 minutes to a particular target and then to obtain a test of immediate recognition by pairing the previously exposed stimulus with a novel target. The infant was revisited once either hours, days, or weeks later and was presented with the previously exposed and novel target as a test of delayed recognition. The second experiment in the Fagan (1973) series explored delayed recognition for photographs of faces (e.g., man versus woman) at intervals of 3 hours, 1, 2, 7, or 14 days. The results were quite straightforward. Tests at each delay were significantly greater than chance, and no reliable decline in preference for novelty occurred at any retention interval. Along with these demonstrations of long-term memory, it was also found that under certain conditions failure to recognize face photographs occurred when the infant's attention was drawn to other faces interpolated during the retention interval (Fagan, 1973, Experiment IV). In particular, the kind of intervening face and the timing of intervention were shown to be important determinants of such forgetting. A more extensive series of experiments was undertaken recently (Fagan, 1977) in an attempt to verify and extend the results from the 1973 study on the perceptual and temporal factors associated with the infant's failure to demonstrate recognition. The aims of the recent experiments were to observe the effects of interpolated faces on 5-to 6-month-old infants' subsequent recognition of face photographs. A number of experimental manipulations with regard to the timing of intervention was made to obtain some estimate of how strong or lasting were the effects of interference. The general results of the Fagan (1977) experiments were that infants 22 weeks of age failed to demonstrate recognition of face photographs only when specific faces (usually other properly oriented faces) were presented in the interval between familiarization and recognition testing. The deleterious effects of such intervention, however, were limited. Recovery of recognition was found after a minute's rest and, even within the effective temporal domain of a distractor, recognition loss was prevented by further, brief exposure to the familiar photograph. In other words, the kind of interpolated face shown the infant emerged as the chief source of interference, a point to which we return in a later section on face orientation. For our present purposes, however, the most important information gained from the Fagan (1977) study was that, even given an effective distractor, any amnesic effects could either be prevented or shown to be short-lived. In short, the infant's face recognition appears to be robust, that is, it lasts over time and is not easily blocked.

In summary, we might conclude that the 5- to 7-month-old behaves toward faces much as he does toward abstract patterns. Specifically, subtle discriminations are made within each class of stimuli, and memory for both are long lasting and not easily disrupted. Such parallelism, of course, does not necessarily indicate a common process governing the recognition of abstract patterns and face patterns. The choice of particular faces and patterns in these experiments may have been fortuitous in revealing common behavior. Nevertheless, although direct comparisons of the infant's recognition performance when faces or when abstract patterns serve as discriminanda are, by definition, not possible, a consistent demonstration of similar responding on the part of the infant when faces or abstract patterns are to be recognized does not lend support to the assumption that face recognition is governed by processes separate from those determining the recognition of abstract patterns. I return to this point about the necessity (or lack of necessity) of assuming separate processes for face recognition and for abstract pattern recognition as we proceed through the chapter.

LIMITING CONDITIONS

We noted earlier that some limits on the infant's ability to recognize face representations are set by individual differences in age. For example, face recognition improves at 5 to 7 months. This section includes a more complete discussion of the growth of face discrimination over the first 5 months. Cognitive status and sex are also considered as possible sources of individual differences in the infants' recognition of faces. Inter-item similarity was also mentioned earlier as a stimulus factor limiting face recognition. In this section, I focus on boundaries imposed on recognition by the orientation and the fidelity of face representations. Where relevant, the relations between infant and adult functioning are noted, and the similarities between infants' recognition performance when faces and when abstract patterns serve as discriminanda are explored.

Individual Differences

The infant's ability to discriminate among and to recognize faces varies with age and with cognitive status. The sex of the infant, however, is not related to facility in facial recognition.

Age.   Early findings by Fantz (1961, 1963) that patterns representing the human face elicit sustained fixation early in life provoked a number of studies that focused on the extent to which patterns varying in degree of facial resemblance controlled infant attention over the first 5 months of life. In general, these studies included experiments in which little effort was made to control the various stimulus characteristics present in a facial configuration (e.g., brightness, number of elements, and symmetry), which might, in and of themselves, influence visual preferences, and they included experiments that did attempt such control. The latter typically compared representations of faces with stimuli composed of rearrangements of the same elements, either "scrambled" or rotated versions of a face. In addition to these studies of the relative attention value of more or less facelike targets, another set of studies (as we have noted throughout) investigated discrimination and recognition by pairing novel and previously exposed faces.

To gain some closure on the results of all this activity, let us consider the infant's developing ability over the first 5 months to discriminate faces from other stimuli and faces from one another. Our summary is based on findings from all the various approaches and focuses on discrimination possible at the neonatal, 4-month, and 5-month periods. In the first few weeks of life, the infant can discriminate a facelike pattern from other patterns that differ widely from a face (Fantz, 1966; Stechler, 1964). Neonates, however, are visually responsive to gross aspects of patterning such as the size, number, and form of contour of pattern elements (Fantz, et al. 1975, pp. 279–287). Hence, the newborn's distinctions between faces and nonfaces may be based on such elementary characteristics rather than on pattern configuration. This simple explanation of the basis of neonatal preferences for faces gains support from the fact that infants at this age show no evidence of discrimination when the two patterns (face and nonface) differ only in arrangement of internal elements. In addition, Maurer and Salapatek (1976) note that the 2-month-old is much more likely than the 1-month-old to scan the internal features of a face. However, by 4 months (specifically, by 16 weeks) the proper arrangement of facial elements can be discriminated from a scrambled pattern (Haaf, 1977; Haaf & Bell, 1964; McCall & Kagan, 1967) or from a rotated face (Fagan, 1972, Experiment II; McGurk, 1970, Experiment II; Watson, 1966). Also by 4 months, individual face features that contribute more or less information for discrimination can be identified (Caron, Caron, Caldwell, & Weiss, 1973). Not surprisingly, the ability to distinguish among abstract, nonface patterns composed of rearrangements of the same elements (e.g., collections of squares) also emerges at about 16 weeks (Fagan, 1970; Fantz et al., 1975, pp. 274–276). At the same time, the 4-month-old infant appears to be limited to a general discrimination of proper from improper face patterning, since more subtle pattern configuration discriminations of one face from another are not evidenced at 16 weeks (Fagan, 1972, Experiment II). By 5 months, as we have already seen, one face can be discriminated from another. Again, subtle pattern configuration discriminations are also possible at 5 months when tests are made with nonface, abstract figures. The fact that studies allowing subjects relatively brief study of achromatic photographs of unfamiliar faces have failed to find evidence of discrimination among faces prior to 20 weeks (Cornell, 1974; Fagan, 1972; Miranda & Fantz, 1974) does not mean that such discriminations are not possible earlier. It is quite likely that highly familiar instances or representations with more fidelity might be discriminated from novel ones prior to 5 months. Fitzgerald (1968), for example, reported differential pupillary dilation to videotapes of a mother's face versus that of a stranger at 17 weeks, and Cohen, Deloache, and Pearl (1977) found recovery of response to a novel target following habituation to a criterion when chromatic photographs of women, men, and babies were presented to 18-week-old infants. In any case, at least a rough approximation of the growth of face perception during the initial months of life can be made, and important age periods in this progression can be identified. The initial differentiation is a general discrimination of facelike from nonfacial patterns by two weeks. A more refined distinction of proper from altered facelike patterns appears at 16 weeks. By at least 20 weeks, differentiations among individual faces are easily accomplished. A parallel age progression may also be noted in the infant's ability to make successively finer discriminations among abstract patterns.

Cognitive Status.   As we have seen, the infant's ability to recognize faces grows with age. We will now see that facial recognition tests also discriminate "normal" from "retarded" infants. The approach of the study reviewed here was to compare groups of infants on recognition tests when there was some reason to expect that later in life one sample would be of higher cognitive status than the other. Specifically, the comparison was between normal and Down syndrome infants, because Down syndrome is diagnosable at birth and virtually certain to result in retarded intelligence. Miranda and Fantz (1974) matched samples of Down syndrome infants with normal controls for sex and length of gestation and tested each sample at 13, 24, and 36 weeks. One of the tasks administered at each age was based on abstract targets differing in arrangement of pattern elements, and another involved a discrimination of photographs of faces (woman versus baby). The results from each task indicated a clear superiority on the part of the normal infants. Distinctions among face photographs and between targets varying in arrangement of pattern elements were accomplished on recognition tests by 24 weeks for normals. Down syndrome infants preferred a novel face photograph at 36 weeks but showed no recognition when abstract targets varying in pattern were to be differentiated. Additional testing ruled out the possibilities that the Down syndrome infants' lack of recognition resulted from either difficulties in simple visual functioning, such as an inability to resolve a pattern or an incapacity to exhibit preferences for novel stimuli per se. In short, Down syndrome infants suffer a deficit in visual recognition memory when discriminations among faces or among abstract patterns are required. Recent studies by Boat (1977) and by Dirks and Neisser (1977) indicate that differences in recognition that are due to cognitive deficit are not limited to the early months of life. Rather, Boat found that recognition memory for complex, not easily labeled visual stimuli (faces of children or of newborns) differentiate normal from trainable retarded children at 8 years. Dirks and Neisser showed that educable retardates at 10 to 12 years perform at about the level of normal first graders for recognition on new items added to a previously seen photographic display of common objects. In other words, recognition memory is sensitive to variations in cognitive status not only in infants but in older children as well.

Sex.   Ellis (1975), in his review of the face recognition literature, cites evidence to indicate that females (older children and adults) are more facile at recognizing faces, particularly faces of other females, than are males. The explanation advanced by Ellis and by others to account for this female advantage is based on the female's more frequent exposure in our culture to a variety of female faces (e.g., in magazine advertisements). Such an experiential explanation, however, appeared to be contradicted by the observation (Fagan, 1972, Experiment III) that 5- to 6-month-old females were better able to recognize face photographs than were their male counterparts. An infant female superiority in recognition of face patterns also runs contrary to repeated demonstrations of no reliable sex effects when infants are asked to discriminate among or to recognize abstract patterns (Fagan, 1970, 1971, 1973, 1974; Fantz et al., 1975, p. 306). Since that initial report in 1972 of an advantage in face recognition on the part of female infants, however, a host of studies has become available that offer no confirmation of such a female advantage. Specifically, 23 separate experiments that include comparisons of male and female infants for face recognition are available: 19, including five from the Fagan (1972) report, are contained in one related series of studies (Fagan, 1972, 1973, 1974, 1976, 1977); two are reported in Cohen et al. (1977); and the other two are those of Cornell (1974) and Miranda and Fantz (1974). The experiments include infants who range in age from 4 to 7 months, a comparison of normal and retarded infants, tests made with masks, achromatic and chromatic photographs and line drawings, variations in the subtlety of discriminations required, measures of both immediate and long-term recognition, studies of resistance to interference, variations in the kind of faces exposed for study and in the length of study allowed, and successive as well as simultaneous discrimination procedures. The upshot of all this work is that in only one of the 23 comparisons (Fagan, 1972, Experiment III) is there reliable female advantage, a result certainly to be expected on the basis of chance. In short, if there are sex differences in face recognition, they do not begin in infancy.

Orientation

In the present section I am not concerned with the infant's ability to discriminate one orientation of a figure from another (e.g., up from down), a topic pursued in more detail in the Pick, Yonas, and Rieser chapter in this volume. Rather, the focus is on ease of discrimination between two patterns when the two are both in one orientation rather than being in another. For example, the type of question concerning us here is whether discrimination is easier between a man's face and a woman's face when both are properly oriented than it is when the same two faces are rotated 180°. Comparisons of ease of discrimination among patterns presented in one orientation rather than in another have an important conceptual advantage. Because the same pattern in two different orientations is identical in simple stimulus characteristics such as brightness, amount of detail, and length of contour, it would be difficult to invoke those characteristics to explain why discrimination should be easier between two patterns in one orientation than between the same two patterns in a different orientation. In other words, differential ease of discrimination as a result of orientation allows us to infer that the discrimination is based on the relation among the elements making up a pattern.

The 5-month-old infant evidences improved discrimination when certain abstract patterns are presented in one orientation rather than in another. Support for such a contention comes from an unpublished study in which 22-week-old infants were tested for recognition when the abstract patterns used as discriminanda were different arrangements of either small diamonds or small squares. In an earlier section we saw that 22-week-old infants were able to discriminate among the different arrangements of diamonds pictured in pairs in the top left illustration in Figure 4.1. Rotating those arrangements of diamonds by 45° produces patterns made up of small squares. The top right illustration in Figure 4.1 pictures two pairings of rotated diamonds (i.e., squares). The first pairing includes an intact overall square pattern paired with a pattern with two elements displaced. The second pair is composed of the pattern (to the left) with two displaced elements and a target with four elements displaced from the original intact square. It is evident that the corresponding pairs of diamond patterns appear in Figure 4.1 immediately to the left of the two pairings of squares. Unlike their counterparts tested for recognition of patterns of diamonds, a sample of eight infants who were required to discriminate the intact square from the square with two displaced elements showed no reliable preference for novelty. A similar failure to demonstrate recognition was found for an additional eight subjects given the patterns with two and four displaced squares. Thus, discrimination proved to be much easier among patterns composed of small diamonds than among the same patterns composed of small squares. No obvious methodological explanation for such a set of results emerged from further analyses of the data. For example, mean study times actually spent during the 60-second familiarization periods preceding recognition testing were virtually identical for infants given the intact arrangements versus the arrangements with two displaced elements (24.5 seconds for squares and 24.9 seconds for diamonds) and for subjects tested on pairings of two with four displaced elements (26.9 for squares, 26.7 for diamonds). Nor is there any directly comparable body of findings in the adult literature on recognition of abstract patterns that can be appealed to for possible elucidation, although Garner's (1974) work on ease of recognition as determined by the kind of internal arrangements of a dot pattern seems most relevant. In other words, it is hard to know why patterns of diamonds should enjoy greater discriminability than patterns of squares for the 5-month-old. However, the demonstration that some abstract patterns are more easily discriminated in one particular orientation than in another provided evidence that facilitation of the infant's discrimination ascribable to orientation is not limited to naturally occurring patterns.

Because we know from our own experience that faces are distinguished on the basis of internal patterning, we are not surprised to find that adults and older children find properly oriented faces easier to discriminate one from another than they do rotated faces (e.g., see reviews by Carey & Diamond, 1977; Ellis, 1975). In the present exposition, we will see that attention to the internal relations of a face pattern begins early in life. An additional main finding that emerges from studies of the adult and older child's recognition of patterns in various orientations is that the advantage of customary orientation is relative rather than absolute, that is, rotated faces are themselves discriminable one from another. We will see that the benefits of proper orientation for discriminations among faces is also relative during infancy. A study by Fagan (1972), noted earlier, found support for the hypothesis that infants' recognition memory is greater when upright rather than rotated faces must be discriminated. Infants in an initial experiment differentiated among photographs of a woman and a baby and among women, babies, and men. Subjects in a third experiment discriminated photographs of a man and a woman, a man and a baby, and a woman and a baby. In a fifth experiment, differentiations among face masks were shown. In each instance in this series of experiments when upright faces were differentiated by 5- to 6-month-old infants, the same stimuli inverted 180° were not. In addition, 7-month-old infants were tested for discriminations between the three-quarter views of the two highly similar men in the third and fourth rows of Figure 4.3 when both faces were rotated 180°. No recognition occurred when the faces were rotated as had occurred for infants tested with upright versions of those faces.

Although it is evident that infants find properly oriented faces easier to recognize than rotated faces, there is also recent work to indicate that the infant, under certain conditions, can distinguish among rotated face photographs. One instance was found in the Fagan (1977, Experiment II) study mentioned earlier. In that study, some rotated photographs interpolated during a retention interval interfered with delayed recognition of an upright face photograph, but other interpolated inverted photographs did not produce such interference. This finding of differential interference implies that 5- to 6-month-old infants can differentiate at some level among rotated face photographs. These instances of differential forgetting occurred only following relatively long (120-second) familiarization periods during which the infant was allowed prolonged study of the to-be-remembered photograph. In the report cited earlier (Fagan, 1972) in which no evidence for discrimination of rotated photographs was found, familiarization periods of 60 seconds were employed. Hence, an empirical relation is indicated with regard to length of familiarization and discrimination among rotated faces. Increased age from 5 to 7 months also facilitates recognition of rotated face photographs. In a recent unpublished study, a sample of 24 subjects with a mean age of 30 weeks was presented with face photographs (woman or baby) for a 40-second familiarization period during which the targets elicited an average of 23.5 seconds of fixation. Separate groups of 12 infants were tested for recognition of upright or rotated faces. As was found (Fagan, 1972, 1973, 1974) for younger, 22-week-old infants, the 30-week-old infants in this study who were shown upright photographs devoted more attention to the novel targets on test. Unlike younger subjects, the 30-week-old sample presented with rotated photographs also gave evidence of recognition, as had their age-mates who were shown properly oriented faces. In short, both increased study time at younger ages and advanced development per se reveal the infant's ability to discriminate among rotated faces on a recognition test.

In summary, differential ease of discrimination between two faces as a function of orientation gives us some evidence that the infant is basing his discrimination on the pattern of features in a face rather than on some simple characteristic such as brightness. In addition, given more study time or with more development, the infant, like the adult, is also able to discriminate among rotated faces. Finally, the facilitation of recognition ascribable to orientation is not confined, for the infant, to faces but occurs for abstract patterns as well.

Fidelity

Some face representations are more true to life than are others. An appropriately sculpted, tinted, bewigged, life-sized mask, for example, is more akin to a real face than is an achromatic photograph which, in turn, is more representative than a schematic line drawing. We begin with a demonstration and a discussion of the fact that discrimination among representations of faces becomes more likely for the infant as the fidelity of the representations to real faces increases. The remainder of the exposition is devoted to a consideration of the fact that infants are capable of recognizing some face representations following long retention intervals whereas other, equally discriminable representations are quickly forgotten.

Figure 4.2 contains examples of the three types of face representations that served as stimuli in the studies (Fagan, 1972, 1973, 1974) to be discussed. The first row of Figure 4.2 illustrates masks of a man, a woman, and a baby. The masks of the man and the woman were constructed from sculpted styrofoam wig models approximately the size and shape of a real head. Watercolors and make-up were employed to give the masks a realistic tint. Both were equipped with wigs, and the woman wore red lipstick and false eyelashes. Both had brown enamel irises with black enamel pupils. The baby mask was a plaster of paris, flesh-colored display mannequin with light brown hair (paint) and green-gray eyes. Each of the achromatic photographs in the second row of Figure 4.2 measured approximately 11.4 centimeters from hairline to chin to yield faces of infants and adults approximately equal in size, and each was mounted on a 15.2-centimeter square of white posterboard. The line drawings (bottom row) were rather stark, unembellished schematics constructed by tracing the prominent features that remained after successive Xeroxing of the photographs shown in the second row. The finished line drawings were then mounted on 15.2-centimeter black backgrounds.

The infant's facility in discriminating among faces on a recognition task depends on the kind of representation employed. In an initial study (Fagan, 1972), discrimination among face masks (Experiments V and VII) or among photographs (Experiments I and III) were readily accomplished by 5- to 6-month-old infants, whereas subjects tested with less veridical representations (line drawings) gave no evidence of discrimination or recognition (Experiment IV). These results were confirmed in a second study (Fagan, 1974) in which 5- to 6-month-old subjects again recognized face photographs but showed no differentiation of novel and previously exposed line drawings. In a recent unpublished experiment, a sample of 24 7-month-old infants was tested on line drawings (woman versus baby). The infants were allowed a 40-second familiarization period during which they spent an average of 28.9 seconds of fixation and then were tested for recognition. No reliable preference for the novel line drawing was obtained. The failure of these 7-month-old infants to show discrimination among line drawings is all the more striking given the positive demonstrations (discussed earlier) from other 7-month-old samples who made subtle discriminations among photographs of highly similar men (Fagan, 1976) or even among rotated photographs of a woman and a baby. Clearly, infants are at a disadvantage when the faces to be recognized are presented in the form of line drawings rather than as masks or as photographs. However, infants are not unique with respect to the difficulty imposed on perception by representations of low fidelity. Children and adults find it easier to identify photographs of objects than they do line drawings of those objects (e.g., see review by Gibson, 1969, pp. 102–105). Adults' recognition memory for a photograph of a scene is superior to their memory for a line drawing of that scene (Loftus & Bell, 1975). Whether infants also find photographs of nonfacial objects more interdiscriminable than line drawings of those objects remains an interesting empirical question. More germane to face perception is the fact that children and adults find some representations of faces easier to identify as faces than others. Mooney (1957) created a number of ambiguous black and white patterns that could be seen by children and adults either as faces or as meaningless figures. On a phenomenal level it is striking to experience the abrupt perceptual reorganization that occurs when one of

Mooney's figures, initially perceived as a black and white blob, becomes a coherent face. Not surprisingly, adults find these ambiguous patterns to be much more discriminable on a recognition test when the stimuli are seen as faces rather than as meaningless patterns (Wiseman & Neisser, 1974). Perhaps for the infant a line drawing of a face is as meaningless a pattern as an unorganized view of one of the Mooney patterns is for an adult. In other words, the infant's failure to distinguish one line drawing from another may be due to a failure to see the line drawing as a face. One could argue that the line drawings are seen as faces by the infant but that line drawings are simply impoverished with respect to whatever informative detail aids discrimination and recognition. Whatever the explanation, it is indeed the case that infants, like adults, find more realistic face representations to be more discriminable than less faithful renderings.

Infants also behave differently toward masks from the way they do toward photographs of faces. Infants, as we have noted, find it easy to discriminate among masks or among photographs on immediate recognition tests. But 5- to 6-month-old infants, capable of long-term recognition of photographs of faces over a two-week period give no evidence of differential responsiveness to novel and familiar face masks over a relatively brief, 3-hour delay (Fagan, 1973, Experiment III). Obvious explanations for the infant's differential forgetting of photographs and masks may be ruled out. For example, one might argue that infants viewing face masks attend to stimulus dimensions other than patterning (e.g., color or brightness differences) which, although sufficient for immediate recognition, fail for delayed recognition. This is unlikely, however, because the same face masks rotated 180° do not yield even immediate recognition (Fagan, 1972, Experiment V). Another possibility is that three-dimensional stimuli per se cannot be recognized after more than a few seconds delay. Both Super (1972) and Martin (1975), however, have shown that 4- to 5-month-old infants have at least 24-hour retention for solid, colored, abstract objects. A more likely explanation of the infant's failure to differentiate novel from familiar face masks after a 3-hour delay lies in the fact that face masks are most akin to patterned objects in the infant's natural environment, that is, real faces, and his attention to people during the retention interval interferes with his subsequent ability to remember which of two masks he has seen before. As noted earlier, infants tested for recognition of face photographs provide some confirmation of the idea that exposure to perceptually similar material during a retention interval is a source of subsequent failure to distinguish novel from familiar faces. The adult literature offers no comparable studies of memory for faces when the stimuli are either photographs or objects. We might infer, however, that a similar phenomenon exists for adults by linking the demonstrated high accuracy of long-term (up to 50 years) recognition for photos of faces of classmates (Bahrick, Bahrick, & Wittlinger, 1975) with the fact that the adult's memory for people seen in important life events leaves much to be desired (see discussion by Loftus & Loftus, 1976, pp. 115–118). In any case, there is evidence of differential forgetting for face masks and photographs on the part of the infant, a pattern of results that is not contrary to what we know from studies with adults. We do not know, of course, whether this differential forgetting on the part of the infant is unique to faces. It may be that collections of objects forming a scene (e.g., different arrangements of eating utensils) are more easily forgotten by the infant than are photographs of such scenes, but this remains an empirical question.

DETECTION OF INVARIANT FEATURES

We recognize a person even though that person has aged, put on weight, or altered his or her hair style. We are capable of detecting quite subtle constancies in even highly schematic face representations, for example, the identity of a person's profile over age (Pittenger & Shaw, 1975). Similarly, we recognize a word even though it is printed in various typefaces or written by different hands. This constancy or permanence of pattern perception depends on our ability to detect the invariant features of a pattern, those unchanging relations among the elements of a pattern that are its meaning or identity. In this present section, we see that the ability to detect invariant features of abstract patterns and of faces begins in infancy.

Abstract Patterns

A number of examples of the infant's ability to recognize invariance in patterning have been reported. McGurk (1972) showed that 6-month-old infants recognize the form of a simple stick figure despite changes in its orientation. Verification of McGurk's finding that infants faced with abstract figures can detect invariance in patterning over changes in orientation has been provided in a study by Cornell (1975). The lower left illustration in Figure 4.1, for example, pictures two different arrangements of small black triangles, each arrangement contained within an overall pyramidal shape. Cornell (1975) employed these patterns, along with versions of each of them rotated 180°, to explore the 18-week-old infant's ability to detect invariance in pattern arrangement. Specifically, an initial group of infants demonstrated that each arrangement of triangles pictured in Figure 4.1 could be differentiated from a version of itself rotated 180°. To test for recognition of invariance in pattern arrangement, an additional group of infants was presented with one arrangement for study (e.g., the arrangement to the left in Figure 4.1) and then given a recognition test pairing with both pattern arrangements rotated (e.g., with the apexes of both pyramidal shapes in Figure 4.1 now pointing down). Infants responded to invariant patterning, preferring the novel arrangement (the arrangement to the right in Figure 4.1 but rotated 180°) even though the familiar arrangement appeared in a new orientation and such a change in orientation could be readily discriminated.

A second example of the infant's detection of the invariant patterning common to related abstract figures comes from an unpublished study employing 22-week-old infants. The bottom right illustration in Figure 4.1 pictures patterns made up of particular arrangements of 20 small black squares. The arrangements were made by placing five sets of four squares per set in different cells of a 3 X 3 matrix. These patterns may seem familiar because they were modeled after the patterns described and studied extensively in experiments with adults by Garner (1974). For our present purposes, however, these patterns are useful because, by placing each of the five sets of four elements in different positions in the 3 X 3 matrix (e.g., as is the case for the two patterns that are paired in the bottom row under TEST), we can create targets that are unrelated in form. By rotating a particular arrangement (e.g., the patterns in the top row under TEST are rotated versions of each other), we can provide targets that are related in form. These patterns were employed to test 22-week-old infants' ability to detect invariance in patterning. An initial experiment with 14 infants demonstrated that the related patterns pictured in the top row under TEST could be discriminated on a recognition test with a mean of 58.7% of test fixation paid to whichever rotation served as the novel target, following an average of 25.9 seconds of study fixation. A second step was the demonstration, with 12 additional subjects, that the two patterns in the bottom row under TEST were of equal attention value when simply paired together. The final test included a sample of 19 infants who were observed to see if they would respond to a particular pattern as being familiar on recognition testing (i.e., the pattern to the left in the bottom pairing under TEST) if a related pattern (i.e., the pattern under TRAIN) had been shown for study. After spending an average of 23.4 seconds of fixation during study, these 19 subjects showed a preference for the novel unrelated pattern reliably greater than chance, indicating that the relation in patterning between the pattern presented for study and its rotated version presented on test had been detected. Thus, we have three experiments—Cornell (1975), McGurk (1972), and the study illustrated in Figure 4.1 — all employing different abstract figures from the others and all concurring in finding the 5- to 6-month-old infant capable of detecting the invariant pattern of a figure.

Faces

The infant's ability to recognize invariant characteristics of a pattern is not confined to abstract figures but extends to facial representations as well.

A systematic examination of the 7-month-old infant's ability to detect invariant aspects of faces is contained in Fagan (1976). As we have seen, two initial experiments in the Fagan (1976) study demonstrated the infant's ability to discriminate among photographs of different men's faces, as well as among poses of the same man's face. A third study examined the infant's attention to unique aspects of a particular face. Specifically, identification of face patterning was tested by asking whether the infant would respond to a particular man's face as being familiar on a recognition test pairing of that man with another man even though a different pose of the "familiar" man's face had been the previously exposed target. A procedural example is given in the top pairing under TEST in Figure 4.4. In this procedure infants are presented with profile poses of two men after having seen a full-face view (e.g., under TRAIN) of one of the men. A similar test condition (not shown) paired the three-quarter poses of each of these two men after familiarization to the full-face pose of one of them. A sample of 32 infants received both problems. In each condition, the results were the same. Infants devoted more attention to the novel man's face even though the "familiar" man appeared

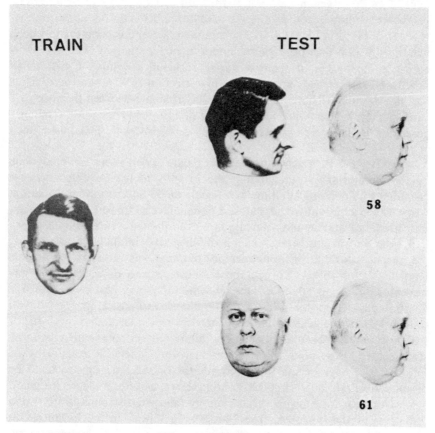

TRAIN   TEST

58

61

FIG. 4.4.   Summary of the results and design of experiments on infants' recognition of invariance in face pattern and in face pose.

in a novel pose. The mean scores across problems averaged 58.4% to the novel man. In short, infants did recognize the familiar man on test even though he had appeared in a different pose during familiarization and even though such a change in pose could be easily discriminated (Fagan, 1976, Experiment II). A recent study by Cohen (1977), who employed photographs of women's faces as stimuli, provides independent confirmation of the Fagan (1976) finding that the 7-month-old infant is able to detect invariance in face patterning over changes in pose. In effect, infants show recognition of certain features of a face, features that remain invariant from one pose to another and that serve to identify that face.

A second aim of the third experiment in the Fagan (1976) report was to test the infant's identification of invariant pose by exposing the infant to a particular man and then showing the infant a new man in two poses, one pose having been the one assumed by the man presented during familiarization. Infants were shown one of two men in either profile or full-face pose (e.g., TRAIN target in Figure 4.4) for study followed by recognition test pairings of full-face and profile views of the other man (as in the bottom row under TEST in Figure 4.4). The infants tested in this manner did indeed identify invariance in pose over changes in face patterning with the novel pose eliciting 61.3% of fixation during recognition testing, a preference significantly different from chance. This detection of invariant pose could not have been ascribable to a failure to discriminate between the face patterns of the two men who, in the present design, held the same "familiar" pose from training to testing (Fagan, 1976, Experiment I). Thus, invariance in pose was identified.

A fourth and fifth experiment in the Fagan (1976) series explored some of the circumstances surrounding the infant's ability to detect general characteristics defining adult male or female faces. Specifically, the question was whether an infant would choose a female face as "novel," for example, on pairings of a male and a female face even though a different male face had been shown for study. The possibility that infants are capable of recognizing sex as an invariant feature of faces was raised in a study by Cornell (1974). In the Cornell report, however, no direct evidence was presented to show that a face shown for study could be reliably discriminated from the same-sex "familiar" face used for recognition testing. Hence, the generalization assumed to be demonstrated by Cornell's infants could have been ascribable to a failure to discriminate the previously seen face from the same-sex face presented for recognition testing. In the Fagan (1976) experiments, however, photos of faces demonstrated to be discriminable within a same-sex pairing served as discriminanda to guard against the explanation that infants simply failed to differentiate study and test items of the same sex. The 7-month-old infants in the Fagan (1976) report did indeed evidence detection of sex as an invariant feature. However, because the provision of multiple instances of the same-sex face during study aided the identification of sex as an invariant feature, the results of these experiments are treated more extensively later, when I discuss facilitation of recognition. In any case, the Fagan (1976) report contains three examples of the 7-month-old infant's ability to detect invariant face features: The facial pattern common to different poses of a man's face was recognized; infants responded to invariance in pose; and infants identified a face as familiar on recognition testing when another instance of that same-sex face had been presented for initial examination.

Given these demonstrations of the 7-month-old infant's ability to recognize rather subtle invariant aspects of face photographs, it is not surprising to find that younger, 5-month-old infants are capable of abstracting more obvious invariant features such as those common to an object and its photographic representation. Recent studies have shown, for example, that 5-month-old infants will respond to photographs of dolls (Strauss, DeLoache, & Maynard, 1977) or to photographs of people (Dirks & Gibson, 1977) as familiar after having been habituated to the actual doll or person. Such recent demonstrations of the 5-month-old infant's ability to identify commonalities between objects and their pictorial representations underscore an earlier contention (Fagan, 1972) that 5-month-old infants "can generalize the disctinctive features abstracted from three-dimensional, chromatic, moving, real faces to two-dimensional, achromatic, still representations such as photos [p. 473]," a contention based on the finding that photographs of faces were more readily distinguished one from the other when presented in an upright rather than in a rotated orientation.

FACILITATION OF RECOGNITION

Thus far, we have described the comparative ease with which the infant discriminates among and recognizes faces and other patterns. We have also discussed various limitations on such abilities set by stimulus factors (e.g., orientation) and individual differences (e.g., age). In this section, we focus on circumstances that facilitate the infant's recognition of patterns. Specifically, we note that improved recognition results from providing the infant with related instances of a to-be-remembered pattern characteristic during study. Such facilitation occurs for both face representations and for abstract patterns.

Abstract Patterns

Facilitation of recognition ascribable to exposure to related instances of a pattern during study occurs when abstract figures are to be discriminated and recognized. Figure 4.5 illustrates the design of an unpublished recognition study in which 22-week-old infants were required to discriminate, on a recognition test, between the abstract black and white patterns composed of

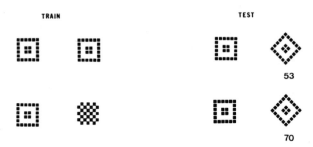

FIG. 4.5. Summary of the results and design of an experiment on facilitation of abstract pattern recognition.

24 small squares or 24 small diamonds pictured under TEST in Figure 4.5. The overall-square pattern, which always served as the familiar target in this study, had proved in pilot studies to elicit equal fixation when paired with the diamond pattern. For one group of 16 infants (design pictured in the top row of Figure 4.5), a standard procedure was followed in which duplicates of the square were paired for a 30-second study period prior to the two 5-second recognition test pairings of square with diamond. During study, these 16 subjects averaged 15.3 seconds of fixation, and did not evidence recognition on TEST with roughly equal fixation paid to square and diamond. A second group of 13 infants was presented during study with the square pattern and with a checkerboard arrangement of 24 small squares (see bottom row, Figure 4.5) for two 15-second pairings. During study, the checkerboard pattern elicited an average of 9.2 seconds of fixation and the square an average of 4.2 seconds (a reliable preference for the checkerboard) for a total TRAIN fixation of 13.4 seconds. Despite this low overall study time, which was apportioned differentially between two different arrangements of small squares, the 13 subjects evidenced reliable recognition of the overall-square pattern on TEST with 70.3% of test fixation paid to the novel, diamond pattern. Hence, the exposure in this example to the same internal elements (small squares) embodied in two different arrangements (overall-square and checkerboard) aided later discrimination of the small squares from an arrangement of diamonds. Whether such facilitation occurs for other abstract figures is an empirical question. In any case, there is evidence to support the view that facilitation of recognition by providing related examples of a target during study is a phenomenon that holds true for infants' recognition of abstract patterns.

Faces

Evidence from a published report (Fagan, 1976) and from unpublished work is advanced to indicate that infants' recognition of faces is facilitated by exposure to multiple exemplars during study. As noted earlier, 7-month-old infants in the Fagan (1976, Experiment V) study proved capable of abstracting the invariant features defining the sex of a face. However, such abstraction and recognition appeared only when two same-sex faces had been shown prior to recognition testing. The experimental design that led to the actual demonstration of successful identification of sexual invariance is shown in the bottom row of Figure 4.6. In the example, the infant was first exposed for 40 seconds to a man (TRAIN₁) followed by a brief TEST₁ pairing of that man with the face of a new man. The preference of 62.9% to the novel man on TEST₁ was reliably greater than chance and indicated that the man serving as familiar could be differentiated from the man who served as novel. After a second study (TRAIN₂) exposure for 40 seconds to the previously seen man, a TEST₂ pairing included a new instance of same sex as the familiar item (another man) and, for the first time, a face of the opposite sex. On TEST₂, the novel sex item (the woman) elicited a greater-than-chance preference of 60.8%. In contrast, another sample of infants exposed simply to the same man for two 40-second study periods (design pictured along the top row of Figure 4.6) evidenced no recognition of invariant sex from study to test, paying equal attention to a new man and a new woman. In other words, providing the infant with related (same-sex) but discriminable instances from a category during the course of study facilitated the infant's later identification of a new instance from that same-sex category as a "familiar" item.

A second unpublished study employing 7-month-old infants was undertaken to test the replicability and the generalizability of the finding (Fagan, 1976, Experiment V) that the provision of multiple exemplars of a face during study aids later recognition. The design of this second study is illustrated in Figure 4.7. The procedure and data shown in the top row of Figure 4.7 are taken from Fagan (1976, Experiment I). As noted earlier, 7-month-old infants were unable to differentiate between two highly similar men when the men were shown in profile view (mean %N of 49 listed under TEST in Figure 4.7, top), following a 40-second study period in which duplicate views of one of the men were shown for study (TRAIN) and an average of 21.1 seconds of fixation was elicited. Further analysis of the Fagan (1976, Experiment I) results also indicated that the profile views of these two men commanded equal visual fixation, that is, one man was not preferred to the other. An additional group of 15 infants was tested for recognition when the discrimination was between these two men in profile pose, with the man pictured as novel in Figure 4.7 serving as being novel across subjects. For these 15 infants, however, the profile pose of the "familiar" man was paired during two 20-second study periods with a full-face and a three-quarter pose of that man. Thus, infants were shown multiple poses of the same man during study and were then tested for recognition of that man when he was paired with a new man. A total of 26.3 seconds was elicited during study. Within that overall looking time, the infants exhibited a decided preference for the full-face over the profile view (8.7 to 4.6 seconds, respectively) and for the

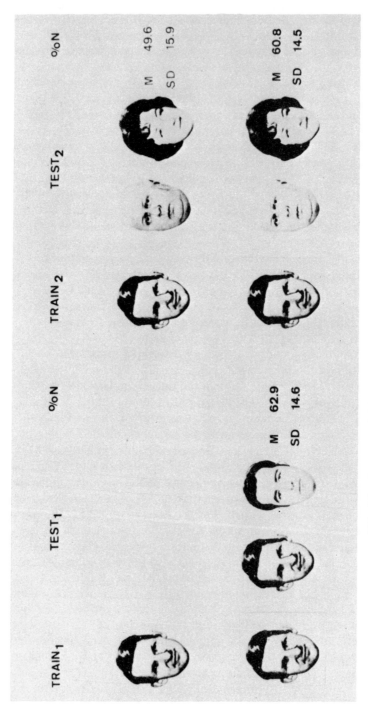

FIG. 4.6. Summary of the results and design of experiments on infants' recognition of invariance in sex.

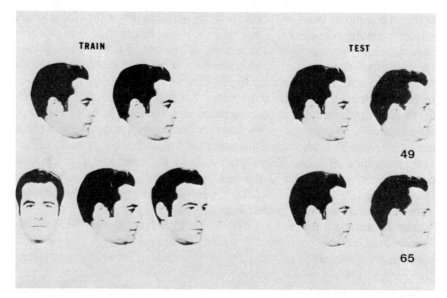

FIG. 4.7   Summary of the results and design of an experiment on facilitation of facial recognition.

three-quarter over the profile pose (8.1 to 5.0). These preferences indicated that during study the full-face and the three-quarter poses were each seen as different from the profile view and, furthermore, that relatively little study fixation (9.6 seconds) was elicited by the pattern (the profile pose) later to be shown as "familiar." Despite this low study fixation to the famliar man's profile, when the two men's profiles were paired on recognition testing, the novel man commanded 64.9% of the total test fixation, a highly reliable preference. In short, results from both the published and the additional experiment lead to the general conclusion that allowing the 7-month-old infant to inspect related examples of a face pattern (i.e., a particular person) or of a facial feature (i.e., sex) during study facilitates later recognition of that face pattern or that face feature.

SUMMARY AND DISCUSSION

This chapter documents the ability of the 5- to 7-month-old infant to recognize facial representations. For the most part, knowledge of the origins of facial recognition was gained by exposing the infant to a photograph of a face and then pairing that target with another. By controlling the manner in which the novel and the previously seen faces varied, the characteristics of the faces upon which the infant based his discrimination and recognition could be inferred. Three main conclusions may be drawn from the results gained by these observations and inferential strategies. The first implication is that the stimulus basis of infant facial recognition lies in the higher-order relations among the internal elements of a target rather than being dependent on simple features such as brightness or amount of detail. This reliance on the information contained in patterning is attested to by the infant's facility in discriminating among highly similar faces and by the improvement in recognition when faces are properly oriented. In addition, the ability to detect invariant facial characteristics and what might be described as the abstraction of common patterning from different instances of a face to aid later recognition also argue for attention to pattern as the basis for infant recognition of faces. These latter abilities to detect invariant or common features, when added to the fact that infant recognition memory for faces is long lasting, also imply that the infant's perception of the patterns in his world has a certain permanence or constancy.

The second main inference is that the infant's recognition of facial patterning need not be considered a special or unique process. As we have noted in every section of this chapter, the phenomena associated with infant face recognition are also associated with the infant's recognition of nonsocial, abstract patterns. To state this another way, although faces are, by definition, a unique class of objects, the processes underlying face recognition do not appear to be unique but hold as well for abstract patterns as for faces. Ellis (1975) has come to much the same conclusion in his review of the adult literature on face recognition. Although this view is disappointing to those who may wish to accord the face a special status in the visual world of the infant, it obviously allows a more parsimonious explanation of early pattern recognition. It also means that investigators who have employed highly artificial stimuli in tests of infant pattern recognition may feel a bit more comfortable about generalizing from their findings in order to make inferences about the infant's processing of more realistic patterns. Furthermore, it serves as a caution to the narrow view that only research employing particular stimuli (natural *or* artificial) contributes relevant data for our understanding of infant perception.

The final conclusion is that most of the essential characteristics of adult facial recognition are present in rudimentary form by the end of the first 7 months of life. Specifically, the infant is able to make subtle discriminations among faces; memory for faces is long-term memory and not easily disrupted; the infant is sensitive to variations in inter-item similarity, to proper orientation, and to fidelity of representation; and the infant is capable of detecting invariant features of faces. In addition, data from infants tell us that sex differences in adult recognition of faces are likely the result of experiential factors, having no origin in infancy. Finally, the infant results raise certain empirical questions that contribute toward further research with older subjects. Such questions include the possible interactive effect of face pose and inter-item similarity on face recognition, the role of orientation in discriminations among abstract figures, the possible differential long-term retention of objects and pictures, and the facilitative effects on face recognition of particular training procedures.

ACKNOWLEDGMENT

The preparation of this chapter was supported by a Career Development Grant (1 K04 HD-70144) to the author from the National Institute of Child Health and Human Development.

REFERENCES

Bahrick, H. P., Bahrick, P. O., & Wittlinger, R. P. Fifty years of memory for names and faces: A cross-sectional approach. *Journal of Experimental Psychology: General,* 1975, *104,* 54–75.

Boat, B. W. *Recognition memory for faces in children of superior, average, and retarded intelligence.* Unpublished doctoral dissertation, Case Western Reserve University, 1977.

Carey, S., & Diamond, R. From piecemeal to configurational representations of faces. *Science,* 1977, *195,* 312–314.

Caron, A. J., Caron, R. F., Caldwell, R. C., & Weiss, S. E. Infant perception of the structural properties of the face. *Developmental Psychology,* 1973, *9,* 385–399.

Cohen, L. B. *Concept acquisition in the human infant.* Paper presented at the Society for Research in Child Development Meeting, New Orleans, March, 1977.

Cohen, L. B., Deloache, J. S., & Pearl, R. A. An examination of interference effects in infants' memory for faces. *Child Development,* 1977, *48,* 88–96.

Cornell, E. H. Infants' discrimination of photographs of faces following redundant presentations. *Journal of Experimental Child Psychology,* 1974, *18,* 98–106.

Cornell, E. H. Infants' visual attention to pattern arrangement and orientation. *Child Development,* 1975, *46,* 229–232.

Dirks, J., & Gibson, E. Infants' perception of similarity between live people and their photographs. *Child Development,* 1977, *48,* 124–130.

Dirks, J., & Neisser, U. Memory for objects in real scenes: The development of recognition and recall. *Journal of Experimental Child Psychology,* 1977, *13,* 77–78.

Ellis, H. D. Recognizing faces. *British Journal of Psychology,* 1975, *66,* 409–426.

Fagan, J. F. Memory in the infant. *Journal of Experimental Child Psychology,* 1970, *9,* 217–226.

Fagan, J. F. Infants' recognition memory for a series of visual stimuli. *Journal of Experimental Child Psychology,* 1971, *11,* 244–250.

Fagan, J. F. Infants' recognition memory for faces. *Journal of Experimental Child Psychology,* 1972, *14,* 453–476.

Fagan, J. F. Infants' delayed recognition memory and forgetting. *Journal of Experimental Child Psychology,* 1973, *16,* 424–450.

Fagan, J. F. Infant recognition memory: The effects of length of familiarization and type of discrimination task. *Child Development,* 1974, *45,* 351–356.

Fagan, J. F. Infants' recognition of invariant features of faces. *Child Development,* 1976, *47,* 627–638.

Fagan, J. F. Infant recognition memory: Studies in forgetting. *Child Development,* 1977, *48,* 68–78.

Fantz, R. L. A method for studying early visual development. *Perceptual and Motor Skills,* 1956, *6,* 13-15.

Fantz, R. L. The origin of form perception. *Scientific American,* 1961, *204,* 66-72.

Fantz, R. L. Pattern vision in newborn infants. *Science,* 1963, *140,* 296-297.

Fantz, R. L. Pattern discrimination and selective attention as determinants of perceptual development from birth. In A. Kidd & J. L. Rivoire (Eds.), *Perceptual development in children.* New York: International Universities Press, 1966.

Fantz, R. L., Fagan, J. F., & Miranda, S. B. Early perceptual development as shown by visual discrimination, selectivity, and memory with varying stimulus and population parameters. In L. Cohen & P. Salapatek (Eds.), *Infant perception: From sensation to cognition: Basic visual processes* (Vol. 1). New York: Academic Press, 1975.

Fitzgerald, H. D. Autonomic pupillary reflex activity during early infancy and its relation to social and nonsocial visual stimuli. *Journal of Experimental Child Psychology,* 1968, *6,* 470-482.

Garner, W. G. *The processing of information and structure.* Hillsdale, N. J.: Lawrence Erlbaum Associates, 1974.

Gibson, E. J. *Principles of perceptual learning and development.* New York: Appleton-Century-Crofts, 1969.

Goldstein, A. J., Harmon, L. D., & Lesk, A. B. Identification of human faces. *Proceedings of the IEEE,* 1971, *59,* 748-760.

Haaf, R. A. Visual responses to complex facelike patterns by 15- and 20-week-old infants. *Developmental Psychology,* 1977, *13,* 77-78.

Haaf, R. A., & Bell, R. Q. A facial dimension in visual discrimination by human infants. *Child Development,* 1964, *38,* 893-899.

Lewis, M., & Brooks, J. Infants' social perception: A constructivist view. In L. Cohen & P. Salapatek (Eds.), *Infant perception: From sensation to cognition: Perception of space, speech, and sound* (Vol. 2). New York: Academic Press, 1975.

Loftus, G. R., & Bell, S. M. Two types of information in picture memory. *Journal of Experimental Psychology: Human Learning and Memory,* 1975, *104,* 103-113.

Loftus, G. R., & Loftus, E. F. *Human memory: The processing of information.* Hillsdale, N. J.: Lawrence Erlbaum Associates, 1976.

Martin, R. M. Effects of familiar and complex stimuli on infant attention. *Developmental Psychology,* 1975, *11,* 178-185.

Maurer, D., & Salapatek, P. Developmental changes in the scanning of faces by young infants. *Child Development,* 1976, *47,* 523-527.

McCall, R. B., & Kagan, J. Attention in the infant: Effects of complexity contour, perimeter, and familiarity. *Child Development,* 1967, *38,* 939-952.

McGurk, H. The role of object orientation in infant perception. *Journal of Experimental Child Psychology,* 1970, *9,* 363-373.

McGurk, H. Infant discrimination of orientation. *Journal of Experimental Child Psychology,* 1972, *14,* 151-164.

Miranda, S. B., & Fantz, R. L. Recognition memory in Down's syndrome and normal infants. *Child Development,* 1974, *45,* 651-660.

Mooney, C. M. Age in the development of closure ability in children. *Canadian Journal of Psychology,* 1957, *11,* 219-226.

Pittenger, J. B., & Shaw, R. E. Aging faces as visual-elastic events: Implications for a theory of nonrigid shape perception. *Journal of Experimental Psychology: Human Perception and Performance,* 1975, *1,* 374-382.

Stechler, G. Newborn attention as affected by medication during labor. *Science,* 1964, *144,* 315-317.

Strauss, M. S., DeLoache, J. S. & Maynard, J. *Infants' recognition of pictorial representations of real objects.* Paper presented at the Society for Research in Child Development Meeting, New Orleans, March, 1977.

Super, C. M. *Long-term memory in early infancy.* Unpublished doctoral dissertation, Harvard University, 1972.

Watson, J. S. Perception of object orientation in infants. *Merrill–Palmer Quarterly,* 1966, *12,* 73–94.

Wiseman, S., & Neisser, U. Perceptual organization as a determinant of visual recognition memory. *American Journal of Psychology,* 1974, *87,* 675–681.

5 Spatial Reference Systems in Perceptual Development

Herbert L. Pick, Jr.
Albert Yonas
John Rieser
University of Minnesota

INTRODUCTION

Perception is relationally determined. The Gestaltists emphasized this in their summary statement that the whole is more than the sum of its parts. J. J. Gibson (1966) argued the same way in stressing the importance of higher-order relational properties of stimuli such as optical flow patterns and texture gradients. However, both these examples tend to focus on *intra*-stimulus relations. These is another sense in which perception is relational; it is in the relation between a stimulus and its context. This is the sense captured by E. J. Gibson (1969) in her analysis of the impact of information theory on perception. *The* stimulus is no longer absolute; what is important is the set of alternative stimuli. *The* response is no longer absolute; what is important is the task confronting the subject. More recently, the relationship between stimulation and context has been noted in the concept of frame as used by researchers in the area of artificial intelligence (e.g., Minsky, 1975) and by sociologists (e.g., Goffman, 1974). The basic idea of the concept of frame is that a situation is uninterpretable unless its context is known, which is true for computers trying to recognize patterns and for humans trying to understand social situations. Neisser (1976) provides a succinct discussion of the concept of frame.

Reference systems or frames of reference provide a way of describing or conceptualizing the relational determinism particularly relevant to spatial perception. A frame of reference is defined here as a locus or set of loci with respect to which spatial position is defined. Thus, a single concrete point could serve as a frame of reference, and a limiting case of spatial orientation would be relative distance from this single point. At the other extreme would be a complex abstract Cartesian reference system with an arbitrary origin and three (or more) orthogonal axes.

In this chapter we examine the development of space perception as organized with respect to various frames of reference. In the first part of the chapter, we suggest that these reference systems change with development as the child is confronted with different tasks. In synopsis, the child's spatial behavior at birth consists primarily of sense organ adjustments, accomplished on the basis of egocentric frames of reference. As the infant gains more control over his behavior and can adjust his position, egocentric frames of reference become more differentiated to provide the infant with position constancy. The infant must rely on geographic "up-down" frames of reference when he begins to stand, and he depends on geographic "layout" frames of reference when he starts to crawl or walk.

In the second part of the chapter, attention is focused on the way frames of reference are used. In particular, we examine two aspects of the functioning of reference systems that may show developmental trends: flexibility in the use of reference systems and the coordination of reference systems. We conclude by suggesting a relationship between the frames of reference used in maintaining orientation and the type of mental representations one has of space.

Before beginning, we must point out that *frame of reference* is not a tight explanatory concept. We find it a useful way of thinking about a number of developmental trends in perception. As noted, examination of space perception in terms of reference systems may imply nothing more than that perception is relational. However, using frames of reference to analyze spatial problems is a convenient way of organizing information about a great deal of spatial behavior, and it helps to generate new and, we believe, fruitful experiments.

TASKS AND REFERENCE SYSTEMS

Sense Organ Adjustment and Egocentric Frames of Reference

The primary spatial behavior in which newborn and young infants engage is adjustment of the sense organs. The findings by Wertheimer (1961) that the newborn infant will turn his head and eyes in the direction of sound and by Rieser, Yonas, and Wikner (1976) that the newborn will turn away from an odorant illustrate both the approach and avoidant aspects of such sense organ adjustment. Other examples include Harris and MacFarlane's report (1974) that a newborn will orient his eyes toward a bright light and Prechtl's finding (1958) that when stimulated tactually near the mouth, a newborn will turn his head toward the locus of the touch. All of these behaviors involve the reorienting of the sensory surface to maximize or minimize stimulation.

To accomplish this reorientation, the sensory surface must be differentiated with respect to position and direction. In short, the sensory surface provides an initial frame of reference for the registration of spatial information. This egocentric frame of reference is inappropriate for much subsequent spatial behavior that must be adapted to the space of the external environment, but it is appropriate for orienting the sense organ toward or away from a source of stimulation.

Saccadic eye movements are the most obvious example of sense organ adjustment that implies the functioning of an egocentric frame of reference in infants. Although the accuracy of saccadic eye movements to peripheral targets has not been directly investigated in newborns, the newborn's eye movements are clearly not directionally random to peripheral stimuli. Harris and MacFarlane (1974) found that if the newborn is presented with light in the periphery, the newborn will shift orientation of the eye to the side of the field in which the light is presented. They found that if the original fixation target remained on, newborns would respond only when the peripheral target was with with 15°. However, if the central fixation target was turned off when the peripheral target was introduced, the newborn would respond to targets as far as 25° in the periphery. Although this study gives us some evidence that the newborn may have a rather small effective visual field, it tells us little about the accuracy of the eye movements that were observed because observers judged only whether the eyes were moved in the correct direction at the presentation of the peripheral light.

A study that provided more information about the direction and especially the extent of saccadic eye movements was conducted by Aslin and Salapatek (1975) with 1- and 2-month-old infants. The infants were presented with a peripheral light at three distances from the stimulus along horizontal, vertical, and diagonal axes. The observers judged that the infants' initial eye movements were directionally appropriate, although rather gross directional errors could be detected. The most interesting result of the study was the finding that the extent of the initial saccade is tied to the distance of the peripheral target, although generally only about one-half of the distance to it. Instead of making a single saccade to a peripheral target as an adult does, the infant makes a series of saccades. Aslin and Salapatek raised the interesting possibility that the eye movements of the young infant may be accurate but are programmed with the expectation that the head would be rotating in the same direction. Because of the immaturity of the motor capacities, the head does not rotate, and the eye movement does not reach the target.

It seems probable that retinal local signs undergo differentiation due to the maturation of neurophysiological substrates. The poor acuity of the neonate certainly suggests that fine differences in spatial structure cannot be detected; later, improvement of acuity indicates that differentiation does occur. It is unlikely that there exists a "built-in" and unchanging linkage of specific retinal locations to specific motor programs for bringing a peripheral target to the fovea. During early development, there is a shift in the lcoation of the fovea, bringing it closer to the optic axis (Mann, 1964), in addition to other anatomical changes.

Given these changes, a mechanism for altering the motor programs that are evoked by retinal location would seem to be very useful. McLaughlin (1967) found that adults adapted the size of saccadic eye movements when the target being fixated was changed in position during the saccade. A problem that we are beginning to explore in our laboratory deals with the nature of this adaptation. Is retinal–motor space organized as a whole so that, for example, minification of saccades in one direction would transfer to all other directions? Or is adaptation specific only to the retinal location that is adapted? That retinal location is basic to the control of eye movements is clear; however, we do not yet know whether the retina acts as a unified frame of reference.

A second visual phenomenon that involves a retinal frame of reference in both adults and infants is differential responsiveness to lines of different orientation. It has long been known that human adults have higher acuity for vertical and horizontal lines than for lines of other orientations. Ogilvie and Taylor (1958) demonstrated that this orientational anisotropy was determined by the orientation of the lines relative to the eye. They found that acuity was best for lines oriented 45° to gravity when the subject's head was also tilted 45°. Such orientational anisotropy has also been reported in young infants, implying a "built-in" aspect of the human visual system (Leehey, Moskowitz-Cook, Brill, & Held, 1975). Annis and Frost (1973), however, have argued that there is an experiential basis for the differential sensitivity to oblique and rectilinear lines. They found a lack of such differential sensitivity in rural Eskimos as compared with urban whites and suggested that the carpentered ecology of the urban environment provided basic experience with rectilinear lines. This experiential hypothesis gains some support from comparative physiological studies. A number of investigators have found that the distribution of orientation-sensitive cells in the visual cortex of kittens may be altered by rearing the kittens in an environment containing lines of only certain orientations (e.g., Blakemore & Cooper, 1970; Hirsch & Spinelli, 1970; Stryker & Sherk, 1975).

The results of Leehey et al. (1975) implying a "built-in" mechanism and those of Annis and Frost (1973) implicating experience may not be in conflict. An experiential effect can reinforce an innate predisposition. In this regard, Leventhal and Hirsch (1975) found that cats exposed only to horizontal or vertical contours have cortical cells sensitive only to this orientation, whereas cats with exposure to diagonal lines alone have cells sensitive to horizontal and vertical as well as diagonal lines. They argue that neurons sensitive to horizontal and vertical contours do not need specific visual input for maintenance or for development but that neurons responding preferentially to diagonal lines require visual input specific to that orientation.

There is other evidence that some aspects of visual sensitivity to orientation in human adults are still organized with respect to a retinal frame of reference. Many sensory aftereffects show an orientational specificity, not to the gravitational or geographic frame of reference but rather to the retinal orientation. Perhaps the best known of these is the orientation-contingent color aftereffect reported by McCullough (1965). After viewing an adaptation grating composed of black and green vertical stripes alternated with a grating of black and red horizontal stripes, the subject was shown a pair of black and white test gratings at right angles to each other. The vertical test grating appeared to be tinted with pink, and the horizontal test grating appeared to be tinted with green. As the subject tilted his head 90°, the vertical grating appeared to change from tinted pink to black and white to tinted green. Thus, a black and white test grating at the same retinal orientation as the adaptation grating appears to be tinted with the color that is complementary to the adaptation grating.

Results such as these suggest that various perceptual phenomena are still mediated in adults by a retinally relevant spatial organization. In young infants this may be the primary organization of spatial information. In adults most spatial behavior demands orientation to geographic frames of reference. However, certain types of spatial behavior (sense organ adjustments such as saccadic eye movements) reflect a retinal frame of reference as do various types of orientation sensitivity.[1]

Frames of Reference and Position Constancy

The spatial tasks that confront even a young infant quickly go beyond the very simple sense organ adjustments just described. As the infant starts to reach, at about 3 or 4 months of age, it is not enough that the retinal local sign accurately control eye movements to bring peripheral stimulation to the

---

[1]A line of research suggests that the topological relationship of inside–outside is appreciated by the visual system of the human infant perhaps from birth. Salapatek (1969) and several others (e.g., Bergman, Haith, & Mann, 1971; Donnee, 1973; Maurer & Salapatek, 1976) have shown that when presented with a compound figure, 1-month-old infants visually scan an outer figure and tend not to fixate on the internal elements of a display, and Milewski (1976) found that 1-month-old infants discriminated only the external shapes of figures and not the internal figures. In contrast, 4-month-old infants discriminated both internal and external shapes. Milewski (1976) and others have ruled out a number of simple explanations for the finding. e.g., poor acuity, lateral intereference, and capture by the first contour. Although these findings suggest that infants prefer the external parts of a pattern (perhaps to aid in the segregation of figure from ground), Milewski (1976) found that when a large figure was presented adjacent to a small shape, its discrimination by 1-month-old infants was as poor as it was when the small shape was presented within the larger figure.

fovea. The problem for the infant in determining the visual direction for reaching to a point in external space is immensely complicated by the fact that the eye and the head (and by about 6 months, the whole infant) are constantly in motion. One possible solution to the problem of azimuth perception would require that the retinal local sign be adjusted to take into account information specifying the position of the eye relative to the head and information specifying the relationship between the head and the trunk. Competing theories have proposed that it is either stretch receptors in the eye muscles or the motor commands to the eye muscles that provide information about eye position. If either of these theories is correct, and if in early infancy this adjustment process is not fully functioning, direction might be registered only in relation to the retina. This possibility could be examined by having an infant learn to anticipate that a light would appear at a peripheral location when a tone occurred; the infant would saccade from a fixation point to that location before the stimulus appeared. Then the initial fixation point would be changed. Of interest is whether the eye movement from this new location would be the same size as the original saccade or whether it would take into account the changed position of the eye.

Bower (1974) has proposed that neither stretch receptor "inflow" nor motor command "outflow" is required to correct retinal local sign for eye position in the head. He suggested that the image of the nose and eye socket acts as a stable frame of reference for judging radial direction relative to the head. If this is the case, one should not be able to learn to anticipate the location of a peripheral target in the dark with changes of eye position. Shebilske and Nice (1976) have recently found that the projection of the nose in the visual field does not aid in adults' judgments of what is straight ahead. No developmental data are available on this question.

The complication described in the case of reaching arises because of the increased differentiation and control of several response systems — specifically, the head and trunk. However, this complication is only an example of a more general constancy problem that confronts the infant. To what extent is the infant able to perceive and orient toward a stable world in the face of changes in sensory stimulation? In the example of reaching described above, the successful infant is coordinating the local sign of a retinal frame of reference with self-produced head and trunk positions. However, much of an infant's movement is not self-produced. Can the infant modulate his spatial behavior in the face of passive changes in position? There is not a great deal of evidence on this question. Acredolo (1976a) has reported one relevant study in which infants of 6 months of age were conditioned to look to the left (or the right) upon presentation of an auditory signal straight ahead in the center of the room. On each training trial, the signal sounded and was followed after a short interval by an experimenter popping up on the left (or right) from behind a screen and saying "peekaboo." Infants soon began to anticipate the experimenter's position by looking in the appropriate direction before the experimenter appeared. When an infant had correctly anticipated that direction five times in a row, the infant was moved to the opposite end of the room and again faced toward the center for the next trial. Would the infant continue to look in the same direction, that is to the left (or right), or would he look at the same place in the room when the auditory signal was presented? The infants all continued to look to the left (or right) and not to the same place. Thus, they were not modulating their egocentric response in the face of changes in position. The same infants were seen in this experiment at 12 months and 18 months of age, and there was a gradual shift to looking at the same place in the room rather than turning in the same direction.

This example may pose a severe test of the ability of an infant to modulate his spatial behavior in relation to passive changes in position. After all, a movement across a room followed by a 180° turn is well beyond possible active movements of many 6-month-old infants. Perhaps passive movements within the range of a child's own active movements would be the first conditions under which a child would modulate his spatial behavior to take into account passive changes of position. There do not appear to be relevant data, although Acredolo's experiment could serve as a model for such research. For example, an infant might be conditioned to anticipate the appearance of an experimenter 45° to the right of center and then be tested with the head turned beyond 45°. Similarly, an infant could be conditioned to look upward and then be tested after being tilted sideways. Would the infant continue to raise his eyes with respect to the body or would the infant move his eyes laterally with respect to the body (and upward in the room)?

Of course, if these experiments were to demonstrate the ability of the infant to modulate spatial behaviors in relation to a passive change in position, it would not necessarily be clear what reference system or systems were involved. For example, a change in head orientation could be signaled by proprioceptive and vestibular stimulation or by visual stimulation. Additional experiments would need to be done to tease these possibilities apart.

An analogous problem in position constancy occurs when it is not the infant who moves but the objects in the environment. Here the problem for the infant is not coordinating a reference system with self-movement but remembering location with respect to appropriate frames of reference. Tests of object permanence can be used to infer the nature of encoding and memory of spatial relations in infants as young as 6 months of age. Consider the following pattern of behavior: An attractive lure is hidden under one of two covers. After a delay (3 to 5 seconds), the infant is allowed to reach for the lure, retrieving it from the appropriate cup. Six-month-old infants succeed at such tasks, encoding the lure's location. Is their code relevant to distinctive characteristics of the visual framework (e.g., NEAR THE RED COVER), or to the infant's body (e.g., TO MY LEFT)? Butterworth (1978) investigated these questions using numerous simple tests. In one test the infant was seated in front of two cups that were symmetrically spaced left and right of midline. The left and right halves of the surface were distinctively colored (red and black, respectively). The infant watched as a lure was hidden inside the left (or right) cup, on top of the red (or black) surface. During a 5-second delay and out of the infant's view, the left-right position of the surface colors was reversed. Did infants reach toward the original egocentric location (i.e., their left) or toward the original visual landmark (i.e., toward the red surface)? Butterworth's results are very informative. Across repeated trials, about half the infants reliably reached egocentrically, whereas the other half reached reliably toward the appropriate landmark. Although there was excellent inter-trial consistency, infants varied from day to day. Thus, one individual might consistently reach egocentrically on one day, whereas the next day his reaches would consistently follow the visual landmark. From these results it seems reasonable to infer that 6-month-old infants can encode spatial relations relevant to either frame of reference. In Butterworth's experimental situation, neither reference system was preferred.

It seems likely that use of visual landmarks does change with age, however. The critical characteristic may be the landmark's spatial proximity to the lure's location. Indirect support from this hypothesis can be inferred from the study by Acredolo (1976a) mentioned earlier. In addition to the previous results described, Acredolo also found that the presence or absence of visual landmarks did *not* influence the responding of the 6-, 9-, and 12-month-old infants tested. Why might infants use visual landmarks in Butterworth's experimental situation but not in Acredolo's? The landmark-to-lure distances differed in the two experimental situations. In Butterworth's study they were coincident, whereas in Acredolo's they were separate. We propose a developmental trend in the use of visual landmarks as frames of reference for spatial relations: With age the ability to use landmarks that are increasingly distal to the target location increases. The hypothesis can be plausibly related to trends described for the development of attention and search-scanning eye movements. One attentional mechanism serving the use of increasingly distal landmarks would be Piaget's demonstrations that with age children increasingly decenter their attention from the object (or characteristic) of immediate concern, relating more peripheral characteristics to their perceptual judgments.

Millar and Schaffer (1972), for example, conditioned infants to make instrumental bar-press responses to signal lights in order to see an interesting rewarding event. They varied the spatial contiguity of the signal light, response manipulandum, and rewarding event. Six-month-old infants were successfully conditioned only when the distances varied from 0° to 5° of visual angle. Older infants were easily conditioned over spatial separations up to 60° of angle. From these demonstrations with infants, as well as others describing changes in the scanning eye movements of children searching for needed information (Vurpillot, 1968; Wright & Vlietstra, 1975), one can infer that younger subjects seem to center both their scanning eye movements *and* their distribution of "internal" attention more narrowly than do older subjects. The hypotheses proposed here are that with age infants and children utilize increasingly distant landmarks as frames of reference and that this attentional change mediates the change in the use of visual landmarks as frames of reference.

Which Way is Up?

When the infant begins to stand at the end of the first year or beginning of the second year of life, information about posture is again potentially signaled by both proprioceptive and vestibular stimulation and visual stimulation. In this case, recent evidence (Lee & Aronson, 1974) suggests that infants rely more on visual stimulation. In this study, infants just over a year of age were place on the floor of a room, the walls of which could be moved backward and forward. When the walls were moved in the direction an infant was facing, the baby behaved as if he were starting to fall backward and to prevent this he swayed forward sometimes to the point of falling over. Conversely, when the walls were moved toward an infant, the baby swayed backward as if to counter his falling forward. Similar experiments with adults also produce marked swaying in the direction of wall movement.

It is reasonable that an infant's standing behavior is organized with respect to what is ordinarily an extremely reliable visual frame of reference. In this case, an external reference system is defining the up-down position of the self. But how does the infant define the up-down spatial layout of the world? Is it defined in relation to an external frame of reference, or is it defined in relation to an egocentric frame of reference? When the infant begins to manipulate objects, his up-down orientation becomes important. Some objects are stable only when positioned base-down. Other objects are containers that spill (much to the chagrin of parents) if they are not positioned right-side up. Of course, for these practical tasks orientation with respect to gravity is important, but presumably differences in orientation must be detectable in order to coordinate specific orientations with gravity.

As far as the infant is concerned, little is known outside of the fact that differences in the vertical orientation of stimuli can be detected. Familiar stimuli — faces — were shown to 8- and 14-week-old infants by Watson (1966). With the 14-week-old infants, upright faces elicited more smiling with shorter latency than did faces rotated 90° or 180°. The discrimination between upright and 180° rotation of faces was replicated by McGurk

(1970) using an habituation paradigm.[2] McGurk also found evidence for discrimination of orientation of a funnel-shaped object with infants as young as 6 weeks of age. Although these experiments were not designed explicitly to investigate the relevant frames of reference, it is possible to infer that the infant's discrimination behavior was based on a retinal frame of reference. This inference is based on the fact that Watson's infants were tested in a supine position with the stimuli presented in a horizontal plane above the eyes. Thus, the only effective frame of reference would seem to be retinal.

Braine (1976) has suggested the intriguing hypothesis that the first thing children perceive about orientation is the difference between right-side up and other orientations, which would be consistent with Watson's (1966) results in which there was no differential responding to stimuli presented at 90° or 180°. Braine reported an experiment with 2-year-olds who were taught to discriminate between pictures of common objects that were right-side up and upside-down, but the children were unable to learn to discriminate between objects that were upside-down and rotated 90°. A possibly related privileged status of vertical orientation has been demonstrated by Berman (1976) and her colleagues (Berman, Cunningham, & Harkulich, 1974; Berman & Golab, 1975). She found that children of 4 to 5 years of age reproduced the orientation of vertical lines significantly more accurately than the orientation of horizontal or oblique lines.

What frames of reference are effective beyond infancy in determining the up-down orientation of objects? On the basis of many years of work, Braine has suggested a two-stage process for children's judgments of whether an object is right-side up or upside-down (Braine, 1976; Ghent, 1961; Ghent & Bernstein, 1961). According to Braine, this judgment is based on the congruence of two tendencies operating when children examine shapes. One tendency is to attend serially to the features of a shape in a downward direction. The second tendency is to look initially at a focal point of the shape. If the focal point is at the top of the figure, the downward "scanning" tendency can operate efficiently. If the focal point that attracts initial attention is at the bottom of the figure, "scanning" downward would take one's attention away from the object. But with respect to what frame of reference is this *downward* direction defined? Braine concludes that it is retinally rather than evironmentally defined, because children looking through their legs at environmentally upright shapes judge them to be upside-down. Even adults seem to be sensitive to retinally defined direction insofar as how uprightness affects their perception. An example is the relative ease of reading retinally upright, environmentally inverted text

---

[2]Harris and Allen (1974) have argued that most research designs with infants do not permit one to separate discrimination of orientation from discrimination of two patterns as different objects. In either case for present purposes, the difference in orientation is the relevant stimulus variable.

viewed through one's legs. Similar systematic evidence has been reported by Rock (1956) using ambiguous figures perceived as one thing in an upright orientation and another thing in an inverted orientation. He found that the retinal orientation determined the perception.

Braine and Knox (1975) have pointed out that perceptual discrimination based on orientation, such as in Rock's experiment, must be distinguished from direct judgments of orientation. The determiners of these behaviors may not always be the same. Thus, it is quite plausible that experienced readers would find when looking through their legs that retinally upright print is easy to read but at the same time they would identify that print as being upside-down if asked to make an orientation judgment. Indeed, Braine and Knox found a developmental trend in judgments of the orientation of a scene that was viewed by children while they were upside-down. The judgments of younger children (3 to 4 year old) were determined primarily by a retinal frame of reference whereas older children's (5 and 9 years old) judgments were determined more by a gravitational reference system. The conclusion of Braine and Knox was that older children make their orientation judgments on the basis of a rule that says to use remote frames of reference of the external world in deciding about orientation. Younger children decide on the basis of a more esthetic judgment, perhaps involving the focal points and scanning mechanisms mentioned earlier.

This account stresses a shift in a rule used for making judgments rather than a developmental change in perceptual sensitivity. An alternate and less intellectual account is that, although the retinal frame of reference is salient and effective early in development, environmental reference systems become increasingly effective during the early school years. Yonas, Kuskowski, and Sternfels (unpublished observations) have investigated the use of frames of reference in perceiving pictoral depth information. In their study, 3- to 8-year-old subjects discriminated convexity and concavity by employing attached shadow information. With such displays, subjects assume that the light is coming from the *upper part* of the photography and interpret a circular shape, in which the upper part is brighter than the lower, as a convexity (see Figure 5.1). Which frames of reference would determine the upper part of the photograph? Retinal and gravitational-geographic frames were manipulated, and the location of the primary source of illumination was varied. Although all three frames of reference were effective to some degree for all age groups, the retinal reference system was powerful for the youngest subjects and did not increase in effectiveness with age. A significant increase in effectiveness with age did occur for the gravitational-geographic and illumination source frames. Because subjects were not asked to judge orientation in this task but rather simply to "point to the bump," it seems unlikely that an intellectual decision rule was determining the results.

The importance of the retinal frame of reference in these experiments is puzzling, because for many practical purposes, it is important to perceive ob-

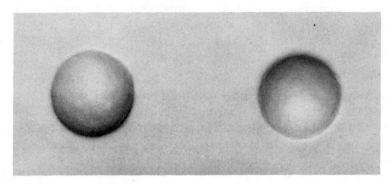

FIG. 5.1.   Surface protuberance and indentation (bump and hole). Depth
quality is determined solely by shadow information.

jects or determine orientation with respect to the external world, especially
gravity. This puzzle may be partially clarified by considering perception and
judgments of orientation from less awkward positions—for body or head tilts
up to 90°. In such cases, the results of a relatively large literature agree that
both perception and orientation judgments are determined primarily by external visual and/or gravitational frames of reference rather than retinal (e.g.,
Attneave & Olson, 1967; Braine & Knox, 1975; Olson & Boswell, 1975; Rock,
1956, 1973). Rock (1956), for example, showed adult subjects ambiguous
stimuli that appeared to be one object (a dog) in one orientation and another
object (the profile of a chef) if rotated 90°. When viewing these stimuli, subjects had their heads tilted 90° so that, for example, the configuration was
oriented as a dog with respect to the retina and as a chef with respect to the
environment. In such situations, the subjects' perception was over-
whelmingly determined by the environmental frame of reference.

These results with rotations up to 90° implicate an environmental frame
of reference. The results previously described with rotations of 180° implicate retinal frames of reference. Why should the mechanism for perceiving be different for rotations of the perceiver up to 90° as opposed to
upside-down? Many activities of primates involve head and body tilts of
moderate amounts. It would be reasonable to assume that a constancy
mechanism might evolve that would coordinate the pattern information on
the retina with a moderate tilt of the body relative to gravity signaled by the
vestibular system. Physiological evidence for such a coordination has been
summarized by Frederickson, Schwartz, and Kornhuber (1974). Single units
in the parietal lobe of rhesus monkeys have been identified that jointly respond to vision and vestibular information. This mechanism could serve the
purpose of constancy while viewing from tilted positions, as well as the purpose of perceived constancy during observer movement.

Which Way Should It Be Pointing?

Discrimination of left-right orientation doesn't become important in our culture until a child begins to read. Indeed, differentiation of objects in the world on the basis of left-right orientation would actually operate against a tendency toward constancy in which symmetrical objects from the other side are the same object e.g., chairs: Һ is ᖇ (E.J. Gibson, 1969). Thus, it is not surprising to find, as Bornstein, Gross, and Wolf (1978) did, that 4-month-old infants did not discriminate left-right mirror images of a bar-c, that is, ⊏ vs. ⊐. They found that infants habituated to looking at the stimulus in a series of trials in which the pair of stimuli were randomly interchanged as rapidly as in a series of trials that consisted only of repetitions of the single stimulus, ⊏. In contrast, looking behavior was shown to habituate more slowly in a series of trials in which ⊏ and ⊓ or ⊏ and ⊔ were randomly presented.

When a child begins to read English, however, left-right discrimination is useful for telling apart lower case p from q and b from d. It has long been known (e.g., Davidson, 1935) that such discriminations are difficult for children learning to read. Discrimination is probably not a correct term for the difficulty. Rather, the difficulty is in identification when the letters are to be named. Similar difficulty is found with mirror-image nonsense stimuli when they are to be associated with an arbitrary name or choice response or when they are to be matched to a standard from memory (Huttenlocher, 1967; Rudel & Teuber, 1963).

When left–right mirror image stimuli are presented simultaneously, children are able to make accurate same-different judgments (e.g., Over & Over, 1967). The difficulty in identification on the basis of left-right orientation appears to be one of *encoding* orientation rather than discriminating it. If so, then procedures that help encoding should ease the identification problem. One such procedure involving motor training was found to be successful by Jeffrey (1958). Preschool children were presented with a discrimination problem with stick figures that differed only in the direction the arm was pointing. In some figures, the arm pointed to the left, in others to the right. Prior training to make a lever response in the direction of a pointing arm on a stick figure facilitated the children's learning to discriminate. Another procedure for helping encoding is to place distinctive external cues near critical features of a stimulus. When this is done, identification on the basis of orientation is easier (Bryant, 1973; Smothergill, Hughes, Timmons, & Hutko, 1975; Thompson, 1975).

The use of distinctive external features to aid identification sheds light on a possible root of the difficulty. Without distinctive external features, a child is forced to rely on an egocentric frame of reference. Corballis and Beale (1970) suggest that an egocentric frame of reference may be difficult to use for encoding for left-right identification with a bilaterally symmetric body and nervous system. In fact, employing an egocentric frame of reference for left-right identification may conflict with a more natural egocentric frame of reference for ordinary lateral position. This is a frame of reference defined in terms of a dimension outward from the midline. Evidence in support of such a natural frame of reference comes from Staller and Sekuler (1976). Using stimuli somewhat like those of Bornstein et al. (1978), they instructed one group of adults to respond "same" to pairs of stimuli oriented in the same direction with respect to the midline, that is, ⊏ ⊐ or ⊐ ⊏ , and "different" to pairs of stimuli oriented in opposite direction with respect to the midline, ⊏ ⊏ or ⊐ ⊐. A second group of adults received the opposite instruction. Reaction times for the first group were faster, suggesting a fundamental sort of stimulus-response compatibility. Analogous results were obtained by the same investigators in a parallel learning experiment with preschool children. [A related experiment was reported by Ettlinger and Elithorn (1962). Monkeys were trained tactually to select one stimulus, for example ⊏ as opposed to ⊐, with one hand and then were tested for transfer with the opposite hand. In transfer they chose the stimulus consistent with orientation toward the midline, that is ⊐ in the example.] If a left-right lateral frame of reference conflicts with a more natural midline-outward frame of reference, it is not surprising that young children have such difficulty making left-right identifications. They may not be as flexible as adults in their use of different spatial reference systems.

A particular aspect of the left-right orientation problem that has received a great deal of attention is the identification of left and right oblique lines. (This is also related to the up-down orientation previously discussed.) In particular, learning to identify right and left oblique lines is considerably more difficult than learning to identify horizontals and verticals, or horizontals and obliques, or verticals and obliques [see, for example, Bornstein et al. (1978) for infants and Rudel and Teuber (1963) and Sekuler and Rosenblith, (1964) for preschoolers]. A recent analysis by Corballis and Zalik (1977) suggests there are actually two problems involved in identification of left and right obliques. One is the left-right mirror-image problem, and the other is general difficulty of identifying obliques as opposed to rectilinear lines. In support of this view, Corballis and Zalik had preschool children perform a delayed matching-to-sample task. The sample, a line 0°, 30°, 60°, or 90° from vertical, was presented and then removed. Five seconds later a pair of stimuli was presented for matching. One stimulus was the same as the standard; the other differed from the standard in left-right orientation, in angle from vertical, or both. Children matched at chance level when the matching stimulus had either a difference in angle alone or a difference in left-right orientation alone. They were significantly better than chance when both angle and orientation differences were present. Apparently, both of these dimensions, orientation and degree of obliqueness, contribute to identification.

The difficulty caused by left-right orientation differences is presumably attributable to the same reference system factors discussed earlier. The difficulty caused by the difference in angle from vertical may be attributable to the various frames of reference available for judging orientation with respect to up-down. Bryant (1974) has suggested that horizontal and vertical stimuli are normally privileged with respect to a visual framework such as a room or a table that has horizontal and vertical main axes. Thus, identification of these can be accomplished simply by noting whether the stimuli match one or the other of the axes of the visual framework. Bryant showed that if an immediate relevant frame of reference is available, children can identify obliques relatively well. In one condition of his study, a diagonal reference line was placed on every stimulus card. Under such conditions, preschool children learned to identify obliques easily and had great difficulty in identifying horizontals and verticals. Apparently, the frame of reference must be very salient and obviously relevant to the identification, because Fellows and Brooks (1973) tried unsuccessfully to replicate Bryant's experiment using diamond-shaped backgrounds as the relevant frame of reference.

The most systematic investigation of the frames of reference used in identification of diagonals and rectilinear lines was described by Olson and Boswell (1975). They considered three reference systems that might be relevant to identification of lines on the basis of up-down orientation: the orientation of the head (which determines orientation of the stimulus on the retina), the immediate visual surround (stimulus card), and the alignment of the stimuli on the stimulus card. These frames of reference could be compatible, or they could be placed in conflict. Thus, horizontal and vertical lines could be viewed with the head tilted. Or, a diamond-shaped stimulus card could contain stimuli aligned horizontally and vertically, that is, ⬦, and be viewed with the head tilted. In this case, the stimuli would be oblique with respect to the retina and the visual frame, but they would be rectilinear with respect to the horizontal alignment of the stimuli themselves. Olson and Boswell demonstrated that the more frames of reference there were that were aligned with the diagonal stimuli, the easier was the identification of the diagonals. However, even when all the frames of reference were compatible with the diagonal stimuli, their identification was no better than that for horizontal and vertical lines without aligned frames of reference.

Paradoxically, when there is a minimum of relevant frames of reference, identification of obliques may also be relatively good. Harris, Le Tendre, and Bishop (1974) trained preschool children to identify diagonals and rectilinear lines presented within a circular framework or a square framework. In both framework conditions, the rectilinears were more often correctly identified than were the diagonals. However, diagonals were identified at a level significantly better than chance when presented within the circular framework. We found similar results (Rieser, Pick, & Warren, unpublished). Preschool children were trained in identification of rectilinear and diagonal lines within circular, square, or diamond frames.[3] Identification of diagonals remained at chance for the square and diamond frames but was well above chance for the circular frames. Finally, Berman et al. (1974) found that children who were asked to copy lines in different orientations presented in a circular background performed significantly better than chance with diagonals. It seems as if frameworks with salient vertical and horizontal axes distract the attention of young children. Children do not make identifications that they otherwise could when the stimuli are presented in circular frames. Young children seem to attend inflexibly to angular framework features in the immediate visual surround. This is another example that flexibility in use of frames of reference may be a significant aspect of perceptual development.

Frames of Reference and Spatial Layout

What reference systems do children use to orient themselves when moving around their environment? It would make functional sense if they used geographic rather than egocentric frames of reference. It would seem to be more important to know where one was in a space rather than how one got there or what one did the last time one was there. Research by Acredolo (1976b) begins to answer this question. The basic paradigm she used was similar to the place- versus response-learning paradigm of traditional learning theory. A child was brought to a particular place in a room and was asked to find that place again after a change of starting position and/or a change in the layout of the room. In one experiment, a child was escorted into a small, relatively uniform room that contained one table standing beside either the right or left wall. The child was taken to the far corner of the table and was blindfolded. The child was then taken by a circuitous route either to the entrance end of the room or to the opposite end. In the meantime, the table had been moved from its original position to the other side of the room. The blindfold was removed, and the child was instructed to return to the place where he had been blindfolded. The child could define that place in terms of an egocentric frame of reference (the direction of heading when first entering the room), in terms of objects in the room (the table), and/or in terms of the shell of the room (the wall where the table was originally standing).

By noting which way a child walked when the blindfold was removed, it was possible to infer which frame of reference was effective in marking place for the child. For example, if the child's blindfold was removed at the entrance end and he went to the table, an object reference system must have been serving as the basis for response because both an egocentric frame of reference or a wall frame of reference would predict a response to the side

---

[1]The diamond framework had no distinctive sides, so that even though a child might register that the stimulus was parallel to one side of a frame, he could not remember which side.

opposite the table. Or if a child starting from the end *opposite* the entrance went to the table, that response could be based on either an object frame of reference or an egocentric frame of reference. In this way it was possible to make inference as to the determinant frames of reference.

Children from 3 to 5 years went through this procedure. In general, the 3- to 4-year-olds responded in terms of an egocentric reference system; the 4- to 5-year-olds responded in terms of an object reference system, that is, tended to go to the current table position. Thus, this experiment suggested that the younger children were "response" responders and the older children were "place" responders. However, in this experiment, an egocentric frame of reference always coincided with either an object frame of reference or a shell frame of reference. How would the egocentric frame of reference fare by itself, when pitted against both the object and shell frames of reference? To answer this question, a replication was conducted with slight modifications. One condition was added: Children were taken on their blindfold walk to opposite end from the entrance, but the table was not moved. The child was again asked to return to the place where the blindfold was put on. Under this condition, if a child turned in the same direction as when first entering the room, he would be using an egocentric frame of reference against both object- and shell-defined frames of reference. A second modification was made in this experiment—a somewhat smaller room was used, 7 feet by 12.5 feet as compared to 10 feet by 15 feet. Finally, in addition to the 3- to 5-year-old children, an older 9- to 10-year-old group was tested. In this small room, the majority of children of all ages used the shell-defined reference system. However, a significant proportion of both the 3- to 4-year-old and the 4- to 5-year-old children responded in terms of the object frame of reference. No children consistently responded in terms of an egocentric reference system.

The results of both experiments together suggest that the 3-year-olds are in transition from relying on an egocentric reference system to a geographic reference system. This geographic reference system is defined in terms of objects in the space, if the shell of the space is slightly removed as in the larger room in the first experiment. If the shell of the room is close by, it acts as a frame of reference for older children and, to a considerable extent, even for younger children. In short, as the child grows older, more remote frames of reference are used for maintaining orientation.

HOW FRAMES OF REFERENCE ARE USED

In this section we discuss certain aspects of the way reference systems are used. Specifically, we consider flexibility in the use of reference systems, the coordination of different reference systems, and the relation between frames of reference and mental representations of spatial layout. Where possible, we illustrate the concepts and issues with developmental experiments. We speculate that there is increased flexibility in the use of reference systems with age and increased coordination of frames of reference. However, there are too few developmental data to make any firm conclusions.

Flexibility in the Use of Reference Systems

As noted, in normal life there are often multiple redundant frames of reference with respect to which spatial behavior may be organized. For behavior concerned with up-down orientation, there is gravity, the visual world, and the axes of the body. For behavior concerned with spatial layout, there are objects in the visual field, the boundaries of the visual space (such as walls, horizon, etc.), and again the body axes. Are some of these frames of reference more often used or more heavily weighted than others? Or do they all function equally and simultaneously for the organization of behavior? If some frames of reference have a preferred status, is it nevertheless possible to organize one's behavior with the less preferred reference systems? These are questions of flexibility in the use of reference systems.

To demonstrate flexibility in the use of reference systems, it is not enough to show that any one of several frames of reference can serve independently in modulating spatial behavior. It is possible that under normal conditions, several different reference systems contribute to spatial behavior. If a particular form of spatial behavior persists in the absence of some reference systems, it may well be that the remaining reference systems normally contribute to that spatial behavior and there is no special flexibility being demonstrated. For example, Rock (1956, Experiment II) presented Figure 5.2A to subjects and noted whether they reported it as looking like a profile of a person or an outline of a map of the United States. When subjects had their heads tilted 45° to the left, they predominantly reported it as a profile; with their heads tilted 45° to the right, they reported it as a map outline. Since the visual and gravitational frames of reference are neutral with respect to these alternatives, the subject's reports indicate the use of a retinal or head axis reference system. However, we do not know from this evidence whether such body axes play a role in normal perception or not. In the same study (Experiment I) Rock presented Figure 5.2B to subjects who had their heads tilted 90° to the left. In that experiment, subjects tended to call the figure an outline map, which indicates that their response was more determined by gravity or the axes of the visual field than by the body reference system. Under these conditions an environmental reference system appears to dominate a body reference system. When an environmental system is absent, subjects may use the body reference system. However, this result does not unambiguously demonstrate flexibility because we do not know whether the body reference system is functioning when it is present but not dominant.

To demonstrate flexibility, it must be shown that a frame of reference

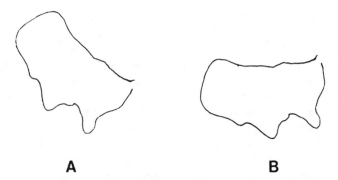

A   **B**

FIG. 5.2.   Spatial reference systems and ambiguous figures. (Adapted from Rock, 1956.)

that is normally utilized may be replaced by another frame of reference. There are two ways in which this substitution could occur. If a preferred frame of reference is deleted, a normally unused frame of reference might be substituted. Or, if two reference systems are providing conflicting spatial information, a less preferred reference system might be used in place of the more preferred system. An interesting example of the second sort of substitution comes from Attneave and his colleagues. Attneave and Olson (1967) taught subjects to identify lines of various orientations. The lines were flashed singly in a tachistoscope, and subjects responded as rapidly as possible with an identifying name. Horizontal and vertical lines were identified significantly faster than were diagonal lines. To determine which reference systems accounted for this difference in reaction time, the environmental and retinal frames of reference were put in conflict. Some subjects performed the task with heads tilted 45° so that environmentally diagonal lines were horizontal or vertical on the retina and environmentally horizontal and vertical lines were diagonal on the retina. The environmentally horizontal and vertical lines were identified faster than were the retinally horizontal and vertical lines. The dominance of the environmental reference system was confirmed even more strongly when subjects were asked after the original learning to change their head tilt either from vertical to 45° or from 45° to vertical. With a change of head tilt, how would subjects identify lines — with respect to their new retinal orientation or with respect to their same old environmental orientation? In this experiment some subjects were instructed to continue to identify the lines with respect to the environment, that is, to use the same names for lines of the same environmental orientation. They continued to respond very rapidly. Other subjects were instructed to continue to identify the lines with respect to their retinal orientation, that is, to use the same names for lines of the same retinal orientation. These latter subjects showed a marked decrement in speed of performance, which suggests that environmental orientation was a clearly dominant frame of reference in comparison with retinal orientation.

In spite of this, Attneave and Reid (1968) demonstrated that the reference system used for such a task is very much under voluntary control. They gave subjects the same initial task as had Attneave and Olson — to assign identifying names to lines at various orientations. Half the subjects performed with their heads tilted 45°. In addition, half the subjects were instructed to think of "up" as the direction of the top of their heads rather than to think of up as its direction in the environment. The first important result was that those subjects who had their heads tilted 45° and were told to think of the top of their heads as up had faster reaction times for the *retinally* horizontal and vertical lines. After learning, subjects were again asked to change their head tilt. The second important result was that subjects could respond with the same names for lines of the same retinal orientation after changing their head tilt. They could use their retinal reference system, however, only if they had *originally* been instructed to think in terms of a retinal or head-relevant frame of reference. This work by Attneave and his associates seems to indicate that an environmental reference system is normally preferred for the basis of identification of lines of different orientations. However, that basis can be changed simply by instructions the subject to rely on a retinal or head–axis frame.

The use of reference systems is not always so optional. Two of the authors of this chapter (Rieser & Pick, 1976) performed a tactual experiment modeled after those of Attneave. Subjects were again asked to identify lines at various orientations that were presented tactually by drawing against the skin of the forehead or haptically by having subjects grasp a rod held in front of them. After learning identifying labels for lines of different orientations, subjects changed their body orientation 90° — from upright to lying on their side or vice versa. They were asked to continue identifying the lines from the new body position. When subjects were presented with the line tactually, they responded in the new body position using a body reference system. However, when the lines were presented haptically, the identifications in the new position were made on the basis of a gravity or environmental reference system. In a subsequent unpublished experiment, subjects were taught the original identifying labels with insructions for the subjects presented with tactual lines to think of the environmental directions of the lines and for the subjects perceiving the haptic stimuli to think of the orientation of the lines with respect to the body. Again after learning, the body position was changed 90° and subjects continued to identify the lines. The subjects presented with lines tactually continued to respond with labels appropriate for a body reference system. However, approximately half of the subjects presented with lines haptically showed flexibility and did respond in terms of the line orientation with respect to the body.

What might account for this difference in flexibility between tactually and haptically presented stimuli? One suggestion is that haptic judgments made in terms of an environmental frame of reference logically seem to require a convergence of two types of information. There is proprioceptive information specifying the perceiving limb's orientation relative to the body. This must converge with vestibular information specifying the direction of gravity. Given that the proprioceptive information is being used anyway, it is not so surprising that it would be available in an unconverged form when subjects are instructed to use a body reference system. On the other hand, the tactual judgments made in relation to a body frame of reference do not require such a convergence of information. A possible neural mechanism for such convergence in the case of haptic judgments has been found by Schwartz and Frederickson (1971), who found single units in the parietal lobe of squirrel monkeys to be responsive to both vestibular stimulation and joint receptor stimulation. No such convergence was found in the case of tactual stimulation.

Another form of flexibility in the operation of reference systems is illustrated by adaptation to visual distortion. As an example, consider the kind of distortion produced by wedge prisms worn as spectacles with bases oriented right or left. Prisms produce a lateral shift of the visual field toward the apex side of the prism. Subjects wearing such spectacles will tend at first to misreach for objects by deviating laterally in the direction of the prism apex. This effect is reduced after a short period of wearing the spectacles. Part of this adaptation under certain conditions is attributable to a change in the registered position of the eye. As a consequence of wearing the spectacles, for example, the eye position registered as "straight ahead" is actually one directed slightly toward the apex of the prism. Therefore, after the prisms are removed, a person asked to identify the point that is straight ahead will indicate one too far toward the apex side. He will make similar errors when asked to indicate the position of an invisible sound source. Given that the direction thought to be straight ahead has changed, it is reasonable that all visual azimuths are shifted correspondingly. This type of flexibility is not flexibility in the sense of shifting from one response system to another but in the sense of recalibration within a reference system.

Little is known about how flexibility in use of reference systems develops with age. Recent work on the development of selective attention suggests that flexibility in strategies of attention increases with age. Older children are better able than younger children to adjust their attention to the requirements of the task (Pick, Christy, & Frankel, 1972). For example, in a task requiring children to compare complex visual stimuli along specific dimensions, knowing the dimensions beforehand facilitated the performance of the older children to a greater extent than it helped the younger children. To the extent that use of one reference system rather than another is analogous to selective attention, one would hypothesize that older children would be better able to use the one that is appropriate for a given task.

Radial direction or azimuth is a spatial property for which there are three normally redundant reference systems. Auditory, visual, and proprioceptive "straight ahead" normally coincide, and in general any target has the same azimuth in all three reference systems. However, it is possible to decalibrate these reference systems and determine to what extent a person is able to change from one reference system to another. A common example occurs in movie theaters in which loud speakers may be displaced from the screen. Although the sound may be coming from the side, the viewer tends to refer it to the appropriate source on the screen. However, it is often possible to attend specifically to the sound and notice the discrepancy between its location and the appropriate visual source. Much smaller discrepancies, as between a ventriloquist and his dummy, are usually not noticed.

This type of decalibration was studied experimentally (Pick, Warren, & Hay, 1969; Warren & Pick, 1970). If a small sound source was viewed through a wedge prism, its visual position was displaced relative to its auditory position. Subjects were asked to indicate where they *saw* the source and where they *heard* it. Subjects showed a strong visual bias, localizing the sound source very close to its optical position with a slight bias toward its acoustic position. When asked to indicate the sound's auditory position, subjects again exhibited strong visual bias, localizing the sound approximately half way toward its optical position. The degree of its visual bias seemed to decrease with age from second grade to college level, reminiscent of the change in flexibility found in the selective attention studies. However, when analogous discrepancies were generated between proprioceptive and auditory azimuth and between visual and proprioceptive azimuth, the age trends were not as clear or as consistent.

Are there any developmental changes in flexibility in the other sense of the term, in the sense of recalibration with a reference system? The only direct developmental data on this question come from a study examining adaptation to visual distortion in second-grade to college-age subjects (Pick & Hay, 1966). In this study, both proprioceptive and visual adaptations were measured, and both showed comparable changes at all age levels.

Coordination in the Function of Reference Systems

Normally, spatial behavior occurs in the presence of several partially redundant frames of reference. How are these multiple reference systems coordinated?

Perhaps a primary form of coordination is simple *addition*. If a particular spatial behavior is carried out with respect to one reference system, is it enhanced by additional redundant reference systems? The study with children by Olson and Boswell (1975) referred to earlier in connection with frames of reference in the identification of diagonals and rectilinear lines is relevant to this question. It will be recalled that the more frames of reference there were aligned with the diagonal stimuli, the more easily they were identified. This study suggests that there is a cumulative effect of redundant frames of reference. However, this would occur only if the subjects were sensitive to the additional reference systems. If some reference systems become effective later in development than others, one might not find a cumulative effect of additional reference systems. Although Olson and Boswell did not find a developmental change in effectiveness of additional reference systems, the age range in their study was small (4½ to 5½ years).

A second way in which reference systems are coordinated is in the successive use of various frames of reference. Such successive use would occur when, as behavior progresses, there is differential use of particular frames of reference. A common example is found in the following set of directions: "Proceed east along County Road C until you come to the church. Then turn right." First employed is a geographical reference system, followed by a landmark reference system, followed by an egocentric reference system. The change from geographical to landmark system presumably occurs because direction is easy to specify geographically, whereas distance is easier to specify by landmark. The switch from landmark to egocentric frame of reference probably occurs because direction again is easier to specify egocentrically than by a landmark. Here direction could also be specified by a return to the geographical reference system: "When you get to the church, turn south." Of course, it would be possible to use a salient landmark for direction as well, but that might require more search behavior: "When you get to the church, turn toward the lake."

The successive application of frames of reference is illustrated by a study by Pufall and Shaw (1973), who asked children ranging in age from 4 to 13 years to place a marker on a spatial array lying in front of them. The marker's location and orientation were specified by the position of an experimenter's marker placed on a similar array in front of the experimenter. The spatial arrays generally included a variety of possible frames of reference: color coded quadrants, distinctive edges, colored pegs within the quadrants, and the like. In the conditions most relevant to the present discussion, the experimenter's spatial array was rotated 180° from the child's. Analysis of the child's errors in placement revealed that children of 6 years were biased by an egocentric reference system for setting the orientation of the marker but were sensitive to landmarks or other cues for determining the position of the marker. However, 4-year-olds were biased by an egocentric frame of reference for both orientation and position. It appears, then, that these two aspects of spatial orientation, orientation and position, are processed independently, each showing a developmental course from egocentric to geographical.

Another example of the successive use of reference systems comes from the work of Cooper (1976) on shape constancy in picture perception. In ordinary perception with shape constancy, if an object such as a cube is viewed from an oblique angle, it will project to the eye a network of edges and surfaces that do not at all meet in right angles. Nevertheless, the cube will be seen as a cube, and subjects will easily discriminate true cubes from noncubic six-sided polyhedrons. Suppose a picture of the outline of a six-sided polyhedron is taken from an oblique angle. When viewed "head-on," this picture also projects a network of nonparallel edges to the retina. However, people are very good at discriminating between pictures of cubes and noncubes (Perkins, 1972, 1973). The intrinsic relations of the angles of the figure specify "possible cubeness." However, now suppose these two situations are combined: A picture hanging on a wall is viewed from an angle; the picture is that of a cube taken from an oblique angle. Differentiating cubes from noncubes would seem to require that the picture as an object first be seen with respect to its real-world frame of reference. This would enable the perceiver to register the objective shapes on the picture plane. Then the relation between these objective shapes and the pictorial reference system would have to be processed to reach a decision of "cube" or "not cube." Cooper found that children 3 years old and under, in contrast to older children and adults, showed rather poor shape constancy in this complex pictorial constancy situation. At the same time, the young children demonstrated a high degree of constancy in either simple constancy situation.

Contingent use of reference systems is the third type of coordination of reference systems. This occurs when the way in which one reference system is used depends on prior information derived with respect to a different reference system. An example of how such contingent use of reference systems might work can be taken from a place- versus response-learning experiment reported by Acredolo (1977). In her study, children walked from one end of a room to its center and then turned right or left to find a reward hidden under a cup. When they had learned to find the goal consistently, they were started from the opposite side of the room. Their behavior under these changed conditions enabled Acredolo, as in previous experiments, to infer whether they had learned to turn right or left (i.e., response learning) or whether they had learned to go to a particular side of the room (i.e., place learning). Under one condition the starting locations were distinctively coded by color and shape in an otherwise very uniform room. In this case, in order to consistently make place responses, the child would have to note where he was starting on the basis of the distinctive coding and then, contingent upon that, choose a particular egocentric response. That is, since there were no distinctive landmarks in the room except the coded start locations, the child would have to use an egocentric response to get to the goal. However, the egocentric response would differ depending on the location at which he started. Children as young as 3 and 4 years made consistent place responses, demonstrating the contingent use of reference systems.

Although this experiment demonstrates contingent use of frames of reference by relatively young children, it would be easy to conceive of complex contingencies that would not be solvable by children and could even be difficult for adults. An important developmental question is to what extent the environment demands these types of contingent behavior and whether there are developmental trends in responding contingently to ecologically valid spatial situations.

Relation Between Reference Systems and Mental Representations of Space

To introduce this topic, let us describe an experiment reported by Lockman, Hazen, and Pick (1976). Children between 3 and 6 years of age were taught a route through a series of rooms arranged in two columns as depicted in Figure 5.3. The rooms were identical in size, and each had a door in every wall. Each room was identifiable by a small toy animal placed on the floor. For example, the first room might be the cow room, the second the dog room, and so on. Children were taught a U-shaped path or a zigzag path. They were required to learn the path, so that they could lead the experimenter from room to room and correctly anticipate each room's animal in succession. After learning the route, they were given a series of test probes to ascertain just what it was they knew about the "house." The first probe required that they go backward along the route anticipating each room's animal in reverse order. In the second probe they were asked to state what room was behind doors through which they had never gone (Figure 5.3), requiring that they make spatial inferences. In the third probe the children were asked to construct a model of the house out of small boxes by putting miniature animals in the appropriate boxes.

Children across the entire age range were able to learn the initial problem. They might have done this on the basis of an egocentric frame of reference simply noting that first they turned left, then right, then right, then left, and so on. They also would have had to learn the order of animals for correct anticipation. Alternatively, they could have learned a series of landmark response sequences: cow—turn left, dog—turn right, and the like. This would be sensory motor knowledge in Piaget's terms. Again, they would have had to know the successive order of the animals. All the children were able to reverse the route correctly. However, the 3-year-olds had difficulty in anticipating the animals in the reverse order. They did not seem to have a serial order of animals that they could run off in reverse order. Similarly, it seems unlikely that they would have been able to reverse a long series of motor responses either. Rather, the best guess is that the 3-year-olds had learned the landmark response sequences and were reversing these one by one but were not even able to anticipate the next animal in the reverse order.

Performing well on the second probe involving spatial inferences would seem to require using reference systems that included direction and distance as well as simply landmarks and egocentric responses. The 3- and 4-year-olds performed very poorly compared to the 5- and 6-year-olds on this task. The induction of spatial relations involved in these inferences implies at least

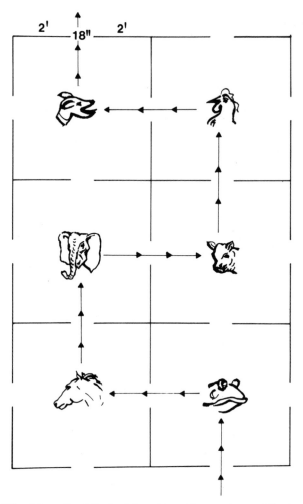

FIG. 5.3.   Schematic of "animal house" used in experiment of Lockman, Hazen, and Pick (1976). Arrow line represents one of the routes children learned.

the rudiments of configurational knowledge of the layout of the house.

However, the main test of configurational knowledge was the third probe — building the model. Configurational knowledge as evidenced by good models would seem to imply, even more strongly than the spatial inferences, that original learning involved reference systems that maintained directional coordinates and distances throughout the house. It was of particular interest that 4-year-olds as well as 5- and 6-year-olds could build models since the 4-year-olds had done poorly on the spatial inference probe. However, these children began to lay out the model, box by box in the order of the path in the house, taking into account the turns they had made in the house as they positioned each box. Lo and behold, the correct configuration evolved. The 4-year-olds seemed to generate the configuration as a consequence of building the model and did not build the model on the basis of configurational knowledge.

There is a dispute in the literature as to whether mental representations of space are propositional or analog in nature (e.g., Norman & Rumelhart, 1975; Pylyshyn, 1973). This is a complex issue and may turn out to be a pseudoproblem. The important questions, as Norman and Rumelhart suggest, are what operations can be carried out on the mental representations and whether these operations are like those that can be carried out in perception. We believe that children are capable of carrying out perceptual-relevant operations on their mental representations operations such as mental rotation (Hardwick, McIntyre, & Pick, 1976; Marmor, 1975) and induction of spatial relations (Kosslyn, Pick, & Fariello, 1974; Lockman, et al., 1976; Trabasso, 1975).

We would like to suggest a different distinction in mental representations between perceptual-relevant representations and motor-relevant representations. Motor-relevant representations would be equivalent to sets of directions for getting around a space and would be sequential in nature. It might be difficult to make spatial inferences on the basis of such representations. Mental rotation would be more difficult, but reversibility would be possible. It seems likely that motor-relevant representations would be generated when perceptual orientation was maintained by an egocentric system, and perceptual-relevant representations would be constructed on the basis of orientation through geographical reference systems. To the extent that older children seem to orient themselves in the environment on the basis of increasingly remote geographical frames of reference, they would be developing more perceptual-relevant representations. This is reasonable because for spatial layout, geographical frames of reference provide more constancy than egocentric frames of reference. A person will often move around a space in different directions. Generally, more remote frames of reference will be more stable than proximal frames. For example, the furniture of a room is more likely to be relocated than the walls, the houses on a block more likely to be changed than the streets, and so on.

However, for other spatial tasks, egocentric reference systems are more useful, and motor-relevant representations are likely to be developed. Typically, these are tasks that have an invariant relation between the performer and the space. Consider typewriting, for example. There is an invariant relation between performer and the work space. Skilled typists have a splendid motor representations of the keyboard and can type the series of letters *m, n, b, v, c, x, z,* with great speed, but if they are asked to *name* the bottom row of keys from right to left, they do so with considerable difficulty. Even adults, under the appropriate circumstances, will use an egocentric frame of reference and develop motor-relevant representations. Of course, adults have a strong tendency to avoid using egocentric reference systems. In teaching typing, the key tabs are often removed so that pupils cannot look at the keys.

It is not known whether young children would have a relatively easier time in using an egocentric reference system in such a task. Although at some stage for some tasks they may be less geographically oriented than older children, once they have shifted toward geographic frames of reference, they may be less flexible than adults in moving back to egocentric frames.

ACKNOWLEDGMENT

The preparation of this chapter was supported by a Program Project Grant HD 05027 from the National Institute of Health to the Institute of Child Development of the University of Minnesota and by the Center for Research in Human Learning of the University of Minnesota.

REFERENCES

Acredolo, L. P. New directions for environmental cognition: We *can* get there from here. Paper presented at Eastern Psychological Association Meetings, New York City, April, 1976.(a)

Acredolo, L. P. Frames of reference used by children for orientation in an unfamiliar space. In G. Moore & R. Golledge (Eds.), *Environmental knowing.* Stroudsburg, Pa.: Dowden, Hutchinson, & Ross, 1976.(b)

Acredolo, L. P. Developmental changes in the ability to coordinate perspectives of a large-scale space. *Developmental Psychology,* 1977, *13,* 1-8.

Annis, R. C., & Frost, B. Human visual ecology and orientation anisotropies in acuity. *Science,* 1973, *183,* 729-731.

Aslin, R. N., & Salapatek, P. Saccadic localization of visual targets by the very young human infant. *Perception and Psychophysics,* 1975, *17,* 293-302.

Attneave, F., & Olson, R. K. Discriminability of stimuli varying in physical and retinal orientation. *Journal of Experimental Psychology,* 1967, *74,* 149-157.

Attneave, F., & Reid, K. W. Voluntary control of frame of reference and slope equivalence under head rotation. *Journal of Experimental Psychology,* 1968, *78,* 153-159.

Bergman, T., Haith, M. M., & Mann, L. Development of eye contact and facial scanning in infants. Paper presented in Biennial Meetings of the Society for Research in Child Development, Minneapolis, 1971.

Berman, P. W. Young children's use of the frame of reference in construction of the horizontal, vertical, and oblique. *Child Development,* 1976, *47,* 259-263.

Berman, P. W., Cunningham, J. G., & Harkulich, J. Construction of the horizontal, vertical, and oblique by young children: Failure to find the "oblique effect." *Child Development,* 1974, *45,* 474-478.

Berman, P. W., & Golab, P. Children's reconstructions of the horizontal, vertical, and oblique in the absence of a rectangular frame. *Developmental Psychology,* 1975, *11,* 117.

Blakemore, C., & Cooper, G. F. Development of the brain depends of the visual environment. *Nature,* 1970, *228,* 477.

Bornstein, M. H., Gross, C. G., & Wolf, J. Z. Perceptual similarity of mirror images in infancy. *Cognition,* 1978, *6,* 89-116.

Bower, T. G. R. *Development in infancy.* San Francisco: Freeman, 1974.

Braine, L. G. A new slant on orientation perception. Invited address, American Psychological Association Meetings, Washington, D. C., September, 1976.

Braine, L. G., & Knox, C. Children's orientation judgments: Retinally or environmentally determined? *Perception and Psychophysics,* 1975, *17,* 473–479.

Bryant, P. E. Discrimination of mirror images by young children. *Journal of Comparative and Physiological Psychology,* 1973, *82,* 415–425.

Bryant, P. E. *Perception and understanding in young children.* New York: Basic Books, 1974.

Butterworth, G. *Thought and things: Piaget's theory.* In A. Burton & J. Radford (Eds.), *The study of thinking.* London: Macmillan, 1978.

Cooper, R. Developing sensitivity to geometric information for viewing shape and size in pictures. Paper presented at Conference on Pictorial Perception, Center for Research in Human Learning, University of Minnesota, Minneapolis, July, 1976.

Corballis, M. C., & Beale, I. L. Bilateral symmetry and behavior. *Psychological Review,* 1970, *77,* 451–464.

Corballis, M. C., & Zalik, J. Why do children confuse mirror-image obliques? *Journal of Experimental Child Psychology,* 1977, *24,* 516–523.

Davidson, H. P. A study of the confusing letters, B, D, P, and Q. *Journal of Genetic Psychology,* 1935, *47,* 458–468.

Donnee, L. H. Infants' developmental scanning patterns to face and non-face stimuli under various auditory conditions. Paper presented at the Biennial Meetings of the Society of Research in Child Development, Philadelphia, 1973.

Ettlinger, G., & Elithorn, A. Transfer between the hands of a mirror-image tactile shape discrimination. *Nature,* 1962, *194,* 1101.

Fellows, B. J., & Brooks, B. An investigation of the role of matching and mismatching frameworks upon the discrimination of differently oriented line stimuli in young children. *Journal of Child Psychology and Psychiatry,* 1973, *14,* 293–299.

Frederickson, J. M., Schwartz, D. W., & Kornhuber, H. H. Cortical projections of the vestibular nerve. In H. H. Kornhuber (Ed.), *Handbook of sensory physiology. VI/1. Vestibular system, Part 1: Basic mechanisms.* New York: Springer–Verlag, 1974.

Ghent, L. Form and its orientation: A child's-eye view. *American Journal of Psychology,* 1961, *74,* 177–190.

Ghent, L., & Bernstein, L. Influence of the orientation of geometric forms on their recognition by children. *Perceptual and Motor Skills,* 1961, *12,* 95–101.

Gibson, E. J. *Principles of perceptual learning and development.* New York: Appleton-Century-Crofts, 1969.

Gibson, J. J. *The senses considered as perceputal systems.* Boston: Houghton Mifflin, 1966.

Goffman, E. *Frame analysis.* Cambridge, Mass.: Harvard University Press, 1974.

Haith, M. M. Visual competence in early infancy. In R. Held, H. Leibowitz, & H. L. Teuber (Eds.), *Handbook of sensory physiology* (Vol. 8). New York: Springer–Verlag, 1978.

Hardwick, D. A., McIntyre, C. W., & Pick, H. L., Jr. Content and manipulation of cognitive maps in children and adults. *Society for Research in Child Development Monographs,* 1976, *41,* Serial No. 166.

Harris, L. J., & Allen, T. W. Role of object constancy in the perception of object orientation. *Human Development,* 1974, *17,* 187–200.

Harris, P. L., & MacFarlane, A. The growth of the effective visual field from birth to seven weeks. *Journal of Experimental Child Psychology,* 1974, *18,* 340–348.

Harris, P. L., Le Tendre, J. B., & Bishop, A. The young child's discrimination of obliques. *Perception,* 1974, *4,* 261–265.

Hirsch, H. V. B., & Spinelli, D. N. Visual experience modifies distribution of horizontally and vertically oriented receptive fields in cats. *Science,* 1970, *168,* 869–871.

Huttenlocher, J. Discrimination of figure orientation: Effects of relative position. *Journal of Comparative and Physiological Psychology*, 1967, *63*, 361–365.

Jeffrey, W. E. Variables in early discrimination learning: Motor responses in the training of a left–right discrimination. *Child Development*, 1958, *29*, 259–275.

Kosslyn, S. M., Pick, H. L., Jr., & Fariello, G. R. Cognitive maps in children and men. *Child Development*, 1974, *45*, 707–716.

Lee, D. N., & Aronson, E. Visual proprioceptive control of standing in human infants. *Perception and Psychophysics*, 1974, *15*, 529–532.

Leehey, S. C., Moskowitz-Cook, A., Brill, S., & Held, R. Orientational anisotropy in infant vision. *Science*, 1975, *190*, 900–902.

Leventhal, A. G., & Hirsch, H. B. Cortical effects of early selective exposure to diagonal lines. *Science*, 1975, *190*, 902–904.

Lockman, J., Hazen, N., & Pick, H. L., Jr. Development of mental representations of spatial layouts. Paper presented at American Psychological Association Meeting, Washington, D. C., September, 1976.

Mann, I. *The development of the human eye*. London: British Medical Association, 1964.

Marmor, G. S. Development of kinetic images: When does the child first represent movement in mental images? *Cognitive Psychology*, 1975, *7*, 548–559.

Maurer, D., & Salapatek, P. Developmental changes in the scanning of faces by young infants. *Child Development*, 1976, *47*, 523–527.

McCullough, C. Color adaptation of edge-detectors in the human visual system. *Science*, 1965, *149*, 1115–1116.

McGurk, H. The role of object orientation in infant perception. *Journal of Experimental Child Psychology*, 1970, *9*, 363–373.

McLaughlin, S. C. Parametric adjustment in saccadic eye movements. *Perception and Psychophysics*, 1967, *2*, 359–361.

Milewski, A. E. Infant's discrimination of internal and external pattern elements. *Journal of Experimental Child Psychology*, 1976, *22*, 229–246.

Millar, W. S., & Schaffer, H. R. The influence of spatially displaced feedback on infant operant conditioning. *Journal of Experimental Child Psychology*, 1972, *14*, 442–453.

Minsky, M. A framework for representing knowledge. In P. H. Winston (Ed.), *The psychology of computer vision*. New York: McGraw-Hill, 1975.

Neisser, U. *Cognition and reality*. San Francisco: Freeman, 1976.

Norman, D. A., & Rumelhart, D. E. *Explorations in cognition*. San Francisco: Freeman, 1975.

Ogilvie, J. C., & Taylor, M. M. Effects of orientation on the visibility of fine wires. *Journal of the Optical Society of America*, 1958, *48*, 628–629.

Olson, R. K., & Boswell, S. L. Children's difficulty with right–left diagonal discrimination is based on orientation of a retinally independent Cartesian reference system. Program on Cognitive and Perceptual Factors in Human Development, Report No. 5, University of Colorado, 1975.

Over, R., & Over, J. Detection and recognition of mirror-image obliques by young children. *Journal of Comparative and Physiological Psychology*, 1967, *67*, 467–470.

Perkins, D. Visual discrimination between rectangular and nonrectangular parallelopipeds. *Perception and Psychophysics*, 1972, *12*, 396–400.

Perkins, D. Compensating for distortion in viewing pictures obliquely. *Perception and Psychophysics*, 1973, *14*, 13–18.

Pick, A. D., Christy, M. D., & Frankel, G. W. A developmental study of visual selective attention. *Journal of Experimental Child Psychology*, 1972, *14*, 165–175.

Pick, H. L., Jr., & Hay, J. C. The distortion experiment as a tool for studying the development of perceptual-motor coordination. In N. Jenkin, & R. H. Pollack (Eds.), *Perceptual development: Its relation to theories of intelligence and cognition*. Proceedings of a Conference Sponsored by Institute of Juvenile Research, Illinois State Department of

Mental Health and National Institute of Child Health and Human Development, 1966.

Pick, H. L., Jr., Warren, D. H., & Hay, J. C. Resolution of sensory conflict between vision, proprioception and audition. *Perception and Psychophysics,* 1969, *6,* 203-206.

Prechtl, H. The directed head turning response and allied movements of the human baby. *Behavior,* 1958, *13,* 212-242.

Pufall, P. B., & Shaw, R. E. Analysis of the development of children's spatial reference systems. *Cognitive Psychology,* 1973, *5,* 151-175.

Pylyshyn, Z. W. What the mind's eye tells the mind's brain: A critique of mental imagery. *Psychological Bulletin,* 1973, *80,* 1-24.

Rieser, J. J., & Pick, H. L., Jr. Reference systems and the perception of tactual and haptic orientation. *Perception and Psychophysics,* 1976, *19,* 117-121.

Rieser, J., Yonas, A., & Wikner, K. Radial localization of odors by human newborns. *Child Development,* 1976, *47,* 856-859.

Rock, I. The orientation of forms on the retina and in the environment. *American Journal of Psychology,* 1956, *69,* 513-528.

Rock, I. *Orientation and form.* New York: Academic Press, 1973.

Rudel, R. G., & Teuber, H.-L. Discrimination of direction of line in children. *Journal of Comparative and Physiological Psychology,* 1963, *56,* 892-898.

Salapatek, P. The visual investigation of geometric pattern by one and two month old infants. Paper presented at the American Association of the Science Meetings, Boston, 1969.

Schwartz, D. W., & Frederickson, J. M. Rhesus monkey vestibular cortex: a bimodal projection field. *Science,* 1971, *172,* 280-281.

Sekuler, R. W., & Rosenblith, J. F. Discrimination of direction line and the effect of stimulus alignment. *Psychonomic Science,* 1964, *1,* 143-144.

Shebilske, W. L., & Nice, D. S. Optical insignificance of the nose and the Pinocchio effect in free-scan visual straight-ahead judgments. *Perception and Psychophysics,* 1976, *20,* 17-20.

Smothergill, D. W., Hughes, F. P., Timmons, S. A., & Hutko, P. Spatial visualizing in children. *Developmental Psychology,* 1975, *11,* 4-13.

Staller, J., & Sekuler, R. Mirror-image confusions in adults and children: A nonperceptual explanation. *American Journal of Psychology,* 1976, *89,* 253-269.

Stryker, M., & Sherk, H. Modification of cortical orientation selectivity in the cat by restricted visual experience: A reexamination. *Science,* 1975, *190,* 904-906.

Thompson, G. B. Discrimination of mirror image shapes by young children. *Journal of Experimental Child Psychology,* 1975, *19,* 165-176

Trabasso, T. Representation, memory, and reasoning: How do we make transitive inferences? In A. D. Pick (Ed.), *Minnesota symposium on child psychology* (Vol. 9). Minneapolis: University of Minnesota Press, 1975.

Vurpillot, E. The development of scanning strategies and their relation to visual differentiation. *Journal of Experimental Child Psychology,* 1968, *6,* 632-650.

Warren, D. H., & Pick, H. L., Jr. Developmental study of sensory conflict in sighted and blind Ss. *Perception and Psychophysics,* 1970, *8,* 430-432.

Watson, J. Perception of object orientation in infants. *Merril-Palmer Quarterly,* 1966, *12,* 73-94.

Wertheimer, M. Psychomotor coordination of auditory-visual space at birth. *Science,* 1961, *134,* 1962.

Wright, J. C., & Vlietstra, A. G. The development of selective attention: From perceptual exploration to logical search. In H. W. Reese (Ed.), *Advances in child development and behavior* (Vol. 10). New York: Academic, 1975.

6 Commentary

E.J. Gibson *and*
Students in Psychology 561
Cornell University

This book, taken in overall perspective, points up rather dramatically the two lines of growth that have characterized developmental psychology since its inception with Darwin. Everything written about the nature of "the child" before that time derived from philosophers, theologians, educators, and politicians, with little or no reference to naturalistic observation, let alone experiment. From Darwin's time, there began to accumulate a body of scientific knowledge, beginning with the careful observations found in many baby biographies. The earlier biographies tend to be factually oriented, full of excellent observations, in a sense establishing a data base for a new discipline. Such a base is an invitation to theorists. The first wave of fact finding was followed by a kind of borrowed theorizing deriving from the still-prevalent tradition of British empiricism; true developmental theorists such as James Mark Baldwin appeared at or soon after the turn of the century. A new wave of fact finding based on experimental methods had begun by 1920, and then of course a new wave of theory making began. In more recent times we have seen the same juxtaposition: a marvelous spurt in the technology of studying the psychology of quite young children and an eager interest in theory exemplified by the near-adulation of Piaget. Books such as Cohen and Salapatek's (1975) collection of essays on *Infant Perception* testify to the former, and a society devoted to Piaget to the latter. Many other examples could be cited in more circumscribed areas, such as the detailed records of early speech development concentrating on short multiword utterances in individual children, and following upon its heels, the elaboration of theories — grammatical, semantic, pragmatic, socially oriented and so on — to interpret the facts.

This book includes examples of both trends. However, probably because we have just witnessed a kind of climax of fact finding, the theoretical trend predominates. A number of the authors who contributed papers to this book have departed from a predominantly empirical approach and are groping for a framework to organize the data. Moreover, there is a noticeable dissatisfaction with the midcentury "schools of psychology" — behaviorism (S–R learning theory), Gestalt psychology, and even information processing — and instead a search for a truly developmental theory. There is an emphasis on concepts or mechanisms of change but not learning theory (with the exception of Papousek, who discusses learning of operant contingencies as a way of adapting to the environment, both physical and social). Sometimes the attempts to see the whole picture are written on a cosmic level that encompasses too much. Loosely defined concepts and an overabundance of metaphor are the result, but the search for principles is surely timely.

It is interesting to look for persistent themes in chapters of the book and to ask whether any that might have been appropriately incorporated are absent. In nearly all the chapters there is an unquestioned acceptance of a constructionist view. Sometimes it is out-and-out Piagetian (cf. Elkind), sometimes neo-Piagetian (cf. Schaffer, Kagan, and Sameroff & Harris). Along with the constructionism go stages and an emphasis on discontinuity between structures of the various stages. A constructionist approach is a structuralist approach, although not all the authors emphasize description of the structures (e. g., McCall who derives his stages inductively from a psychometric data base).

Despite the structuralism and the emphasis on discontinuity, which could underlie a rather undynamic stairstep progression motivated by maturation alone, there is a search for the motive power for development. What instigates the move from one stage to the next? Sameroff and Harris, Nelson, and Kagan particularly address this question, introducing such concepts as discrepancy, contradiction, coordination of two worlds ("social" and "object"), and discovery of the utility of language as potential igniting forces. Other reviewers will examine these concepts. It would have been rather nice to have a chapter by a Genevan included. We think of Pierre Mounoud's paper (1975), which discusses development as a series of "revolutions" and proposes that there must be a "decomposition" of an earlier organization, a differentiation or analysis of it. An initial organization is "shattered" as certain behaviors become individualized and certain properties of objects isolated or dissociated. This differentiation precedes a new organization with new properties.

Related to the search for dynamics of change is a process–structure distinction. It is most evident in Kagan's chapter in Part II, but it underlies many, perhaps because it is inevitable in a constructionist approach. The structures seem to get more attention than the processes. It may occur to some readers (as it did to us) that the functionalist tradition, a concern with evolution and the adaptiveness of behavior, is neglected by most of the authors. There is also a conspicuous absence of an ethological point of view, and as a corollary to that, there is hardly any attempt to consider ecology or the nature of the information in the world that cognition, to be adaptive, must extract. The latter effort would help the structure-oriented theorist out of a dilemma that is occasionally apparent: How are the stages separated from the tasks chosen (by the experimenter) to represent or describe them? More attention to the natural environment of the child as he matures, accompanied by a consideration of Brunswikian "representative design," would enrich the book. The first four chapters (those of Part I) on which we were specifically asked to comment come the closest to an ecological and functional approach. These chapters are more factually oriented and empirical than the later ones. We had better not exaggerate this quality, because no present-day psychologist (including ourselves) can resist theorizing. Nonetheless, these chapters do present a marked difference from the others in their proportion of factual content and in the more circumscribed questions addressed when theory does emerge.

In her chapter, "Perspectives on Infant Motor System Development," Kopp proposes to show that motor development can be meaningfully placed within a general psychological framework. Traditionally, motor development has been studied in isolation, as a topic apart from intellectual and social development. Exceptions are the work of Piaget, Bruner, and the Soviet psychologists for whom activity is the prime source of knowledge. Although they stress the importance of motor behavior, they fail to specify how motor behavior molds psychological development.

Kopp makes three important points. First, she maintains that there is a genetic program that leads to a species-general development of motor behavior in the first year of life. The unfolding of motor skills, in terms of their forms and function, is remarkably similar across infants. Cross-cultural studies attest to the universal nature of this development. Even infants with visual, auditory, and neuromuscular impairments and infants with Down's syndrome proceed through the same invariant process, although their rate of development may be slower than normal. Only severe neuromuscular insult will lead to disruption of this process. Because motor abilities are basically the same in all infants, behaviors that are dependent on those abilities ("functions of the emergent skill") are also quite similar across infants. What varies among infants is the rate of development and the frequency of particular behavior. Although Kopp does mention Gesell in passing, it should be emphasized that Gesell also argued, on the basis of 40 years of research, for the existence of a species-typical program of motor development.

Second, Kopp points out that motor precocity in the first year is often thought to have long-term cognitive and social developmental effects. She challenges this belief and suggests that motor precocity may be overrated in terms of its long-term effects on cognitive and social development. Her argument is as follows (based on Blank, 1964). There is large variation in ability when a motor skill is first emerging (the "focal period"). It so happens that during the focal period there is a significant positive correlation between development of this motor skill and cognitive development (as measured by mental tests, quality of play, etc.). That is, infants who exhibit motor precocity have high scores on the various "psychological" measures, whereas slower developers have low scores. The behaviors that are measured in the psychological tests may indeed be functions of the emergent skill, but if one looks at these correlations after the focal period, the relationship between motor and cognitive development has disappeared. It seems as if the long-term effects of the motor precocity of a skill are not predictive of later intellectual development.

Besides pointing out a possible misconception concerning the role of early motor precocity, Kopp implies a caution that often goes unheeded: One should not be too hasty in concluding that correlations are stable throughout development when only a specific age range has been sampled. McCall makes a similar point in his chapter.

Third, Kopp suggests that it is only after the first year that special experience becomes an important factor, in that different experiences will lead to different "competences" or abilities. At this time, motor precocities may have long-term influences, as in the famous case of Johnnie, the practiced twin who demonstated continued agility years later. Other examples Kopp discusses are the role of early manipulation of objects in developing attentional skills and the role of locomotion in learning the spatial layout, options for action, and self-awareness.

Kopp's chapter is a valuable addition to this volume. She provides a different perspective on motor development from the usual one. Motor behavior should not be catalogued and considered per se, nor should it be considered as a necessary but relatively uninteresting device through which the infant gathers knowledge. Rather, it should be viewed as part of psychological development, assuming in our theories the same kinds of roles (e.g., enabling, enhancing, depriving) that are assigned to the more traditional psychological factors.

The major contribution of Bornstein's Chapter 3 is an expert and full presentation of what is generally referred to as categorical perception of phonemes and of hues. Bornstein refers to categorical perceiving as "feature perception." Whatever the nomenclature, he is referring to man's tendency to perceive certain qualitative properties of things (if we may refer to speech as a thing) with minimal discrimination inside rather definite boundaries and sharp discrimination across boundaries. The classic example is the categorical perception of phonemes varying in voice onset time. Bornstein takes voice onset time as his case for discussion of phonemes and presents the evidence for generalized perception within categories compared to sensitivity between categories in detail for human adults, infants, infrahuman organisms (monkeys and chinchillas), deprived populations, children of different ages developing in a normal (for the species) environment, and different cultural and language groups. Bornstein is convinced that there is an innate physiological basis for the qualitative generalizations — that is, that they reflect "native sensory functions." Boundaries between "perceptual features" may sharpen during the course of development and plateaus within boundaries may broaden, but the mechanism is laid down genetically.

A similar case is made for four primary qualities of hue. The evidence is presented in great detail for discontinuity of wavelength discrimination in the human infant. Babies at 4 months old partition the physical spectrum into qualitative categories much as do adults. The basic hue categories of blue, green, yellow, and red are perceived categorically, and interhue boundaries between these are discriminated sharply before language or cultural differences could play a role. Much of the work here is Bornstein's own, and he has attacked the problem with a variety of methods. From an empirical standpoint, his work is admirable. His argument that the processes responsible for the categorical perception of hue are rooted in the biological nature of the sensory system is easy to accept. The differences in perceptual partitioning of the spectrum by other species (e.g., bees) is a more convincing argument for genetic propensities than is the similarity between man and chinchilla for phonetic categorization. The data from electrophysiological research on the primate visual system that identifies four classes of chromatic sensitive cells in primates makes the case for an innate basis particularly persuasive.

A difficulty in Bornstein's paper is the use of the term *feature*. It is unusual to refer to a categorically perceived phoneme or hue as a feature, whether or not there is a physiological, genetically determined basis for the categorical nature of the perception. Traditionally, the term has been used by linguists and psychologists to refer to the contrastive feature differences, always relational and in no way elements or structures, that distinguish members of a set such as phonemes. Voiced-unvoiced would be such a contrastive relationship, but the phonemes so distinguished, even if they are perceived categorically, are not themselves features.

Bornstein defines *feature* as a "qualitative generalization". Occasionally "qualitative differences" are referred to as features, which gets a little closer to the classical use of the term. However, the substitution itself is confusing, because the terms *equivalence* and *generalization* appear with far greater frequency. It may be that the term *feature* is being used to suggest a neurological construct, a "trigger feature." In that case, it would help the reader to have a straightforward presentation of the reason for the term's usage. To many psychologists, categorical perception is not easily reconciled with descriptions of perceptual differentiation by means of distinctive features.

Actually, such a reconciliation is quite possible if one thinks of features as being contrastive properties that distinguish among members of a set. The features are shared by the members in different degrees and distributions, so that each "bundle" is unique. However, there may be a member of the set that shares the greatest number of features with other members. That member, to use Rosch's terminology, may be perceived as the "focal" member of the set and may in that way represent a category. Reconciliation of this usage with a trigger for a hypothetical detector in the nervous system is not easy, however. Bornstein is not using the term contrastively. That is his privilege, of course, but it would help the reader to bring the issue into the open.

In a final section of the chapter, Bornstein considers the functional utility of categorical perception, a welcome but not entirely successful attempt. Discontinuous discriminability produces contrasts and oppositions. The observation comes as a surprise at this point and is not developed further. Rather, features are also said to be "good patterns" and "holistic". Invariance and constancy are mentioned as functional contributions, but the "information encoded into features" is said not to rely on context. Color constancy will prove to be a tough problem because context must be considered in order to understand it, and it is surely pertinent to Bornstein's discussion. Perhaps this criticism is unfairly based on terminological disagreements, but it might be better to point up the differences between categorization and invariance and to admit the relational nature of contrasts rather than try to squeeze all these concepts into one.

The point about the cognitive economy of categorical perception is a sound one and is well supported. The conclusion, that categorization is ubiquitous, is hard to deny, but to present these two cases — phonemes and hues — as prototypes of such a ubiquitous process may be misleading. Nevertheless, the summary of all the evidence is a service to the researchers in the field, and any disagreements about terminology may lead to resolutions that will help us on our way.

In the chapter "Spatial Reference Systems in Perceptual Development," Pick, Yonas, and Rieser analyze developmental changes in spatial behavior in terms of the types of reference systems employed. They suggest several developmental trends in the acquisition and use of various frames of reference. First, they propose that as an individual's repertoire of spatial behaviors increases with age, there is a corresponding increase in the different types of frames of reference used to organize the behaviors and a differentiation of those frames already in use. The infant engaging in spatial adjustment of perceptual organs toward or away from a source of stimulation relies on egocentric frames, such as loci on a sensory surface. The child learning to stand orients his body by way of an external reference system, specifically a geographic "up-down" frame of reference, and the child beginning to locomote uses geographic "layout" frames of reference to guide his movements. The authors argue that as the individual becomes older, his spatial behaviors reveal the use of increasingly more remote frames of reference, which tend to be more stably anchored in the environment. Second, two developmental trends related to the use of these reference systems are presented. It is proposed that there is an increase with age in both the degree to which an individual is flexible in his use of various frames of reference (i.e., is able to substitute one frame of reference for another when necessary) and in the extent to which he is able to coordinate different frames of reference appropriately, either by successive use, contingent use, or making maximal use of redundant reference frames. The authors conclude by suggesting a new distinction by which to characterize mental representations — motor-relevant (spatial knowledge by means of egocentric reference systems) and perceptual-relevant (spatial knowledge by means of geographical reference systems).

Pick, Yonas, and Rieser (Chapter 5) note that the concept of frame of reference is not "a tight explanatory concept," and in fact their conception of the construct is not perfectly clear to the reader. They present a brief definition of frame of reference ("a locus or set of loci with respect to which spatial position is defined") and refer to a variety of reference systems at different levels of specificity (retinal frame of reference, visual frame of reference, head-axis reference system, environmental frames of reference, landmark reference system, object frame of reference, etc.) without further specifying the nature of the systems or the relationships among them. An elaboration of their conception of the frames of reference and their interrelationships would add to the lucidity of the arguments presented.

Pick, Yonas, and Rieser present a great deal of experimental evidence demonstrating the role of frames of reference in the perception of artificial stimuli, such as pictures and drawings of lines. If the concept of reference frames is to be used as a tool for analyzing the development of space perception, it must be evaluated in terms of its ability to describe perception of real world stimuli. Accordingly, it would be appropriate to place a greater emphasis on research demonstrating the use of reference frames in perceiving objects and spatial layouts in the environment. In this regard, the authors might have included in their discussion more of the research on perspective taking.

Pick, Yonas, and Rieser raise many interesting questions and point out several areas for further research. However, it is not clear that the concept of frames of reference will be useful as an explanatory construct in accounting for all the behavioral phenomena presented here. Although the construct may help in describing age-related differences in the types of relational information attended to in the world, it seems less profitable to characterize such low-level physiologically based (and quite possibly perceptually irrelevant) phenomena as the McCullough effect within this context.

Fagan's Chapter 4, "The Origins of Facial Pattern Recognition," addresses the ability of young infants to discriminate and recognize faces and
abstract patterns. Most of the work summarized is his own. A preference
method was used to compare unique characteristics of a particular face in
different poses, a particular pose over faces, sex distinctiveness of faces,
and patterning in abstract figures. Factors are discussed that might influence
facial or pattern recognition—orientation of the figure, age of infant, sex of
infant, and presentation of multiple examples of a class. Three major conclusions are drawn from the host of experiments: that the basis of facial
recognition is in "higher-order relations" within the face; that facial
recognition is paralleled by a like ability to discriminate between abstract
patterns; and that those aspects of face recognition demonstrated by adults
are present "in rudimentary form" by the age of 7 months.

Fagan points out three cases where the extraction of "invariants" can occur—recognizing facial patterns in different poses, distinguishing the same
pose over different faces, and picking out the same-sex face as had been
presented earlier. This detection of invariants contributes to "the permanence of pattern perception." Fagan's use of the term *invariant* needs
elaboration, however. His stimulus materials are mostly two-dimensional
static ones, but in the more usual sense, invariants are extracted from
transformations occurring over time. Fagan's examples of invariants can in
most cases be thought of as common features, characteristics such as having
hair or being bald, or having a nose in profile. Higher order relations, in
turn, are usually thought of as transposable. Fagan's conception of these
relations is illustrated by his description of a diamond pattern used in one
study (see Figure 4.5): "a compact, regular symmetrical form" discriminated
from "random arrangements of small diamonds having no distinctive or obvious general configuration." Analogous arrangements of squares were not
discriminated by infants as one might expect on the basis of higher-order
structure and transposability. This exception is used, however, to strengthen
another hypothesis: that orientation can facilitate recognition in the case of
abstract forms as well as faces. In view of Fagan's later emphasis on higher-
order relations and reliance on common patterning for recognition, one
wishes that "invariant patterns" were defined and in fact specified in the particular experiments. What are the invariant patterns that specify sex, for instance, or even the same face in different poses? Given invariant patterns,
how can they be systematically varied on each presentation?

Throughout the chapter Fagan minimizes any differences that might be
found between face and the recognition of abstract patterns. He reassures
investigators who have used artificial stimulus materials that they may be
more relaxed about generalizing from such work, given his results. Perhaps
we need fewer reassurances and some encouragement to employ more
natural displays. Fagan does find that an infant's facility in discriminating

among faces on recognition tasks is contingent on the type and fidelity of representation used. Continuing in this vein, he might have urged more work by others using both real faces and faces in motion.

The reader may be agreeably surprised by the ability of infants to recognize faces and abstract patterns over long intervals—two days for patterns, two weeks for photographs of faces—given an initial 2-minute period of familiarization. For some reason this ability does not carry over to more life-like displays. Although infants discriminate among masks very well, recognition of masks is not retained even as long as 3 hours. Fagan suggests that retroactive inhibition explains this counter-intuitive result.

Fagan's chapter provides an extensive and detailed review of one area of research on facial recognition. Parallels between abstract pattern recognition and face recognition are emphasized. However, most of the experiments cited used photographs of faces, stimulus materials that are more similar to pictorial patterns than are three-dimensional, moving faces. Furthermore, Fagan refers only to results found with a preference paradigm. Similar studies with habituation measures or some other method would have been a valuable addition to the chapter. Overall, the "Origins of Facial Pattern Recognition" is not perfectly convincing because of the imprecise vocabulary and the extrapolations from rather specialized materials. There is work yet to be done in this area.

These four chapters are concerned with some very basic problems. They make valuable contributions to arguments about fundamental issues that are currently of major concern.

ACKNOWLEDGMENT

These comments are the result of discussions of all the chapters by a seminar including Lorraine Bahrick, Debra Clark, Diana Dee-Lucas, Maria Ginieri-Coccossis, Katherine Loveland, Margaret McMahon-Rideout, Jane Megaw-Nyce, Cynthia Owsley, Arlene Walker, and David Zola.

REFERENCES

Blank, M. A focal periods hypothesis in sensorimotor development. *Child Development,* 1964, *35,* 817–829.

Cohen, L. B., & Salapatek, P. (Eds.), *Infant perception: From sensation to cognition.* New York: Academic Press, 1975.

Mounoud, P. *Revolutionary periods in early development.* Paper presented at a conference on "Dips in Learning and Development Curves." (CNRS-OECD). Foundation Maeght, Saint-Paul-de-Vence, France, March, 1975.

II | COGNITIVE DEVELOPMENT

7

Structure and Process In the Human Infant: The Ontogeny of Mental Representation

Jerome Kagan
Harvard University

INTRODUCTION: WHAT WE ASK OF THE INFANT

The human infant plays at least three roles in our current construction of development, functioning at different times in the roles of transition, projective screen, and preview. Although the language of developmental psychology has the ring of modernity, one of its presuppositions bears a relation to the pre-Darwinian image of a great unbroken chain of being from jellyfish to man. That idea, which was modified in form but not substance by evolutionary theory, has tempted psychologists to treat the infant as a dynamic link between ape and human adult and to search for similarities in language, play, and parent–child bonding in chimpanzees and 2-year-olds in order to affirm the gradualness in nature that Aristotle postulated. On occasion, we also cast the child in our shadow, attributing to the infant the opposite of a valued trait we wish the adult to attain. For example, the West values autonomy, the ability to resist complete dependence on another, and increasing individuation. Erikson (1959) views the task of development as attainment of an articulated ego identity, Mahler (1963) of a firm body boundary, Schafer (1968) of a sense of separation of self from others. In the middle of the nineteenth century, Emerson (1876) called this quality *self-reliance:* "Trust thyself, every heart vibrates to that iron string ... Whoso would be a man must be a nonconformist ... Nothing is at last sacred but the integrity of our mind [p. 36-37]."

Because development is seen as a progression toward this ideal, many theorists have assumed that the infant was undifferentiated, without autonomous function, and hopelessly dependent—qualities the young child would outgrow unless he were improperly socialized. However, these evaluative descriptions of the young child are not universal. Japanese parents, who prize intimate interdependence among adults, believe infants are too autonomous, and they attempt to seduce them into a more dependent role (Nakane, 1972). Finally, since infancy is seen as the first leg of the journey to adulthood, parents and scientists try to preview in thrashing arms or quiet concentration the future athlete or scholar.

These views of the infant shape contemporary research on early development, a great deal of which rests on two central premises. The first is that the infant inherits structures, competencies, and dispositions that have homologues in lower forms. The second is that some of the structures established during infancy are highly resistant to change. There are good reasons why we maintain a faith in these two assumptions. Modern man seeks to defend his ethics with natural law. Hence, any evidence that human and animal infants are similar in a fundamental way makes it easier for the citizen to treat established facts about animal behavior as a guide to resolution of moral issues. The belief in continuity has more varied sources, including the compelling, subjective conviction that the present moment is tied to the distant past, the Puritan imperative to prepare early for possible future calamity, and the ideological commitment to a linked, linear causality that can be found in Plato as well as in Thomas Aquinas's brief for God as the original unmoved mover.

THE HISTORICAL BASES FOR FAITH IN CONTINUITY

The assumption of a thick cord of connection between developmental stages —a contingent relation between earlier and later structures—is attractive to the Western mind because we like the classical Greek notion of simple, unitary, deep structures that explain phenotypically diverse performances. Modern stage theories satisfy our deep longing for a hidden unity that weaves all past experience into a seamless fabric and makes our lives seem coherent and our decisions rational.

The belief in an unbroken relation between infancy and later childhood is present in Plato's assumption in the *Timaeus* that all events have prior causes and in the arguments proposed by medieval philosophers to affirm the existence of God. Thomas Aquinas's defense bears a strong resemblance to contemporary arguments for the origins of adult personality in infant experience. Aquinas accepted the Greek premise that all dynamic events had a prior cause. Hence, if one traced all movements back to the original incentive, one would arrive at the original unmoved mover which, for Aquinas, was God. Psychologists who believe that adult behavior is derived in part from early experience tacitly suppose that some adult dispositions must have a connection to earlier ones and the earlier ones to stil earlier events. In this regression, one arrives at the nursery convinced that in a newborn's thrashing or lethargy one sees the origins of antisocial behavior.

The belief that the structures laid down by experience during the first 3 years of life had a primacy not easily muted was strong prior to the nineteenth century, and evolutionary theory strengthened this idea considerably. Darwin reclassified the human infant as a member of the category "animal" by positing a continuum in evolution. Because animal behavior was regarded as instinctive, inflexible, and therefore resistant to change, a paradox was created. How was it possible for man to be varied in custom and habit — so flexible and progressive — if he were such a close relative of creatures whose behavior appeared to be excessively stereotyped and rigid? One way to resolve the dilemma was to award a special function to what seemed to be the more prolonged period of infant helplessness in human beings as compared with animals. Since most scholars assumed that all qualities of living things had a purpose, it was reasonable to ask about the purpose of man's prolonged infancy. John Fiske (1883), among others, argued that infancy was a period of maximal plasticity, the time when adults were to teach children skills and ideas they would carry with them throughout life.

In a lecture at Harvard in 1871, Fiske noted that man's power to control his environment and to enhance progress had to be due to his educability—a potential Fiske believed animals lacked. How then to explain why man was so educable? Following popular rules of inference, Fiske looked for other major differences between man and animal, and of the many candidates he could have selected — language, the opposable thumb, upright stature, an omnivorous diet, sexual behavior throughout the year—he selected the prolongation of infancy. The logic of the argument consisted of two premises and a conclusion. Nature had to have an intended purpose for the initial 3 years of human incompetence and dependence. Since the most likely purpose was to educate the child, it must be the case that the child is maximally malleable to training during that early period. That conclusion was congruent with a deep belief in continuity of character from infancy to later childhood; it served to keep parents self-conscious about their actions with their babies; and it was an argument for building good schools. It also provided an experiential explanation for individual differences in adult success —which was attractive to a democratic and egalitarian society (Fiske, 1883). America and England, the two major Protestant nations in the Western community, wanted to believe in the eventual attainment of an egalitarian society in which, if conditions of early life were optimal, all citizens potentially could attain dignity and participate effectively in the society. Indeed, during the years just prior to the American Revolution, clergy and statesmen wrote impassioned essays stressing the importance of early family treatment and proper education in the prevention of crime and the safeguarding of democracy. Despotism could be eliminated if all children were well nurtured and properly educated — a conviction not unlike Plato's assumption that if one knew what was good, immorality was impossible.

Finally, we do not like to see anything wasted or thrown away. Perhaps that is why the principle of conservation of energy is so aesthetic. The possibility that the intensity, variety, and excitement of the first years of life, together with the extreme parenting effort those months require, could be discarded like wrapping paper that is no longer needed is a little threatening to our Puritan spirit. We want to believe it is possible to prepare the child for the future as one saves for a rainy day. Application of that maxim to psychological development leads to the deduction that if children are treated optimally during the early years of life, the healthy beliefs and behaviors established during that first era will be adequate protection against later trauma.

From America's birth until the present, a majority has believed that the correct pattern of experiences at home and school would guarantee a harmonious society. This view, which was in accord with the doctrine of infant malleability, invited each generation of parents to project on to the infant their hopes for the future. Every infant was a fresh canvas, and the community was ready to receive any psychological theory that would make social experience the major steward of growth.

The Evidence for Continuity

Recently published data have led a small group of psychologists to question the traditional belief in the long-term effects of early experience on future behavior (Kagan, 1976). For the first time in the modern history of child psychology, one senses a beginning skepticism toward the strong form of the continuity assumption. The belief in psychological continuity within an individual life led, during the 1930s, to the initiation of several long-term longitudinal studies whose goal was to document the continuity that many were certain had to be present. The twin assumptions that the infant is malleable to experience and that early structures persist for decades, which were seen as necessarily correlated, are now regarded as independent (see McCall, Chapter 7, this volume). If the young child is malleable in his current environment, then a change in context might alter the profiles produced by the prior context. The nineteenth century commitment to the malleability of the infant is being taken seriously because the young child seems to have an extraordinary capacity for change, given new adaptation demands and proper encounters. That insight was disguised in the past, perhaps because we implicitly assumed that the average child's environment would not — or could not — change. In a more stable America, most children remained in the same family context and neighborhood until it was time to embark on adult responsibilities. The continuity of behavior noted by relatives and friends was attributed to forces within the child rather than to the environmental context in which each played out his or her role. If a small marble placed on a trough on an incline rolled unerringly in a straight line, one would not credit the marble with the capacity to maintain continuous linear movement (Waddington, 1977). We did not apply that principle to development but concluded instead that children had a mysterious power to sustain their psychological direction without the help of a guiding track.

COGNITIVE DEVELOPMENT IN INFANCY

Although search for evidence favoring the assumption of continuity from infancy to adolescence has not been enormously successful, the data are still so inconclusive that many developmental psychologists remain committed to demonstrating the ways early experience affects future talent and character, which in earlier periods meant the ways experience released or molded the behavior of the infant—feeding, toileting, sociability, and fearfulness. Because cognitive processes dominate contemporary thinking, scientists are more prone to ask how experience affects the infant's perception and construction of the world. This work, unlike the investigations of the 1940s, is being implemented at a time of deep interest in the role of biological maturation. Each year more child psychologists acknowledge the effect of maturation on cognition during the early years (see Bornstein, Chapter 3, this volume). That attitude leads one to study the ways experience monitors the time of emergence and the profile of what appear to be the universal competencies of infancy. One of these competencies is the creation of representations of experience. That theme takes us directly to a discussion of the nature of cognitive functioning during infancy.

Before we turn to that issue, it may be useful to defend, although briefly, the contemporary emphasis on cognition, because some scholars promote the view that the only significant events are those that change the world. However, even such pragmatists acknowledge that the exquisite armor of bone and muscle that erects buildings, heals the distressed, and destroys enemies takes some orders from a central executive. With only a few exceptions—for example the tremor of old age—any action can be stopped as fast as the mind decides. Furthermore, the pleasant states that have always been commanding criteria for action and legislation are, in the end, influenced by mental processes. If they were not, we would never have invented words like *love, appetite,* and *gratified* because *orgasm, hunger,* and *satiety* should have done the job quite well. Thus, whether constructive action, sensual pleasure, or quiescent relaxation are the criteria, one must turn to mental processes as the origin.

The Initial Structure: The Schema

We assume that the infant's first cognitive structure is a schema, which is defined as an abstract representation of an event that retains the relations among the physical dimensions of the original experience — be it object, sound, smell, or dynamic sequence. The event represented is of a figural component in a context. The child perceives a round shape with a clear, dark contour on the sandy background of a dirt road and forms a schema for that scene — a stone in the road. If the stone were moved to the child's bedroom, he might not recognize it in the new context. In a recent study in our laboratory, we found that a few 20-month-olds who could recognize their faces in a mirror did not recognize a Kodachrome slide of themselves when it was paired with the face of another child and projected on a screen in a small laboratory room.

The mechanism of schema formation is controversial, in part, because of the reasonable desire to base the process of cognitive development on one principle. Those who wish to make cognition dependent on motor action, the Piagetians being the clearest example, insist that the first structures are functional in nature. The representation is assumed to include both the properties and the envelope of actions with an object in one dynamic Gestalt.

A less extreme position separates the child's actions from the functions of the object, but this position regards functions as the defining dimensions of the schema. Both of these views are apt to be incomplete. A 5-month-old infant can develop a schema for a static horizontal arrangement of three geometric forms differentiated from the background frame on which the forms are mounted. After infants were habituated to the horizontal arrangement of the three elements, they were shown a 45° oblique arrangement of those same elements. They reacted with increased interest, indicating that they noticed and were aroused by the change in the figure. If the background was altered by a 45° change in orientation but the three elements remained horizontal, infants also reacted but with less sustained attentiveness. These data suggest that the child cannot only develop a schema for a static visual event without actively manipulating it but that he or she also naturally distinguishes salient from less salient aspects of events (Wiener & Kagan, 1976).

Super (1972) demonstrated that 2- to 3-month-old infants can remember for 24 hours aspects of a novel event (an orange sphere moving up and down in front of them in a regular cycle) that they had seen for only a few minutes. The fact that a 10-week-old infant who had seen this event on a previous day became bored more quickly than one who was watching it for the first time tempts us to conclude that a young infant can create a schema for an event merely by attending to it. This is not to say that manipulative interaction with the object does not facilitate schema formation or produce a different quality of schema. But there is no need to choose between action versus no action as the basis for early schema formation. It is likely that both mechanisms mediate the early acquisition of schemata.

A preference for the Piagetian view of infancy may be a derivative of a materialistic and mechanistic bias. If we make overt interaction necessary for new knowledge, we can control and study our hypothetical mechanisms more easily because overt behavior is public. If we allow knowledge to be gained secretly, we lose some control. Scientists prefer hypothetical mechanisms that are subject to empirical tests, interpretations that permit intervention, and phenomena that are observable. Hence, they are most receptive to explanations that meet those criteria, and they move away from those that do not.

Galileo's assumption that falling bodies should obey a mathematical law and Copernicus's assertion that the orbits of the planets are circular provide additional examples of the delicate tension between the facts and the Platonic idealism many theorists carry deep in their hearts. When there are no facts inconsistent with the ideal, it is useful to retain it. However, when the ideal view is inconsistent with empirical knowledge, one must begin to question it, as twentieth century physicists did when they abandoned parts of the elegant structure of Newtonian mechanics in order to accommodate to the new information generated by quantum mechanics.

Available evidence is consonant with the view that infants can acquire knowledge of an event by looking, listening, or smelling; it is not always necessary that they manipulate it (see also, Kopp, Chapter 2, this volume).

How Much Abstraction: The Prototype or Schematic Category

It is not clear how much abstraction of common dimensions across events occurs during infancy. How quickly can the young child extract a prototype of an event from its invariant features? It appears that the 4-month-old infant has clearly done so for some events, for he will smile to unfamiliar faces, implying that he has abstracted a set of critical dimensions from repeated encounters with people. He possesses a prototypic schema (or schematic category) for that class of events. What is not clear is whether he can extract such a core set of salient dimensions from the very first exposure.

The process of creating a prototype is not to be confused with differentiating a figural object from its background context. A schematic prototype is a representation of the shared dimensions of events that vary in specific form and context. Adults possess generalized schemata for melodies since variations on an infinite number of themes can be recognized, whether they are played by unaccompanied piano, trumpet, violin, or 60-piece orchestra. All of us possess generalized schemata for various animal species and recognize a heron in a picture book or on a sandy spit, a tulip standing in a dense, green field or in an orange pot on a florist's shelf. We have schematic categories for sequences of movements and for patterns of internally generated sensations. The prototypic schema, which may be the most frequently used unit of knowledge, permits immediate recognition of a new event before we can name it. It allows us to know if the strange object in the road in front of us is an odd shaped rock or an animal, a discarded suit or a crumpled piece of paper.

The opportunity for dynamic interaction with an event, especially interaction that changes the object, probably facilitates the establishment of a prototype. Small objects amenable for play and adults who respond reciprocally and contingently to the child possess this property. They provide consistent variation in response to imposed action. The object (toy or person) responds with a uniform transformation to an imposed action permitting the child to create a schematic prototype. Similarly, the child probably possesses a better articulated schematic prototype for faces than for beds because of the many more variations on the former.

It is possible that some schemata remain relatively unchanged for long periods of time. The schema of my first-grade teacher has probably retained some stability for 40 years, despite no renewal (I believe I could recognize her face in an array of 100 photographs) because the schema has not been transformed as a result of encounter with similar events. However, the schema for my younger brother, which was created at the same time, is probably lost because continued contact with him produced serious transformations in the original structure. The stability of a particular structure may be less a function of elapsed time than of the frequency with which it is reexperienced in the same form and the degree to which it participates in experiences that transform it. Some schema may be completely lost after one exposure. We recently showed 38 pairs of chromatic slides to 68 10-year-olds who had seen 22 of the pictures in our laboratory when they were 27 months old. Of these 22 scenes, 16 were ecologically valid illustrations of people or animals, whereas six were unusual (e.g., a man wearing a dress, a man with four arms, a woman with no head; see Kagan, 1971, for details). Each child was told that he or she had seen one of the members of each pair eight years earlier and was asked to decide which one it was. No child did better than chance, suggesting that if a schema for the original scene were still "present," it was not retrievable, even under these relatively optimal recognition–memory conditions.

Schemata for Individual Dimensions: The Sign

As the schema for an event becomes better articulated as a result of continued encounter the child is able to assimilate events that represent only one of the salient dimensions of what was originally an entire set. He will recognize the sound of footsteps on the stairs as representative of his father, a bark as representative of a dog. Langer (1957) has called these events *signs*. The single element predicts the larger whole just as a wet driveway in the morning announces a shower during the previous evening. At an intuitive level the process involves more inference than assimilating the whole event to a schema. It is useful, we suppose, to differentiate a schema for an entire event from the representation of one of its elemental dimensions. We see no reason why Langer's term *sign* should not be used as a descriptive label for the latter structure. The construction of signs may proceed simultaneously with the creation of schematic categories, with whole and part becoming better articulated with experience and maturity. This knowledge grows quietly and is used as surreptitiously as it is gained because the mind continually detects similarities in, and extracts categories from, experience with the regularity of the dance of returning honeybees.

The Symbolic Category

The queen of structures is the symbolic category—an arbitrary representation of the shared dimensions of a set of events. The symbolic category, unlike the schema, bears little or no veridical relation to the event it summarizes. We view the difference between schema and symbol as engaging the ancient debate between materialistic and idealistic views of nature. The schema bears a lawful relation to reality. Although it is not a replica, it is related to the physical qualities of the event, as a reflection in a distorting mirror bears a veridical relation to the object being reflected. However, symbols and concepts divide nature more arbitrarily. The most common symbolic category is, of course, a linguistic structure. The child acquires a symbolic "word" by coordinating an event in the auditory mode with a schematic category. This process may be different from coordinating the voice and face of a person because, in the latter instance, both are spatially contiguous and form a Gestalt. In the case of a spoken word, the verbal information is not an inherent part of the referent event. It has its origin in an arbitrary place. Indeed, some 2-year-olds will, when shown two familiar objects and one unfamiliar object and asked by an examiner to, "Give me the zoob," pick up the unfamiliar form, suggesting that they learn some language by inference. Some children, when they returned a month later, asked the examiner for the "zoob." It is generally assumed that the child treats the language of another as a salient dimension of some referential event and coordinates it with an appropriate schematic category acquired earlier. However, the child can on occasion create both at once. Eventually, the linguistic structure can become the salient dimension of the representation.

In the more traditional explanation, it is assumed that the child has a schema for an event that involves, say, a bottle, milk, and the act of drinking. The mother says, "Here is your milk," emphasizing the last word. That envelope of sound may be treated initially as if it were an additional dimension and becomes part of the structure. In those cases in which the label applies to only part of the original schema, the language label promotes a fragmentation of the schematic category. The original schema is destroyed, like a diamond cleft by a jeweler's sharp blow, leaving the child with a symbolic structure, "milk," composed of part of the original schema and the language label, and residual schematic prototypes that have not yet been mapped onto symbolic structures.

In one sense, the introduction of language labels is like a stream of neutrinos bombarding a proton, fragmenting it into a new set of particles and in that dynamic action transforming the original element. Language often hems what was origially a less bounded experience.

Because symbolic structures, unlike schemata, are not defined by the physical features of the events they represent, an event cannot be discrepant from a symbol but can be inconsistent with it, as when different symbolic forms are applied to the same class of events. Although inconsistency, like discrepancy, elicits uncertainty, each may generate a different quality of that state. Hence, it is wise to give this phenomenon a new name — symbolic dissonance, perhaps. Young children usually laugh rather than become afraid when a parent calls a man a dog. Although they cannot assimilate the event, young children do not usually become frightened, perhaps because they are not yet as strongly committed to the permanence of the symbolic form as they are to the physical event.

The symbol is neither figurative nor operative, to use Piagetian terms, for it neither represents reality in a veridical way nor participates in transformations of experience or knowledge. The symbol is a highly condensed and biased summary of an event that promotes certain qualities and ignores others. The word *child* tells us nothing of its sex or family status; the roadside symbol designating a steep hill tells us nothing of the length of the curve or the angle of descent. This indifference to variation leads to those distortions normally called *stereotypes.* The concept *scientist* evokes for some citizens an analytic, morally calloused, overachieving adult in a room full of machines. The mother who screams, "No, that's bad," when her child eats with his fingers or hits a younger sibling tempts the child to mute the difference between those two acts and exaggerate their similarity. (We will ignore the philosophical debate as to the existence of universals. We share Russell's relativistic view that physical and mental events are two distinct but real classes of phenomena. The representation that lies behind the butterfly's ommatidia may exist only for the butterfly, but it is real nonetheless.)

It is understood, of course, that a schematic prototype is a category but one that is not necessarily symbolic. It is likely that 1-year-olds possess schematic categories for animals and human beings that may have no symbolic component. Ross (1976) showed 12-, 18-, and 24-month-olds 10 physically different objects, each representing the same category (e.g., 10 different animals or 10 different edible foods). On the eleventh trial the child was shown a pair of new objects. One was a physically novel instance of a category the child had previously seen, and the other toy was a member of a new category (a human being or an article of furniture). The majority of the children in all three age groups showed a preference to reach for and play with the member of the new category, implying that they assimilated the additional instance of the familiarized category to a structure and treated it as a member of that class.

The Concept

The symbolic category can represent a class of real events or the shared aspects of other symbolic categories. In the latter instance, we might call them symbolic concepts, but this terminology is arbitrary and many regard categories and concepts as being synonymous. The child has a symbolic category for water when he possesses a linguistic structure *water* and applies it only to the colorless liquid in his bottle. When water represents other symbolic categories—the ocean, H_2O, mud puddles, and vapor—he is said to have a symbolic concept.

Schemata versus Categories

It is important to distinguish between a schema and a symbolic category (or concept). Symbolic concepts are more open than are schemata and can assimilate experiences that were not part of the events that created them. This is less true of a schema. My concept of lamp refers to any manufactured object having the potential to give light. I have been in modern hotel rooms where only the assumption that there must be a lamp in the room allowed me to assimilate a peculiarly slim, white floor-to-ceiling pole as a lamp. Assimilation to a category is different from assimilation to a schema, for the latter is a pattern of relations among physical events. Categories are hierarchies of dimensions that can be potentialities or other symbolic categories. As with a schema, the central dimensions of a category are its invariant qualities. The category *lamp* has the central qualitites of the capacity to give light that is contained in some manufactured frame. Although a fire is not a lamp, if we place flaming chips of wood in a glass container, we would assimilate it to our category for lamp. Like a schema, a category has a small set of primary, defining dimensions and a larger set of secondary ones. The defining set of primary dimensions for a table is a raised surface on which objects can be placed. That definition allows the possibility that a particular object could be a chair or a table. Additionally, each event can have a different set of characteristics that differentiate it from others. If I wish to distinguish a table from a man, I emphasize the animate-inanimate distinction, not the raised surface that can accept objects. If I wish to distinguish a table from a bench, I emphasize height from the ground. As with schemata, the dimensions that define a category in the prototypic sense are often different from the dimensions that distinguish it from another category.

The Meaning of Meaning

Pursuit of the meaning of a cognitive structure is slippery along the entire journey. The most popular solution is to assume that the meaning of a schema, symbol, or category is contained in the pattern of its functions, physical attributes, conceptual relations, and evoked psychic reactions. That definition elicits the image of a sticky piece of taffy in a large trunk; as you withdraw the taffy, you pull out all that has become attached to it.

The power to provoke a coherent set of cognitive units is one definition of meaning. The larger and more coherent the set of reactions, the more salient the representation and the more meaningful the event. However, meaning is a continuous and dynamic, not a static, quality. Kenneth Livingston has gathered unpublished data in our laboratory indicating that the ability to name the instances of a category, and to show proactive inhibition, conceptual inference, and clustering in verbal recall tends to appear in a somewhat orderly sequence for the categories *animal* and *living thing,* at least among school-age children. That is, a 7 year-old child who can name many instances of animals or living things and shows inhibition and release in a proactive interference design may not necessarily be capable of inferring either concept in a standard inference task nor cluster the conceptual terms in a verbal recall procedure. However, children who show clustering are likely to show evidence of possessing the concept in all four procedures. Thus, each of the psychologist's experimental probes mirrors a different stage of organization of the concept. A child's failure to display knowledge of a concept in one evaluation situation cannot be treated as evidence that he does not possess the concept.

If the meaning of an event is contained in all the structures it is capable of evoking, then each event has many meanings — one is contained in the schemata for the physical attributes of the event, one in the actions surrounding an event, still another in the symbolic representations of the event.

DEVELOPMENTAL CHANGES IN REACTION TO DISCREPANT EXPERIENCE

Because schemata, symbolic categories, and concepts change following encounter with discrepant or inconsistent events, it is useful to inquire into the developmental course of these processes. Do the processes that mediate detection of discrepancy and creation of cognitive structures change over the first 2 years of life?

The existing data suggest that they do. Changes in scanning strategies from 5 to 7 weeks lead the child to search inside the boundaries of figures and hence detect information he missed when younger. By 8 to 12 weeks, or even earlier, the infant seems capable of recognizing that an event is related to a schema because he is alerted by events that are discrepant transformations of his knowledge.

We also believe that at about 8 months a major change in cognitive functioning occurs due to the emergence of two related competencies. These processes are best conceptualized as (1) an enhancement in the ability to retrieve schemata of past events when minimal cues are available in the perceptual field and (2) the ability to hold representations of past and present in active memory for a longer time to permit prolonged comparison and evaluation. The evidence for this suggestion comes from a coherent and relatively invariant set of changes in the behavior of the infant during the last half of the first year. Let us consider these changes.

Increased Attentiveness

If cross-sectional or longitudinal samples of children are administered interesting visual and auditory events across the period from 3 to 13 months, it is usually, but not always, the case that there is a U-shaped function for attentiveness with a trough at 7 to 8 months of age. We have commented on this growth function in earlier reports (Kagan, 1971, 1976). We consider here some additional data that provide further support for that statement.

A group of 95 children was seen over the period of 3½ to 29 months of age. Thirty-two of these children were attending a day-care center 5 days a week; the other children were being reared at home. One visual and one auditory episode were administered across this entire age interval. The visual event consisted of a box with an orange rod at one end and three light bulbs at the other. In this procedure a hand came out and touched the orange rod, moved it across a traverse of 180° toward three light bulbs that lit when the rod contacted them. This event was repeated 8 or 10 times, followed by five transformations in which the hand touched the rod, but the rod did not move and three seconds later the lights went on. Following these five transformation trials, there were three re-presentations of the original standard. In the auditory episode a child heard a 4-second meaningful phrase for 10 or 12 trials followed by five transformation trials of either a phrase of nonsense or a change in word order, followed by three re-presentations of the standard. The variables of interest were the percentage of total fixation time to the stimulus (during the visual episode) and the percentage of total time searching during the auditory episode. Search was defined as the maintenance of a quiet, alert posture together with saccadic movements of the eyes during the presentation of the auditory episode.

Table 7.1 shows the percentage of total fixation and search time for all children across standard trials two through five, the first three transformations, and the three return trials for these episodes.

TABLE 7.1
Proportion of total fixation time to visual and total search time
to auditory episodes for day-care and home-reared children

Age	Standards 2–5	Trans. 1–3	Returns 1–3
	Visual: Percentage of total fixation time		
3	75.6	43.6	66.2
5	93.6	70.2	68.6
7	91.5	65.0	54.5
9	95.3	71.9	73.5
11	95.9	70.9	72.8
13	93.1	94.3	72.4
20	94.0	92.2	82.4
29	92.2	89.5	85.4
	Auditory: Percentage total search time		
3	66.6	59.3	49.5
5	61.3	55.7	51.3
7	54.2	36.5	36.5
9	67.7	54.0	49.6
11	71.6	56.0	48.9
13	72.5	46.3	38.9
20	81.1	65.3	67.6
29	80.2	69.3	63.5

The data suggest a U-shaped function for all phases of the auditory episode and for the return trials of the visual episode with a trough in attention at 7½ months.[1] There was slightly less attentiveness to the visual episode at 3½ months due, we believe, to the difficulty a very young child has in tracking a moving stimulus. Search movements to the auditory stimulus did not require such tracking, and the U-shaped function held across the period 3½ through 29 months with the trough at 7½ months. Since this was a longitudinal study, it was possible to perform an ipsative analysis and ask at which age each infant showed the least amount of attention.

Inspection of each child's fixation times to the light episode revealed that 76% of the children showed a U-shaped function to the standard, transformation, or return trials (or to two or three of these phases) and that the modal age of the trough was 7½ months. Over 90% of the children who showed a U-shaped function displayed a trough at 7½ or 9½ months. Ex-

---

[1]The growth functions for fixation time were tested for curvilinearity by computing the F-values for the quadratic component of a repeated measures analysis of variance. The F values were significant for the three return trials of the light episode and for all phases of the auditory episode.

amination of the longitudinal data on the auditory episode revealed that 78% of the infants showed a U-shaped function for search to the standard, transformation, or return phases and the modal age for the trough was 7½ months. Of those infants who showed the U-shaped function, 65% displayed the trough at 7½ months of age. Perhaps one reason why the U-shaped occurred for search to the standards of the auditory episode but not for fixation time to the standards on the light episode is the more obvious habituation of attention that occurred to the auditory than to the visual episodes at each age.

A similar growth function emerged for a longitudinal sample of Guatelmalan infants living in rural, subsistence farming villages in the eastern part of the country.[2] These infants were administered the same light episode in a manner comparable to the procedures used in the United States across the period 5 to 13 months. The Guatemalan infants also displayed the U-shaped growth function with a trough at 7½ months (see Figure 7.1). As with the American data, we examined the growth function for total fixation time to each phase of the episode for each of the 137 Guatemalan infants in this longitudinal sample. About half of the children showed a U-shaped function to the standard, transformation, or return trials with a trough at either 7 or 9 months. Occurrence of the trough was almost as frequent at 9 as it was at 7 months, in contrast to the American sample in which more infants showed their lowest fixation times at 7 months.

Finally, we administered the auditory episode to a much more isolated group of 87 Guatemalan Indian children between 5 and 21 months of age who were living on Lake Atitlan in the northwest highlands of the country. Forty-five of these infants lived in the modernizing village of San Pedro with a population of about 5000; the remaining children lived in the much poorer and more isolated village of San Marcos a few kilometers away, with a population of less than 1000. Each child, seated next to the mother in the home, heard a recording of a phrase (best translated as, "Come here, I'll pick you up") in Indian dialect for 12 repeated presentations followed by five transformations that were without meaning, and then three re-presentations of the original standard. The tape recorder, which was located to the right of the child, was not visible. The occurrence of search behavior was coded only once per trial; hence, the maximal score was 20. The infants in both villages showed a U-shaped function for search behavior with a trough at 7 to 8 months of age (see Table 7.2).

Thus, both Cambridge and Guatemalan infants seem to pass through a brief stage at 7 to 8 months when attentiveness to visual and auditory events is at a nadir, after which it increases. If we interpret the trough in attention at 7 months as indicating easy assimilation of the event, why is it that a few

---

[2]These data were gathered as part of a collaborative study with Dr. Robert E. Klein, INCAP, Guatemala City.

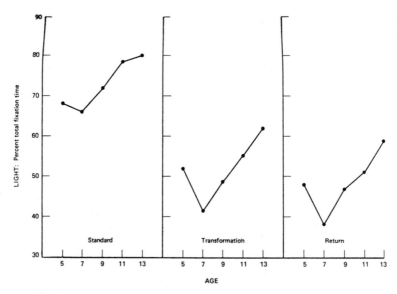

FIG. 7.1.   Percentage total fixation time to light episode for longitudinal sample of Guatemalan infants.

months later the same event seems to be more difficult to assimilate? There are several possibilities. The first is that the child has detected something in the event that he did not notice when younger. Because the infant's schemata for both visual and speech events become better articulated with age, the older child should be prepared to regard the event in a different way. This might be true for the speech episodes, because cognitive representations of morphemes emerge toward the last half of the first year. The child assimilates the auditory event to the schema for a voice at the younger ages, but at 11 months may assimilate the event to representations for language. However, if the growth of a new structure were the primary deter-

TABLE 7.2
Age and village differences in search to auditory:
mean proportion of trials on which search behavior occurred (all trials)

Age	San Marcos	San Pedro	Both Villages
5- 6	100	63	78
7- 8	38	55	46
9–10	44	72	58
11–12	63	73	69
13–14	80	63	70
15–16	89	64	76
17–18	67	84	79
19–21	67	71	69

minant of the U-shaped function, why should the child develop better articulated schemata for the light at about the same age? The "light" is an unfamiliar event the children were not exposed to at home. It seems a little unusual that equivalently articulated cognitive structures would develop for both the light and auditory episodes at the same age and in both cultures. It seems more likely that the growth function for attentiveness is due to a new competence or competencies rather than to a different structure. We suggest that the new function involves the ability to retrieve the schema of the original standard, compare it with the transformed event in the perceptual field, and attempt to resolve the discrepancy between the two. While performing this mental work, the infant remains attentive. The 3- to 6-month-old is attentive to a discrepant event because he or she is trying to assimilate it to an existing schema. Because that process proceeds more quickly at 7 to 8 months, attentiveness is reduced. However, 1-year-olds show more sustained attention because they are better able to retrieve the past and hold representations of the past and present in active memory for a longer period of time. Thus, they have more information and more time to generate the relation between the two structures.

An Invariant Sequence of Performances

More persuasive support for the hypothesis that retrieval capacity improves in a major way after 7 months comes from a longitudinal study of 8 middle-class Cambridge children who were seen monthly in both laboratory and home from 6 to 13 months of age and to whom the following procedures were administered (Fox, Kagan, & Weiskopf, in press).

Vacillation. The child was allowed to play with a single toy for 30 seconds. The toy was then taken away, and 30 seconds later the child was shown the familiarized toy and a new one simultaneously. The examiner coded the degree of looking back and forth between the two toys, a response we called *vacillation*. This procedure was repeated six times with six different pairs of toys.

Object permanence. The child was administered the standard Stage 4 object permanence procedure in four variations: (1) object placed under cloth, (2) cloth put over object, (3) object placed behind screen, (4) screen placed in front of object. The examiner coded the child's reaching for and retrieval of the object.

Object permanence: A-not-B procedure with 3-second delay. The child was administered the standard A-not-B object permanence procedure with a toy and two identical cloths, using a 3-second delay between the hiding of the object at location B and permitting the child to reach for it. The child first found the toy correctly at location A on three successive trials. On the fourth trial, the toy was hidden at location B.

Object permanence: A-not-B with 7-second delay.   The A-not-B procedure was administered as described in the foregoing paragraph. However, this time there was an imposed 7-second delay between the hiding of the toy at location B and permitting the child to reach for it.

Object permanence: absent object.   This procedure was identical to the A-not-B episode described with a 3-second delay, except that when the child went to location B, no object was present. The examiner coded whether the child searched at location A after initially finding no object at location B.

Object permanence: substitute object.   This procedure was identical to the "absent object" task described in the previous paragraph except that when the child went to location B, he found an object different from the one he had seen being hidden. The examiner coded whether the child went to location A after finding this unexpected object at location B.

Object permanence: screened hiding.   An object was hidden under one of two identical cylindrical forms. The examiner then placed a screen between the infant and the forms for 3 seconds. When the screen was lifted, the child was allowed to reach for the toy.

These seven performances formed an impressive invariant scale. All the infants showed vacillation first, at around 6 months of age, a behavior that requires only recognition memory. This victory was followed by simple object permanence at 7 to 8 months—a behavior that requires recall of the location of the hidden toy. A month or two later, at 10 months, the child was able to tolerate a delay of 7 seconds in the A-not-B procedure. By 12 months of age the child was able to recall the location of the object even when it was screened, and he searched at location A after failing to find the original toy at location B in the substitute-object and absent-object conditions.

Table 7.3 shows the order in which each of these behaviors emerged for each of the eight children. The Guttman coefficients of reproducibility and scalability approached 1.0, suggesting intersubject consistency in the order in which these performances appeared. We suggest that one way to view this sequence is to regard it as reflecting the improved ability to retrieve a representation of a past experience and to hold it in active memory for some period of time without external stimulus support.

Additional evidence for this idea comes from the cross-sectional study of Indian children from San Pedro and San Marcos mentioned earlier. The infants, between 5 and 21 months of age, were administered three of the procedures used in the Cambridge study described earlier (vacillation, Stage 4 object permanence, A-not-B with a 3-second delay) and, in addition, inhibition to novelty. In the latter procedure the infant was shown the same identical toy for six repeated trials, each lasting about 8 seconds, with an intertrial interval of about 3 seconds. On the seventh trial, the infant was shown a single novel toy. Latency to reach for the toy was coded on each trial, and the behavior of interest was the tendency to inhibit reaching for the novel toy on the critical seventh trial. The procedure was repeated three times with three different pairs of toys. The criterion for inhibition was an increase of at least 1 second in the latency to reach for the new toy, as compared with the latency on the last presentation of the familiarized toy.

TABLE 7.3
Age at which each of eight American infants mastered
the seven procedures (to the nearest half-month)

Procedure	Infant							
	A	B	C	D	E	F	G	H
Vacillation	6	7	7	7	6	6	6	7
Stage 4 object permanence	7	8	8	8	7	8	7	7
A-not-B 3-second delay	8	8	8	9	9	9	8	8
A-not-B 7-second delay	8	9	9	10	9	10	9	9
Absent object	9	9	10	10	10	11	9	10
Substituted object	10	11	11	11	11	12	10	10
Screened object	11	12	12	12	11	12	12	11

The performance of the Indian children on these four procedures also fell into an invariant sequence. In both locales, vacillation occurred before inhibition to novelty, and both occurred before successful solution of the two object-permanence problems. Table 7.4 presents the earliest age at which any child met the criteria for the task and the age at which half of the children in an age cohort met the criteria for these procedures.

It is of interest that in both Cambridge and Guatemala "pretend" play with a toy-like object first appeared between 12 and 15 months. This behavior requires not only the retrieval of an event witnessed in the past but, additionally, the ability to generate variations on a schematic prototype. For example, the child has a representation of his parents drinking coffee. He can generate and implement in action a variation of that representation with a toy cup, or he can even drink imaginary liquid with his closed right hand.

The Appearance of Inhibition

The period of wariness and inhibition to unusual or unexpected events that usually emerges at 7 to 8 months may be a derivative of the amplified

TABLE 7.4
Sequence of developmental milestones in San Pedro and San Marcos

Response	Youngest age at which any child first met criterion		Age at which 50% of age group met criterion	
	San Pedro	San Marcos	San Pedro	San Marcos
Vacillation (2 of 5 trials)	5 mos.	7 mos.	5–6 mos.	7–8 mos.
Inhibition to novelty (2 of 3 trials)	6	8	9–10	9–10
Stage 4 object permanence	7	9	7–8	11–12
Object permanence A-not-B, with 3-second delay	7	11	9–10	11–12

memorial competence. For example, the occurrence of separation distress shows its steepest slope from 9 to 13 months in Guatemalan, American, Israeli, and !Kung San children (Kagan, 1976), as does irritable fretting to a female examiner in a simple social-interaction situation. The end of the first year also marks a temporary inhibition in the amount of babbling to unusual visual and auditory events as well as maximal vacillation to paired presentation of an old and new toy. Scarr and Salapatek (1970) have also reported a period of fearfulness to a variety of unusual events around the first birthday.

We interpreted the increase in attentiveness after 8 months as being due to the ability to retrieve and hold on the stage of active memory the schema for a prior but absent event that is related to a discrepant event in the perceptual field and to compare the two structures. Because the schema does not vanish quickly, the child has a continual incentive present to provoke attempts at assimilation. The older infant pays a price for the persistence of the trace. If he cannot assimilate the new event and cannot relate the present to his retrieved knowledge, he becomes vulnerable to uncertainty. Hence, the period prior to the first birthday is characterized by signs of inhibition of play and crying to discrepant events because the child is mature enough to compare past and present but not yet mature enough to resolve those inconsistencies. The decrease in these signs of uncertainty and fear later in the first and early in the second year implies that the child has become more capable of interpreting the transformed event. It is for this reason that we regard stranger and separation fear as being dependent in part on the maturation of a new memorial competence.

The new competence may also make it possible for the first symbolic categories to appear. During the first 8 months the child has been extracting schematic prototypes. Toward the end of the first year he is able to relate the common dimensions shared by a sequence of events and hence create a category. This competence requires the amplification of memory (so the child can relate old and new) as well as the disposition to compare similar schemata. In Ross's (1976) paradigm, discussed earlier, the 1-year-old saw different animals, but all shared key dimensions such as shape of head, number of legs, and ratio of body parts. The ability to remember those dimensions over the course of the ten presentations and the disposition to relate those common dimensions to one another and to an existing structure may have been the key processes mediating the 1-year-old's capacity to recognize and habituate to the category presented by the repeated events and, therefore, to reach for the exemplar of the new category when it appeared.

STRUCTURE AND PROCESS

The changes we have described as occurring from 7 to 13 months are likely to be universal; they occur among urban American children as well as those living in more isolated settings. Because this short interval corresponds to the era of sensorimotor intelligence that Piaget calls "object permanence stages 4-6," it is appropriate to ask whether it is theoretically more useful to view the behavioral changes of this period as the product of a new structure —a belief in the permanence of objects—or new processes, specifically the ability to retrieve schemata and to compare them. Some theorists have argued that separation distress waits on the child's ability to believe in the permanence of objects. Our view is that both object permanence and separation protest are dependent in part on the maturation of enhanced memorial processes. How different are these views? At one level it must be true that the 12-month-old believes in the permanence of the hidden object. The child would not search for the toy if he did not believe it was there. The fact that a 12-month-old will appear puzzled and search in another place when he finds no object under the cloth is convincing evidence that he believes objects do not disappear. Whereas Piaget simply posits the emergence of the cognitive structure, we suggest that the belief in the per- manence of the object can occur only after the memorial ability has matured. The new structure is dependent on the prior development of the new competence. There are many analogous examples in development. The formation of the notochord represents an important change in the developing embryo, but the appearance of that structure is dependent on prior changes in the competencies of tissues in the dorsal aspect of the em- bryo. The child cannot acquire a representation of a human face—a struc- ture—until the competence to scan inside the boundary of a figure emerges, somewhere between 5 and 7 weeks. The child cannot learn the meaning of words until he first acquires the ability to treat an event symbolically. (Of course, not all new structures are yoked to the growth of a new competence.) Consider the relation between affective structures and the cognitive processes that permit them to develop. The child of 5 years holds beliefs about right and wrong and, as a result, will apply self-accusatory descriptions following violation of a standard. In the 1940s it was fashionable to say that he possessed a structure called the superego. That structure cannot appear until the child is mature enough to reflect upon his actions, a process that typically appears after 2 years of age.

Whether one prefers to view the change at 8 months as characterized by a growth in memorial capacities or a belief in the permanence of objects depends on one's theoretical purposes. This difference in viewpoint resembles, in a sense, the wave-particle controversy in physics during the first decade of the twentieth century, which Bohr resolved with the now-famous principle of complementarity, a principle that seems to be useful for resolving some theoretical issues in psychological development.

The emphasis on process in interpreting psychological growth is in accord with recent work on cognitive development in older children. The improvement in recognition and recall memory after 6 years of age is due, many claim, to activation of processes involving organization, rehearsal, and retrieval rather than new knowledge (Flavell, Friedrichs, & Hoyt, 1970). The 9-year-old American child can remember many more familiar words than can a 5-year-old because of the way the older child acts on the information. At adolescence the ability to detect inconsistencies in sets of beliefs is as important a cause of uncertainty as new knowledge. It is likely that processes we have not yet discerned are introduced into ontogenesis during the first decade of life. Each of the new competencies permits new structures to be created. Of course, new knowledge can mediate behavioral change, but American psychologists have been more friendly to attributing changes in behavior or performance on cognitive tasks to new knowledge rather than to emergent processes. Knowledge can be manipulated in the laboratory with greater ease than can processes. Hence, it is empirically convenient to draft interpretations in forms that permit a well-designed experiment. Second, individual differences in academic proficiency seem more closely yoked to differences in general information and richness of linguistic repertoire than to memory, perception, or reasoning. Lower- and middle-class 10-year-olds are probably more similar in their cognitive processes than in the knowledge they possess, and it is likely that domestic concern with individual differences is one reason for awarding priority to knowledge.

SUMMARY AND IMPLICATIONS

There seems to be a complementary relation between developing competencies and structures during the opening years of life — and probably throughout development. We have suggested, with a bit more boldness than the data warrant, that some of the changes of the first year should be regarded as the result of the insertion of a new dynamic competence into the stream of development. This attitude invites a view of stage that is slightly less abrupt and more fluid than the one promoted in the past. Structures have a static connotation. When a child learns what *shilling* means, he is changed permanently—and abruptly. Hence, defining stages in terms of the acquisition of structures tempts an analogy to square wave functions. One moment the knowledge is absent, the next it is present. Defining stages as intervals during which new abilities grow suggests a more gradual view of growth, for few new abilities are activated in a large number of contexts at once. A child does not automatically apply a new talent to all possible situations (Rogoff, Newcombe, & Kagan, 1974: Kagan, 1976). The 8- to 10-month-old cannot remember the location of all objects he has watched being hidden, only salient ones. The 12-year-old San Marcos child can remember the order of 10 familiar pictures but fails to recall the orientation of three dolls. It seems useful to regard a developmental stage as the period during which the envelope of contexts in which a competence is activated is enlarged. That perspective awards each competence a long history. As we have written in other places, the age designation for a stage tends to be that time when a particular set of abilities is activated in a large number of appropriate situations.

ACKNOWLEDGMENTS

This paper was written while the author was a Belding Scholar for the Foundation for Child Development. The research described in this essay was supported by grants from the Office of Child Development, National Institute of Child Health and Human Development, Carnegie Corporation of New York, and the Grant Foundation.

REFERENCES

Emerson, R. W. Self-reliance. In *Essays*. Boston: Houghton Mifflin, 1876.

Erikson, E. H. Identity and the life cycle: Selected papers. *Psychological Issues,* 1959, *1,* 1–171.

Fiske, J. *The meaning of infancy*. Boston: Houghton Mifflin, 1883.

Flavell, J. H., Friedrichs, A. G., & Hoyt, J. D. Developmental changes in memorization processes. *Cognitive Psychology,* 1970, *1,* 324–340.

Fox, N., Kagan, J., & Weiskopf, S. The enhancement of memory in the first year. *Genetic Psychology Monographs* (in press).

Kagan, J. *Change and continuity in infancy*. New York: Wiley, 1971.

Kagan, J. Emergent themes in human development. *American Scientist,* 1976, *64,* 186–196.

Langer, S. K. *Philosophy in a new key*. Cambridge: Harvard University Press, 1957.

Mahler, M. S. Thoughts about development and individuation. *Psychoanalytic Study of the Child,* 1963, *18,* 307–324.

Nakane, C. *Japanese society*. Berkeley: University of California Press, 1972.

Rogoff, B., Newcombe, N., & Kagan, J. Planfulness and recognition memory. *Child Development,* 1974, *45,* 972–977.

Ross, G. *A study of conceptualization in young children.* Unpublished doctoral dissertation, Harvard University, 1976.

Scarr, S., & Salapatek, P. Patterns of fear development during infancy. *Merrill–Palmer Quarterly,* 1970, *16,* 53–90.

Schafer, R. *Aspects of internalization.* New York: International Universities Press, 1968.

Super, C. M. *Long term memory in infancy.* Unpublished doctoral dissertation, Harvard University, 1972.

Waddington, C. H. *Tools for thought.* London: Paladin, 1977.

Wiener, K., & Kagan, J. Infants' reaction to changes in orientation of figure and frame. *Perception,* 1976, *5,* 25–28.

8 Qualitative Transitions in Behavioral Development in the First Two Years of Life

Robert B. McCall
Center for the Study of Youth Development
Boys Town, Nebraska

INTRODUCTION

For decades, American developmental psychologists have perceived the description of continuities and stabilities of major behavioral attributes across age to be one of their principal missions, despite the fact that the concept of development implies change (Wohlwill, 1973). The historical orientation toward studying consistency rather than change may have stemmed from two progenitors, one conceptual and one methodological.

First, it is difficult to escape the inherent truth that "the child is father to the man." Consistency is more parsimonious and orderly than is change. Second, we are loyal to certain methodologies. McCall (1977; McCall, Eichorn, & Hogarty, 1977) has argued that the heavy reliance on simple cross-age correlations locks developmentalists into finding stability of individual differences and ignores transitions in the absolute levels of behaviors over age. However, there is an aura in the contemporary Zeitgeist signaling a reversal in this attitude. Developmentalists are now becoming more interested in describing changes, discontinuities, and instabilities. Kagan (Chapter 7, this volume) has outlined several factors that may be stimulating this revolution.

This chapter subscribes to this new look in developmental research by emphasizing transitions and changes in addition to continuities and stabilities. It is a primitive attempt to present a modest conceptualization of some of the major transitions in the mental development of infants in the first 3 years of life and to relate those transitions to changes in a variety of mental and social/emotional events typical of this period.

GENERAL ORIENTATION

This presentation is guided by two general conceptual orientations. One concerns the different ways in which developmental transitions may be manifest, and the second represents a developmental orientation toward the nature–nurture issue.

Two Realms of Developmental Analysis

Consistency and change over age can occur in two different realms. Suppose Figure 8.1 is a plot of the growth of an attribute over age — for example, verbal fluency. The heavy line depicts the average of a group of subjects, and the thinner lines represent each of the five individuals in the sample. Statistically, the distinction to be made is simply the difference between the absolute value of the average curve at different ages on the one hand and the stability of relative rank orderings of individuals from one age to the next on the other. Just as the correlation between two sets of scores is independent of the means of those two distributions, so too the absolute value of a trait in a group is independent from the relative stability of individual differences.

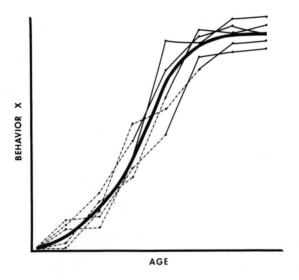

FIG. 8.1.   Hypothetical plot of the development of behavior X for five subjects illustrating the developmental function (heavy line) and the stability/instability of individual differences (thinner lines). Cross-age correlations are low across the early years (dashed lines) but become higher later (solid thin lines). Reprinted from McCall, Eichorn, and Hogarty (1977) with permission of authors and publisher (Society for Research in Child Development).

Developmental function.   The measured value of a given attribute plotted across age defines the *developmental function* of that characteristic. If the developmental function represents an average over a random sample of a given species, then that developmental function is an estimate of the *species-general developmental function* for that attribute. In Figure 8.1, the heavy line might represent an estimate of the developmental progress of human beings in verbal fluency. As in other estimation procedures, the accuracy of this function is determined by the representativeness of the sample and the adequacy of the measurement.

Developmental functions for individuals, groups, or species are either *continuous* or *discontinuous* (Emmerich, 1964). A developmental function is continuous when changes over age are quantitative rather than qualitative, that is, when the fundamental nature of the attribute does not change. A plot of height over age would be continuous because the fundamental character of height is the same at every age even though the average measured value is not. The developmental function for vocabulary would also be continuous. In contrast, the plot of Piagetian sensorimotor development would be discontinuous because its specific behavioral character is different from one stage to the next.

Individual differences.   Another sphere in which consistency and change in development have been assessed involves the relative stability of individual differences. That is, do individuals maintain the same relative rank ordering within their group at two different ages, or does the relative rank ordering change from one age to the next? The term *stability* refers to the relative consistency of such individual differences across age. Therefore, in the hypothetical plot in Figure 8.1, individual differences are not stable during the early years but become more stable later.

Confusing developmental function and individual differences.   It should be apparent that the developmental function and individual differences are potentially independent distinct types of information about the developmental process, and the factors that govern one realm may be different from those that influence the other. Furthermore, the continuous or discontinuous character of the developmental function does not necessarily reveal anything about the relative stability of individual differences. That is, there may be stable (or unstable) individual differences for both discontinuous and continuous developmental functions.

Developmental psychologists have sometimes lost sight of the potential independence of these domains. For example, Bloom (1964) suggested that 50% of a child's adult intelligence is developed by 4 years of age, basing this conclusion on the statistical fact that the correlation between IQ at 4 years and IQ at 17 years is approximately 0.71. But this claim for the development of intelligence in general is based solely on the stability of individual differences — it completely ignores the fact that the average child's mental age (i.e., the "amount" of mental skill displayed) will increase by more than four times during this interval. This approach is rather like predicting a 30-foot difference in the heights of mature Sequoia trees from seedlings while ignoring the fact that all the trees grow to be over 300 feet tall.

The discussion of heredity and environmental influences on intellectual performance is similarly clouded by the failure to distinguish between individual differences and developmental function. For example, if data showed that there was a strong correlation between IQ test performance and genetic circumstance, we would be prone to conclude that IQ is determined mostly by heredity. Conversely, if IQ scores correlated very highly with some environmental circumstance, we would decide that IQ was mostly governed by environmental factors. The proper conclusion in either of these cases is that individual differences — not intelligence in general — are governed by one or the other set of factors in the available sample and under the circumstances of the assessment. Actually, all methods of assessing the genetic influence on a trait depend on individual differences. *We have no methods of assessing the heritability of the species-general developmental function for intelligence or any other characteristic.*[1]

Although the developmental function and individual differences are statistically and conceptually independent, they actually may not be so independent in nature. That is, if a given set of assessments is made across age and there is a relative dip in the size of the cross-age correlations at 8 months, that period of relative instability of individual differences may signal an underlying discontinuity in the developmental function of specific behaviors contributing to those assessments. This possibility requires that the determinants of individual differences and developmental function are in part the same. However, this is an empirical question, and inferences across these two realms should not be made carelessly.

Canalization

Every theory of development must deal with the nature–nurture issue. Although this topic has dominated thought for decades, relatively little progress seems to have been made on its resolution. I submit that one reason may be that we persist in casting the issue in simplistic polarities: Is trait X governed by hereditary or environmental circumstances? What percentage of the variation in trait X is attributable to genetic heritage? Persisting in this traditional mode leads to paradoxes. For example, among normal infants

---

[1]The heritability of *individual differences* in developmental functions (but not the species-general function itself) can be estimated by methods that correlate individual differences in individual developmental functions with genetic or environmental circumstance (e.g., McCall, 1970; McCall, Appelbaum, & Hogarty, 1973; Wilson, 1972).

neither socioeconomic class nor genetic circumstance correlates with individual differences in performance on standardized assessments of "mental" development in the first 18 months of life (McCall, Hogarty, & Hurlburt, 1972; McCall, 1976). Are we to conclude that development prior to 18 months has no obvious environmental or genetic cause?

We need some fresh thinking in this domain—conceptions that consider the process of development (Anastasi, 1958) as it is reflected in the developmental function as well as in individual differences. One such approach rests on the concept of canalization, which has been most recently discussed by Scarr–Salapatek (1976) and subsequently by McCall (in press).

The basic concept.   Canalization implies a species-typical path, called a *creod*, along which nearly all members of the species tend to develop. However, development typical of the species occurs along the creod only as long as species-typical appropriate environmental circumstances predominate. While such circumstances exist, development proceeds "normally"; when such environmental circumstances deviate markedly from typical rearing conditions, development can go awry. Therefore, the utility of the concept of canalization depends on the breadth of experiences and circumstances that define species-typical environments and the extent to which individuals will return to the creod after periods of exposure to atypical circumstances.

Mental development in human infants seems to be highly canalized at the start. That is, infants proceed along the species-typical path under a wide range of environments, and there is a strong self-righting tendency should extreme circumstances deflect an infant from this path. However, mental development becomes progressively less canalized with age, beginning in a substantial way at approximately 18 to 24 months. This conception can be metaphorically illustrated by considering a special bowling alley that resembles a funnel cut in half lengthwise. In contrast to the usual flat surface, this alley consists of a trough that has steep walls at its beginning, but these sides progressively flatten out until the entire alley is a level plane. Now consider what happens when a bowling ball is rolled down such a trough-like alley. First, should a ball deviate from the median, there is an extraordinarily strong self-righting tendency, but this becomes weaker as the ball proceeds down the alley. Therefore, environmental perturbations occurring during the early stages of development are likely to induce some wobbling in the developmental trajectory of the organism, but the earlier they occur the more likely the child will return to a species-typical developmental path (Waddington, 1977).

Early insults and self-righting.   The impact of early major biological adversity has recently been reviewed by Honzik (1976), J. V. Hunt (1976),

Sameroff and Chandler (1975), and Scarr–Salapatek (1976). These authors conclude that the effects of nutritional deprivation, prematurity, anoxia, and other neonatal risk factors produce contemporaneous depression in infant test scores. But if these infants are subsequently reared in adequate environments, the effects of these early circumstances are diminished by 3 years and are often absent by 6 years. However, if such infants are not reared in species-typical environments but are exposed to markedly inferior circumstances, the effects of early insults can persist.

Early individual differences.   The second implication of the canalization position is that as long as the sides of the trough are steep, individual differences will be relatively insignificant in terms of their contemporaneous and long-term implications and predictions. One can imagine a ball initially set in motion somewhat obliquely to the center line of the trough. It would bounce back and forth between the steep sides of the alley at first, but eventually it would trace a more stable path down the alley. Consequently, early deflections from the average are likely to be short-lived because of the self-righting tendency, and therefore the power of such early individual variations to predict later development is limited. Of course, if the early insult actually damages the biological-maturational system or if rearing circumstances continue to depart from those typical of the species, aberrant development can persist and be predicted. However, within a broad range of environmental circumstances, individual differences will have very modest contemporaneous and long-term predictive significance, if any (McCall, 1976; McCall, in press; McCall et al., 1972).[2]

Given this view, individual differences in mental test performance prior to 18 to 24 months should reveal genetic or general environmental circumstances during the early months of life. Such is the case, although the implications of the data are still being debated (Golden & Birns, 1976; Honzik, 1976; McCall, 1976; McCall, Appelbaum, & Hogarty, 1973; Scarr–Salapatek, 1976). Presumably, many of these individual differences may be attributable to temporary circumstances of testing and fluctuating temperamental states of the infant. Note that while individual differences may not show substantial

---

[2]Although the data tend to be consistent with this prediction, exceptions apparently exist (McCall, in press). For example, certain environmental circumstances not only have contemporary correlations with infant test performance. They also predict scores later in childhood, and sometimes the predictive coefficients are higher than the contemporary *r*s. However, McCall (in press) has suggested that the dynamics underlying these predictive correlations are unclear. For example, it may be that the early environmental circumstances have a causal relation to contemporary performance but not to future performance; the predictive correlations occur because parents who provide functional experiences for their younger children also provide salient stimulation when their children are older. The correlation between parental behavior across age, not the early stimulation per se, may produce the longitudinal predictions. At the very least, the empirical issue is still unclear.

heritability, the species-general developmental function or creod is under strong, inherited, biological-maturational influence.

The decline of canalization. The third feature of the proposed model concerns the progressive decline over age in the strength of the canalization system and thus the potency of the self-righting tendency. As the canalization of the developmental function begins to weaken at approximately 18 to 24 months of life, a greater range of environmental or genetic factors generating individual differences will produce individual variation that may persist over relatively longer periods of time if such circumstances continue. Contemporaneous as well as longitudinal correlations do increase between 1 and 6 years, and they first become significant in research samples between 18 and 24 months of age (Honzik, 1976; McCall, in press; McCall, et al., 1972).

The end of plasticity? The fourth implication pertains to the continuing potential of experience to influence mental development after canalization weakens. During the past two decades, psychologists have emphasized the malleability of human development during the early years of life (e.g., J. McV. Hunt, 1961; B. L. White, 1976). However, acceptance of Bloom's (1964) claim that more than half of the child's "intelligence" is established by 4 years seemed to place a time limit on such plasticity. The belief emerged that experiences prior to approximately age 6 can have massive and nearly indelible effects on subsequent mental performance, but (by implication) environmental circumstances implemented after this period will have relatively little impact. Environmental and genetic factors gradually do produce meaningful and enduring individual differences beginning at approximately 2 years of age, and mental development appears to become more plastic during this age period. Furthermore, longitudinal correlations in mental test performance approach an asymptote by 6 years. However, do these data imply that the die for future mental accomplishment is irrevocably cast at this point?

I think not. I believe the consistency observed after 6 years is more associated with the perseveration of the environmental circumstances than with any indelible or inherent characteristic of the child stamped in by salient environmental circumstances before the age of 6. The potential for change remains, although naturalistic circumstances typically conspire to favor stability. The facts that experience is cumulative and that children are a dynamic force in the selection and creation of their own environments promote environmental stability. Moreover, children tend to live in the same family until age 18, they go off to schools matched to their early life circumstance, and as adults they are likely to select experiences that are also commensurate with the intellectual environment they experienced in childhood.

Reports of plasticity in the mental performance of children 6 years and older are not unknown. Substantial shifts in IQ at 5 to 7, 11, and 14 years of age occurred in the Fels sample with little evidence for a genetic determinant of these inflections (McCall, 1970; McCall et al., 1973). Moreover, the apparent mental renaissance of children tragically reared in isolation for the first 6 years of life (Mason, 1942) and the dramatic shift in mental performance during midchildhood as an apparent function of cultural circumstances (Kagan & Klein, 1973) also speak for the potential of children to remain susceptible to alterations in salient aspects of their environment (Clarke & Clarke, 1976). Therefore, I do not believe that mental capability is essentially imprinted by age 6, although naturalistic circumstances favor environmental stability.

OVERVIEW OF THE CONCEPTUAL ORIENTATION

The following discussion represents a stage conceptualization of early mental development that transpires within the general framework of the canalization position outlined earlier. It is derived principally from Piaget (1952) and Uzgiris (1976) and rests heavily on data reported by McCall et al. (1972) and McCall, Eichorn, and Hogarty (1977). No claim is made for the originality of the notions presented, but it is hoped that the organizational scheme, the implications of these ideas for a variety of developmental phenomena, and the emphasis on consistency and change in both developmental function and individual differences will have heuristic value for future methodology and theory.

General Qualifications

Every theoretical presentation has certain limits of application. Some qualifications for this scheme follow.

Stage orientation. Stages differ from a sequence of developmental events in the breadth of behaviors functionally associated with the fundamental characteristic defining each stage (Wohlwill, 1973). Because a major feature of this presentation is the implication of the hypothesized mental advances for a variety of cognitive and social behaviors, I believe this conceptualization fits the criterion of a stage theory.

Number of stages. The number of stages that may be postulated in the course of development is nearly unlimited, depending on the level of analysis. Therefore, a single stage presented here might be broken down into several substages. Consequently, the absolute number of stages is less important than the sequence and implications of the specific mental capabilities described here.

Ages. The age boundaries of each stage are intended to be approximate. Not only will one infant make a stage transition at a different age than another infant, but whether a transition will be seen at all depends on how those behaviors are assessed. Therefore, the proposed stages describe a sequence of qualitative shifts in fundamental ability across age and represent discontinuities in the general developmental function, but infants do not precipitously jump from one stage to the next.

Horizontal décalage.   Although it will be proposed that an advance in a certain mental skill permits the emergence of a variety of new behaviors, these related changes will not necessarily occur at the same age as the primary transition. Piaget (1941) called this variation in the onset of related behaviors a *horizontal décalage.* Ample data demonstrate that task, procedural, and experiential variables affect the diagnosis of Piagetian stages and the existence of such décalages (Barratt, 1975; Fischer, 1974; Goldschmid, 1971; Inhelder, Sinclair, & Bovet, 1974; Jackson, Campos, & Fischer, 1978; Salatas & Flavell, 1976). Therefore, the empirical demonstration of parallel developments across task domains or even different assessment procedures within a single task is likely to be difficult.

Perspective.   I have adopted the perspective of describing early mental development and its implications for a variety of other behaviors. This may give the impression that mentality is primary and advances in other domains are merely epiphenomena. I do not subscribe to this opinion—presumably, one could write a theory of affective development and consider mentality a "mere" derivative (Sroufe, in press). Eventually, such diverse perspectives will be integrated.

The function of mental behavior.   Consistency in overt mental behaviors is nearly absent during infancy, and this chapter emphasizes discontinuity and instability more than many of its predecessors. Nevertheless, all developmental consistency should not be denied. I believe consistency is more likely to be found in the biological function of mental behavior (i.e., its adaptive significance for the organism and species) than in its specific behavioral manifestations. Therefore, although the specific behaviors and abilities change radically from one age to the next, these heterogeneous behaviors serve a common function across the life span. Piaget suggested that these functions were assimilation and accommodation; I prefer another perspective.

One function is the *acquisition of information,* its intake, storage, and retrieval. A second but corollary function is *to influence the environment,* both animate and inanimate. These two dispositions are inherent characteristics of human beings and probably many other animals, although one species will differ from another in the level and strength of such tendencies. It is the disposition toward such functions that energizes much behavior that we call mental. The adaptive significance of each function is obvious — survival, adaptation, and modification of the environment are dependent on them. The similarity between acquiring information and influencing the environment and Piaget's assimilation and accommodation are readily apparent, and influencing roughly corresponds to R. W. White's (1959) notion of "effectance."

Locating Transition Points

What kinds of general evidence support a stage theory of mental development?

Theoretical. Others have offered stage conceptions of development. Piaget (1952) proposed the major contemporary stage theory of sensorimotor development, and many of his notions have been supported by research employing assessments especially designed to test his postulated stages (e.g., Corman & Escalona, 1969; Uzgiris, 1976; Uzgiris & Hunt, 1975). The present conceptualization is appropriately considered to be "modified Piaget."

Recently, other scholars from varying vantage points have also offered stage-type theories. Emde, Gaensbauer, and Harmon (1976) and Parmelee and Sigman (1976) point out that a variety of psychobiological functions undergo profound transformations at approximately 2 months of age and perhaps again at 7 to 8 months. Fischer (in press) has proffered a multistage conception of mental development with implications for perceptual-cognitive, language, and social development. And Sander (1962, 1969) and Sroufe (in press) have proposed stage theories of social-affective development with implications for mental behavior. Although these diverse efforts have evolved rather independently, I believe they are more similar than different in the proposed ages of major transitions and the qualitative nature of such changes in the developmental function.

Empirical (infant testing literature). The most direct evaluation of a stage theory requires the creation of a pool of behavioral items that directly assess the hypothesized fundamental characteristic of each stage as well as behaviors encompassed by proposed horizontal décalages. Such items would be administered frequently to a longitudinal sample, and the sequence of transitions and their consistency across behavioral domains would be observed. The research and conceptualizations of Uzgiris (1976, 1977) exemplify this view.

However, although many longitudinal data on mental behaviors were not originally guided by specific theories, they may be marshaled post hoc to support a stage theory of mental development. For example, the Berkeley and Fels longitudinal studies administered traditional infant mental tests frequently during the first years of life. McCall (McCall et al., 1972; McCall, Eichorn, & Hogarty, 1977) subjected the individual items to principal components analyses separately at each testing age. The first principal component represents the best distillation of the item pool and therefore estimates the predominant character of mental behavior at that age. Changes across age in the item composition of the first principal components were interpreted as signaling discontinuities in the developmental function. At certain ages, cross-age correlations of component scores showed dips in the level of stability of individual differences surrounding the developmental function. Although potentially independent, the points of discontinuity in developmental function and the nodes of instability of individual differences both occurred at the same ages—approximately 2, 7, 13, and 21 months. Because the ages and the qualitative nature of the stages that emerged from these studies are similar to those offered by Piaget (1952) and Uzgiris (1976), I propose stage boundaries at approximately 2, 7, 13, and 21 months as the working framework for this paper.

Do other longitudinal studies using different samples and other test instruments conform to these hypotheses? Table 8.1 presents additional results from the Berkeley Growth Study plus data from the Louisville Twin Study that are consistent with locating stage boundaries at 7, 13, and 21 months (the 2-month stage was not considered in these early reports). This table displays median correlations determined over intervals of various lengths in which some correlations span hypothesized stage boundaries while others cover intervals of the same size but that are totally contained within a stage. If the determinants of individual differences change at a stage boundary, the correlation across a stage boundary should be lower than the correlation within a stage. These data are concordant with such a prediction. When the interval is only a month or two, one would expect such correlations to be rather high regardless of whether they straddle a stage boundary or not. Therefore, the data from the Berkeley Growth Study reported at the top of Table 8.1 are consistent with the hypothesis, but the magnitude of the effect is substantial only when longer intervals are involved. The Louisville results (bottom of Table 8.1) are based upon longer time spans and are more compelling.

The proposed stage boundary at approximately 13 months also shows up in a variety of forms in the literature on Piaget-inspired assessment procedures. Not only is there a break in the developmental function as hypothesized by Piaget (1952) at approximately this time, but the scalability of items within a Piaget-type test is lowest (Kopp, Sigman, & Parmelee, 1974) and there is less concordance in stage rankings across different tasks between 12 and 15 months (Lézine, Stambak, & Casati, 1969).

TABLE 8.1
Average Bayley Test Score Correlations Across Various Age Spans
as a Function of Whether Those Spans Are Within a Stage
or Cut Across a Stage Boundary at 7, 13, or 21 Months of Age

	Age Span in Months [Bayley (1933)[a]]				
	1	2	3	4–9	
Within a stage	0.84	0.75	0.82	0.82	
Across 1 stage boundary	0.80	0.74	0.77	0.68	
	Age Span in Months [Wilson & Harpring (1972)[b]]				
	3	6	9	12	15
Within a stage	0.52				
Across 1 stage boundary	0.45	0.39	0.37		
Across 2 stage boundaries			0.29	0.28	0.20

[a]Averages of 2 to 6 correlations. Data from 1 to 4 months have been omitted because reliability and cross-age *r*s are known to be low for this period for reasons irrelevant to this comparison.
[b]Averages of 1 to 4 correlations for members of twin pairs. Reproduced from McCall, Eichorn, and Hogarty (1977) with permission from authors and publisher (The Society for Research in Child Development).

Therefore, when infants have been repeatedly assessed with tests of general mental performance, transitions in the predominant nature of mental behavior and the pattern of stability of individual differences across age appear at approximately 2, 7, 13, and 21 months.

Empirical (other longitudinal studies).   Kagan (1971, and Chapter 7, this volume) has conducted two large-scale longitudinal studies involving a variety of different assessments of attentional behavior to nonsense designs and facial stimuli as well as habituation and response to discrepancy paradigms over the first 3 years of life. Kagan (Chapter 7, this volume) reports a dip in fixation time to animate and inanimate stimuli and discrepancies plus a decline in search for an auditory stimulus at approximately 7 months of age for American and Guatemalan infants. In addition, the period between 7 and 13 months, an interval defining one stage hypothesized below, was characterized by several unique behavioral events. For example, 7- to 13-month-old infants displayed the maximum amount of anticipatory fixation to a repeated event, searched more for the source of an auditory stimulus, increased their attention to a variety of visual stimuli, and evidenced greater vocal quieting to stimulus discrepancies in an auditory episode. Moreover, search behavior for the locus of an auditory signal correlated most highly across age, and fixation time as a percentage of total looking time changed very little during this 7- to 13-months period.

Whatever cognitive processes are reflected by these diverse measures (Kagan in this volume hypothesizes an increase in memory capability) infants seem to undergo some fundamental change at 7 and 13 months.

DESCRIPTION OF STAGES

Stage I: The Period of the Newborn (0 to 2 Months)

The primary characteristic of the first 2 months of life is the substantial governance of behavior by internal or endogenous factors. Although the infant is responsive to external stimuli and can demonstrate rudimentary learning, most activities are under major internal control, dependent on biological states and inborn dispositions (Karmel & Maisel, 1975). The exercising of inborn behavioral action patterns described by Piaget (1952) exemplifies this period, and Sroufe (in press) has similarly characterized this period from the perspective of emotional development.

Emde and his colleagues (Emde et al., 1976; Emde & Robinson, 1976) and Parmelee and Sigman (1976) have summarized evidence indicating that the neonatal period runs until approximately 2 months when a cluster of psychobiological transformations occur pertaining to the ease and permanence of conditioning, the habituation of response to a repeated stimulus, perceptual strategies and organization, social smiling and eye contact, sleep states, reflexes, responses cortically and visually evoked that are presumably indicative of perceptual information processing, and neuroanatomy.

Because behavior is so governed by internal factors that undergo rapid and massive ontogenetic metamorphoses, there is relatively little stability of individual differences during this period. For example, cross-age correlations of the first principal component from infant tests given monthly do not reach notable levels until after 2 months (McCall, Eichorn, & Hogarty, 1977), the same age that the reliability of such tests attains acceptable standards (McCall et al., 1972). The test behaviors typical of this period include reflexive looking, alerting, and visual tracking.

Stage II: Complete Subjectivity (2 to 7 Months)

The second stage in this proposed scheme represents a shift toward greater influence of exogenous factors, but the infant interacts with the environment from a completely subjective orientation. That is, knowledge of the world is limited to and indistinguishable from the infant's past or present perceptual and motor actions with it. This stage corresponds approximately to Uzgiris's (1976) Stage I, Piaget's (1952) Stages II and III, and Fischer's (in press) sensorimotor levels 1 and 2. The fact that Piaget and Fischer see more than one level of performance occurring within this period suggests that substages are possible.

TABLE 8.2
Hypothesized Stages of Development During Infancy — Stage II

Code............................	Infant/Entity
Stage Description...................	Complete Subjectivity
Approximate Ages..................	2 to 7 Months
Similar to:	
Piaget Stages...................	II, III
Uzgiris Stage...................	I
Fundamental Cognitive Attribute......	The world is known only through the infant's own actions, which are not distinguished from external objects or events.
Representative Test Items............ (BGS Study)	Selectively attends to stimuli and explores objects, especially those producing obvious perceptual consequences: "Looks, reaches, closes on red ring;" "Regards, reaches, picks up cube;" "Lifts cup, by handle, obtains cube;" "Smiling playful response to mirror image;" "Paper play;" "Bangs in play."
Object Notion and Permanence........	Objects are known only as inseparable aspects of the infant's own actions; infant does not solve a visible displacement, returns to place where action was successful.
Attention/Exploration..............	Attends to best blend of new but processable information; explores entities that provide contingent perceptual responses with simple undifferentiated actions but without a separable goal (commonly applies means that have been successful in the past or that are accidentally discovered).
Imitation.........................	Pseudoimitation—imitation only of behaviors already in the infant's repertoire.
Language	Vocalizations; can be increased in frequency by contingent events and imitation.
Social...........................	Schemes may be reinforced with contingent social behaviors; attends to people as stimuli; physically manipulates them (e.g., eyes, nose, mouth) as other objects.

Reproduced from McCall, Eichorn, and Hogarty (1977) with permission of authors and publisher (The Society for Research in Child Development).

Fundamental cognitive attributes. The characteristics of this stage are summarized in Table 8.2. The distinguishing feature of this period is the infant's total subjective or egocentric contact with the environment — the world is known only through direct physical or perceptual commerce with it.

No environmental entity possesses an independence of its own, nor are stimuli or events distinguishable from the child's perceptual or physical actions with them.

Because this stage is characterized by a totally subjective view of the world limited to and synonymous with the infant's contemporaneous perceptual and physical actions with it, I have symbolized this stage with the notation *Infant/Entity* in which "entity" refers to any stimulus (object or person) or stimulus event in the infant's environment, and the slash implies that the infant "knows" such entities only in conjunction with its perceptual or physical actions with them.

General evidence.   In McCall, Eichorn, and Hogarty's (1977) analysis of the Berkeley Growth Study, the first principal components of the mental tests given after 2 months of age were consistently intercorrelated until a relative dip in the cross-age stability of individual differences at 8 months. Moreover, the fundamental character of the first principal components was essentially the same throughout this period. The items loading most prominently on these components reflected selective attention to stimuli, direct visual and physical exploration of objects, and manipulative acts that contingently produce obvious perceptual consequences (see Table 8.2).

In addition to high cross-age correlations during this period for the first principal components of standardized infant tests, there are other reports that correlations between behaviors involving the acquisition of stimulus information and the influencing of the environment are related within an age during this period. For example, Uzgiris (1973) and Kopp et al. (1974) observed correlations between the infant's tendency to obtain a partly or totally covered object (Object Permanency Scale) and the likelihood of attempting to locate a sound, follow a trajectory, grasp an object, or look for a fallen object (Object Relations in Space Scale)—behaviors similar to those characterizing this stage as described in Table 8.2. These were the highest correlations observed in the 5- to 8-month age period. Therefore, there seems to be some cohesiveness across specific tasks and contexts with respect to the predominant mental behavior during this stage.

The exploration of environmental entities that characterizes this period, despite its subjectivity, serves the first function of mental behavior—acquiring information (Weisler & McCall, 1976). Moreover, the manipulative production of contingent stimulation (Rovee & Rovee, 1969) also contributes in rudimentary form to the second function — influencing the environment. However, true influencing is not possible at this stage because there is no separation of means and ends. That which is influenced is indistinguishable from the infant's actions. Therefore, although exploratory and manipulative behavior are reinforced by contingent perceptual events, there is no goal-oriented influencing.

Memory. The infant in this stage can obviously learn and remember. Numerous reviews of the literature on infant learning are available (e.g., Brackbill & Koltsova, 1967; Fitzgerald & Porges, 1971; Lipsitt, 1963; Sameroff, 1971), and recent studies show the infant's recognition memory for past stimulus events to be quite good (Cohen & Gelber, 1975; Fagan, Chapter 4, this volume). However, although the infant is certainly capable of recognition memory provoked by the presence of stimuli identical or similar to entities encoded into memory, to my knowledge no evidence suggests that the infant of this age period retrieves a memory from storage in the absence of an eliciting stimulus. Out of sight is out of mind (see Kagan, Chapter 7, this volume). Sroufe (in press) has made similar points, using the literature on affect as a base.

Object notion and permanence. Because objects exist for the infant only in conjunction with perceptual and motor actions and because the ability to remember an object in the absence of a provoking stimulus is not yet present, the infant cannot solve the object permanency test. Typically, object permanency is assessed by getting the infant to locate repeatedly an attractive object under a cover and then hiding the object under an alternative occluder. (The task is called a *visible displacement* if the infant is allowed to view the second hiding.) When presented with a single visible displacement, infants in this stage typically do not search at all for the object or they look under the initial cover, despite the fact that they watched the object being hid under the second cover. Infants do not usually search for the object under the second cover until 8 to 10 months of age (e.g., Appleton, Clifton, & Goldberg, 1975; Corman & Escalona, 1969; Gratch & Landers, 1971; Kopp et al., 1974; Uzgiris, 1976; Uzgiris & Hunt, 1975). Presumably, the failure to solve this problem is attributable to the infant's conception of the world that is tied directly to actions with it, and this reliance on actions overrides the perceptual sighting of the object being hid in another place. Hence, infants search where their actions led them to find the object in the past.

Attention/exploration. As in the previous period, the infant attends to stimulus information that matches the neurological organization of the perceptual system (Karmel & Maisel, 1975) and pays special attention to events that represent a moderate departure from well-remembered standards (McCall, Kennedy, & Appelbaum, 1977; McCall, 1971; McCall & McGhee, 1976; Weisler & McCall, 1976). Moreover, infants of these ages manipulatively favor objects in the environment that provide contingent perceptual consequences (McCall, 1974; Rovee & Rovee, 1969; Watson & Ramey, 1972; Weisler & McCall, 1976). However, the child's exploration is seriously limited by the cognitive inability to distinguish between actions, objects, and the consequences of actions. As a result, exploratory behaviors are not well differentiated or extensively molded to the specific nature of the object. Although particular actions may be increased or decreased in frequency by a contingent outcome, they are not easily modified qualitatively by the specific nature of that feedback (Uzgiris, 1976). Moreover, there is no systematic, goal-directed examination or investigation of an object.

An important implication of the ability to alter the frequency of a behavior is the potential of the infant to learn not to respond, a state called "learned helplessness" in its extreme form (Seligman & Maier, 1967). If influencing the environment is a fundamental disposition of the organism and a cornerstone of mental behavior, then an infant who lives in a totally noncontingent environment might never develop such a disposition or extinguish a preexisting tendency. The literature indicates that this is possible in human infants (Ramey, Starr, Pallas, Whitten, & Reed, 1975) children (Dweck & Repucci, 1973), rats (McCulloch & Bruner, 1939), dogs (Seligman & Maier, 1967), and human adults (Thornton & Jacobs, 1971). Moreover, infants who are given special experience in controlling stimulation subsequently learn to increase their response rate to other contingent stimulation (Ramey et al., 1975), and infants given experience with *non*contingent stimulation later may fail to learn a simple response contingency that infants with no particular experience acquire. Therefore, although I believe that the disposition to influence is largely an inborn tendency, it obviously requires environmental nurturance.

Imitation.   The act of imitating a new behavior displayed by another individual demands that infants be able to distinguish between themselves and the other person. Therefore, it is not surprising that no evidence exists (to my knowledge) demonstrating that infants in the first 7 months of life readily imitate behaviors not already in their repertoire. However, there are several reports that young infants, even in the first months of life, can increase the frequency of tongue protrusions, vocalizations, and simple limb movements that already exist in their behavioral repertoire as a function of seeing another person perform such actions (Gardner & Gardner, 1970; Maratos, 1973; Meltzoff & Moore, 1977). I prefer to call this behavior *social facilitation,* not imitation.

Language.   Vocalizations can be increased by reinforcement (Rheingold, Gewirtz, & Ross, 1959). However, new sounds or sound combinations are not typically produced by imitation or reinforcement during this stage, and the imitation of vocal behavior in general tends to lag behind gestural imitation for reasons yet unknown (McCall, 1975; McCall, Parke, & Kavanaugh, 1977; Uzgiris, 1971).

Social behavior.   I believe that early social behavior develops within the limitations of the infant's cognitive system and the availability of social experiences. Thus, the human face represents an optimal stimulus to be explored by the infant—not because it is a face, but because it embodies in a single stimulus numerous attributes that are known to capture the attention of infants even when those attributes are presented in the form of inanimate stimuli such as brightness contrast, contour, circularity, dark dots, movement, sound, and the like (Fagan, Chapter 4, this volume; Schaffer, 1971). Moreover, reciprocal imitation (i.e., facilitation) games and contingent responsiveness of parents can lead to simple conditioning of vocal and gestural behavior that may foster social blossoming and attachment (Schaffer, 1971; Watson, 1972). Finally, smiling falls increasingly under greater exogenous control, leading to more positive interactions with the caretaker (Sroufe, in press). However, the infant's social behaviors, although more truly social and subject to parental reinforcement, are essentially egocentric: Infants do not distinguish between their actions and the social consequences of those actions. That is, separate social entities possessing their own dynamic properties do not exist for the infant in this stage.

Environmental correlates. Since the predominant tendency during this period is the attention to and exploration of stimulus information and response-contingent events, one might expect a correlation between the presence of stimuli in the infant's environment and performance on infant tests (assuming the tests have items similar to those described earlier for this period). Correlations can be found. For example, the amount of visual experience and the internal decor and colorfulness of the home were related to 7-month Uzgiris-Hunt (Piaget-inspired) performance (Wachs, Uzgiris, & Hunt, 1971), and the presence of a variety of play objects, especially responsive toys, showed correlations with contemporary and future test performance from 5 to 36 months of age (Baldwin, Kalhorn, & Breese, 1945; Bradley & Caldwell, 1976; Elardo, Bradley, & Caldwell, 1975; Moore, 1968; Wachs, 1976; Yarrow, Rubenstein, Pedersen, & Jankowski, 1972). Of course, the infant and toddler must be able to explore this varied environment, so it is not surprising to find correlates between freedom to explore and mental test performance (Baldwin et al., 1945; Beckwith, 1971; Wachs, 1976).

Stimulation can also be social, and the variety of social stimulation (e.g., play, encouragement of motor acts, range of affect displayed by parents, and number of different physical settings in which social relations occur) showed more correlations than other measures of experience with certain item clusters from the Bayley Infant Scale for upper-middle-class, black, 5-month-old infants (Yarrow et al., 1972). Interestingly, these social stimulation variables revealed their highest relationship with Bayley items in which the infant reached for objects (a cluster that Yarrow et al. termed *goal orientation)* and with items reflecting Piagetian secondary circular responses (the repetition of responses producing contingent perceptual events), actions that I suggest characterize mental behavior at this age (see Table 8.2). In another study of 40 adopted children administered the Cattell test at 6 months of age, Yarrow (1963) found rather high correlations with mental test performance for ratings of stimulus adaptation ($r = 0.85$), achievement stimulation ($r = 0.72$), and social stimulation ($r = 0.65$).

These data imply that experiences directly exercising the mental functions of acquiring information and influencing the environment show correlations with mental test performance during this period. However, the stimulation must match the capabilities and limitations of the infant in this stage. Therefore, distinctive stimulus events, responsive objects and people, and varied environments correlate with mental performance, but parental language model does not (although correlations are observed in later stages when language becomes a salient behavior of the infant). The fact that the specific environmental factors that correlate with mental test performance during this period are behaviors and experiences that conceivably match and promote the specific skills proposed as primary attributes of the infant's mental behavior supports the interpretative emphasis given these characteristics as major attributes of mental behavior at this time.

Stage III: Separation of Means from Ends (7 to 13 Months)

Stage III, the separation of means from ends, characterizes the infant between approximately 7 and 13 months. It corresponds roughly to Piaget's Stage IV, Uzgiris's Stage II, and Fischer's sensorimotor levels 2 and 3. Its important features are summarized in Table 8.3.

Fundamental cognitive attribute.   Several cognitive changes occur at approximately 7 months. In my view, the most fundamental of these is the beginning of the infant's emerging ability to distinguish between means and ends and between the infant's actions and the environmental entities acted upon. However, although environmental entities are discriminable from the infant's actions with them, they are not yet totally independent from those actions. Therefore, the infant cognizes that actions and their consequences are different, but objects and people are not yet totally independent, dynamic entities, and the infant's knowledge about the environment remains intimately tied to actions with it. Therefore, I have symbolically coded this stage as *Infant* ⟶ *Entity*. The arrow implies both the distinction between infant and entity as well as the fact that entities are still known through the infant's action with them.

General evidence.   In many respects, this period is a transitional one. Seven months marks the beginning of the separation of means from ends,

TABLE 8.3

Hypothesized Stages of Development During Infancy — Stage III

Code.............................	Infant ⟶ Entity
Stage Description....................	Separation of Means from Ends
Approximate Ages...................	7 to 13 Months
Similar to:	
Piaget Stage.....................	IV
Uzgiris Stage....................	II
Fundamental Cognitive Attribute......	Means and ends (cause, effect) are now distinguished, but the world is still known only through the infant's own actions with it.
Representative Test Items............. (BGS Study)	Manipulative exploration plus imitation and vocal behavior: "Looks, reaches, closes on red ring;" "Regards, reaches, picks up cube;" "Manipulates and rings bell;" "Pulls string, imitates ring;" "Smiling, playful response to mirror image;" "Imitates scribbling;" "Listens, imitates familiar words;" "Vocal interjections;" "Says several syllables;" "Says da-da or equivalent."
Object Notion and Permanence........	Objects are now distinguished from the infant's action, but objects are still known predominantly in association with infant's own actions; solves a single visible displacement.
Attention/Exploration...............	Action schemes are now distinguished from objects, goals can direct actions, means can be generalized to new ends, action schemes can be coordinated and are differentiated according to the nature of the object.
Imitation.........................	Imitation of only those new responses that bear some similarity to previous action schemes; approximates those behaviors by applying familiar action schemes.
Language.........................	Vocalizations may be generalized from one context to another.
Social............................	Separation and stranger distress begin because of the infant's response uncertainty engendered by a person who is now distinguished from the infant's actions and who is accorded permanence upon departure; people are now objects to be explored, physically manipulated, and imitated.

but complete independence between the infant and external entities does not occur until the beginning of the next stage at approximately 13 months. Therefore, many new behaviors make their developmental entrance at approximately 7 to 8 months but do not become fully articulated until later. Moreover, the first principal components of the Berkeley tests are defined by several behaviors including manipulative exploration, sensorimotor and vocal imitation, and means/ends differentiation (Table 8.3). Despite the gradual growth and transitional character of this stage, correlations in mental test scores during this period are relatively high (Kagan, Chapter 7, this volume; Kopp et al., 1974; McCall, Eichorn, & Hogarty, 1977) with delimiting points of relative instability at approximately 7 and 13 months (Emde et al., 1976; Kagan, Chapter 7, this volume; McCall, Eichorn, & Hogarty, 1977).

Memory.   The infant is now capable of operating with a memory of an entity in the absence of eliciting stimuli (see Kagan, Chapter 7, this volume). In an exemplary study, Millar (1974) allowed 6- or 9-month-old infants to be rewarded with sound and light changes contingent upon moving a manipulandum. However, for some subjects, a distinctive green ring marked the location where the rewards would appear, whereas this mediating stimulus was not available for other subjects. The reinforcements were effective for the 9-month-olds with or without the mediating stimulus, but the 6-month-old infants increased their response rate only if the green stimulus was present. Millar concluded that 9-month-old infants were capable of making spontaneous use of centrally held information and relating it to ongoing activities, a conclusion shared by Schaffer (1971).

Object notion and permanence.   The fact that entities in the external world are beginning to take on an identity of their own apart from action with them plus the increased memorial capability permit the infant to cognize the existence of objects even when they are out of hand and out of sight. Therefore, a single visible displacement can be solved—the infant immediately heads to the second cover after seeing an object placed there rather than doing so only after exploring the first cover (Corman & Escalona, 1969; Décarie, 1965; Gratch & Landers, 1971; Kopp et al., 1974; Uzgiris, 1976; Uzgiris & Hunt, 1975). However, an invisible displacement (i.e., after several hidings of an object beneath a cover, the object is surreptitiously hid beneath an alternative cover) or a series of successive visible displacements apparently remove the object too far beyond the infant's memory capability and are not solved forthrightly.

Kagan (Chapter 7, this volume) has laid heavy theoretical emphasis on the proposition that the infant's ability to use the memory of an object in the absence of an eliciting stimulus is the salient cognitive advance that permits object permanence and separation protest. My position is that the capacity to retain, retrieve, and use the memory of a stimulus in the absence of that stimulus is a necessary condition for object permanence, but the infant's searching for the object reveals that means and ends are distinguished and that the object exists beyond the infant's actions. Both memorial factors and means/ends differentiation are fundamental to object permanence and separation protest (see Chapter 7).

Attention/exploration/play. Because actions are now distinguished from environmental entities, the infant is able to generalize an action pattern from one entity to other similar entities, action schemes can be coordinated with one another in the exploration of an object, and the nature of exploration becomes progressively more tailored to the specific physical features of the object (McCall, 1974; Uzgiris, 1976). As a result, the infant's exploration of objects appears to be more goal-directed; there is a more systematic search for information and for the possible consequences that can be elicited from an object. Moreover, the infant can now modify the quality of action with an object as a result of feedback from the object—a process previously rendered impossible by the cognitive unity of action–entity. These new skills greatly increase the infant's ability to acquire information and make possible the first attempts to truly influence the environment (e.g., secondary circular responses).

Distinguishing means from ends and the decentering of thought from action allows the infant to use two objects simultaneously in some type of joint play. Fenson, Kagan, Kearsley, & Zelazo (1976) observed 7- and 9-month-old children playing with a tea set and recorded the number of "simple relational acts," a category consisting of associations between two objects but not necessarily in an appropriate way (e.g., touching a spoon against a pot, hitting the lid against the side of the cup, etc.). Although only 9% of the 7-month-old infants displayed one or more instances of such simple relational acts, 92% of the 9-month-old infants did so. However, it was not until 13 months that substantial numbers of infants used two objects together in an appropriate manner (e.g., placing the lid on the pot, the cup on the saucer, the spoon in the cup, etc.) or imitated socially appropriate behavior (e.g., eating, drinking, pouring, or stirring), acts that presumably require complete independence of action and the environment.

Imitation. The imitation of another person's novel behavior requires the child to internalize an event that the child has not directly acted on and to use that encoded perception to guide subsequent behavior. Because this stage marks the beginning of such a distinction, the imitation of new behaviors, in contrast to the facilitation through modeling of behaviors already in the infant's repertoire, becomes more and more likely during this period. At first, the infant may vocalize or gesture after a behavior is modeled, but there may be little or no correspondence between the child's actions and the details of the model's behavior (Uzgiris, 1976; Uzgiris & Hunt, 1975) unless the target action is very similar to behaviors already in the infant's repertoire. Then the capability of modest generalizations from previously practiced action schemes to new situations emerges, followed by the imitation of relatively new simple behaviors near the end of this period (Abravanel, Levan–Goldschmidt, & Stevenson, 1976; McCall, 1975; McCall, Parke, & Kavanaugh, 1977).

Language. Athough vocal imitation lags behind gestural imitation (McCall, 1975; McCall, Parke, & Kavanaugh, 1977; Uzgiris, 1971), the infant's vocalization patterns undergo development comparable to that described in the foregoing paragraph. Near the end of this period, infants frequently learn to utter sounds that adults interpret as words. I predominantly regard these sounds as reinforced operants that are not accorded a cognitive existence apart from their utterance until Stage IV.

Social behavior.   The distinction between means and ends that produces the advances in exploration and influencing described earlier can also be applied to social entities. Thus, infants now take a more active role in initiating social interaction (Escalona, 1968; Sander, 1962) and play social games (Sroufe & Wunsch, 1972). Emotions become more articulated (Sroufe, in press), including the expression of wariness and fear when the infant is separated from its caretaker or confronted by a stranger (Sroufe, 1977).

The cognitive advance of this stage permits *response uncertainty* to occur. Prior to this point, when the infant's action and its consequence are not distinguished cognitively by the infant, response uncertainty cannot exist because action and consequence are not separable. Once such a distinction is made, then responses can be understood to have several possible consequences and situations can be understood to require one of several possible responses. I believe that wariness, fear, crying, and seeking familiar contexts (i.e., "security") are the inherent consequences of a state of response uncertainty.

With respect to separation protest, consistent with Stage III, the data suggest a typical onset age of 7 to 8 months (Ainsworth, Bell, & Stayton, 1972; Schaffer & Callender, 1959; Schaffer & Emerson, 1964; Stayton, Ainsworth, & Main, 1973; Tennes & Lampl, 1964). Wariness exhibited prior to this age appears to be an inherent response to the departure of *any* conspecific (Schaffer & Emerson, 1964; Stayton et al., 1973). Kagan (Chapter 7, this volume) has summarized the case for assuming that a necessary condition for separation protest is the infant's new ability to remember an entity without the presence of associated cues. Although such a memorial

capacity is obviously a necessary requirement, I do not believe it is sufficient. Why does the infant display wariness rather than some other response?
Memory alone cannot explain this disposition. I believe the wariness is a
consequence of the infant's uncertainty over what response will bring the
return of the departing or absent parent.

I share my belief that response uncertainty is instrumental in stranger
protest as well as separation wariness with Shaffer, Greenwood, and Parry
(1972) and Sroufe (1977), who has recently contributed a penetrating review
of the literature which need not be recapitulated here. True wariness tends
to occur initially between 7 and 9 months (Sroufe, 1977), again at the beginning of Stage III. Moreover, it is not simply the sight of a stranger that produces protest, that stranger must approach, intrude upon, or touch the infant (Sroufe, 1977) — circumstances that are likely to instigate response
uncertainty. Moreover, Bronson (1972) has proposed that infants who can
resolve their response uncertainty in the face of a stranger by crawling away,
display less upset than those who are restrained from so responding.

Evidence implicating response uncertainty in separation protest is
flimsy, but the propensity to display wariness and upset at separation is
reduced when the infant has a response to make—typically crawling after the
parent (Ainsworth et al., 1972; Coates, Anderson, & Hartup, 1972; Stayton
et al., 1973).

Direct experimental tests of the proposition that response uncertainty is a
necessary factor in stranger anxiety have been rare, but a recent study by
Rafman (1974) is instructive, despite certain limitations. Rafman reasoned
that if an infant shows fear because of uncertainty over what response to
make, then fear should not be displayed as frequently if the stranger
behaves in a manner that reminds the infant of a specific response in the infant's repertoire. Therefore, each mother in the study was asked to show the
experimenter simple games she typically played with her baby that required
a specific response from infant (e.g., peek-a-boo, pat-a-cake, ring around
the rosy, question and answer games, etc.). In the test phase the infants
were approached three times, once by the mother, once by the stranger acting as a stranger, and once by the stranger imitating the behaviors taught
by the infants' mothers. Eleven of the 17 infants (8 to 15 months of age)
displayed a negative response when the stranger behaved idiosyncratically,
and all of them responded more positively to the stranger when that stranger
displayed behavior that had been associated with specific responses of the
infant. Moreover, Rafman reported that when the stranger first began to
imitate the mothers' behavior, infants tended to freeze and look puzzled until *they tried out* the previously associated response several times. The smile
or other positive response always came after such response exploration.
Therefore, it was as if the infant were faced with a situation in which a
response was required, some uncertainty prevailed concerning what to do,

the behavior of the stranger elicited the memory of a response the infant had made in previous circumstances, the infant tried out the response, and only then did the infant show a positive reaction to the stranger.

The theoretical argument can be summarized as follows. At approximately 7 months of age, the child's cognitive development first permits the separation of means from ends and infant from environment. Whereas previously the infant's response and its consequences were unitary, now their separation introduces an element of response uncertainty — either, "will this response have a desired consequence?" and/or "which of several responses shall I make?" Fear will be displayed only when the stimulus condition provokes such response uncertainty—that is, when the stimulus (the stranger) prompts the infant to action and when the infant has sufficient experience with such a stimulus to attempt to generalize several previously learned response patterns to such a new stimulus.

Readers should notice that the foregoing discussion was focused on hypothesizing that response uncertainty made possible by the emergence of the distinction between action and the environmental entity acted on contributes to the developmental function of separation and stranger protest. Other factors (e.g., the affective) also contribute (Sroufe, 1977; in press), and this discussion has not considered individual differences at all.

Stage IV: Objectification of Environmental Entities (13 to 21 Months)

In Stage IV the infant can cognize objects quite independently of actions with them. As such, the stage is roughly comparable to Piaget's Stage V and parts of VI, Uzgiris's Stage III, and Fischer's levels 3 and 4. The characteristics of this stage are summarized in Table 8.4.

Fundamental cognitive attribute. With the advent of Stage IV, means and ends become totally separable, and environmental entities take on an independent existence of their own—that is, the existence and capabilities of entities are not dependent on or tied to the child's actions with them. The most important implication of this development is that infants are able to operate mentally on entities in the environment without the necessity of direct physical action with those entities, and therefore it is possible for the infant to appreciate simple relationships between two entities without having to act on either component. I have symbolized this ability by *Entity–Entity,* in which the dash represents an association or relationship but one that is not necessarily defined by the action of the infant on one or the other entity. In brief, this is the start of serious mental decentration of the infant from the environment.

TABLE 8.4
Hypothesized Stages of Development During Infancy — Stage IV

Code.............................	Entity–Entity
Stage Description...................	Objectification of Environmental Entities
Approximate Ages..................	13 to 21 Months
Similar to:	
Piaget Stage....................	V
Uzgiris Stage....................	III
Fundamental Cognitive Attribute......	Objects and events now have an existence and even dynamic character independent of the infant's own actions, and those entities can be compared and associated with one another without the infant acting on them.
Representative Test Items............ (BGS Study)	Consensual vocabulary and perceptual relations: "Names 1 to 3 objects;" "Names 1 to 6 pictures;" "Points to 3 to 7 pictures;" "Gesell form board;" "Bayley board, correct and speed;" " Wallin peg board, pegs and speed;" "Names watch (fifth to third trial)."
Object Notion and Permanence........	Objects have an existence of their own and apart from the infant's own actions; infant solves a series of successive visible displacements.
Attention/Exploration..............	Schemes are independent of available objects and context; child experiments with causal chains by deliberately varying actions with objects and modifies action as a function of feedback on the outcome relative to goal.
Imitation........................	Since action schemes are independent of entities and since Entity–Entity relations can be cognized without action, true imitation of new behavior is possible.
Language	Separation and independence of external objects from actions permit consensual verbal labeling of entities.
Social...........................	The intensity of distress to both separation and strangers peaks during this stage because the infant can more fully appreciate the absent rather than the departing parent and can understand the implication of a stranger who carries with him associations and dynamic properties; it is now possible to influence people without touching them through imitation/modeling and vocal/verbal behavior.

Reproduced from McCall, Eichorn, and Hogarty (1977) with permission of authors and publisher (The Society for Research in Child Development).

General evidence.   Shortly after the first year of life, dramatic shifts in capabilities occur, often accompanied by radical upheavals in the consistency of individual differences across age (Bayley, 1933; Fenson et al., 1976; Kagan, 1971, 1976; King & Seegmiller, 1973; Kopp et al., 1974; Lezine, 1973; Lezine et al., 1969; Lowe, 1975; McCall, Eichorn, & Hogarty, 1977; Uzgiris, 1976).

Correlations across two different tasks both requiring Entity–Entity relationships should be observed during this period. For example, Uzgiris (1973) found some of the largest correlations (0.61 to 0.85) during the 14- to 19-month period across Piaget-type object relations tasks (building a tower, using a string to obtain objects, or being aware of the location of people) and the development of means (infant wants the experimenter to repeat an action with an object, imitates a new behavior, etc.). Similarly, Kopp et al. (1974) observed the highest cross-task correlations during the 13- to 18-month period to occur between exploratory behavior and means–ends relationships. Correlating scores on seven Hunt–Uzgiris subtests across 14-, 18-, and 22-month assessments, King and Seegmiller (1973) found only five of 21 correlations to be significant, but the largest cross-age r was for the causality scale (which assessed Entity–Entity relationships in causal sequences) between 14 and 18 months.

Entity–Entity relations should permit children to group objects according to similarities or differences in their form, color, or function. Two studies support the proposition that such behavior begins with the onset of Stage IV and increases during this period (Nelson, 1973a and Chapter 13, this volume; Ricciuti, 1965). Moreover, Nelson (1973a and Chapter 13, this volume) suggests that infants in the second year of life group objects that are similar in function before they group objects similar in form or color, presumably supporting the proposition that Entity–Entity relationships grow out of a previous stage in which knowledge of the world is dependent on active physical commerce with it.

Object notion and permanence.   Because objects now have a true existence of their own independent of the infant's actions with them, a succession of visible displacements can be followed (Corman & Escalona, 1969; Décarie, 1965; Kopp et al., 1974; Uzgiris, 1976; Uzgiris & Hunt, 1975). However, at this stage the infant cannot make *inferences* regarding the relationship between external objects. Therefore, a series of invisible (rather than visible) displacements, which presumably requires such a symbolic inference, cannot be solved at the beginning of this stage.

Attention/exploration/play.   The exploration of objects now appears to be quite deliberate and goal-oriented, deriving from the fact that action schemes are independent of external objects. The infant can search through a repertoire of exploratory subroutines to find one that suits a perceived goal at a particular moment. Moreover, true experimental variation of actions with objects occurs for the purpose of observing their diverse consequences, and such feedback is incorporated into the system to modify qualitatively further exploration (Uzgiris, 1976).

Fascination with the novel takes on new meaning because novelty now resides within the object and is no longer simply a new consequence to old action patterns. The salience of novelty or discrepancy is not unique to this stage (e.g., Friedman, 1972; Friedman, Bruno, & Vietze, 1974), but the ways in which the infant investigates it and accords it a status independent of action are new.

Three developmental studies of the qualitative nature of children's play converge on a common transition at the beginning of this stage. Specifically, children incorporate into their play appropriate relations between two external entities. That is, whereas prior to this stage two objects may have been brought into some physical contiguity with each other, there was no obvious appropriate relationship involved. Now there is a clear relationship between these two external entities—for example, the lid is put on the teapot, the cup placed on the saucer, the spoon is placed in the cup (Fenson et al., 1976; Lézine, 1973; Lowe, 1975). Fenson et al. (1976) reported especially impressive data documenting this transition. Whereas 92% of their 9-month infants displayed behaviors involving the association of two objects in *non*appropriate ways, only 33% of the 9-month infants associated objects in appropriate ways. By 13 months, 100% of the infants displayed such appropriate relational activities. These data imply that although the 9-month infant has the motor skills to bring objects together, it is not until 12 to 13 months that infants are mentally able to relate two external entities to one another appropriately.

Moreover, the objectification of external entities permits the child to imitate seriously behaviors seen in others (see page 211). Therefore, we would expect play to include socially appropriate behaviors the infant has observed in others, including eating, drinking, stirring, sweeping, and the like (Fenson et al., 1976; Lézine, 1973; Lowe, 1975; Watson & Fischer, 1977). These actions of the infant have often been called *symbolic* because they are applied to replicas of real objects (miniaturized utensils and cleaning implements) and because there is an imaginary component (e.g., "pretend" food, tea, or dirt). However, it is not clear that the "symbolic" entity is truly symbolized by the child until later (e.g., Stage V). For example, when a 13-month-old child pours "tea," is this merely an imitative action the child does with a teapot and cup or does the child actually imagine the tea? When 13-month-old children sweep with a broom, do they sweep imaginary dirt? Moreover, if the tea or food were really imagined, why is it that only the children themselves in this stage drink or eat "imaginary" entities and uniformly do *not* pretend to have a doll eat or drink until 21 months (Lézine, 1973; Lowe, 1975; Watson & Fischer, 1977)? Perhaps the child does not yet have true symbolism and is only performing appropriate actions generalized to miniature objects that are not accompanied by imaginary elements.

Imitation.   Because actions are independent from external entities, infants can now readily cognize the association between an action displayed by another person and the consequences of that action by observation alone. Therefore, they can easily imitate elementary events not currently in their repertoire. Focused studies of the imitation of simple novel motor events indicate their emergence and rise of frequency during this period (Uzgiris, 1976; Uzgiris & Hunt, 1975). For example, McCall, Parke, & Kavanaugh (1977) found that 12-month-old infants imitated 28% of the elementary motor actions modeled by a strange adult, but they imitated 76% at 24 months of age. Interestingly, when the modeled event involved a coordinated sequence of two actions, imitation did not begin to occur until 18 to 24 months. Presumably, the objectification of entities in the external world must be fairly firm before novel Entity–Entity relationships can be readily encoded and used to guide subsequent behavior. In addition, if a delay was introduced between modeling and the infant's performance, imitation of coordinated sequences of actions in this deferred context did not occur until at least 24 months of age (Stage V). Presumably, as the symbolic and memory demands of the task increased, the age of performance also increased.

Language.   I believe that the onset of consensual vocabulary occurs during this stage with the permission of Entity–Entity cognition. Although a child's verbal utterances may be shaped by reinforcement to correspond to words and may be used appropriately by the infant, he cannot acquire vocabulary through observation until Entity–Entity cognition is available. Only then can the infant cognitively relate a sound with an external object, preserving the independence of each. Given the newly emergent skills of imitation and consensual vocabulary, it is not surprising that marked increases in elicited and spontaneous imitation of vocabulary occur near the end of this stage (Stewart & Hamilton, 1976). Nelson (Chapter 13, this volume) has described more fully the language behavior of children of this stage.

Social behavior.   A major accomplishment of this stage is the infant's appreciation of the complete separation of action and the environmental entities acted on, even to the point that external entities may be understood to possess their own dynamic properties — they act independently of the infant's own actions. According to the analysis made previously, distress reactions should peak at approximately 12 to 14 months of age for both separation (Ainsworth, Bell, & Stayton, 1971; Ainsworth et al., 1972; Stayton et al., 1973) and stranger situations (Benjamin, 1963; Greenberg, Hillman, & Grice, 1973; Morgan & Ricciuti, 1969; Scarr & Salapatek, 1970). As more experience with response alternatives accumulates and symbolic processes become available at approximately 21 months of age (see page 213), these phenomena should cease (Scarr & Salapatek, 1970; Tennes & Lampl, 1964).

A fundamental transition in social behavior as well as in mental activity is the shift from a dependence on physical interaction with the environment to interaction with that environment at a distance. In the context of peer–peer social relations, infants prior to this stage deal with one another (if at all) in a physical manner, typically a struggle over a toy desired by each. Social relations are largely egocentric and revolve around the child's actions or the object of those actions rather than around the social partner. However, when the child is capable of Entity–Entity relationships, the exploration of environmental entities becomes more systematic, flexible, and goal-oriented, and the infant is able to imitate new behaviors observed in other individuals. Therefore, another child is now a dynamic entity independent of the infant and worthy of being explored with the new skills now available. The lack of dependence on physical action as well as the ability to cognize relationships between two entities without directly acting on either permits the child to interact socially with another being at a distance, without touching.

McCall, Parke, and Kavanaugh (1977) conducted an experimental study to determine whether the infant's perception of being imitated would lead to greater social influencing than if the other individual contingently performed a qualitatively different act. The experiment involved 15-, 18-, and 24-month old infants who were permitted to play with pairs of toys. When an infant displayed a preordained target behavior with one of the toys, the adult exerimenter either forthrightly imitated the infant's behavior or performed a qualitatively different behavior with the other member of the toy pair. Presumably, if infants detected that their behavior had influenced the experimenter, the infant would again perform an action and then pause to observe the examiner's subsequent behavior—as if to ask, "Will my action again produce a consequence in this adult's behavior?" This behavioral scenario occurred more frequently at 15 and especially at 18 months when the infant was imitated by the examiner than when the examiner performed a nonimitative behavior contingent on the infant's initial action.

Therefore, it is possible that reciprocal imitation games present the infant with an experience maximally conducive to the discovery that the child's behavior influences another without touching the other. When such reciprocal imitation games are played, the infant of this stage may develop a cognition of social influencing that is independent from specific actions and specific social entities, an ability not possible until Entity–Entity relations have evolved.

Environmental correlates. Prior to this stage, the infant's commerce with the environment was restricted to perceptual and physical actions with entities and their immediate consequences. Therefore, it was not surprising that the variety of stimulation and the presence of responsive objects and people correlated with infant mental test performance. Now in an epoch of Entity–Entity relations, ratings of the adequacy of verbal stimulation and the verbal responsivity of the parent first began to correlate with mental-test performance, which is also more verbal in character (Beckwith, 1971; Elardo et al., 1975; Wachs, 1976; Wachs et al., 1971).

If social stimuli become maximally intriguing to the infant because of their dynamic and variable quality during this period, then one might expect relations between parental involvement with the infant and mental test performance to increase throughout this period. Although the nature of the social involvement with a parent may be different for males and females (McCall, in press), a variety of studies shows relationships between mental performance on the one hand and maternal involvement and the child's social experience on the other (e.g., Beckwith, 1971; Bradley & Caldwell, 1976; Caldwell, Heider, & Kaplan, 1966; Elardo et al., 1975; Haviland, 1976; Yarrow, 1963; Yarrow et al., 1972; Yarrow & Pedersen, 1976). However, it should be observed that parental involvement and social variety provide experiences salient to mental performance in all stages described here, and therefore it is not surprising that such variables have been found to correlate with contemporary and future mental performance beginning at least as young as 5 months. Nevertheless, these relationships attain their highest levels at the end of Stage IV and thereafter, at which time the mental test becomes more verbal and when experience relevant to such verbal assessments derives predominantly from such social interaction.

Stage V: Symbolic Relations (21 + Months)

The final stage to be described is that of symbolic relations, a phase similar to Piaget's Stage VI, Uzgiris's Stage IV, and Fischer's sensorimotor level 4. This stage emerges initially at approximately 21 months, and its features are outlined in Table 8.5.

Fundamental cognitive attribute. The major advance characterizing the onset of this stage is that relations between entities can exist independent of specific actions and of specific entities, and the relationship itself as well as the associated entities may be symbolic. Thus, the child is able to relate two symbols or comprehend a symbolic relation between entities, symbolic or otherwise.

General evidence. Because longitudinal studies begun early in infancy do not often persist through the second year of life, evidence that a major

TABLE 8.5
Hypothesized Stages of Development During Infancy — Stage V

Stage Description...................	Symbolic relations
Approximate Ages..................	21+ Months
Similar to:	
Piaget Stage....................	VI
Uzgiris Stage...................	IV
Fundamental Cognitive Attribute......	Relations can exist independent of actions and specific entities (i.e., as concepts), and the relation and/or entities can be symbolic.
Representative Test Items............ (BGS Study)	Consensual vocabulary, symbolic perceptual and verbal relations, verbal fluency: "Points to 3 to 7 pictures;" "Names 1 to 6 pictures;" "Points to size opposites;" "Names watch (fifth to third trial);" "Understands 2 to 5 prepositions using objects;" "Imitates/copies block structures;" "Recalls 1 to 9 object pictures;" "Form cards, match-to-sample;" "Names action–agents, levels I to VI;" "Describes pictures, levels I to VI;" "Describes pictures, levels I to IV;" "Recognizes 1 to 7 remembered forms;" "Verbalizes 1 to 7 opposites."
Object Notion and Permanence.......	Objects and relationships between them may be symbolized and mentally manipulated; solves a series of successive invisible displacements by inferring location of object.
Attention/Exploration..............	Relations between certain entities exist in the abstract and can be applied to a totally new context or to new entities, entities may be symbolized and not actually present, problems can be solved by mental combination (i.e., "insight") in anticipating outcome.
Imitation........................	Infant can now imitate sequences of actions, defer imitation, imitate isolated constituents from total modeled sequence, and imitate an action in a new context.
Language	Symbolism and abstraction of relationships apart from actions or specific objects permits true two-word utterances.
Social..........................	Goal-directed social influencing through mental combinations by words that express agent–action and other directives.

Reproduced from McCall, Eichorn, and Hogarty (1977) with permission of authors and publisher (The Society for Research in Child Development).

transition occurs between 18 and 24 months is more sketchy than for the 7-and 13-month stage boundaries. Nevertheless, the Berkeley Growth Study data (McCall, Eichorn, & Hogarty, 1977) reveal a transition at this point, both in the nature of the developmental function as well as the stability of individual differences across age. First, a dip in the cross-age correlations of first principal component scores occurs at approximately 21 months of age for both sexes (although an additional dip at 30 months may exist for females). Second, the major change in the nature of the items marking this boundary involves the symbolic requirements of the task (see Table 8.5). For example, items newly added to the first principal component at 21 months included understanding of two to five prepositions, pointing to size opposites after the examiner uses a verbal comparative, and reconstruction of a block configuration after the sample has been removed from view. Some months later, verbal fluency items (e.g., naming action-agents, describing pictures, and verbalizing opposites) appear, further illustrating the symbolic relational character of the predominant mental behavior during this period. The additional dip in cross-age correlations at 30 months for girls may reflect the fact that the test becomes thoroughly saturated with verbal-relational items at 30 months, a cognitive medium that may have greater salience for girls than for boys.

Predictions to later IQ also emerge with this stage. Reviews of the literature on the prediction of later IQ from infant test scores reveal that sizable correlations to later IQ do not occur until approximately 18 to 24 months, although the precise age may depend on the sex of the infant and the particular test (Golden & Birns, 1976; Honzik, 1976; McCall, 1976; McCall, in press; McCall et al., 1972). Specifically, in the Berkeley Growth Study protocols, individual differences on the first principal component do not predict later IQ until 21 months, at which point the correlations immediately become substantial and project to age 36 months for boys. The pattern is less abrupt for girls, although longitudinal correlations also begin at 21 months but are not consistently established until 30 months when the first principal component becomes highly verbal in character. Therefore, it appears that symbolic relational behavior, especially within the verbal mode, may be associated with the first substantial and consistent correlations with later IQ (see McCall et al., 1972, for a review of exceptions to this principle).

Object notion.   Because objects may be represented by symbols that can be used in the absence of the object and can be mentally related to other entities, the child is able to solve a succession of invisible object displacements (Corman & Escalona, 1969; Miller, Cohen, & Hill, 1970; Uzgiris & Hunt, 1975).

Attention/exploration/play.   The exploration and play of children becomes more clever and "insightful" as characteristics of objects and consequences of actions can be inferred through mental combination. Furthermore, the content of the child's play becomes more symbolic and imaginative, sometimes involving the relationship between more than one imagined entity. For example, whereas prior to this stage children would pretend to feed themselves, they now direct such pretending toward others (e.g., they feed a doll instead of themselves). In fact, three studies show the transition from self- to other-directed imaginative play to occur at 21 months (Lézine, 1973; Lowe, 1975; Watson & Fischer, 1977).

Imitation.   Piaget (1962) interpreted the child's display of deferred imitation—imitating a model no longer available to the child—to signify the presence of the semiotic or symbolic function. Focused studies show that imitation of a simple motor act may be successfully deferred at 15 to 18 months, but if a symbolic relation between two entities is required, then deferred imitation does not occur with any substantial frequency until after 21 months (McCall, Parke, & Kavanaugh, 1977). Encoding, remembering, and retrieving a symbolic relationship between two external entities (i.e., a coordinated sequence of two motor acts with a set of objects) presumably must await the emergence of Stage V, symbolic relations.

Language.   From the perspective of the current theory, the establishment of symbolic relations between entities is required before creative two-word utterances can be produced in which two words learned separately are brought into temporal contiguity to form a new thought. Thus, two-word utterances make their appearance at approximately this time. The fact that a new stage is not achieved between 13 and 21 months may explain why language exhibits relatively little progress during the second year of life (see Nelson, Chapter 13, this volume).

I also believe early language development can be viewed from the standpoint of the two hypothesized functions of mental behavior—acquiring information and influencing the environment. For example, Nelson (1974; Chapter 13, this volume) has proposed a theory of language development in which early language grows out of the Infant⟶ Entity sensorimotor experience characteristic of Stage III. She has observed that children are more likely to group objects together on the basis of their functional attributes (i.e., what one can do with the object or primative influencing) before objects are grouped on the basis of form or color. Palmer and Rees (1969), using Palmer's Concept Familiarity Index, also demonstrated that functional attributes and relations appear to be learned earlier than perceptual ones. From another perspective, Bruner (1975) points out that in Brown's (1973) scheme of early multiword utterances, agent–action (e.g., mommy push), action–object (e.g., bite finger), and agent–object (e.g., mommy milk) are the first categories of expressions to be used and are binary subsets of the agent–action–object triad. Thus, the first thing a child attempts to express symbolically in multiword language is an Entity–Entity contingency that is typically an example of influencing. Bruner (1975) concludes, "These various sets of data suggest that the child, in using language initially, is very much oriented toward pursuing (or commenting upon) action being undertaken jointly by himself and another. This includes not only agent, action, and object, but also control, as represented by possession [p. 7]."

A second category of early utterances involves calling the attention of other people to, or commenting on, acquired pieces of information or attributes of objects—the categories of nomination, demonstrative marking, nonexistence, greeting, and locating. Indeed, Nelson (1973b), Ryan (1974), and Bruner (1975) emphasize the nature of a parent's interpretation of the child's ambiguous actions and utterances as being either an attempt to carry out an action or an attempt to influence or to acquire information. According to Bruner, in many early utterances "the child is not so much trying to DO something as he is trying to FIND OUT ABOUT something [p. 12; capitalization in original]." Therefore, I regard the pattern of language acquisition as potentially both falling within the stage sequence framework proposed here as well as serving the general functions of mental behavior—the acquisition of information and the disposition to influence the environment. However, as with any other behavioral domain, language development will also have its own unique parameters.

Social behavior. The ability to symbolize relationships between perceived or symbolic entities also allows children to view themselves as objective entities, thereby fostering the possible emergence of self-concept (Sroufe, in press). Moreover, one might speculate that when toddlers conceive of themselves and others as being totally independent dynamic entities, they are likely to explore creatively the patterns of reciprocal influencing between themselves and others. When the exploration of such social influencing is more important to toddlers than the positive or negative character of the social outcomes of any particular action–reaction episode, one may well have the "terrible twos."

EPILOGUE

Although an attempt has been made to articulate a molar theory of mental development in the first three years, a potentially more important theme in this chapter may be its approach. In my view, developmental psychology must unshackle itself from searching for consistency only in development— that is, continuity and stability. Rather, development implies change (Wohlwill, 1973), and we need to entertain thoughts and methods that will describe the qualitative, as well as quantitative, transitions in developmental function and individual differences and to explore the patterns of such developmental changes across traditional content domains.

Moreover, we may have to abandon our traditional investment in specific observed behaviors and their consistency across contexts and age. Rather, higher order concepts that subsume diverse specific behaviors may be more meaningful and consistent across context and age as well as be capable of integrating otherwise anomalous findings. I have suggested the acquisition of information and the disposition to influence the environment as being two superordinate notions of the function of mental behavior. Sroufe and Waters (1977) have made a similar case for the study of *attachment* during infancy, proposing that attachment be regarded as an organizational concept and that diverse behaviors be considered with respect to their function. When this is done, Sroufe and Waters find considerable consistency across a variety of behaviors and contexts as well as across age in the nature and individual differences of attachment behaviors.

Consequently, I press my colleagues to study discontinuity and instability as vigorously as they do continuity and stability, remembering that these are potentially (but not necessarily empirically) independent realms in the study of development. Furthermore, we must look beyond specific behaviors and explore the common functions of diverse actions, wherein I suspect Nature has cloaked the order we seek.

ACKNOWLEDGMENTS

Portions of this paper and the research presented in it were supported by the Samuel S. Fels Fund. I thank Cindy Kennedy, Kurt Fischer, Jerome Kagan, Sandra Scarr, and Alan Sroufe for their helpful comments on an early draft of this paper, and Carol Dodds, Karen Phelps, and Joanne Steinhilber for preparing the manuscript.

REFERENCES

Abravanel, E., Levan-Goldschmidt, E., & Stevenson, M. B. Action imitation: The early phase of infancy. *Child Development,* 1976, *47,* 1032–1044.

Ainsworth, M. D. S., Bell, S. M., & Stayton, D. J. Individual differences in strange situation behavior of one-year-olds. In H. R. Schaffer (Ed.), *The origins of human social relations.* London: Academic Press, 1971.

Ainsworth, M. D. S., Bell, S. M., & Stayton, D. J. Individual differences in the development of some attachment behaviors. *Merrill–Palmer Quarterly,* 1972, *18,* 122–143.

Anastasi, A. Heredity, environment, and the question "How?" *Psychological Review,* 1958, *65,* 197–208.

Appleton, T., Clifton, R., & Goldberg, S. The development of behavioral competence in infancy. In F. D. Horowitz (Ed.), *Review of child development research* (Vol. 4). Chicago: University of Chicago Press, 1975.

Baldwin, A. L., Kalhorn, J., & Breese, F. H. Patterns of parent behavior. *Psychological Monographs,* 1945, *58* (3, Whole No. 268).

Barratt, B. B. Training and transfer to combinatorial problem solving: The development of formal reasoning during early adolescence. *Developmental Psychology,* 1975, *11,* 700–704.

Bayley, N. Mental growth during the first three years: A developmental study of 61 children by repeated tests. *Genetic Psychology Monographs,* 1933, *14,* 1–92.

Beckwith, L. Relationships between attributes of mothers and their infants' IQ scores. *Child Development,* 1971, *42,* 1083–1097.

Benjamin, J. D. Further comments on some developmental aspects of anxiety. In H. S. Gaskill (Ed.), *Counterpoint.* New York: International Universities Press, 1963.

Bloom, B. S. *Stability and change in human characteristics.* New York: Wiley, 1964.

Brackbill, Y., & Koltsova, M. Conditioning and learning. In Y. Brackbill (Ed.), *Infancy and early childhood.* New York: Free Press, 1967.

Bradley, R. H., & Caldwell, B. M. Early home environment and changes in mental test performance in children from 6 to 30 months. *Developmental Psychology,* 1976, *12,* 93–97.

Bronson, G. W. Infants' reactions to unfamiliar persons and novel objects. *Monographs of the Society for Research in Child Development,* 1972, *37* (3,Whole No. 148).

Brown, R. *A first language.* Cambridge, Mass.: Harvard University Press, 1973.

Bruner, J. S. The ontogenesis of speech acts. *Journal of Child Language,* 1975, *2,* 1–19.

Caldwell, B. M., Heider, J., & Kaplan, B. *The inventory of home stimulation.* Paper presented at the meetings of the American Psychological Association, New York, September, 1966.

Clarke, A. M., & Clarke, A. D. B. *Early experience: Myth and evidence.* London: Open Books, 1976.

Coates, B., Anderson, E. P., & Hartup, W. W. Interrelations in the attachment behavior of human infants. *Developmental Psychology,* 1972, *6,* 218–230.

Cohen, L. B., & Gelber, E. R. Infant visual memory. In L. Cohen and P. Salapatek (Eds.), *Infant perception: From sensation to cognition. Basic visual processes* (Vol. 1). New York: Academic Press, 1975.

Corman, H. H., & Escalona, S. K. Stages of sensorimotor development: A replication study. *Merrill–Palmer Quarterly,* 1969, *15,* 351–361.

Décarie, T. G. *Intelligence and affectivity in early childhood.* New York: International Universities Press, 1965.

Dweck, C. S., & Repucci, N. D. Learned helplessness and reinforcement responsibility in children. *Journal of Personality and Social Psychology,* 1973, *25,* 109–116.

Elardo, R., Bradley, R., & Caldwell, B. M. The relation of infants' home environments to mental test performance from six to thirty-six months: A longitudinal analysis. *Child Development,* 1975, *46,* 71–76.

Emde, R. N., Gaensbauer, T. J , & Harmon, R. J. Emotional expression in infancy: A biobehavioral study. *Psychological Issues Monograph Series, Inc.,* (Vol. 10) Monograph #37. New York: International Universities Press, 1976.

Emde, R. N., & Robinson, J. The first two months: Recent research in developmental psychobiology and the changing view of the newborn. In J. Noshpitz & J. Call (Eds.), *Basic handbook of child psychiatry.* New York: Basic Books, 1976.

Emmerich, W. Continuity and stability in early social development. *Child Development,* 1964, *35,* 311–332.

Escalona, S. *The roots of individuality.* Chicago: Aldine, 1968.

Fenson, L., Kagan, J., Kearsley, R. B., & Zelazo, P. R. The developmental progression of manipulative play in the first two years. *Child Development,* 1976, *47,* 232–236.

Fischer, K. W. Cognitive development as problem solving. The meaning of décalge in seriation tasks. *Proceedings of the Fifth Annual Conference on Structural Learning,* 1974. (N.O.R.C. Technical Report, June 30, 1974.)

Fischer, K. W. A theory of cognitive development: Seven levels of behavior and understanding. *Psychological Review,* in press.

Fitzgerald, H. E., & Porges, S. W. A decade of infant conditioning and learning research. *Merrill–Palmer Quarterly*, 1971, *17*, 80–117.

Friedman, S. Habituation and recovery of visual response in the alert human newborn. *Journal of Experimental Child Psychology*, 1972, *13*, 339–349.

Friedman, S., Bruno, L. A., & Vietze, P. Newborn habituation to visual stimuli: A sex difference in novelty detection. *Journal of Experimental Child Psychology*, 1974, *18*, 242–251.

Gardner, J., & Gardner, H. A note on selective imitation by a six-week-old infant. *Child Development*, 1970, *41*, 1209–1213.

Golden, M., & Birns, B. Social class and infant intelligence. In M. Lewis (Ed.), *Origins of intelligence*. New York: Plenum, 1976.

Goldschmidt, M. L. The role of experience in the rate and sequence of cognitive development. In D. R. Green, M. P. Ford, & C. B. Flamer (Eds.), *Measurement and Piaget*. New York: McGraw–Hill, 1971.

Gratch, G., & Landers, W. F. Stage IV of Piaget's theory of infant's object concepts: A longitudinal study. *Child Development*, 1971, *42*, 359–372.

Greenberg, D. J., Hillman, D., & Grice, D. Infant and stranger variables related to stranger anxiety in the first year of life. *Developmental Psychology*, 1973, *9*, 207–212.

Haviland, J. Looking smart: The relationship between affect and intelligence in infancy. In M. Lewis (Ed.), *Origins of intelligence*. New York: Plenum, 1976.

Honzik, M. P. Value and limitations of infant tests: An overview. In M. Lewis (Ed.), *Origins of intelligence*. New York: Plenum, 1976.

Hunt, J. McV. *Intelligence and experience*. New York: Ronald Press, 1961.

Hunt, J. V. Environmental risk in fetal and neonatal life and measured infant intelligence. In M. Lewis (Ed.), *Origins of intelligence*. New York: Plenum, 1976.

Inhelder, B., Sinclair, H., & Bovet, M. *Learning and the development of cognition*. (S. Wedgewood, trans.). Cambridge, Mass.: Harvard University Press, 1974.

Jackson, E., Campos, J. J., & Fischer, K. W. The question of *décalage* between object permanence and person permanence. *Developmental Psychology*, 1978, *14*, 1–10.

Kagan, J. *Change and continuity in infancy*. New York: Wiley, 1971.

Kagan, J., & Klein, R. E. Cross-cultural perspectives on early development. *American Psychologist*, 1973, *28*, 947–961.

Karmel, B. Z., & Maisel, E. B. A neuronal activity model for infant attention. In L. B. Cohen & P. Salapatek (Eds.), *Infant perception: From sensation to cognition: Basic visual processes* (Vol. 1). New York: Academic Press, 1975.

King, W. L., & Seegmiller, B. Performance of 14 to 22-month-old black, firstborn male infants on two tests of cognitive development: The Bayley Scales and the Infant Psychological Development Scale. *Developmental Psychology*, 1973, *8*, 317–326.

Kopp, C. B., Sigman, M., & Parmelee, A. H. Longitudinal study of sensorimotor development. *Developmental Psychology*, 1974, *10*, 687–695.

Lézine, I. The transition from sensory motor to earliest symbolic function in early development. In J. I. Nurnberger (Ed.), *Biological and environmental determinants of early development (Research Publications Association for Research in Nervous and Mental Disease)*. Baltimore, Md.: Williams and Wilkins, 1973.

Lézine, I., Stambak, M., & Casati, I. *Les étapes de l'intelligence sensorimotrice (Monographie No. 1)*. Paris: Les Editions du Centre de Psychologie Appliquée, 1969.

Lipsitt, L. P. Learning in the first year of life. In L. P. Lipsitt & C. C. Spiker (Eds.), *Advances in child development and behavior*. New York: Academic Press, 1963.

Lowe, M. Trends in the development of representational play in infants from 1 to 3 years— an observational study. *Journal of Child Psychology and Psychiatry*, 1975, *16*, 33–47.

Maratos, O. *The origin and development of imitation in the first six months of life*. Unpublished doctoral dissertation, University of Geneva, Switzerland, 1973.

Mason, M. K. Learning to speak after years of silence. *Journal of Speech and Hearing Disorders,* 1942, *7,* 295–304.

McCall, R. B. IQ pattern over age: Comparisons among siblings and parent–child pairs. *Science,* 1970, *170,* 644–648.

McCall, R. B. Attention in the infant: Avenue to the study of cognitive development. In D. Walcher & D. L. Peters (Eds.), *Early childhood: The development of self-regulatory mechanisms.* New York: Academic Press, 1971.

McCall, R. B. Exploratory manipulation and play in the human infant. *Monographs of the Society for Research in Child Development,* 1974, *39*(2,Whole No. 155).

McCall, R. B. *Imitation in infancy.* Paper presented at the meeting of The Society for Research in Child Development, Denver, April, 1975.

McCall, R. B. Toward an epigenetic conception of mental development in the first three years of life. In M. Lewis (Ed.), *Origins of intelligence.* New York: Plenum, 1976.

McCall, R. B. Challenges to a science of developmental psychology. *Child Development,* 1977, *48,* 333–344.

McCall, R. B. The development of intellectual functioning in infancy and the prediction of later IQ. In J. D. Osofsky (Ed.), *Handbook of infant development.* New York: Wiley, in press.

McCall, R. B., Appelbaum, M., & Hogarty, P. S. Developmental changes in mental performance. *Monographs of the Society for Research in Child Development,* 1973, *38*(3,Whole No. 150).

McCall, R. B., Eichorn, D. H., & Hogarty, P. S. Transitions in early mental development. *Monographs of the Society for Research in Child Development,* 1977, *42*(3,Whole No. 171).

McCall, R. B., Hogarty, P. S., & Hurlburt, N. Transitions in infant sensorimotor development and the prediction of childhood IQ. *American Psychologist,* 1972, *27,* 728–748.

McCall, R. B., Kennedy, C. B., & Appelbaum, M. I. Magnitude of discrepancy and the distribution of attention in infants. *Child Development,* 1977, *48,* 772–785.

McCall, R. B., & McGhee, P. E. The discrepancy hypothesis of attention and affect in human infants. In I. C. Uzgiris & F. Weizmann (Eds.), *The structuring of experience.* New York: Plenum, 1976.

McCall, R. B., Parke, R. D., & Kavanaugh, R. D. Imitation of live and televised models in the first three years of life. *Monographs of the Society for Research in Child Development,* 1977, *42* (5,Whole No. 173).

McCulloch, T. L., & Bruner, J. S. The effect of electric shock upon subsequent learning in the rat. *Journal of Psychology,* 1939, *7,* 333–336.

Meltzoff, A. N., & Moore, M. K. Imitation of facial gestures by human neonates. *Science,* 1977, *198,* 75–78.

Millar, W. S. The role of visual holding cues in the simultanizing strategy in infant operant learning. *British Journal of Psychology,* 1974, *65,* 505–518.

Miller, D. J., Cohen, L. B., & Hill, K. T. A methodological investigation of Piaget's theory of object concept development in the sensory-motor period. *Journal of Experimental Child Psychology,* 1970, *9,* 59–85.

Moore, T. Language and intelligence: A longitudinal study of the first eight years. Part II. Environmental correlates of mental growth. *Human Development,* 1968, *11,* 1–24.

Morgan, G. A., & Ricciuti, H. Infant's responses to strangers during the first year. In B. M. Foss (Ed.), *Determinants of infant behavior* (Vol. 4). London: Methuen, 1969.

Nelson, K. Some evidence for the cognitive primacy of categorization and its functional equivalence. *Merrill-Palmer Quarterly,* 1973, *17,* 21–39. (a)

Nelson, K. Structure and strategy in learning to talk. *Monographs of the Society for Research in Child Development,* 1973, *38*(1-2,Whole No. 149). (b).

Nelson, K. Concept, word and sentence: Interrelations in acquisition and development. *Psychological Review*, 1974, *81*, 267–285.

Palmer, F., & Rees, A. *Concept training in two-year-olds: Procedures and results.* Paper presented at the meetings of the Society for Research in Child Development, Santa Monica, Calif., March, 1969.

Parmelee, A. H., Jr., & Sigman, M. Development of visual behavior and neurological organization in pre-term and full-term infants. In A. D. Pick (Ed.), *Minnesota symposia on child psychology* (Vol. 10). Minneapolis: University of Minnesota Press, 1976.

Piaget, J. Le mecanisme du developpement mental et les du groupement des operations. *Archives de Psychologie*, 1941, *28*, 215–285.

Piaget, J. *The origins of intelligence in children* (M. Cook, trans.). New York: International Universities Press, 1952.

Piaget, J. *Play, dreams, and imitation in childhood* (C. Gattegno and F. M. Hodgson, trans.). New York: Norton, 1962.

Rafman, S. The infant's reaction to imitation of the mother's behavior by the stranger. In T. G. Décarie (Ed.), *The infant's reaction to strangers*. New York: International Universities Press, 1974.

Ramey, C. T., Starr, R. H., Pallas, J., Whitten, C. F., & Reed, V. Nutrition response-contingent stimulation and the maternal deprivation syndrome: Results of an early intervention program. *Merrill–Palmer Quarterly*, 1975, *21*, 45–53.

Rheingold, H. L. The effect of a strange environment on the behavior of infants. In B. M. Foss (Ed.), *Determinants of infant behavior* (Vol. 4). London: Methuen, 1969.

Rheingold, H. L., Gewirtz, J. L., & Ross, H. W. Social conditioning of vocalizations in the infant. *Journal of Comparative and Physiological Psychology*, 1959, *52*, 68–72.

Ricciuti, H. N. Object grouping and selective ordering behavior in infants 12 to 24 months old. *Merrill–Palmer Quarterly*, 1965, *11*, 129–148.

Rovee, C. K., & Rovee, D. T. Conjugate reinforcement of infant exploratory behavior. *Journal of Experimental Child Psychology*, 1969, *8*, 33–39.

Ryan, J. Early language development. In M. P. M. Richards (Ed.), *The integration of a child into a social world*. London: Cambridge University Press, 1974.

Salatas, H., & Flavell, J. H. Perspective taking: The development of two components of knowledge. *Child Development*, 1976, *47*, 103–109.

Sameroff, A. J. Can conditioned responses be established in the newborn infant 1971? *Developmental Psychology*, 1971, *5*, 1–12.

Sameroff, A. J., & Chandler, M. J. Reproductive risk and the continuum of caretaking causalty. In F. D. Horowitz (Ed.), *Review of child development research* (Vol. 4). Chicago: University of Chicago Press, 1975.

Sander, L. Issues in early mother–child interaction. *Journal of the American Academy of Child Psychiatry*, 1962, *1*, 141–166.

Sander, L. The longitudinal course of early mother–child interaction—cross-case comparison in a sample of mother–child pairs. In B. Foss (Ed.), *Determinants of infant behaviour* (Vol. 4). London: Tavistock, 1969.

Scarr, S., & Salapatek, P. Patterns of fear development during infancy. *Merrill–Palmer Quarterly*, 1970, *16*, 53–90.

Scarr-Salapatek, S. An evolutionary perspective on infant intelligence: Species patterns and individual variations. In M. Lewis (Ed.), *Origins of intelligence*. New York: Plenum, 1976.

Schaffer, H. R. *The growth of sociability*. Middlesex, England: Penguin, 1971.

Schaffer, H. R., & Callender, W. M. Psychologic effects of hospitalization in infancy. *Pediatrics*, 1959, *24*, 528–539.

Schaffer, H. R., & Emerson, P. E. The development of social attachments in infancy. *Monographs of the Society for Research in Child Development*, 1964, *29*, (3, Whole No. 94).

Schaffer, H. R., Greenwood, A., & Parry, M. H. The onset of wariness. *Child Development,* 1972, *43,* 165–175.

Seligman, M. E. P., & Maier, S. F. Failure to escape traumatic shock. *Journal of Experimental Psychology,* 1967, *74,* 1–9.

Sroufe, L. A. Wariness of strangers and the study of infant development. *Child Development,* 1977, *48,* 731–746.

Sroufe, L. A. The ontogenesis of emotion. In J. Osofsky (Ed.), *Handbook of infant development.* New York: Wiley, in press.

Sroufe, L. A., & Waters, E. Attachment as an organizational construct. *Child Development,* 1977, *48,* 1184–1189.

Sroufe, L. A., & Wunsch, J. The development of laughter in the first year of life. *Child Development,* 1972, *43,* 1326–1344.

Stayton, D. J., Ainsworth, M. D. S., & Main, M. B. Development of separation behavior in the first year of life: Protest, following, and greeting. *Developmental Psychology,* 1973, *9,* 213–225.

Stewart, D. M., & Hamilton, M. L. Imitation as a learning strategy in the acquisition of vocabulary. *Journal of Experimental Child Psychology,* 1976, *21,* 380–392.

Tennes, K. H., & Lampl, E. E. Stranger and separation anxiety in infancy. *Journal of Nervous and Mental Disease,* 1964, *139,* 247–254.

Thorton, J. W., & Jacobs, P. D. Learned helplessness in human subjects. *Journal of Experimental Psychology,* 1971, *87,* 367–372.

Uzgiris, I. C. *Patterns of vocal and gestural imitation in infants.* Paper presented at the International Society for the Study of Behavioral Development, Nijmegen, Netherlands, July, 1971.

Uzgiris, I. C. Patterns of cognitive development in infancy. *Merrill–Palmer Quarterly,* 1973, *19,* 181–204.

Uzgiris, I. C. Organization of sensorimotor intelligence. In M. Lewis (Ed.), *Origins of intelligence.* New York: Plenum, 1976.

Uzgiris, I. C. Comment. In R. B. McCall, D. H. Eichorn, & P. S. Hogarty, Transitions in early mental development. *Monographs of the Society for Research in Child Development,* 1977, *42,* (3,Whole No. 171).

Uzgiris, I. C., & Hunt, J. McV. *Assessment in infancy: Ordinal scales of psychological development.* Urbana: University of Illinois Press, 1975.

Wachs, T. D. Utilization of a Piagetian approach in the investigation of early experience effects: A research strategy and some illustrative data. *Merrill–Palmer Quarterly,* 1976, *22,* 11–30.

Wachs, T. D., Uzgiris, I. C., & Hunt, J. McV. Cognitive development in infants of different age levels and from different environmental backgrounds: An explanatory investigation. *Merrill–Palmer Quarterly,* 1971, *17,* 283–318.

Waddington, C. H. *Tools for thought.* London: Paladin, 1977.

Watson, J. S. Smiling, cooing, and "the game." *Merrill–Palmer Quarterly,* 1972, *18,* 323–340.

Watson, J. S., & Ramey, C. T. Reactions to response contingent stimulation early in infancy. *Merrill–Palmer Quarterly,* 1972, *18,* 219–227.

Watson, M. W., & Fischer, K. W. A developmental sequence of agent use in late infancy. *Child Development,* 1977, *48,* 828–836.

Weisler, A., & McCall, R. B. Exploration and play: Résumé and redirection. *American Psychologist,* 1976, *31,* 493–508.

White, B. L. *The first three years of life.* Englewood Cliffs, N.J.: Prentice-Hall, 1976.

White, R. W. Motivation reconsidered: The concept of competence. *Psychological Review,* 1959, *66,* 297–333.

Wilson, R. S. Twins: Early mental development. *Science,* 1972, *175,* 914–917.

Wilson, R. S., & Harpring, E. B. Mental and motor development in infant twins. *Developmental Psychology,* 1972, *7,* 277-287.

Wohlwill, J. F. *The study of behavioral development.* New York: Academic Press, 1973.

Yarrow, L. J. Research in dimensions of early maternal care. *Merrill-Palmer Quarterly,* 1963, *9,* 101-114.

Yarrow, L. J., & Pedersen, F. A. The interplay between cognition and motivation in infancy. In M. Lewis (Ed.), *Origins of intelligence.* New York: Plenum, 1976.

Yarrow, L. J., Rubenstein, J. L., Pedersen, F. A., & Jankowski, J. J. Dimensions of early stimulation and their differential effects on infant development. *Merrill-Palmer Quarterly,* 1972, *18,* 205-218.

9

The Figurative and the Operative in Piagetian Psychology

David Elkind
Tufts University

INTRODUCTION

Over the past decade Piaget has introduced in various different books (e.g., Piaget, 1970, 1973) a distinction between figurative and operative knowing, between knowledge of states and knowledge of transformations. Although this distinction has antecedents in Piaget's earlier writings, it did not become prominent until his more recent work on the figurative processes, namely, perception (Piaget, 1969), memory (Piaget & Inhelder, 1973), and imagery (Piaget & Inhelder, 1971). The figurative/operative distinction would seem to be particularly important in the context of this book. In effect, the figurative/operative distinction is one of the ways in which Piaget conceptualizes development from infancy.

Piaget's stages describe the structural and functional changes that mark development, but his distinction between the figurative and the operative has to do with changes in the *content* of thought that occur from infancy through adulthood. Very simply, for Piaget the content of thought develops from the figurative to the operative, from a knowledge of static states to a knowledge of dynamic transformations. In this chapter I elaborate on this important distinction, which is much less well known than the Piagetian stages. In the first section, a detailed discussion of figurative and operative processes is given. In the next section, the distinction between the figurative and the operative is placed in perspective by describing other well-known conceptions of development from infancy. A third section compares and contrasts the figurative/operative notion with the other conceptions of development. A final section describes some implications of the distinction between the figurative and the operative for psychological theory and practice.

THE FIGURATIVE AND THE OPERATIVE

It would be correct but incomplete to say that for Piaget development involves the progressive construction of both intelligence and reality. Such a description is incomplete because it fails to say anything about the nature of the constructive process. And Piaget has given several different answers to the question of how intelligence and reality come to be built up. One of these is the well-known theory of stages and of the functional invariants of assimilation, accommodation, and equilibration. These invariants deal with the construction of the progressively more elaborate systems of mental operations. Accordingly, this answer might be called Piaget's *structural/functional* theory of development.

A second answer to the question of construction is provided by Piaget's distinction between the figurative and the operative, between knowledge of states and knowledge of transformations. In Piaget's view, conceptual understanding proceeds from the figurative to the operative. This answer to how reality is constructed might be called Piaget's (1970) *content* theory of development:

> I shall begin by making a distinction between two aspects of thinking that are different, although complementary. One is the figurative aspect and the other I call the operative aspect. The figurative is an imitation of states taken as momentary and static. In the cognitive area the figurative functions are above all, perception, imitation and mental imagery, which is in fact interiorized imitation. The operative aspect of thought deals not with states but with transformations from one state to another. For example, it includes actions themselves which transform objects or states and it also includes the intellectual operations which are essentially systems of transformations [p. 14].

Piaget's distinction between the figurative and the operative thus make it possible to describe the construction of reality from the standpoint of content as well as from the standpoint of structure and process. Although content has always been important in Piaget's research and theorizing, the figurative and operative distinction is his attempt to deal with content in a more general and systematic way than he had in the study of particular concepts. However, before we turn to the psychological features of this progression from figurative to operative knowledge, something about its epistemological significance needs to be said.

Epistemological Background of the Figurative/Operative Distinction.

Piaget's theory of intelligence, of which the figurative/operative distinction is a part, is first and foremost an epistemology — an answer to the question regarding the nature and origin of knowledge. To appreciate fully the innovations of Piaget's epistemology, it has to be seen in the context of other epistemologies that preceded it. Inasmuch as we are here concerned primarily with the figurative/operative or content aspect of epistemology, we look only briefly at the way this content issue was dealt with by other theorists.

The Empiricists. Every epistemology, of necessity, builds on the systematic knowledge of the world available at the time. The empiricist philosophers Locke (1695/1975) and Hume (1947 edition) were very much influenced by the Newtonian, or mechanical, view of the universe. These men took reality as an external given and asked how it was possible for the mind to acquire knowledge of that reality. The processes they advocated for acquiring knowledge were atomistic and mechanical, in keeping with the physics and chemistry of their time. Bishop Berkeley (1947 edition), who is sometimes grouped with the empiricists, nonetheless regarded physical reality as an entirely psychological construction.

What characterizes the empiricists, then, is that for them the important problems of epistemology are in the question of *how* knowledge is acquired and not in the nature of knowledge, taken as a fixed given, itself. In fact, however, the idea that reality is a fixed entity outside the person can be looked at as a kind of reverse nativisim. The empiricists were empiricists only with regard to the acquisition of knowledge. With regard to the content of knowledge, they were nativists in the sense that they regarded reality as fixed, and prior to, experience.

It was Immanuel Kant (1781/1943), "awakened from his slumbers" by Hume's critique of inductive knowledge, who recognized the importance of content for epistemological discussions. He argued that the long-held distinction between reason and reality was relative rather than absolute. For Kant, reason was not "pure" because it could operate only in relation to experience. What were *a priori* (prior to) experience were the mental categories for apprehending experience, space, time, and so on. From a Kantian standpoint, collective knowledge, whether in science or in any other domain, is important because its organization reflects the organization of the mind. Kant thus extended epistemological analysis to the science of his time and found parallels between the structure of knowledge and the processes of knowing.

Hegel (1953 edition) wanted to restore "pure" reason to where it had been before Kant. Although he followed Kant in regarding knowledge (in Hegel's case historical and political knowledge) as data for epistemological analysis, he postulated a higher order intelligence or reason that regulated the interaction of mind and reality. Today we recognize that both Kant and Hegel were probably wrong in their conclusions regarding the nature of physical and historical reality, but this does not detract from their methodological innovation which was the inclusion of knowledge itself as a central component in epistemological discussions.

The Logical Positivists.   Every action provokes a reaction. Kant reacted to Hume, and the logical positivists reacted to Kant. In a sense, they took the Kantian premise — the importance of collective knowledge for a theory of knowing — to an extreme. They concluded that mental constructions had validity only insofar as they could be brought into conformance with sense data. From this standpoint, the methods of science were the only true epistemological methods, and epistemology became the philosophy of science.

The logical positivist approach, as exemplified in the writings of men such as Reichenbach (1951), denied a constructive role to reason, which was either "analytic" and empty (as in syllogistic reasoning where the conclusion is already embedded in the premise) or "synthetic" and founded on sense experience with no contribution of its own: "For astronomical and for sub-microscopic dimensions they [the Kantian categories of space, time, etc., etc.] had to be replaced by the laws of the new physics and this fact alone makes it obvious that they were empirical laws and not forced on us by reason itself [p. 125]."

The positivist position thus retreats to a pre-Kantian position in denying that the subject plays a constructive role in the knowing process. Indeed, the role of the philosophy of science is to remove, insofar as possible, subjective elements from collective knowledge and to ensure that nothing creeps into scientific knowledge that is not warranted by the canons of scientific method.

The emphasis of the logical positivists on abiding methods of verification, in contrast to transient and changing contents of knowledge, led to a devaluation of the contents of knowledge that persists today. The contemporary psychological emphasis on the process of learning, independent of the contents learned, is a reflection of the logical positivist bias against content as important in the construction of knowledge. Thus, the logical positivists, although they started from the Kantian position that analysis of the content of knowledge was important for epistemology, ended up by asserting that only the processes employed in putting together collective knowledge had any epistemological significance.

Piaget, in contrast, goes a bit further than Kant. He argues that the forms of knowing (Kant's *a priori* categories of space, time, causality, etc.) are themselves rooted in experience. Mental operations are not innate and simple products of maturation; rather, they are abstracted from the child's experience of transformation. A child who is playing with 10 pebbles may rearrange them into a variety of different shapes (square, circle, and so on) and discover that no matter how they are arranged, they always make 10. From this standpoint, reason itself is a kind of knowledge derived from experience by "reflective abstraction," abstraction from the results of the child's own actions on things.

If reason is itself derived from experience, albeit a different kind of experience that is rooted in the child's own behavior, what happens to the logical positivist's clean separation between empty reason and informative sense data? In essence, the distinction between *analytic* and the empty and the *synthetic* and the informative is rendered invalid. For if reason is itself derived from experience, then it must also be, from the standpoint of logical positivism, synthetic and valid. A child's conservation concepts are a case in point. Such knowledge is both analytic (in the sense that in any given instance conservation is a deduction from the premise that the two quantities are equal to begin with and that changing the appearance does not change the quantity) and synthetic (in the sense that the mental operations involved are derived from experience and in the sense that the conclusion can be tested by empirical methods).

From a Piagetian standpoint, rational knowledge is every bit as synthetic as knowledge derived from sense data. Not because such knowledge is synthetic *a priori* but rather because its genesis is at one or another point in development traceable to sense experience (Apostel, Mays, Morf, & Piaget, 1957). Looked at in this way, the familiar epistemological dichotomies—between reason and sense data, between the synthetic and the analytic, and between the inductive and the deductive—are rendered relative rather than absolute. All knowledge is derived, in part, from experience. *Even those operations that take us beyond experience are themselves an outgrowth of experience.*

Piaget's position in this regard clearly grows out of his view that human intelligence is an extension of biological adaptation and that it is always a product of subject–object interaction. To understand that interaction, one must look at *both* the subject and the object, at both the process and the content. To understand the child's conception of geometry, one must look at the child struggling to learn geometry. And to understand the child's conception of causality, one has to look at the child attempting to look at causal relations. The process of knowing these contents is not separate from, but rather dependent on, the contents to be known.

The foregoing discussion seemed necessary to make two points about Piaget's figurative/operative distinction. First of all, it seemed important to demonstrate why, from a Piagetian perspective, content is important in knowledge and to contrast this with the empiricist and logical positivist positions. Second, and equally important, it was necessary to emphasize that Piaget's conceptualization of content (reflected in the figurative/operative distinction) is closely tied to his structural/functional theory of development. As suggested earlier, structures and functions derive from contents just as contents can be derived from structures and functions. Indeed, that is why Paiget has spent more than 60 years studying how children acquire particular contents of knowledge. With this philosophical discussion behind us, we can now look at the figurative/operative distinction at the level of psychology.

Psychological Facets of the Figurative/Operative Distinction

The foregoing discussion suggests that Piaget's content distinction between the figurative and the operative is intimately tied to his structural-functional theory of development. In effect, Piaget emphasizes the fact that structures and functions can be derived from contents just as contents can be derived from structures and functions. This assertion emphasizes Piaget's (1970) basic position, namely, that human intelligence is an extension of biological adaptation. From the biological perspective, structure and function, content and process, are but different ways of looking at the living organism. Although these distinctions are essential for theoretical and philosophical discussion, in the living, behaving child, they cannot be dissociated. We need now to turn to a further delineation of the figurative and the operative at the level of psychology.

First, it has to be emphasized that both figurative and operative processes involve the activity of the subject. The construction of images, a figurative process, is not a simple passive prolongation of perceptual processes. On the contrary, the construction of images involves considerable activity on the part of the subject. For example, the child who draws a profile with two eyes òr transparencies (drawing something one would not ordinarily see like the far leg of a horseback rider) shows that he is not simply copying reality. The child draws what he knows, not what he sees. In the same way, even rote memorizing reveals the activity of the subject. The well-known serial position curve, on which the first and last items are recalled before the middle ones, reflects the imposition of the subject's activity on the simplest figurative process. The progression from the figurative to the operative is *not* a progression from the passive to the active.

Second, although some processes of knowing, such as imitation and imagery, are more figurative than others, such as reason, they may be "invaded" by operativity. Piaget and Inhelder's (1971) work on imagery makes this point. For example, anticipatory images, which predict the results of transformations, do not usually appear until after the age at which children have attained concrete operations. In effect, the operations "invade" the imagery processes and render them more operative. The same occurs in perception. Although the perception of the young child is largely static and figurative, older children act on the perceptual givens (reverse figure and ground, find hidden figures, and so on), which renders perception more operative than it was before. Piaget (1970, 1973) says that perception, imagery, and imitation are nonetheless figurative processes because even when they are "invaded" by operations, they never attain the fully reversible and equilibrated structures that hold true for intelligence proper.

Third, the progression from the figurative to the operative is always relative to the child's level of development. That is, operative constructions at one level of development may serve as material for figurative knowledge at another level. (Much as for Aristotle, form could become the matter for a still higher form.) To illustrate, object concepts constructed by the infant are externalized and are conceived as existing outside the self (Piaget, 1954). However, at the preoperational level, these objects come to be known figuratively with respect to their form, color, size, and so on. A child who calls a large block "daddy" and a small block "baby" has a figurative concept of size. Later, after the attainment of concrete operations, these dimensions of form and size are themselves operationalized.

It should be clear, then, that in a strict sense the conceptualization of development as progression from the figurative to the operative holds only within stages and not between them. On the other hand, speaking loosely, one could say that knowledge at the earlier stages of development is relatively more figurative than it is at the later stages. This is true because the extents of reversibility and transformations within the system are greater at the more mature levels of development than they are at the earlier ones.

Finally, although the figurative is frequently built on the operative, the operative is very often blocked or impeded by the figurative. The well-known horizontal décalages in the Piagetian literature are a case in point. Although the conservation of both number and length requires concrete operations for its attainment, length conservation is usually attained about a year after number conservation (Elkind, 1961a, 1966; Piaget & Szeminska, 1952). Likewise, the conservation of discontinuous quantities (beads) precedes by about a year the conservation of continuous quantities (liquids) (Elkind, 1961b; Piaget & Szeminska 1952). In both cases the décalage concerns the figurative properties of the materials involved. It is easier to conserve discontinuous elements than continuous ones because the discontinuous elements are already separate in perception. However, perceptually continuous quantities present a certain "resistance" to operational understanding. It is in this sense that the figurative can impede the operative.

This, then, is the Piagetian conception of the figurative and the operative. To appreciate fully the originality of this distinction it is necessary to place it in the context of other approaches to development and to see in what way it adds to or improves on these existing conceptions. It is to this endeavor that the next two sections are devoted.

CONCEPTIONS OF DEVELOPMENT FROM INFANCY

How shall development be conceived? In contemporary psychology a number of different conceptualizations are available. It is useful to describe these as a way of highlighting the uniqueness of the figurative/operative formulation. It should be said, too, that although I am a Piagetian, I do not necessarily reject the other positions or necessarily accept Piaget's—at least in its entirety. There is, I believe, some merit in each of the conceptualizations in the following paragraphs.

Differentiation and Hierarchical Integration

For Heinz Werner (1948) a single "orthogenetic principle" describes development, whether it be in biology, psychology, history, or any other field. According to Werner (1957): "Wherever development occurs it proceeds from a state of relative globality and lack of differentiation to a state of increasing differentiation, articulation and hierarchical integration [p. 126]." To illustrate this position, Werner uses the example of the child who believes that dreams are outside the self. In this instance the child fails to distinguish what comes from outside from what comes from within. As the child progressively differentiates inner processes from outer events, he is gradually freed from the domination of the immediate situation.

At the descriptive level, the orthogenetic principle does seem to encompass a great deal of developmental data. For example, the results of many of Piaget's investigations can be described in terms of age-related progressions of differentiation and heirarchical integration. In the attainment of number concepts (Piaget & Szeminska, 1952), for example, the child begins with a global concept of numerousness when numbers are "nominal" and not differentiated from names. Then the child attains an "ordinal" concept of number wherein numbers stand for a position in a series. Only toward the age of 5 or 6 do children attain a true "interval" concept of number in which numbers stand for units that are at once nominal (the same as every other unit) and ordinal (different from them in order of enumeration).

What holds true within a given cognitive domain holds true between cognitive processes as well. In the young infant, for example, many psychological processes such as motor action and perception are not clearly differentiated one from the other. The young infant does not distinguish clearly between that which disappears as a result of his own movements or as a result of the object's own movements. Infancy is marked by a progressive differentiation of sensory and motor processes (e.g., Bower, 1974). Later in childhood, however, there appears to be a higher-order integration of sensory processes (Birch & Belmont, 1965).

There is obviously considerable validity to the orthogenetic principle, but it is more a program to be filled out than a specific answer to the question of development from infancy. In each case, the concepts of globality, differentiation, and hierarchical integration have to be defined for the particular investigative domain under consideration. This limits the generality of the concepts.

Language and Mediation

A second view of development is that it moves from unmediated to mediated processes. From this perspective, language plays a central role in the development and comes progressively to control and direct behavior. The work of the Kendlers on reversal shift behavior is a well-known elaboration of this position (Kendler & Kendler, 1975). The Kendlers have demonstrated that before the age of five or six, children respond to particular stimuli, whereas after that age they begin to respond to general categories and relations. This shift from single-unit responding to mediated responding between the ages of about five to seven has been found by many different investigators using a variety of paradigms (see White, 1965, for a review of these studies).

Russian psychologists have also emphasized the role of language in the development of higher-order mental processes. In Russia, however, the theory of development is much more visibly tied to political ideology than is true in the United States. From the standpoint of dialectical materialism, social reality is primary and antedates individual consciousness and knowledge. Language, which is a social construction and is part of social reality, is progressively internalized until it becomes mental process. For the Russian psychologists, therefore, language is the primary means for the development of socialized behavior and thought. This orientation is evident both in the writings of Luria (e.g., Luria & Yudovich, 1968) and in the well-known work of Vygotsky (1962).

Although the foregoing is only an encapsulated presentation of the mediation standpoint, it may suffice as an indication of what is meant by those who advocate mediation, or internalization, or overt processes as a major dimension of development. In American psychology, to be sure, the emphasis is on the behaviors that are being internalized as well as the process of internalization. For Russian psychology, the social origins of the internalized responses are emphasized as well. Nonetheless, for both groups, development is viewed as a movement from overt to covert behavior.

In some respects the problem with the mediation theory is the opposite of that posed by the orthogenetic principle. That is, the concept of development as internalization is perhaps too specific to account for the full range of developmental phenomena. To be sure, many behaviors develop from the overt to the covert, but this process is far from characteristic of all developmental processes. Perception is a case in point. Perception changes with age (Elkind, 1975; Piaget, 1969), but it could hardly be said that perception in the young child is more "overt" than it is in the older child and adult. And, in the case of the development of memory, it might even be said that development occurs in the other direction. The development of complex memory strategies (e.g., Niemark, 1971) in older children and adults might be taken as an instance of the *externalization* of covert processes. The use of memory aids such as date books is an illustration of the fact that some mental processes can move from the covert to the overt with increasing age.

There is also the question of whether all internalization is of the same order. Vygotsky's (1962) lovely example of "whispering" as a stage in the internalization of language suggests that there is merely a reduction in quantity — that internalization is a kind of miniaturization of response. Hull's (1952) "fractional anticipatory goal response" is another instance in which internalization is assumed to be accomplished by miniaturization. However, such reductions of size could hardly explain the internalization of the operations described by Piaget. Operations permit mental actions not possible on the plane of motor response. For example, an object can be thought of as being on the left of one object and on the right of another, but motorically a right hand can never be a left hand and vice versa. A simple internalization of right–left discriminations could hardly give rise to an operational understanding of right and left.

The internalization theory of development is clearly an important one that holds true in some domains. However, it is far from being sufficient to account for the whole of development. It is also true that the concept of internalization as a kind of quantitative miniaturization of response will hold for some but certainly not for all processes of internalization.

Development as Representation

A somewhat different approach to development has been taken by Jerome Bruner (1964) who argues that cognitive development involves the growth of representational processes. In Bruner's view, knowledge is first encoded through action (*enactive* encoding), then through representations that resemble or are similar to their referents (*ikonic* encoding), and finally, by symbols that bear no resemblance to the referents (*symbolic* encoding). As a result of this increasingly sophisticated representation of reality, children become progressively more familiar with the more complex aspects of the world. From Bruner's perspective, representational systems are the child's primary tools for coming to know the world.

The central role of language in knowing reality has an anthropological origin and can be traced back at least as far as Sapir (1949) and Whorf (1956). Bruner's (1975) own anthropological bent is evident in a theme that keeps occurring in his work, namely, cognitive processes are thought of as tools that extend man's adaptive capacities. From this perspective, language extends the possibilities of human thought much as shovels, hoes, and tractors extend the possibilities of human agriculture.

The conception of mental growth as the development of representational tools emphasizes the evolutionary as well as the cultural nature of thought.

Bruner's conception of language as a tool for the construction of reality sets his view apart from that of the Russians. From the standpoint of dialetical materialism, social reality is a given, and language may or may not represent it accurately. It does not create it. The idea that language might create reality is "idealism" from the Russian perspective. The identification of thought with representational systems raises some serious problems. Language itself presupposes a set of rules that are not themselves representational. Chomsky's (1957) deep structures are not the same as the surface structures they govern. If language, or any other representational system, is said to include the deep structures, then it is no longer purely representational — a structural or operational component has been added. This component organizes representations but is not itself symbolic. The nonsymbolic rules and operations are what constitute thought. Hence, to describe development in terms of representations ignores the nonsymbolic elements present in any representational system. As Cassirer (1953) following Kant (1781/1943) has pointed out, symbols or representations are what mediate between thought and reality, but they should not be identified with either one.

Development as Exactness and Competence

A number of different conceptual orientations have in common the idea that cognitive development involves increased exactness and competence in performance. This idea is common to those concerned with operant learning (e.g., Skinner, 1971), to the perceptual theory of Gibson (1974), and to psychometric approaches to intelligence development (e.g., Horn 1975, 1976). Each of these different but related views stresses the fact that the young organism is relatively inefficient and that growth (conceived as diminished errors in responding) involves action that becomes more eonomical as a consequence of experience.

This orientation is quite clear in the operant approach to behavior (Skinner, 1971): "The environment is obviously important but its role has remained obscure. It does not push or pull, it selects, and this function is difficult to discover and to analyze. The selective role of natural selection in evolution was formulated only a little more than a hundred years ago, and the selective role of the environment in shaping and maintaining behavior is only beginning to be recognized and studied [p.25]." The environment selects or shapes behavior in desirable (or undersirable) directions and thus renders it more efficient in attaining its goal. Cumulative records (on all sorts of organisms) document the increased efficiency of behavior as a consequence of environmental shaping.

Another approach which suggests that development is a matter of increased efficiency is the perceptual theory of E. J. Gibson (1974):

Perceptual learning, as I see it, is characterized by an increased specificity of correspondence between stimulation   and the precision of the responding organism's discrimination. My husband and I argued many years ago that the essence of perceptual learning was differention rather than enrichment and that this kind of learning was not adding something like a response or an image to sensations, but rather was a change in *what* was responded to uniquely and specifically [p. 25].

And Gibson (1974) extends this idea to other cognitive processes: "I propose the hypothesis that the meanings of words, like the meanings of things and events, are gradually differentiated and converge, eventually, with the meanings of things and pictures of things, which are differentiated very early [p. 26]." From this point of view, conceptual no less than perceptual development involves a progressively more differentiated and exact correspondence with external reality. Because Gibson assumes that there is a fixed reality outside the individual that is to be known, she is closer to the Russians than she is to Bruner or to Werner.

A third orientation within the general rubric of development as increasing exactness is that of the psychometricians. From a psychometric standpoint, development from infancy is seen as the quantitative change with age in a number of mental abilities. On the Wechsler Scales (1958, 1967, 1974), for example, the same types of subtests are given at the preschool, school-age, and adult levels of intellectual functioning. There is a presumed continuity of intellectual functioning across age levels, with age changes contributing only a facilitative effect, at least through adolescence. In recent years the widely held conception that intelligence declines in the adult years has been challenged (e.g., Schaie & Labouvie–Vief, 1974). Other writers have argued that there are two types of intelligence, one that continues to improve with age and another that does show a decline (Horn, 1975).

In general, the psychometricians have little use for a stage, or qualitative, description of mental growth, despite the fact that the items on intelligence tests for different age levels tap manifestly different cognitive processes. For example, on the Information subtest of the Wechsler Intelligence Scale for Children (1974), the correct answers to the following two questions are given equal numerical credit. The first question has to do with the identification of a finger as the thumb. The twenty-ninth question has to do with the identification of Charles Darwin. It would seem that the difference between the questions is one of process as well as sheer quantity of knowledge. Yet the psychometricians do not always concede this possibility, as the following recent statement of their position indicates (Horn, 1976): "It is clear that children at one age fail to solve problems which most of them solve at a later age, but it is by no means always clear that this is indicative of a reorganization of the kind specified by Piagetian theory and is not just as parsimoniously interpreted as difficulty as specified by other theories [p. 456]."

The concept of development as an increase in the proficiency of performance is thus shared by the operant learning, perceptual discrimination, and psychometric orientations. And there is certainly considerable validity to this position. In general, behavior becomes more economical and more efficient with increasing age. On the average, the adolescent can read faster and comprehend more than can the elementary school pupil. A very important advantage of this view of mental growth is that it makes development easily measurable.

Although there are advantages to the "improved performance" approach to development, there are disadvantages as well. At one point or another, numbers have to be interpreted if they are to be applied to human behavior. When this occurs, those who advocate the quantitative approach nonetheless have to resort to qualitative descriptions. Such descriptions inevitably go beyond the notion of development as the mere improvement of performance. When Skinner (1971) talks about "freedom and dignity," he has to venture beyond the realm of cumulative records and behavioral regulation. Likewise, when Gibson talks about learning to read (e.g., Gibson & Levin, 1975), she has to go beyond quantitative changes in perceptual processes and talk of motivation, childrearing practices, and the like. Finally, in the psychometric domain, the failure of tests to predict much of anything in the way of vocational success has recently been demonstrated by several writers (e.g., Jencks, Smith, Acland, Bane, Cohen Gintis, Heyns, & Michelson, 1972; McClelland, 1973). And in clinical work, quantitative scores have to be coupled with qualitative analyses to be of much diagnostic utility (Schafer, 1948).

So the conception of development as improved performance with age has its limitations. However, the limitations are somewhat different, say, from those of the verbal mediation approach. The major limitation of the verbal mediation approach is one of process, in the sense that internalization is simply not sufficient to account for the whole of development. The limitation of the growth as quantifiable improvement, on the other hand, is one of content. A quantitative approach always has to be coupled with a qualitative interpretation if it is to have practical and theoretical as well as empirical significance.

Development as Geographic Progression

Within Freudian psychology, development tends to be viewed geographically (Freud, 1920). In the course of psychosexual development, the instinctual forces move from the oral to the anal to the genital areas of the body. The Freudian stages thus describe the progressive erogenic development of various body zones. This theme is carried forward by Anna Freud (1946) in her discussion of ego defenses in adolescence. According to her, intellectual processes can be taken over by instinctual drives after puberty.

This geogrpahic conception of development is present even in the work of some of Freud's most contemporary followers. The psychosocial stages of

Erik Erikson (1950), for example, could be interpreted geographically. Although Erikson does not talk about biological drives, he does believe that all the psychosocial dichotomies (trust versus mistrust, identity versus role diffusion, and so on) are present in some form from the beginning of life. At different times in development, one or another of these dichotomies is brought to the forefront of the individual's existence and constitutes one of a series of psychosocial crises. Because all the dichotomies exist from the beginning of life, the successive crises again constitute a kind of geographical shift of energies to various "sectors" or "fronts" of psychosocial or interpersonal interaction.

The geographical-shift conception of development highlights the biological and physical changes that accompany growth. And it is certainly true that these changes affect and are interrelated with changes in cognitive development. Again, this view of growth is incomplete, even on its own terms. The derivation of ego defenses from the evolution of drives cannot account for their differing levels of cognitive complexity. Denial, for example, is much less complex structurally than is rationalization (Elkind, 1976). This difference cannot be explained geographically. Likewise, Erikson's theory cannot fully explain why identity crises occur in adolescence other than that empirically this happens to be the case. The appearance of formal operations in adolescence, as described by Piaget (1950), can provide an explanation. It is only in adolescence that young people have the conceptual wherewithal to construct a cohesive identity from the disparate experiences of their life histories. Dynamic theories need to be complemented with cognitive developmental theories to give a more complete explanation of behavior.

In this very brief review of conceptions of development, I have tried to show some of the virtues as well as some of the limitations of several extant conceptions of development from infancy. It is time now to compare these conceptions with Piaget's distinction between the figurative and the operative. This distinction presents a very different conception of the nature of development.

THE FIGURATIVE/OPERATIVE DISTINCTION AND OTHER CONCEPTIONS OF DEVELOPMENT

What, then, are the advantages and disadvantages of the figurative/operative conception of cognitive development, particularly in regard to the other views of development from infancy that have already been described? First, like Werner's (1948) orthogenetic principle, the distinction is quite general and can encompass the development of scientific knowledge as well as the development of individual knowledge. In science, concepts such as the earth's roundness were eventually arrived at from reasoning about such things as the earth's shadow on the moon and the disappearance of ships on the horizon, but this transformational conception was preceded by the more static, figurative conception of the earth's flatness. The figurative/operative distinction is particular as well in that it refers to specific mental processes (imagery, imitation, and perception) in connection with the figurative knowing and other processes (the various operational groupings of intelligence) in connection with operative knowing. However, the description of development as moving from the figurative to the operative still has to be filled out with regard to specific content. In the sense that Piaget's studies deal with content as well as process, the whole corpus of Piaget's work would be said to be a detailed exposition of how knowledge moves from the figurative to the operative.

The Piagetian distinction of the figurative and operative also has advantages in comparison to the mediation viewpoint. It was argued earlier that the mediation view is too narrow because it includes only one process with a limited definition. However, in Piaget's distinction between the figurative and the operative we have a recognition that development involves both internalization and externalization. We also saw that the externalization of an operative product could be the basis for a new, operative internalization. In addition, Piaget recognizes that internalization is not a simple miniaturization of response. He has introduced the concept of *reflective abstraction* (Piaget, 1970) to explain how the child derives operations from experience. So, although Piaget recognizes that internalization is an important process of development, he also recognizes that it is coupled with externalization and that it is never a mere miniaturization of response.

If we now compare the Piagetian position with that of Bruner, other advantages are seen. Bruner (1964) identifies thought with representation and ignores the nonrepresentational elements in any symbolic system. However, this separation between the representational and the operational is built into the distinction between the figurative and the operative. The figurative processes, imitation, and imagery perception are the basis for representational systems, including language (Piaget, 1951), but representational systems including langauge are not the same as operational systems although there is considerable interaction between them. Some aspects of language are largely figurative (accent and inflection) whereas others are largely operative (grammar and syntax). The figurative/operative distinction thus embodies the distinction between representational systems and thought that are dealt with as a unity by Bruner.

It is probably easy to see how Piaget's conception of the figurative and the operative answers the criticisms that were earlier leveled at the views that see development as being essentially the improvement of performance over time. The trouble with such views, it was said, was that although they stressed the quantitative, the qualitative always had to be taken into account

if the quantified results were to be interpreted either theoretically or empirically. If anything, Piaget can be faulted in the other direction, that of not
being sufficiently concerned with the quantification of behavior. That
criticism is correct, but it is also true that the quantification of Piaget's findings is probably much more easily accomplished (e.g., Goldschmidt &
Bentler, 1968) than is the qualitative interpretation of findings from operant
conditioning, discrimination learning, or psychometric testing.

In comparison with the conception of development as geographical progression, Piaget's constructions stand up well. A major advantage of the
psychoanalytic views was that they took seriously the relation of mental
development to physical maturation, to biology. Piaget's work, too, is
closely tied to the biological nature of the organism, but Piaget's view implies that development is more than a matter of shifting from one organ
system to another. Rather, it is a matter of unending change from structure
to function, from those that are static to those that are dynamic. This process, in turn, is effected through the development of new mental structures.
So, although Piaget respects the contributions of biology to development,
he does not limit his conception of development to shifting "zones" of interaction with the environment.

Perhaps the major advantage of the figurative/operative conception of
development, in comparison to the others that have been mentioned, is that
it takes *reality* into account. All the other positions — differentiation and
hierarchical integration, mediation, representation, increased exactness of
performance, and geographical progression — pay little, if any, heed to reality. Like the pre-Kantian empiricists, such orientations take reality for
granted and center on the mental processes of knowing as if these were
separate and apart from the content to be known. In psychology, this exclusive focus on process to the exclusion of content leads to the use of
nonsense syllables in the study of memory and simple geometric forms in the
study of concept attainment.

For Piaget, however, the content known is every bit as important as the
processes of knowing, as must be the case if the very operations of knowing
are themselves derived from experience. To understand how the child arrives
at the operations for dealing with the physical world, one has to study how
the child deals with the physical world. It is not surprising, therefore, that
all of Piaget's books deal with *relevant* content, space, time, number, quantity, geometry, physical causality, and so on. The empiricist notion that one
can study mental processes in isolation from relevant content is an illusion
that has befogged psychological and educational research for decades.
Simply put, if one does not study relevant content, then one will never
observe the mental processes necessary to their conceptualization.

However, the figurative/operative distinction is, not without its own
limitations. It is a fairly general distinction that is sometimes difficult to

draw in particular instances. Lanaguage processes are particularly troublesome in this regard. Speech clearly has both figurative and operative aspects, and reading also involves a complex of figurative and operative processes. Moreover, it may not be clear without investigation whether a child's response to a particular problem is figurative or operative. A child may count correctly without having a true or unit concept of number. The only way to make the determination would be to test the child for the conservation of number. In short, criteria will have to be decided on in particular instances as to what constitutes figurative and operative knowledge.

In addition and equally important is the fact that Piaget has left the whole domain of social reality out of consideration. With the exception of the work on moral development (Piaget, 1965), he has been little concerned with the child's construction of social reality. One would expect the figurative/operative distinction to hold in this domain as well. And one would also assume that the construction of social reality would be best understood in studies of important social concepts and situations. These are questions that need to be answered by future research. Although it does not provide them explicitly, Piaget's work suggests important directions for research in the expanding field of social cognition.

IMPLICATIONS

Piaget's distinction between the figurative and the operative would seem to bear both general as well as specific implications for psychology. It is clearly not possible to discuss all these implications within the confines of a single chapter, but I would like to deal with one general implication and with one specific application. The general implication concerns the role of content in psychological theory and research. The practical application concerns a cognitive developmental analysis of several of the subtests of the Wechsler Intelligence Scale for Children (WISC) (Wechsler, 1974).

Content in Psychological Theory and Research

In my opinion Piaget's emphasis on the importance of content in the study of mental process is perhaps the most important contribution of the figurative/operative distinction. In this section I will consider some of the reasons why content has been neglected in contemporary psychology and re-emphasize the importance of content in psychological research and theory.

It is rather surprising that an empiricist psychology, such as that which predominates in the United States, should be so disinterested in the content of knowledge. Contemporary information-processing approaches to learning, for example, like the earlier S-R theories, regard the content of learning as secondary to the processes that deal with it (see, e.g., the studies reported in Levine, 1975). The divorce of psychological theory from content is also evidenced in the many "mathematical models" that periodically appear to explain one or another psychological phenomenon. In a very real sense these models are really too advanced for the state of the discipline. Our knowledge of behavior is simply not exact enough to warrant such models. Yet such model building is encouraged as long as one holds to the belief that process can be dealt with separately from content.

The divorce of psychological theory and research from relevant content is probably due in large measure to the precedent set by the empiricist philosophers and by the logical positivists. Historically these two traditions gave rise to related emphases in psychology. Empiricism gave rise to contentless learning theories such as those of Hull (1952) and of Skinner (1938). Logical positivism gave impetus to "operationism" as a scientific credo (Bridgman, 1927). These two developments have often been conjoined and are generally believed to be complementary. In fact they are, if anything, contradictory. Learning theory attempts to reduce knowledge to human behavior. Logical positivism seeks to reduce knowledge or behavior to sense data. Learning theory tries to psychologize knowledge whereas logical positivism tries to depsychologize it. Considering the difference in orientation, it is interesting that so many psychologists adopted a scientific credo that was decidely antipsychological.

In my opinion, Piaget has tried to reconcile these opposed viewpoints by recognizing the importance both of the processes of knowing and of the content to be known in the construction of reality. Perhaps the best example of this twofold approach to psychological investigation is given by Piaget's two books, *The Origins of Intelligence in Children* (Piaget, 1952) and *The Construction of Reality in the Child* (Piaget, 1954). In the *Origins* book Piaget focuses on the psychological processes of construction, primary and secondary circular reactions, and so on. In the *Construction* book he focuses on the content of the child's experience, the construction of permanent objects, and the progressive differentiation between states and transformations, between the figurative and operative. Taken together, these two books demonstrate the utility and fruitfulness of a psychology that recognizes that the analysis of content is a necessary corollary to the analysis of process.

In psychology, and particularly educational psychology, the artificial separation betwen process and content has impeded theoretical progress. For example, as long as concept formation, problem solving, and memory were explored with simple materials, only simple processes could be observed. As soon as investigators began presenting subjects with complex problem solving, concept attainment, and memory tasks, it was discovered that the human learner employs a variety of sophisticated strategies, constructs and tests hypotheses, and so on. The failure of the early workers to observe these processes was a direct result of their use of simple materials.

In educational psychology the bifurcation of process and content has led to disastrous curriculum errors. During the 1960's, for example, curriculum development went to one or another extreme. In some areas of curriculum development, such as the new math, the focus was on content to the extent that the concepts were much too difficult for the age groups to which they were presented. On the other hand, the focus on discovery learning in other areas of curriculum development made content incidental to acquiring the ability to think. Current attempts by community and social psychologists to teach school children problem solving and communication skills, independent of curriculum content, are equally one-sided. The current back-to-basics movement is, at one level, an attempt to get process *and* content back into the curriculum.

There is some evidence that learning theory in the United States is also beginning to recognize the importance of content in psychological investigations. One of the most interesting lines of research spearheading the contemporary revolution in learning theory starts from recent work on "super learning". For rats, the taste of food is by far the most important stimulus, and the rat will avoid a place where poisoned food was even when the poison did not take effect immediately (Riley, 1974). Among other animals "super learning" occurs in other domains. Quail, for example, avoid the visual rather than the gustatory aspects of poisoned food (Wilcoxon, Dragoin, & Kral, 1971). Apparently, animals of different species vary in their readiness to learn through particular sensory avenues. Even at the animal level, therefore, the content of what is to be learned cannot be separated from the process. The laws of learning simply do not apply across all contents and all species. A truly comprehensive theory of learning will have to take content as well as process into account.

A Cognitive Developmental Analysis of Several WISC Subtests

As a practical demonstration of the utility of the figurative/operative distinction, let us analyze some of the subtests of the Wechsler Intelligence Scale for Children (Wechsler, 1974). I chose the WISC because many of the items deal with relevant content and because a cognitive developmental analysis of the subtests is long overdue. This is true because the well-known qualitative analysis of the Wechsler Adult Intelligence Scale (WAIS) by Rapaport, Gill, and Schafer (1945) has often been uncritically adopted as a model for the qualitative analysis of the children's scales. That is, the Rapaport et al. interpretations (e.g., that similarities measure "concept formation," that digit span measures "attention," and so on) are still employed by clinicians and school psychologists in their diagnostic work.

As we will see, however, a cognitive developmental analysis of some of the WISC subtests in terms of figurative and operative processes gives us quite a different picture. It must be remembered, however, that the pioneering work of Rapaport et al. (1945) was done without our contemporary knowledge of cognitive psychology. When they did their research, the distinction between the operative and the figurative had not yet been made, nor was the distinction between divergent and convergent thinking clearly formulated. And the notion that concept attainment and problem solving involved hypothesis testing had not been seriously considered. It is no disrespect to these writers to say that a reevaluation of the WAIS as well as the WISC is very much in order.

Because a comprehensive cognitive analysis of the WISC would be a major work in itself, I illustrate only the potential fruitfulness of such an analysis with a few items from several different subtests. We will look at some items from General Information (said to measure the ability to learn from experience), from Similarities (said to measure concept formation), and from the Block Design (said to measure concentration).

General Information. The first item on the General Information subscale is the question, "What do you call this finger (show thumb)" which requires simple figurative/knowledge — labeling an object. However, the very next item, "How many ears do you have?" already involves some operative understanding — to the extent that number and counting are involved. Of course, some children may know the answer on a purely figurative basis, by rote, but others will know it on an operative level. Qualitatively, success or failure on this item is ambiguous because the reasons for success or for failure cannot be known without further inquiry. Many of the items on this subtest have the same ambiguity.

It should also be said that the items range all the way from the preoperational to the formal operational insofar as their logical substructure is concerned. "What do you call this finger?" is a preoperational question. However, the question, "How many pennies make a nickel?" poses a concrete operational problem. It requires that the child understand that one thing (a single coin) can represent many coins. In logical terms, the substructure of the task is analogous to that involved in the hierarchical organization of classes (boys and girls = children) and becomes prominent once children attain concrete operational thought.

Many of the later test items presuppose formal operational processes. The question, "What causes iron to rust?" involves an understanding of the process of oxidation. Understanding oxidation requires the knowledge that air and water contain oxygen and that oxygen interacts with metal to cause rust. Of course, on this item as on many others, a child may be correct on a purely figurative basis because he has merely heard someone say that oxygen causes rust and many not understand the processes involved. For example, a subject may also know the answer to the question, "How far is it from New York to Los Angeles?" without having a true (formal operational) conception of geographical space.

The cognitive heterogeneity of this subtest is exemplified by the last item, "What does turpentine come from?" — essentially a concrete operational question. In this case, the difficulty of the item is its unfamiliarity rather than its logical difficulty. Accordingly, on the General Information Subtest we have a cognitively quite heterogeneous set of items that may assess figurative or operative learning (at any one of three different levels) as well as an openness to learn extraneous bits of information. Without really examining a child's responses item by item, it would really be misleading to attribute his performance to a single construct such as "fund of general information." At the very least, one would want to know how much of the information was figuratively acquired, how much was acquired operatively, and the highest level of operativity involved. On the other hand, if one really wanted to assess a child's capacity to learn from experience, a whole range of items, all at the same operative level, would do the job much better.

Similarities.   According to Rapaport et al. (1945), the Similarities Subtest measures concept attainment. Presumably this is true because the subject is required to find a common feature or quality that joins two different objects. However, concept attainment can occur at many different levels and in many different ways. The Similarities Subtest is far from being a homogeneous measure of processes involved in concept attainment.

The first item of the test is: "In what way are a wheel and a ball alike? How are they the same?" This is a figurative task in that a perceived quality, roundness, is the correct answer. So, too, is the problem posed by the next item, Candle–Lamp. But the next two items, Shirt–Hat and Piano–Guitar, are operative in that they require the nesting of classes associated with concrete operations. Through item 11, the test moves developmentally. The early items are preoperational, the next are concrete operational, and the later items are formal operational. For example, item 10 (Pound–Yard) and item 11 (Anger–Joy) require higher-order, formal operational thought for a two-point answer. The correct answers, "measurement" and "emotions", are second-order abstractions characteristic of adolescent thinking.

Thereafter, however, the items take a different turn. Item 12 (Scissors–Copper pan) like the last item (Salt–Water) is concrete operational in its logical substructure. What these items seem to measure is not so much conceptual level as divergent thinking. Indeed, many items of this sort appear in tests of creativity. And category breadth and narrowness are often used as measures of divergent thinking (see Wallach and Kogan, 1965, for a discussion of this issue).

The Similarities Subtest, therefore, measures both figurative and opperative knowing (at several different levels) and also divergent thinking. To interpret performance on this subtest as a straightforward measure of concept attainment ability would be simplistic. As in the case of the information subtests, interpretations should probably be made with respect to performance on particular items, or groups of items, rather than on the basis of the subtest as a whole.

Block Design.   The Block Design Test is a familiar one in which the subject is requested to reconstruct with a set of blocks a design depicted on a card. From a cognitive developmental point of view, the Block Design is one of the purest subtests of the WISC. It is almost entirely a test of perceptual regulations—concrete operations in the service of perceptual analysis. It is a largely operative task because the difficulty of the items has almost nothing to do with the discrimination of the various forms depicted on the cards. Even young children can discriminate these forms and can match them to a sample if required to do so. The difficulty of the task is of a different order, lying in the necessity of analyzing the design into component parts. In this regard, it is not unlike the conservation of continuous quantities (such as liquids and clay) wherein the subject must mentally divide the material into units to arrive at a correct solution.

Rapaport et al. (1945) said that the Block Design test was a measure of concentration. That it may be, but it is also a very good measure of Block Design Subtest correlates so highly with performance on the verbal subtests (Wechsler, 1974). It might correlate even more highly if it tapped a wider range of operational structures. However, the Block Design primarily measures concrete operations, and the difficulty among the various items would seem to be largely a matter of horizontal décalage, that is, the figurative complexity of the various designs.

These brief examples may provide some evidence for the practical utility of the figurative/operative distinction. At the very least, this distinction offers tools for analyzing many different contents from mental tests to school curricula. And it provides a new way of thinking about the cognitive processes involved in these materials.

CONCLUSIONS

In this chapter I have tried to accomplish four things: (1) to provide an in-depth review of Piaget's conception of the figurative and the operative; (2) to provide a brief review of others' conceptions of development from infancy; (3) to compare Piaget's position with each of the others reviewed; and (4) to suggest   some   theoretical   and   practical   implications   of   Piaget's figurative/operative distinction. I hope that I have shown how the figurative/operative conception adds to other conceptions of development and how it has considerable value both for theoretical and applied child development.

REFERENCES

Apostel, L., Mays, W., Morf, A., & Piaget, J. *Les liaisons analytiques et syncretiques dans les comportements du sujet.* Paris: Presses Universitaires de France, 1957.

Berkeley, S. A treatise concerning the principles of human knowledge. In S. Commens & R. N. Turscott (Eds.), *Man and spirit: The speculative philosophers.* New York: Random House 1947.

Birch, H. G., & Belmont, L. Auditory-visual integration, intelligence and reading ability in school children. *Perceptual and Motor Skills,* 1965, *20,* 295–305.

Bower, T. G. R. *Development in infancy.* San Francisco: Freeman, 1974.

Bridgman, P. W. *The logic of modern physics.* New York: Macmillan, 1927.

Bruner, J. The course of cognitive growth. *American Psychologist,* 1964, *19,* 1–15.

Bruner, J. Child development: Play is a serious business. *Psychology Today,* January 1975, 81–83.

Cassirer, E. *The philosophy of symbolic forms.* New Haven: Yale, University Press, 1953.

Chomsky, N. *Syntactic structures.* The Hague: Mouton, 1957.

Elkind, D. The child's discovery of the conservation of mass, weight and volume. *Journal of Genetic Psychology,* 1961, *98,* 219–227.(a)

Elkind, D. The development of quantitative thinking. *Journal of Genetic Psychology,* 1961, *98,* 37–46.(b)

Elkind, D. Conservation across illusory transformations. *Human Development,* 1966, *25,* 389–400.

Elkind, D. Perceptual development in children. *American Scientist,* 1975, *83,* 533–541.

Elkind, D. Cognitive development and psychopathology: Observations on egocentrism and ego defense. In E. Schopler & R. J. Reichler (Eds.), *Psychopathology and child development.* New York: Plenum, 1976.

Erikson, E. *Childhood and society.* New York: Norton, 1950.

Freud, A. *The ego and the mechanisms of defense.* New York: Hogarth, 1946.

Freud, S. *A general introduction to psychoanalysis.* Garden City, N. Y.: Garden City, 1920.

Gibson, E. Trends in perceptual development. In A. D. Pick (Ed.), *Minnesota symposia in child psychology* (Vol. 8). Minneapolis: University of Minnesota Press, 1974.

Gibson, E. J., & Levin, H. *The psychology of reading.* Cambridge, Mass.: MIT Press, 1975.

Goldschmidt, M. L., & Bentler, P. M. Concept assessment, kit, conservation. San Diego, Cal.: Educational and Industrial Testing Service, 1968.

Hegel, F. *[Reason in history]* (R. S. Hartman, trans.). New York: Liberal Arts Press, 1953.

Horn, J. Psychometric studies of aging and intelligence. In S. Sershon & A. Roskin (Eds.), *Geriatric psychopharmacology: The scene today.* New York: Rowen Press, 1975.

Horn, J. Human abilities: A review of research and theory in the early 1970's. In M. R. Rosenzweig & L. W. Porter (Eds.), *Annual review of psychology,* 1976, *27,* 437–486.

Hull, C. L. *A behavior system: An introduction to behavior theory concerning the individual organism.* New Haven: Yale University Press, 1952.

Hume, D. An enquiry concerning human understanding. In S. Commins & R. N. Tunscott (Eds.), *Man and spirit: The speculative philosophers.* New York: Random House, 1947.

Jencks, C., Smith, M., Acland, H., Bane, M., Cohen, D., Gintis, H., Heyns, B., & Michelson, S. *Inequality: A reassessment of the effect of family and schooling in America.* New York: Basic Books, 1972.

Kant, I. *Critique of pure reason.* New York: Wiley, 1943. (Originally published, 1781.)

Kendler, H. H., & Kendler, T. S. From discrimination learning to cognitive development: A neobehavioristic odyssey. In W. K. Estes (Ed.), *Handbook of learning and cognitive processes* (Vol. 1). Hillsdale, N. J.: Lawrence Erlbaum Associates, 1975.

Levine, M. J. *A cognitive theory of learning: Research on hypothesis testing.* Hillsdale, N. J.: Lawrence Erlbaum Associates, 1975.

Locke, J. *An essay concerning human understanding.* New York: Oxford University Press 1975. (Third original edition printed, 1695.)

Luria, A. R., & Yudovich, F. Y. *Speech and the development of mental processes in the child.* London: Staples, 1968.

McClelland, D. C. Testing for competence rather than for intelligence. *American Psychologist,* 1973, *28,* 1-14.

Neimark, E. D. An information processing approach to cognitive development. *Transactions of the New York Academy of Sciences,* 1971, *33,* 516-528.

Piaget, J. *The psychology of intelligence.* London: Routledge & Kegan Paul, 1950.

Piaget, J. *Play, dreams and imitation in childhood.* New York: Norton, 1951.

Piaget, J. *The origins of intelligence in childhood.* New York: International Universities Press, 1952.

Piaget, J. *The Construction of reality in the child.* New York: Basic Books, 1954.

Piaget, J. *The moral judgment of the child.* N. Y.: Free Press, 1965.

Piaget, J. *The mechanisms of perception.* London: Routledge and Kegan Paul, 1969.

Piaget, J. *Genetic epistemology.* New York: Columbia University Press, 1970.

Piaget, J. *The child and reality.* New York: Grossman, 1973.

Piaget, J., & Inhelder, B. *Mental imagery in the child.* New York: Basic Books, 1971.

Piaget, J., & Inhelder, B. *Memory and intelligence.* London: Routledge & Kegan Paul, 1973.

Piaget, J., & Szeminska, A. *The child's conception of number.* New York: Free Press, 1952.

Rapaport, D., Gill, M., & Schafer, R. *Diagnostic psychological testing.* Chicago: Year Book Publishers, 1945.

Reichenbach, H. *The rise of scientific philosophy.* Berkeley: University of California Press, 1951.

Riley, A. L. *Learned aversions to the location of toxic water supply.* Paper presented at the meeting of the Western Psychological Association, San Francisco, April, 1974.

Sapir, E. *Culture, language and personality.* Los Angeles: University of California Press, 1949.

Schafer, R. *The clinical application of psychological tests.* New York: International Universities Press, 1948.

Schaie, K. W., & Labouvie-Vief, G. Generational versus ontogenetic components of change in adult cognitive behavior: A fourteen-year cross-sectional study. *Developmental Psychology,* 1974, *10,* 305-320.

Skinner, B. F. *The behavior of organism: An experimental analysis.* Englewood Cliffs, N. J.: Prentice Hall, 1938.

Skinner, B. F. *Beyond freedom and dignity.* New York: Knopf, 1971.

Vygotsky, L. S. *Thought and language.* Cambridge, Mass.: MIT Press, 1962.

Wallach, M. A., & Kogan, N. *Modes of thinking in young children.* New York: Holt, Rinehart and Winston, 1965.

Wechsler, D. *The measurement and appraisal of adult intelligence* (4th ed.). Baltimore, Md.: Williams & Wilkins, 1958.

Wechsler, D. *Wechsler preschool and primary scale of intelligence.* New York: Psychological Corporation, 1967.

Wechsler, D. *Manual for the Wechsler intelligence scale for children* (Rev. ed.). New York: Psychological Corporation, 1974.

Werner, H. *Comparative psychology of mental development.* Chicago, Ill: Follett, 1948.

Werner, H. The concept of development from a comparative and organismic point of view. In O. B. Harris (Ed.), *The concept of development.* Minneapolis: University of Minnesota Press, 1957.

White, S. H. Evidence for hierarchical arrangement of learning processes. In L. P. Lipsitt & C. C. Spiker (Eds.), *Advances in child development and behavior* (Vol. 2). New York: Academic Press, 1965.

Whorf, B. L. *Language, thought, & reality.* Cambridge, Mass.: MIT Press, 1956.

Wilcoxon, H. C., Dragoin, W. B., & Kral, P. A. Illness-induced aversions in rat and quail: Relative salience of visual and gustatory cues. *Science,* 1971, *171,* 826–828.

10 From Adaptive Responses to Social Cognition: The Learning View of Development

Hanuš Papoušek
Max Planck Institute for Psychiatry, Munich

INTRODUCTION

Adaptive processes characterize the early development of the human infant, and learning in infants has been analyzed previously by numerous skilled discussants including Brackbill and Koltsova (1967), Horowitz (1968), Reese & Lipsitt (1970), and Stevenson (1972). Moreover, the relationship between adaptive responses and early cognitive development has been reviewed by Kessen (1966), Elkind (1967), Charlesworth (1968), and Bower (1974). Yet, for all the simplicity and uniformity of theories of learning, each empiricist or theoretician has his own points of view, and the opportunity and challenge to discuss two decades of my own attempts to learn something about the infant's learning and to learn about the infant's cognitive and social development therefore represents too attractive an opportunity to pass by.

INFANT OBSERVATION AND EXPERIMENTATION AS A BEGINNING

Twenty years ago in the United States Hullian and Skinnerian theories of learning prevailed. They represented a culmination of the tendency toward "scientific" psychology. This psychology was devoted to the analysis of observable behaviors, and it avoided all "black-box" phenomena. Vygotsij, Gestalt psychology, system theory, and even Piaget still had a touch of exoticism. In Europe, the Zeitgeist was quite the opposite. Schools of thought indigenous to Europe sensitized European researchers to the close relationship between learning and central cognitive processes. In Prague, for example, developmental and comparative biology influenced the minds of psychology students. Next to physically standardized stimuli and narrowly selected behavioral responses, the psychology in which I was trained also cared for general behavior of the whole organism, including for example, its biorhythms.

In particular, the impetus in developmental psychology at that time was to study the earliest period of development, infancy, and this impetus derived from two influeces. One was Gestalt psychology, with its focus on "cognitive" processing of "perceptual" information and the structure of complex environmental stimulation, and the other was learning, with its focus from Pavlov on "physiology of higher nervous functions." These dual influences brought experimental methods to the study of early development and at the same time raised basic questions about the ontogeny and organization of learning.

In addition to principles of learning, we in infancy studies were exposed to several lines of evidence that implicated organismic constituents in early development. The orienting response (OR), described by Pavlov (1927) and analyzed in greater detail by Sokolov (1963), first drew experimental attention to primary organismic or adaptive processing of environmental stimulation. Whether a stimulus situation is or is not new to a subject does not depend solely on its physical qualities. Rather, its status is determined by preceding experience, its engram, and the subject's capacity to detect similarities or differences between past and current stimulation. Likewise, comparative biology emphasized a second category of organismic determinant, namely, species-specific sensitivity to environmental stimulation, phylogenetically conditioned. It is obvious, for example, in the difference between birds depending largely on visual cues and nocturnal rodents depending on olfactory or auditory cues. One lesson derived from this principle was to take greater care to avoid zoomorphisms, or exaggerated tendencies to apply findings from animal experiments to the interpretation of human behavior. Pavlov himself had repeatedly warned against this, stressing the importance of man's second signal system — language. One further organismic determinant relating to the efficacy of external stimulation is still relatively unknown at present. It is Ukhtomsky's (1952) "principle of a central dominance," according to which one part of the central nervous system (CNS) may respond to stimuli that would otherwise typically elicit responses from another area if the first is in a state of increased excitation. In his classical experiments, Ukhtomsky (1952) showed that a cat responded with a rectal contraction rather that with a flexion of the forepaw to a tactile stimulation of that paw when intra-rectal tension was experimentally increased. Depending, then, on the reinforcement history of the individual, different factors lead to alternative views of strengths of the same stimulus arrangement.

In different ways, then, European developmental psychologists have been exposed to influences beyond physical or laboratory control of stimulus and response. Interest in the complex structures of both stimulus situation and thought processes involved in the integration of adaptive responses obviously had roots similar to the developmental concepts formulated in systems theory (Bertalanffy, 1968), in comparative psychology (Werner, 1948), and to some extent in the epistemology of Piaget (1952). This milieu sensitized us, even two decades ago, to broad conceptions in development.

WHY BEGIN PSYCHOLOGICAL RESEARCH IN INFANCY?

It seemed to us a reasonable strategy to investigate initial and primitive levels of mental development in advance of the complex and difficult problem of the adult mental capacities. Comparative biologists who have studied embryology have realized how helpful it is to observe the recapitulation of somatic development of the species in order to better understand adult anatomy and physiology. Therefore, it seemed realistic to pay similar attention to the early ontogeny of adaptive behavior. Moreover, we wondered to what extent simple beginnings indicate potential.

Infant psychology is ultimately important for its examination of individual differences. Individual infants differ not only along quantitative dimensions but above all in their qualitative behavioral strategies. Human observers are able to detect much more subtle behavioral changes in the human infant than in any other animal. This may be valid for emotional and communicative behavior as it is for observable signs of thinking. Obviously, we all use external signs as feedback elements in communication with others. Therefore, such signs cannot escape our attention whenever we see them in the infant. Every parent is able to list patterns of emotional behavior that significantly exceed that set used to describe emotion in rats, usually the number of boluses or amount of self-licking. Moreover, parents will gladly offer interpretations of emotional behavior in babies, and surprisingly enough, such interpretations will have much to do with though processes.

Here again, even outside of objective experimental work, there is something about the infant that draws our attention repeatedly to the interior of the "black-box."

Several circumstances supported research in infancy in Europe. One was connected with strong traditional interests among Europeans in educational programs. Whereas beliefs that education was inappropriate for infants and toddlers or might even interfere with early personality development seemed to have caused its neglect among parents and educators in the United States (Fowler, 1962), European concern dated back to Comenius (1629) and reached a height of detailed treatment in Montessori (1964). In Europe increasing numbers of children were taken to day nurseries often early in the first year of life, and different European countries emphasized the necessity to elaborate and use early educational programs. For example, Viennese child psychology, represented in research by the Buhlers, stressed the importance of the early experience and was probably the effective impulse for Spitz's (1945) later studies. The Czechoslovakian government fostered educational programs for infants. For the infants reared at our research unit in Prague there was also available a continuing educational program carried out systematically under the regular supervision of psychologists associated with our research team. This made the infants' experimental circumstances comparable and permitted easier analysis of the individual differences among them.

Practically speaking, research in infancy had been neglected and so, consequently, adequate rational care for infants. Difficult access to newborns and infants, together with a prevailing underestimation of what could be learned for studies of subjects so fragile, certainly reflect two major reasons why we then knew so little about early behavior.

Our situation in Prague, where infants with their mothers could be cared for and studied over the first 6 months of life, provided additional reason to concentrate on infancy. Studies of maternal deprivation (Goldfarb, 1945; Lowrey, 1940; Spitz, 1945) had provided first warning signals of the need for research concern, and ethological concepts like imprinting and critical periods in development had had a significant social impact. We needed to study infants systematically in order to understand deprivation, institutionalization, and fashion in child rearing.

CONDITIONING, LEARNING, AND COGNITION

Two decades ago the behavioral sciences offered only a very narrow view to those interested in the early development of adaptive behavior. Learning theoreticians, studying both animals and human beings, hoped very much to be able to interpret most adaptive processes in terms of conditioning. Studies of infantile conditioning were rare and did not allow convincing conclusions on the basic questions of how early and how easily the infant learns even the simplest conditioned response. Conditioning did not offer a wide repertoire of experimental methods, either, although conditioning methods had already been shown to be a new useful tool. For example, in studies of perceptual discrimination, Kasatkin (1948) demonstrated the first norms of infantile discrimination in several modalities.

Early infant-conditioning studies were principally based on motor behavior, and different views, particularly the Piagetian, have emphasized the inter-relation between motor actions and thought processes as being one of the most important preconditions of the development of intelligent behavior in the child (Kopp, Chapter 2, this volume). However, perceptual psychology has had very little to say about the processing of proprioceptive and kinesthetic information coming from the sensory organs to the CNS. Infants demonstrate particularly clearly how much behavior is constituted of motor behavior. Coordination and integration doubtlessly require intricate processes analogous to thought processes—grouping and regrouping, serial and parallel ordering at different levels of hierarchy, coding in memory, conceptualizing, and predicting and testing predictions. All these processes occur nonverbally. In fact, their development precedes the development of speech of vocal communication both in phylogeny and in ontogeny, and it may well be based on systems of structural order and rhythm that are replicated later in the structure of language. (Schaffer, Chapter 12, this volume). One could argue that this replication engages a substantially reduced repertoire of those processes previously used to integrate movements. Imagine a situation in which you are walking on board a ship, balancing out the ship's movements, playing with a key in one hand, fishing for small change in your pocket with the other hand, whistling your favorite melody, and simultaneously searching for your friend in the crowd of passengers with your eyes. All these activities may be carried out in parallel, but as verbal operations, we have to treat them in a serial order. It is like having a single-lane outlet for a thick network of multilane highways: There is good reason for highly selective utilization of such an outlet but no reason for assumptions that knowledge of rules that control the movement through such an outlet presuppose knowledge about all the rules applied prior to the outlet. In the motor system, in fact, quite complex cognitive processes may develop prenatally. We only have to look for methods by which to see them.

Both associative and operant methods of conditioning have been used in the analysis of more complex cognitive processes. Very early, Krasnogorskij with his co-workers elaborated classical salivation methods of conditioning for children (1907) and later attempted to modify these methods toward an objective analysis of logical operations (1958). For instance, they used the word "eighteen" as a verbally conditioned signal reinforced with candied cranberries. The appearance of conditioned salivation, its latency, and its intensity served as indexes of arithmetic operations in experiments when the "pupil" was given tasks like 9 times 2, 90 divided by 5, 72 divided by 4, and so on. In other experiments, bird names were used as verbal signals for a conditioned salivation, and occasionally the word "bird" was tested without ever having been reinforced. "Bird" first elicited no conditioned salivation, but when a sufficient number of bird names had been made conditioned salivation signals, the word "bird" suddenly elicited a conditioned salivation as well. From that moment on, other bird names also functioned as conditioned signals without their ever being reinforced. This certainly was early experimental evidence (1958) of the integrative role of words at different levels of abstraction. Similarly, Fields (1932) used operant conditioning to demonstrate concept learning (of triangularity) in rats, and Herrnstein and Loveland (1964) showed how exact concepts of man are formed in pigeons.

Seeking a motor response that would allow study of both simple forms of learning and higher cognitive processes like concept formation and that in addition would be applicable in newborns and older infants, our laboratory turned its attention to head movements.

Left and right head turns are movements simple enough to be analyzed quantitatively in degress of rotation and recorded polygraphically. They may be used for both operant and associative types of conditioning or in a mixed design in which the latency of a response can be utilized as a parameter of adaption (Papoušek, 1961). The adaptive aspect of head movements can be varied so as to serve as an instrumental act for obtaining food, switching on visual displays, or avoiding unpleasant stimulation. Head turns also belong to the class of orienting responses. Because a head turn can be carried out symmetrically, it can serve in designs of conditioned discrimination if a response to CS_1 is reinforced from the left and to CS_2 from the right. In comparison with the three common ways of measuring discrimination capacities in infants (preference designs in paired comparison, generalization designs, and discrimination between reinforced and nonreinforced stimuli), this design allows an exact analysis of the learning process with the added benefit of exact dependent measures such as the percentages of correct responses, intensity, and latency. (Examples using such designs in concept formation are described later.) Pilot analyses of individual data, moreover, confirmed that head movements deserved particular attention because measures as sensitive as the latency and intensity of the response help to evaluate interesting changes in the behavorial state of an infant. Infants also use head movements adaptively by simply distributing their attention either to facilitate information input in novel situations or to avoid distressing forms of stimulation.

Although we focused on head movements, we paid attention to other behaviors and soon became interested in the regularity with which vocal signs, facial expressions, and so on accompanied the instrumental act. Some of these concomitant components suggested themselves as rudimentary forms of communicative behavior; others appeared as emotional behavior. Confusions over the interpretation of emotional behavior aside, even the simplest categorization of signs of pleasure versus signs of displeasure provides interesting possibilities to understand more about motivational aspects of learning. As is explained in more detail later, this expectancy soon appeared justified and led to a reconsideration of the intrinsic motivation resulting from the cognitive processes in the infant.

The analysis of overt behavior is to some extent easy in infancy because of the opportunity to use evidence of the baby's relatively short preceding life history, because the infant does not yet hide his feelings, and because he has not yet learned to reduce his movements to some economical minimum.

Striking changes in behavior accompany infants' learning in experimental situations, changes that suggest that our results are transferable to natural situations. It is natural to attempt to interpret learning abilities in terms of the infant's play or his interactions with the caretaker, but alas, this is where the narrow concepts of learning leave us dissatisified and where we have to consider adaptive processes other than simplistic principles of conditioning — processes such as identification of attributes, concept formation, learning of rules, and imitation.

The simple principles of conditioning are then limited, even in "chained units." Rather, concomitant adaptive responses seem to be evident in the acquisition of cognitive behavior. In addition, cognitive behaviors are themselves aligned in a hierarchical structure with learning on a simple level and symbolic functions on a complex level. Thinking and problem solving are arrayed between.

After a few years of preliminary conditioning studies, we started more consistent studies of conditioned head movements in human infants between birth and 6 months of age. Infants were to learn, for example, that whenever they heard an electric bell they could obtain a small portion of milk by turning the head to the left: 10 trials per session until they reached a criterion of 5 consecutive correct responses (Papoušek, 1959). The acquisition of such a conditioned response was followed by extinction experiments, by relearning, and by conditioned differentiation during which the infant learned to respond with left turns to the bell and with right turns to a buzzer. The sides of reinforcement were reversed when an infant successfully acquired this behavior, and finally they were reversed once more (Papoušek, 1967). For reasons mentioned earlier, we analyzed the whole process of learning and recorded a wide range of parameters including respiration, heart rate and general motility, types of general movements, state of eyes, facial expressions, oral behavior and vocalization. Thus, we were able gradually to detect regularities in the general behavior of the infant. In addition to head movements appropriate to the experimental design in question, infants also responded in different ways that seemed to be connected with the regulation of information input, information processing, and the organization of adaptive responses. This organization is reviewed in our model of the fundamental adaptive response system (Papoušek & Papoušek, 1975).

Soon after birth the infant is obviously able to identify *aspects of environmental stimulation* and *contingencies of his own behavior.* Both of these are relational invariants determined by the outcome of information processing inside the infant rather than by their physical aspects. Both also affect related categories of responses. First, they elicit increased attention, orienting, or exploratory behavior, and thus they also determine the level of the infant's waking state. Second, they elicit emotional responses appropriate to the course of behaviorial adjustment; these are interesting from the point of view of motivation. The two also seemed to play crucial roles in structuring new stimulus situations and in resultant organismic behaviors. For example, information processing may include the detection of simple regularities in environmental events, such as repetition at regular intervals, to which the organism might then respond with increased orienting, which will soon decrease when it becomes evident that those events are irrelevant. At other times, some environmental events may regularly signal relevant biological situations, for example, the availability of food or the danger of distress, to which the organism might respond with a set to learn associatively.

Yet a third situation arises when an event is contingent on the organism's own activity. Here, the infant shows much stronger orienting responses, approach and exploratory activities, that will be more resistant to habituation and will eventually last as long as is necessary to learn an appropriate instrumental response. More complex stimulus situations will thus call forth multiple discriminations, the formation of behavioral chains, and also formation of concepts and rule learning. These cognitive processes are hidden phenomena. Nevertheless, a careful analysis of overt behavior will reveal graduations in orienting or exploratory responses, a gradual coordination of adaptive movements, activiation of the autonomic nervous system, and adequate emotional signs of displeasure if a false prediction leads to disappointing results instead of successful problem solving. Interestingly enough, the crossing points in behavior that might mean the detection of novelty, identification of familiarity, detection of contingency, successful acquisition of an appropriate adaptive response, or disappointment in an opposite case are also the occasions when vocalization is most frequent, as if the outcome of cognitive processes triggered social messages. Partial vertification of this hypothetical model of behavioral change in the infant came in our studies of concept formation (Papoušek & Bernstein, 1969) and was later grafted onto the analysis of social interactions (Papoušek & Papoušek, 1975).

In summary, according to our model of the fundamental adaptive response system, the organism responds in different stimulus situations, such as those connected with food intake, pain, avoidance, or social interaction, not only with a set of specific reflexes but also with a common set of fundamental responses that serve to regulate information input and information processing. They also help to organize adaptive responses. In one direction, they activate orienting responses, approach and exploratory behavior, and thus guarantee sufficient information for an appropriate adaptation. In the opposite direction, however, they inactivate such mechanisms and lead to detachment from distressing events, from sources of information difficult to identify and conceptualize, or from problems too difficult to solve. In the infant, this detachment suggests a "biological fuse" that protects the organism from supraliminal strain in taxing situations. This system could almost be considered a drive, and it is amazing to observe how much effort the infant exerts in a learning situation that represents a relatively difficult but not insurmountable problem. Other evidence may be addressed to a theory of intrinsic motivation connected with this fundamental adaptive system. We quite regularly observed signs of displeasure that accompanied unsuccessful attempts to organize appropriate responses and signs of pleasure in successful conditioning experiments. For example, smiling appeared earlier than it was observed in the infant's interaction with his mother. By contrast, hunger did not influence the average course of conditioning or conditioned differentation at all (Papoušek, 1967). We saw infants respond perfectly and with pleasure to the conditioning bell signals for the delivery of milk, even when they were fully satiated and refused any further milk reinforcement. Similarly, we often saw in our studies of concept formation that the infant was highly motivated to solve difficult problems but seemingly cared less for a rewarding visual display (Papoušek & (Bernstein, 1969). Others have suggested that incongruency or dissonance plays a greater role as an intrinsic motivation than does the pleasure resulting from successful adaptive processes (Hebb, 1949; Hunt, 1966). However, on the basis of our observations in infants, we believe that in addition to extrinsic motivation, the infant may be as strongly pushed by unpleasant incongruency as he may be pulled by the expectation of pleasure that comes with successful adaptation.

Flowing out of the fundamental adaptive system are concept formation and problem solving, the two main components of cognitive behavior (Bourne, 1966). We first noticed certain evidence of concept formation in infants in experiments on conditioned differentiation in which the infant was to turn his head to the left when stimulated with a bell and to the right when stimulated with a buzzer. Although both conditioned signals were applied in random orders, and incidental and seeming congruence between them and the infant's still undiscriminated responses led to false concepts ("superstitious behavior") that further influenced the infant's responses. Table 10.1 shows two examples that demonstrate such false concepts: One leads to prevailing unilateral responses, typical of the initial phase of conditioned differentiation, and another one leads to an alteration concept.

TABLE 10.1
False concepts of regularity during conditioned differentiation
of two stimuli applied in random orders.

	A: *"Only one side is correct."*	
	DAY n	DAY n + 1
CS:	R L L R L R R L R L	L L R L L R L R R R
CR:	R R L L R R R R R R	R L L L L L L L L R

	B: *"Left-right-left-right is correct."*	
	DAY n	DAY n + 1
CS:	L R R L R L R R L L	L L R L R R R L L R
CR:	L L R R L R L R L R	R L R L R L R L R L

Key:
.... = incidental regularity in randomized conditioning stimuli.
_____ = incidental congruence between *CS* and *CR*.

Further evidence of conceptual behavior appeared in a study of the conditionability of emotional responses in infants (Papoušek, 1967). Head turns to the bell were reinforced from the left with sweet milk, and head turns to the buzzer from the right were reinforced with a bitter solution. After several sessions, the infant responded with signs of pleasure to the sound of the bell and with displeasure to the buzzer. When the kinds of reinforcement were reversed, we observed that for some time the infants sucked the bitter solution as if it were the sweet milk but refused the sweet milk with displeasure. Obviously, belief outstripped sensation!

Toward further analysis of concept formation in infants, we modified an operant version of the head-turn conditioning by rewarding infants with an attractive visual display of blinking, colored lights (Papoušek & Bernstein, 1969). First, the infant had to learn a "switching-on" head movement (see Figure 10.1). Then different rules were introduced. For instance, two to four consecutive switching-on head turns or regularly alternating left and right turns were required to obtain the visual reward. The adaptive coordination of head movements is schematically illustrated in Figure 10.1. The course of successful adjustment, "learning the rule," yields important information on the capacity of cognitive processes in preverbal infants and reconfirmed the power of intrinsic motivation, which in some cases was stronger than the external motivator (the visual reward). These experiments with babies demonstrate quite clearly that the transition between conditioned learning and cognition is subtle. Experimental learning and the role of contingencies of reinforcement are at work constantly in our daily lives and may be particularly salient or important in the lives of infants and young children just coming into contact with the rules. Social interaction

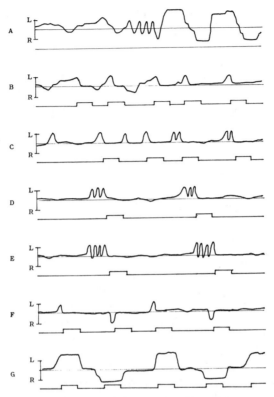

FIG. 10.1.   Schematic representation of adaptive head movements during experiments on concept formation in human infants at the age of 4 to 5 months. A: activated orienting; B: acquisition of switching-on movements; C: concept of "twoness"; D: concept of "threeness"; E: concept of "fourness"; F: "left-right-left-right" concept; G: same concept as in F, but head movement carried out without attention to visual reinforcement. *Upper lines* are records of head movement; marks on vertical lines indicate 45° head turns to the left (L) or right (R). *Lower lines are records of visual reinforcement displayed at the midline.*

and play behavior represent areas that depend to a very large degree on such rules, learning, and experience.

SOCIAL INTERACTION AND PLAY

Two perennial problems in the behaviorial sciences center around the nature of social interaction and play. The fundamental adaptive system, including early preverbal concept formation, appears to be particularly helpful in the interpretation of both social interactions and play—two natural, everyday infant activities.

Narrow concepts within learning theory have by and large failed to provide a satisfactory interpretation of the infant's complex social interactions with his parents or other adult caretakers. Thus, viewing the parent only as a source of rich stimulation that shapes the infant's development or as a dispenser of rewards and punishments sorely underestimated the infant's own cognitive competence and autonomy. However, social interactions, learning, and the problem situations we have studied provide for some stunning parallels.

Social interaction may be viewed as a chain of interlocking elements in which each element gains new dimensions resulting from its position in the chain, from its preceding history in similar interactions, and from the impact this element has in the social situation. Each element simultaneously acts as a response as well as a stimulus. For infants, two aspects of social interaction are of particular importance: One is the degree of familiarity of elements, and the second is their contingency on the infant's own activity. When interacting with infants, parents tend to modify their own behavior into repeated simple patterns in all observable modalities. Such repetitions may elicit expressions of pleasure resulting from recognition. Infants may also limit such behaviors and enjoy manipulating adults. Parents themselves show strong interest in any signs of cognitive capacities in their infants. Obviously, as in adult–adult interactions, adults tend to select the type and dose of stimulation according to their partner's capacity to process, and they are sensitive to feedback cues about such capacities.

Learning and early cognition thereby extend themselves to the social development of the child, and a continuity of function is maintained. In this sense, contingencies are quite important to understanding behavior. For example, the first imitating of the parent may in actuality be an expression of contingent learning. It is the parent who imitates first; she or he imitates the newly born child from the first day. Soon, the child may detect that imitating responses are contingent on his behavior and may learn how to elicit responses irrespective of any similarity between the two behaviors.

Although play is an easily understandable term in everyday parlance, it is particularly difficult to define in behavioral terms. From comparative studies of animal play, we know its descriptive behavioral features (Hinde, 1970). For example, the "play-face" (Hooff, 1962) signals such behavior to social partners. Drive theories failed to explain any motivation for play (Hall, 1904). Piaget (1951) discussed the proportion of accommodation and assimilation — two main aspects of intelligence — in play, leaving aside the questions of definition and motivation. Huizinga (1962) enumerated the elements of creativity in play and ascribed to play a main role in the development of culture. Flitner (1973), however, has stressed the close relations between play and learning.

Although the relations between play and cognitive development have been discussed repeatedly in newer theories, the crucial questions of motiviation and biological meaning have been left open. It is possible, however, to conceptualize these aspects of play from the point of view of fundamental cognitive processes. The essence of cognition is to increase the degree of knowledge of objects and events around us and in us or, in other words, to move from "unknown" to "known." This movement, however, should not exceed certain optimal limits. Too much novelty, incongruity, or uncertainty in the unknown will elicit distress and fear. On the other hand, too little novelty and incongruity may lead to boredom. Two strategies involved in the fundamental adaptive system determine movement from unknown to known (Papoušek & Papoušek, 1977b). They are shown in Figure 10.2. One strategy tends toward integration of available information and comes to a closed and complete concept when the event in question utilizes acquisition of different skills and various forms of learning. This strategy helps the organism to avoid stress resulting from the unknown. The second strategy works in the opposite direction as soon as the first strategy reaches its goal, and it tends to reopen seemingly complete concepts. This process forces what is known into a new light and to be viewed from unusual aspects. Hence we may detect unexpected relations, make the known again more unknown, and thus avoid the danger of boredom. This second strategy is the essence of play, creative arts, and humor, whereas the first corresponds to the mundane goals of formal education. The essence of play is that it is one particular cognitive strategy.

From this point of view, of course, play can begin only when a certain amount of knowledge has already been acquired and integrated. Play reflects a higher processing of experience. It follows, then, that play cannot be seen in the activities of the newborn in the first days of life, even if newborn behaviors otherwise correspond to the descriptive features of animal play (e.g., incomplete sequences of behavioral patterns, unusual orders of patterns in a sequence, etc.). Rather, it is the parent who selects adequate stimulation for the young and who repeats or modifies it in accordance with the infant's interest, providing him thus with the sort of pleasure that somewhat older infants go on to obtain themselves. As in so many other areas of development, children learn play modes of processing experience.

Parents regularly display strong interest in any signs of cognitive capacities in their infants. As adults do with one another, parents select the type and dose of stimulation in accordance with the infant's processing capacity. Moreover, signs of such capacities serve as feedback. We are presently engaged in studying the nature of these interactions.

FUTURE DIRECTIONS

Just two decades ago we asked whether and from what age infants could learn the simplest conditioned responses. Today we know that they are capable of learning from birth, that the speed of learning significantly improves in the first trimester, and that from about the fourth month behavior adapts to rules that infants extract from the structure of complex environmental stimulation. In a score of years, our experimental repertoire has broadened from simple conditioning to studies of concept formation.

Today there is great interest in observing the infant in his natural ecology. Recent studies have revealed that naturalistic learning and

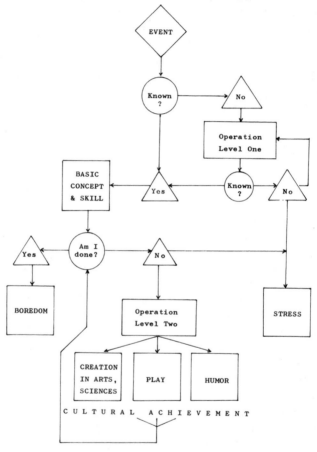

FIG. 10.2. Flow chart of adaptive operations (1) leading to higher levels of learning and cognition and (2) protecting against stress from "unknown" or boredom of trival knowledge. Key to symbols:

⬭ = question; △ = answer; ▭ = operation; and ▯ = outcome.

Operational Level One includes learning of basic skills, categories or rules, and tends to formulate closed concepts. *Operation Level Two* tends to reopen concepts formulated at Level One, view events from nontrivial standpoints, and create new problems and solve them.

problem-solving situations evolve from social interaction with the adult caretaker and from play. Both situations are in many regards different from the laboratory, and these differences raise new important research problems. Observing versus experimenting should not be an "either–or" dichotomy for a student of human development. Rather, the two methods should complement each other so that observation may lead to the isolation of meaningful problems before experimentation, and later, so that observation can serve to verify generalizability of experimental solutions.

Toward this goal, new technologies and methods have been used. Introduction of film and television techniques has helped us in analysis of important aspects of human social interactions that apparently previously escaped the attention of students using real-time observational techniques or simple questionnaires. Clearly, important behaviorial responses occur very fast and often without conscious control (Condon & Sander, 1974; Papoušek & Papoušek, 1977a) so that even our current knowledge of human maternal behavior is far from satisfactory. It is hoped that adequate modifications of film or television techniques (Papoušek, 1977) will facilitate microanalyses necessary to elucidate such behavior.

Interpretations of parent–infant interaction also reveal new functions of individual components of learning and cognitive processes. The same response may act as stimulus, reinforcement, or feedback cue at a given time. Going beyond simple S–R concepts, we have to consider models of interacting complex systems. Moreover, we have to use dynamic rather than static models of interaction in order to assess how both partners develop and change across interactions. For example, the behaviorial states of interacting partners constantly change to reflect external (e.g., circadian rhythms) and internal factors (e.g., satiation of hunger). Their interaction itself elicits further changes in behaviorial states as well. Above all, the infant develops dramatically, and his caretaker has to adapt correspondingly.

Obviously, further study will assign much more autonomy to the infant. Infants have too often been viewed as being responsive to stimulation and parents as being agents of enrichment. In fact, from the beginning the situation is almost the reverse, and it is the parent who first typically adapts his behavior during interactions with the newborn. Parents do so in many relevant ways. Human parents are not only prepared culturally, they are also preprogrammed biologically for this role. Nature offers the parent a very useful and effective model, and it is detrimental to neglect or substitute for nature with less justified artificial models.

Increased attention should also be paid to individual differences. Interest in individual differences has perhaps been inhibited by abandoning past typological trends in biology and by the introduction of statistical analyses in social sciences. We should not blame statisticians but ourselves, because we have persisted in representing our population samples as being homogeneous. Although such posturing may not have mattered much during the time of descriptive analyses of developmental changes, if we now want to understand the processes of development better, and exact analysis of individual differences seems to be necessary. Developmental changes in behavior have complex, multifactorial determinants and cannot be reduced to simple statistical operations and two-dimensional graphs. A more sophisticated application of computer techniques will permit pluridimensional representations of complex relations. Such techniques have already opened new ways for modeling discontinuous, "catastrophic" processes (Thom, 1975).

ACKNOWLEDGMENT

The preparation of this report was kindly supported by grants from the "Deutsche Forschungsgemeinschaft" (Pa 208/1) and from the "Stifterverband fur die Deutsche Wissenschaft." I also owe special thanks to the editors for their kind help.

REFERENCES

Bertalanffy, L. von. *Organismic psychology and systems theory.* Worcester, Mass: Clark University Press, 1968.

Bourne, L. E. *Human conceptual behavior.* Boston: Allyn & Bacon, 1966.

Bower, T. G. R. *Development in infancy.* San Francisco: Freeman, 1974.

Brackbill, Y., & Koltsova, M. M. Conditioning and learning. In Y. Brackbill (Ed.), *Infancy and early childhood.* New York: Free Press, 1967.

Charlesworth, W. R. Cognition in infancy: Where do we stand in the mid-sixties? *The Merrill-Palmer Quarterly,* 1968, *14,* 25–46.

Comenius, J. A. *Schola materni gremii.* (Czech Edition 1964). Prague: State Publishing Agency for Pedagogics, 1629.

Condon, W. S., & Sander, L. W. Neonate movement is synchronized with adult speech: Interactional participation and language acquisiton. *Science,* 1974, *183,* 99–101.

Elkind, D. Cognition in infancy and early childhood. In Y. Brackbill (Ed.), *Infancy and early childhood.* New York: Free Press, 1967.

Fields, P. E. Studies in concept formation. I. The development of the concept of triangularity in the white rat. *Comparative Psychology Monographs,* 1932 (*1,* Whole No. 9).

Flitner, A. *Spielen–Lernen.* Munich: Piper, 1973.

Fowler, W. Cognitive learning in infancy and early childhood. *Psychological Bulletin,* 1962, *59,* 116–152.

Goldfarb, W. Effects of psychological deprivation in infancy and subsequent stimulation. *American Journal of Psychiatry,* 1945, *102,* 18–33.

Hall, G. S. *Adolescence.* New York: Appleton, 1904.

Hebb, D. O. *The organization of behavior.* New York: Wiley, 1949.

Herrnstein, R. J., & Loveland, D. H. Complex visual concept in the pigeon. *Science,* 1964, *146,* 549–551.

Hinde, R. A. *Animal behavior* (2nd ed). New York: McGraw-Hill, 1970.

Hooff, J. A. R. A. M. van. Facial expressions in higher primates. *Symposia of the Zoological Society of London,* 1962, *8,* 97–125.

Horowitz, F. D. Infant learning and development. *Merrill–Palmer Quarterly,* 1968, *14,* 101–120.

Huizinga, J. *Homo Ludens. Vom Ursprung der Kultur im Spiel.* Hamburg: Reinbek, 1962.

Hunt, J. McV. The epigenesis of intrinsic motivation and early cognitive learning. In R. N. Haber (Ed.), *Current research in motivation.* New York: Holt, Rinehart, and Winston, 1966.

Kasatkin, N. I. *Early conditioned responses in human ontogeny.* Moscow: Medical Academy USSR, 1948.

Kessen, W. Questions for a theory of cognitive development. In H. W. Stevenson (Ed.), *Concepts of development. Monographs of the Society for Research in Child Development,* 1966, *31* (No. 3), 55–70.

Krasnogorskij, N. I. [An experience with the acquisition of conditioned responses in children of early age.] *Russkij Vratsh,* 1907, *36,* 1245–1246.

Krasnogorskij, N. I. *[Higher nervous activity in the child.]* Leningrad: Medgiz, 1958.

Lowrey, L. G. Personality distortion and early institutional care. *American Journal of Orthopsychiatry,* 1940, *10,* 576–586.

Montessori, M. *The Montessori method.* New York: Schocken, 1964.

Papoušek, H. New methods for studying the higher nervous functions in early human infancy. *Activitas Nervosa Superior,* 1959, *1,* 130–131.

Papoušek, H. Conditioned head rotation reflexes in infants in the first months of life. *Acta Paediatria (Uppsala),* 1961, *50,* 565–576.

Papoušek, H. Experimental studies of appetitional behavior in human newborns and infants. In H. W. Stevenson, E. H. Hess, & H. L. Rheingold (Eds.), *Early behavior: Comparative and developmental approaches.* New York: Wiley, 1967.

Papousek, H. Zur objektiven Analyse und Mikroanalyse des Verhaltens: Audiovisuelle Versuchsreproduktion mit Hilfe von Film- und Fernsehtechnik. In H. Remschmidt & M. H. Schmidt (Eds.), *Neuropsychologie des Kindesalters* (Vol. 1). Stuttgart: Enke, 1977.

Papoušek, H., & Bernstein, P. The functions of conditioning stimulation in human neonates and infants. In A. Ambrose (Ed.), *Stimulation in early infancy.* New York: Academic Press, 1969.

Papoušek, H., & Papoušek, M. Cognitive aspects of preverbal social interaction between human infants and adults. In M. O'Connor (Ed.), *Parent–infant interaction.* Amsterdam: Elsevier, 1975.

Papoušek, H., & Papoušek, M. Mothering and the cognitive head-start: Psychobiological considerations. In H. R. Schaffer (Ed.), *Studies in mother–infant interaction.* New York: Academic Press, 1977.(a)

Papoušek, H., & Papoušek, M. Das Spiel in der Fruhentwicklung des Kindes. *Paediatrische Praxis,* 1977, *18,* 17-32.(b)

Pavlov, I. P. *Conditioned reflexes. (G. V. Anrep, trans.).* London: Oxford University Press, 1927.

Piaget, J. *Play, dreams, and imitation in childhood.* New York: Norton, 1951.

Piaget, J. *The origins of intelligence in children.* New York: Norton, 1952.

Reese, H. W., & Lipsitt, L. P. *Experimental child psychology.* New York: Academic Press, 1970.

Sokolov, E. N. *Perception and the conditioned reflex.* Elmsford, N.Y.: Pergamon Press, 1963.

Spitz, R. A. Hospitalism: An inquiry into the genesis of psychiatric conditions in early childhood. *Psychoanalytic Study of the Child,* 1945, *1,* 53–74.

Stevenson, H. W. *Children's learning.* New York: Appleton-Century-Crofts, 1972.

Thom, R. *Structural stability and morphogenesis.* Reading, Mass.: Addison-Wesley, 1975.

Ukhtomsky, A. A. The principle of dominant center. In J. M. Sechenov, I. P. Pavlov, & N. E. Vvedeneskij (Eds.), *[Physiology of the nervous system]* (Vol. 1) (3rd ed.). Moscow: Medgiz, 1952.

Werner, H. *Comparative psychology of mental development.* Chicago, Ill.: Follett, 1948.

11 Commentary

Paul Mussen
Institute of Human Development
University of California, Berkeley

Cognitive development has occupied the stage center in developmental psychology for the past 20 years — as cognition dominated the whole discipline of psychology — and it continues to do so. Subsumed under the rubric *cognitive* is a very wide range of psychological processes and an impressive variety of theoretical approaches. Hence, it is not surprising that the four stimulating papers in Part II reflect what is commonly called a "healthy diversity" of fact and theory.

The papers differ markedly from one another on many dimensions: the central issues discussed, underlying assumptions about human nature, the kinds of research cited, the concepts used to explain empirical findings. The experiments and data analyses reported in these papers seem unassailable; each author's work is relevant, rigorous, and careful. However, generally speaking, facts and findings are secondary to theory building in these chapters, and, unfortunately, the theoretical discussions, although presenting many plausible, provocative, and stimulating ideas, are not so impeccable. Because the bulk of this commentary is concerned with the non-empirical aspects of the chapters in Part II, I return to a critique of the theoretical aspects of the papers later. The substance of each paper is summarized first.

For Kagan, cognitive advances during infancy are reflected in the infant's ability to create structures of increasing degrees of abstraction. The first cognitive structure is a schema defined as an "abstract representation of an event that retains the relations among the physical dimensions of the original experience." Then the infant becomes capable of generating the following structures in this sequence: prototypes or schematic categories, signs (schemata for individual dimensions), schematic categories, and, finally, concepts. Apparently, the infant has some rather high-level capabilities right from the outset, since even 10-week-olds can "create a schema for an event by merely attending to it." The structures are described well, but the processes or mechanisms underlying the shifts from one structure to the next, more abstract one are only vaguely defined. Factors of biological maturation are hinted at, but experience also plays a critical role, structures becoming better articulated as a result of "continued encounters." Like other cognitive developmentalists, Kagan maintains that structures change as a result of confrontations with discrepant or inconsistent events.

Kagan's most detailed discussion of process pertains to the infant's "amplified memorial competence," which emerges between 7 and 8 months and improves progressively during the next few months. The improvement in memory gives rise to two related competencies: "enhancement of the ability to retrieve schemata of past events when minimal cues are available" and "the ability to hold past and present in short-term memory for a longer time, permitting prolonged comparisons and evaluations." According to Kagan, these better capacities to retrieve information and to hold it in short-term memory help to explain several other interesting phenomena that are manifested at this time (approximately 8 months), including increases in attentiveness, signs of inhibition in play, separation anxiety, and distress in interactions with strangers.

McCall used factor analyses of the intercorrelations of items on infant tests to derive his five-stage theory of development during infancy. The first principal component, derived at each age period, gives the best distillation of the item pool and thus describes the fundamental cognitive attributes of each stage. The definition of each stage is then expanded by drawing on the findings of many other studies and showing that each stage encompasses a broad range of functionally interrelated behaviors — cognitive, social, linguistic, and affective — including memory, smiling, imitation, vocalizations, play, and interactions with peers. The approximate boundaries of the stages "describe a sequence of qualitative shifts in fundamental ability across age and represent discontinuities in the general developmental functions, but infants do not percipitously jump from one stage to the next." Furthermore, the congruence between the ages and the qualitative nature of the stages that emerge from these analyses and those offered by Piaget and by Uzgiris is impressive.

Papoušek's paper summarizes and reinterprets some of his well-known earlier studies of operant conditioning in infants. The conditioned responses were head movements which, Papoušek emphasizes, have many adaptive functions for obtaining food, avoiding unpleasant stimulation, and for orienting the individual. In his view, the transition between conditioned learning and cognition is a subtle one. Powerful intrinsic (built-in) motivations, as well as complex cognitive processes such as information input, information processing, and the organization of adaptive responses, are involved in the behaviors associated with simple reflexes. Observations and analyses of facial expressions and vocalizations accompanying conditioned head movements indicate that infants are pleased (that is, they smile) in successful conditioning experiments. If they become aware of "an unpleasant incongruency," they are motivated to change their behavior—a notion that is similar to Kagan's hypothesis that discrepancy motivates change. Like Kagan and McCall, Papoušek attributes to the infant high levels of cognitive competency and strivings for autonomy, and he also believes that soon after birth, infants can identify familar environmental stimuli and the contingencies of their own behavior. The adaptive functions of early learning and cognition are also manifested in the domain of social development, specifically in the child's play with peers and in early social interactions.

The orientation and flavor of Elkind's paper are much different from those of the other three papers in Part II. Elkind's principal topic is Piaget's distinction between figurative and operative thought, between knowledge of states and knowledge of transformations. In the course of development from infancy through adolescence, the child's thinking progresses from relatively more figurative — functioning primarily in thought, perception, imitation, and mental imagery — to the operative. In making the figurative/operative distinction, Piaget acknowledged the importance of *content* in the study of the child's thought, just as his structural/functional theory of development—involving stages and the functions of assimilation, accommodation, and equilibration — highlighted the importance of the psychological *processes* involved in constructing reality. Structures and functions can be derived from contents just as contents can be derived from structures and functions, and Elkind maintains that the analysis of content is as necessary as the analysis of process in understanding the child's thought.

The utility of the figurative/operative distinction is demonstrated by thoughtful analyses of the processes and contents involved in responding to various subtests of the WISC. Elkind cautions against interpreting subtest results as being measures of single processes (or operations) of simple figurative knowledge. Elkind states a warning explicitly: "In psychological theory and research, process should no longer be regarded as separate from content." Kagan, McCall, and Papoušek have apparently heeded this caveat, for all of them attempt to show how particular psychological process — for example, memory, information retrieval, or attempting to influence the environment—affect performance on a wide variety of intellectual tasks and social interactions. Elkind's own chapter is further distinguished with a succint and original account of several major conceptions of development.

Because these chapters differ from one another in so many ways, we cannot expect to achieve significant conceptual integrations or to find a great many significant "emerging themes." Nevertheless, in addition to concentration on theory building—perhaps their most striking shared attribute—these chapters have several other characteristics in common. And, given the diversity of theoretical orientations and research approaches, we will pay special attention to overlapping ideas, consistencies in sets of data, and congruent explanatory concepts.

One interesting trend, probably of minor significance, is interest in specifying the historical antecedents of theoretical orientations. The kinds of historical data brought to bear on the problem and the use to which these data are put vary from author to author. Thus, Kagan emphasizes the broad philosophical and sociohistorical forces that produced and maintained a concern with continuity in behavior (rather than discontinuity), whereas Papoušek gives an account of the academic and intellectual forces that have directed the recent history of research and theory in European, particularly eastern European, developmental psychology. Elkind puts Piaget's figurative/operative distinction into the broad context of earlier conceptions of development, most of them from recent history but on occasion borrowing from such ancients as Kant, Locke, and Berkeley.

Diverse as these papers are in orientation, there is no doubt that all four authors find the principles of traditional learning and conditioning theory to be inadequate for the explanation of the critical phenomena of cognitive development. By now, this seems unsurprising. Yet it is interesting to find how prevalent this dissatisfaction with traditional learning theory is. Even Papoušek, whose systematic work is entirely within the conditioning framework, seems much less concerned with S–R connections than with the infant's intrinsic motivations (which, according to Papoušek, are complex—not at all like the simple ones of traditional learning theory), cognitive capabilities, and the functions of cognition in adaptation to the physical and social environment.

Piaget's theory dominates the thinking of all researchers and students of cognitive development, and it has become the standard against which all other theories of cognitive development are to be evaluated and judged. All new theoretical efforts must show how they relate to, or differ from, Piaget's. This is most explicit in the papers of Kagan, McCall, and Elkind, but it is also implicit in Papoušek's interpretations of his observations of infant's behavior accompanying conditioning. However, Piaget's ideas and explanations are not accepted without question, and even some of his basic concepts are now being challenged. For example, Kagan rejects Piaget's notion that object permanence depends on the creation of a new structure and views this phenomenon as the outcome of the 8-month-old's improved ability to remember things. And, although McCall centers his attention on stages of development and compares his stages to those discovered by Piaget, his conception of stages is fundamentally different from that of

Piaget. For Piaget, a major criterion for a stage is the existence of a *unified, logically related,* set of structures. Factor analyses of the interrelationships among a wide variety of disparate, unrelated tasks such as the tasks in infant intelligence tests (McCall's intriguing approach to the discovery of stages) could hardly yield information about such structures or sets of structures.

The abiding concern of these cognitive developmentalists is the "black box"—although only Papoušek labels it this way—that is, with what goes on in the infant's head. The main emphases of these papers is on the structure of mind and thought rather than on the actions, experiences, infant–environment interactions, and processes that regulate the construction and modification of mental structures. Thus, both Kagan and McCall carefully elaborate their descriptions of structures and stages, but they provide much less theory and empirical information about the critical antecedents.

Because the "black box" cannot be explored directly, theorists are tempted to speculate freely about it. Sometimes they make assumptions, often very complicated ones, about infants' intrinsic motivations; see, for example, McCall's functions, essentially motives, to acquire information and to influence the environment. Sometimes they generously attribute to very young infants what appear to be very high levels of abilities; see, for example, Kagan's assertion that 10-week-olds can create representations of events they have encountered. Since these complex motives and abilities are present from birth, they are presumably biologically determined or "wired-in."

Indeed, biological orientations toward development are apparent in many facets of these papers. The profound impact of evolutionary biology is obvious in many of the discussions of the adaptive functions of learning, of mental structures, and of operations. Elkind addresses the question of why we develop. McCall implies that certain goals are inherent in human beings and asserts that human behavior represents attempts to accomplish these goals.

Many of the explanatory concepts invoked by these writers are biological, most explicitly so in Papoušek's and McCall's chapters. One of McCall's central concepts, canalization, is drawn from Waddington's discussion of the "epigenetic landscape" and from Scarr's article on evolutionary perspectives on variations in intelligence. In addition, as noted earlier, the complex motives that energize development are, according to both Kagan and McCall, inherent, innate, or "wired-in," and there are some strong suggestions that transformations in the infant's abilities and mental structures are to a very large degree governed by biological maturation. Maturational factors undoubtedly enable the infant to acquire higher-level abilities and structures, but it hardly seems likely that biological changes in themselves produce cognitive transformations. Yet, judging from Kagan's chapter, experiential factors have virtually no role in cognitive process during infancy. McCall acknowledges that stimulation is related to advances in the later periods but views the shift from Stage I to Stage II as a function of psychobiological, including neuroanatomical, changes. Neither Kagan nor McCall specifies the biological factors involved in cognitive development, nor do they cite any evidence. Implicit in this argument is the notion that these changes would occur regardless of the nature of the infant's experiences and interactions with others.

Although much of the research in cognitive development during the late 1950s and 1960s was designed to challenge the validity of the notion of "developmental stages," particularly those described by Piaget, the chapters in Part II demonstrate that that situation has changed considerably. There is now a prevalent concern with discontinuities in development, as Kagan and McCall point out. Both of them argue convincingly that cognitive development advances in stages during infancy, although the empirical bases for their arguments are vastly different, as are their ideas about the nature and characteristics of the stages and the explanatory concepts behind them. McCall advocates a much stronger form of stage theory than Kagan does and, in fact, stresses discontinuities more strongly than he stresses continuities. Kagan agrees that there are discontinuities and stages, but he also emphasizes the gradualness of cognitive development. In his view, new stages emerge as new abilities are acquired, and development continues gradually as these new abilities are applied in a greater number of contexts. In spite of some major theoretical differences between Kagan's and McCall's approaches, they are agreed on at least one empirical finding: Dramatic cognitive changes occur between the ages of 7 and 13 months, and these are related to changes in underlying processes.

There seems to be general acceptance in these chapters that sequence of events in cognitive development, including the order of stages, is universal and invariant, although evidence on this issue is not unequivocal. Kagan's cross-cultural findings are exemplary in this matter, for they provide convincing data on the validity of the hypothesis—at least for the structures and processes with which he is concerned. Will McCall's stages and the numerous concurrent behaviors included in each stage prove to be universal? Because of the data base from which McCall worked, this seems unlikely, but empirical tests of the question would yield fascinating information. If there is evidence that the same stages occur in the same order in different cultures, hypotheses about biological determinants would seem tenable. If it turns out that the stages vary from culture to culture, investigators might fruitfully examine the influence of experience on mental structures in more fine-grained ways than they have heretofore.

Another emergent theme, potentially of great significance, is the general recognition that cognitive development must be viewed in the broad context of overall psychological growth. Cognitive advances are concurrent with, and have significant impact on, other facets of development, particularly on affective and social behaviors. Thus, Papoušek maintains that the infant's cognitive accomplishments are accompanied by manifestations of feelings of pleasure, Kagan links improvement in memory at 8 months of age with modified reactions to strangers and to separation from the mother, and Mc-Call calls attention to changes in social behavior at each of his later cognitive stages. These authors assume that cognitive changes form the basis for new affective-social responses, rather than the reverse—a plausible, but hardly proven, assumption.

All four writers share an overwhelming enthusiasm from theory construction, and all seem to be striving to formulate a theory that is truly developmental and comprehensive. Intense concern with theory building is entirely admirable and understandable. Psychologists have been impressed with the elegance and utility of theory so frequently that they are uncomfortable with data that are not conceptually integrated or tied together in a sensible theoretical framework. However, these efforts are open to serious criticism, partly because theoretical content generally outweighs the empirical facts, and many traditional and still respected canons of theory building are often disregarded or violated. After all, a few plausible explanations of behavior or behavior change plus some metaphors and analogies do not, in themselves, constitute a systematic theory. Good theory building requires, minimally, clearly defined concepts, specific, logical, rigorous, and internally consistent relationships among concepts and hypotheses, and the establishment of substantial links between objective data and theoretical hypotheses, concepts, and assumptions. Parsimonious explanations are still regarded as being more satisfactory than complicated ones, although there seems to be less stress on parsimony in theory building now than there was in the past. Disregard of these requirements is rampant in these chapters. Many concepts are imprecisely defined, some underlying assumptions seem unwarranted, the authors often make enormous inferential leaps from empirical data to theoretical propositions, and sometimes what is clearly conjecture in the early part of a theoretical presentation becomes "fact" later on in the account. Some of the chapters are rich in metaphor—too rich. Metaphors sometimes seem to be in control, with more attention being paid to amplifying their implications than to reducing the vast discrepancies between theory and findings. Speaking of his own theorizing, Kagan notes that it sometimes involves "a bit more boldness that the data warrant." The statement is applicable to the other writers, too. Good theory building is extremely difficult, as numerous problems of definition and inference encountered in these pages demonstrate. In the interest of developmental psychology, we must underscore the need for constant vigilance and rigorous control in drawing conclusions in the construction of theories.

A number of critical substantive and conceptual issues—issues that must be confronted in any adequate theory of cognitive development—are either underplayed or missing from the chapters in Part II. The roles of experiential factors and the child's own experimentation in early cognitive process need to be analyzed in greater detail, and the relationship between cognitive development or early stages of cognition in infancy and subsequent cognitive progress must be confronted. Some thoughtful hypotheses or insights into this matter would be most welcome because, even if there were marked discontinuities, early cognitive advances must somehow affect development between the ages of 2 and 5 years, the period that has probably received less theoretical and empirical attention than any other.

In spite of these deficiencies, the chapters are stimulating and rich in ideas that are worth pursuing theoretically and empirically. They are an excellent source of hypotheses for future research. Theories in all sciences — and particularly sciences that are still in their formative years — emerge, change, and improve through a series of successive approximations. These theoretical chapters have many of the merits of stages along the way.

III

LANGUAGE AND
SOCIAL DEVELOPMENT

12 Acquiring the Concept of the Dialogue

H. R. Schaffer
University of Strathclyde
Glasgow, Scotland

INTRODUCTION

Participation in social interactions constitutes a regular and inevitable feature of the everyday experience of infants from birth on. All social interactions, irrespective of their content or the age of the participants, involve highly intricate, closely synchronized sets of behavior patterns contributed by two or more individuals. They are dialogues, verbal or nonverbal, generally characterized by impressive "smoothness" and conducted according to sets of rules that are more often than not far from explicit. How such dialogues come to be established during early development and the prerequisities on which they are based form the topic of this chapter.

THE SOCIAL OR THE LONELY INFANT?

Development always occurs in an interpersonal context. In some respects, this is particularly true in the earliest stages, although in the adult, too, behavior has generally a social dimension without which it would lose its most distinctive characteristic. And yet, psychology has always been happier to treat behavior at a purely individual level, as though responses "belonged" to people and were entirely beneath-the-skin events. Take the infant's sucking: We have here one of the very first avenues whereby the newborn comes into contact with the world, one of the principal modes of establishing a relationship with the mother. Yet, as any review of the volumunious literature on this behavior pattern shows (e.g., Kaye, 1967;

279

Kessen, Haith, & Salapatek, 1970), it is generally treated as though no other human being were involved in the act, as though it were a matter of some disembodied nipple descending on the infant, as though no decision were ever made by another being when or how to feed the child, and as though no interplay between two individuals occurred during the activity to determine its course.

Some degree of abstraction is, of course, always necessary, and there can be little doubt that the narrow focus deliberately adopted by investigators of sucking behavior has yielded a great deal of useful material on the structure of this response. To what extent our knowledge of functional aspects has been furthered by examining it only under "ideal" conditions (experimental nipples, carefully controlled rate of liquid flow, infant's bodily position constant and standardized, and so on) is another matter. But let us take another example that makes even clearer the danger inherent in isolating the child from his social context—that of language acquisition. As long as the focus was merely on the individual and language treated as his "property," explanations for its beginnings had to be couched in terms of intrapsychic processes, resulting finally in such a *deus ex machina* as a "language acquisition device" with apparently magical functions. Only with a widening of focus beyond the individual came the realization that, as Jaffe and Feldstein (1970) have pointed out, the dialogue and not the monologue is the basic speech unit; the monologue is merely a special instance of a dialogue with one partner absent or silent. The primary function of speech is thus to communicate, and its beginnings need therefore to be understood in the context of an interpersonal situation — hence, present efforts (e.g., Bruner, 1975, 1977; Schaffer, Collis, & Parsons, 1977; Trevarthen, 1977) to trace continuities between preverbal and verbal communicative modes and to see language arising against a background of already well-established ways of sharing meanings between mother and child.

The view of the lonely infant is now gradually coming to be discarded. The just-quoted example of language acquisition is one indication; other areas showing the same trend are problem solving and skill acquisition (Kaye, 1976; Wood & Middleton, 1975), concept formation (Nelson, 1974), visual behavior (Stern, 1974), attention (Collis & Schaffer, 1975), and even sucking (Kaye, 1977). In each case the infant's behavior is seen as having an interpersonal function and to derive its meaning from occurring within a social relationship. And, ironically, even the example of social responsiveness ought to be added to the list: Here, too, the prototypical way of studying an infant's behavior was to put him into an interpersonal situation but then to examine only his own responses (his smiles, cries, glances, etc.) with little or no reference to those of his partner. It is only recently that parent and infant have begun to be treated as a dyad in which the ebb and flow of their interaction is studied in truly interactional terms (Schaffer, 1977a).

SOCIAL PREADAPTATION

Sociability is multifaceted. It is constituted of a great many diverse functions (communication, imitation, attachment, interpersonal sensitivity, group participation, adherence to social norms, competitiveness, and many others), which may have little in common with one another except for the all-important fact that they jointly define the individual's capacity to participate in social life. It is this capacity that develops in such an extraordinary speedy and diverse fashion in the early years. Consider the infant at birth: Essentially he is as yet an a-social being, for he responds not to other people as such (let alone to specific others) but merely to primitive configurational stimuli. The mother is not yet the mother but a pair of eyes that elicit attention, a voice representing sounds different from inanimate noises, a nipple providing food, and so on. As yet, there is no awareness of a social world *per se*. But within the span of just a year all this has changed. People are no longer interchangeable. The child has developed intense feelings regarding certain specific individuals, he has acquired a set of highly sophisticated communicative skills that he can use appropriately under defined circumstances, he is able to imitate others, and he is starting to acquire some sense of what is approved and what is disapproved by his social group. In his interactions with others he is now beginning to show consummate skill in managing the to and fro of social intercourse. How is all this accomplished so speedily and efficiently?

That the infant learns these skills, that is, that he starts off as a *tabula rasa* on whom a set of specific learning experiences are in some way grafted, is an impossible view. For one thing, the speed as well as the manner of acquisiton makes this unlikely. For another, no existing description or analysis of parental activities provides any indication that social development is built up in the piecemeal fashion demanded by traditional learning accounts. Both the roles of the child and that of the adults in his environment are likely to be of a much more complex nature.

As to the child's contribution, the notion of the *tabula rasa* neonate has long been abandoned. Reviews of our accummulated knowledge of neonatal capacities (e.g., Kessen, et al., 1970; Appleton, Clifton, & Goldberg, 1975) make it abundantly clear that at birth the infant is already well equipped with the psychological means of starting life and has already begun the task of coping with his environment — especially, we want to suggest, with the other people who comprize his social environment. Indeed, the more one learns about the growth of sociability in the early months of life, the more difficult it becomes to escape the conclusion that in some sense the infant is preadapted for social interchange. The manner of this preadaptation needs spelling out.

Structural Characteristics

There are, it is proposed, two aspects of preadaptation that may be usefully distinguished — the *structural* and the *functional*. As to the former, a neonate is born with certain bodily structures that serve to bind him to other members of the species. The most obvious example is a mouth that is precisely adapted to cope with the nipple that the mother provides. A life-maintaining link is thus established analogous to such other species-specific links as the rhesus monkey's grasping reflex that ensures his ability to cling to the fur provided by the mother. Less obvious links, about which we have nevertheless gathered quite a lot of knowledge by now, are found in the infant's sensory equipment, in particular in his visual and auditory apparatus. As shown in detail by Fagan (Chapter 4, this volume), the infant's visual apparatus is structured so that it is highly sensitive to just those forms of stimulation that emanate from other people: pattern, movement, contrast, three-dimensionality, and so on. None of these characteristics is specific to people, yet in combination, together with the fact that during most care-taking activities the mother's face is generally held within the infant's highly confined fixation distance, they ensure that other people become stimulus objects of great potency to the young infant (Schaffer, 1971a). Similarly, the infant's auditory apparatus is such that it is especially attuned to the type of sounds characteristic of the human voice (Bornstein, Chapter 3, this volume; Hutt, Hutt, Lenard, Von Bernuth, & Muntjewerff, 1968). In brief, the infant comes into the world equipped with structures that ensure a basic compatability between himself and his caretakers.

Functional Characteristics

But structural compatability is not enough. A mouth is more than just a hole into which a nipple fits; once contact has been made the infant responds by sucking actively. And similarly, although visual and auditory selectivity serve to direct the infant's attention specifically to other people, this is only the first step, to be succeeded by various intricate interactive maneuvers. Interactions, by definition, are *joint enterprises taking place over time,* characterized by constant dynamic changes and mutual adjustments. For these to take place smoothly, *functional* compatability is required to supplement structural compatability.

The way functional compatability between the infant and his caretakers is achieved is perhaps the major problem to which students of early social behavior must presently address themselves. However, we can start off with two all-important facts: First, that from the beginning all the infant's behavior is organized in particular ways over time; second, that others, in relating to the child, appear to respect the nature of his temporal organization and make attempts to synchronize their behavior with his.

Let us illustrate. Sucking, it has been shown (e.g., by Sameroff, 1967, and Wolff, 1968), tends to be organized in burst–pause patterns. A definite temporal patterning thus underlies this response, which is primarily regulated by an endogenous mechanism in the brain. Infants with congential mouth defects, it has been found (Wolff, 1968), show no disturbance in the cyclical organization of sucking. In some brain-injured infants, on the other hand, the burst–pause rhythm shows marked irregularities. By adopting a wider focus of study and including the mother's as well as the baby's behavior during feeding, Kaye (1977) has been able to show that mothers tend to interact with their infants in precise synchrony with the burst–pause pattern of sucking. During bursts, they are generally quiet and inactive; during pauses, on the other hand, they jiggle, stroke, and talk to the baby, thus taking turns with him in being principal actor. The mother, in other words, allows herself to be paced by her baby. She fits in with his natural sucking pattern, responds to his signals such as ceasing to suck, accepts the opportunity to intervene offered by his pauses, and by this means sets up a dialogue between them.

This example, as we see below, serves as a prototype for a great deal of early interaction. Here let us note that the temporal integration of the two participants' responses is accomplished, first, on the basis of the baby's inherent rhythms and, second, through the mother's sensitivity to the periodicity of his behavior. Thus, there are not only endogenous structures but also endogenous patterns of functioning that underlie the infant's interactions with others.

Rhythms and Behavior

A number of inherent rhythms have so far been isolated in the human infant (Wolff, 1967). Each is based on some centrally located oscillating mechanism, each can thus be interfered with through cerebral pathology, and each imposes its own particular on–off pattern on the relevant functions. Some, like the sleep-waking cycle (Roffwarg, Muzio, & Dement, 1966) are macrorhythms taking place over hours or even weeks. Others, such as sucking or visual scanning (Trevarthen, Hubley, & Sheeran, 1975) are microrhythms with basic frequencies of seconds or fractions of seconds. All may be regarded as being species-specific characteristics, although the possibility of stable individual characteristics relating to some rhythm parameters (e.g., Kron, Ipsen, & Goddard, 1968) has also been raised. They represent intrinsically regulated periodicities especially but not exclusively evident in early life that are initially independent of experiences or of particular kinds of sensory input. According to Lashley (1951), the central nervous system must be regarded as the source of such autonomous oscillators, which thus function as the primary mechanisms for the temporal regulation of rhythmical motor sequences.

Rhythms do not, however, merely function in isolation. They may interact at both an intrapersonal and at an interpersonal level—a possibility considered above all by Condon (1977). In his microanalytic studies of adults' movements during speech, Condon found that these movements could be reduced to units lasting but a fraction of a second. Within each of these units the various parts of the body all move in synchrony, sustaining a particular speed and direction for the brief duration of that unit before all simultaneously change to form another unit. In addition, however, Condon also suggests that the units cut across different functions. When he included speech in his analysis, he found the same units there, linked to the rest of the movement pattern to form a total rhythm system. Intrapersonal synchrony is thus established. According to Condon, however, the same analysis may also be applied to interpersonal synchrony. He found, in the first place, that a similar rhythmic pattern could be discerned in the *listener's* movements during speech and, second, that this was evident even when that listener was a newborn baby (Condon & Sander, 1974). That is, infants are said to move synchronously with adult speech as early as the first day of life. A precise and almost simultaneous entrainment process is thus operating, producing an intricate and subtle dance that is always occurring during interactions.

These results are still preliminary and tentative. If confirmed, they will provide a further indication of the way in which the infant is equipped, from the very beginning, to enter social life and participate in interpersonal activities. They point to a biological foundation that enables human beings to participate together within a wider communicational context. It appears that the very structure of behavior is such that it lends itself to social interplay. However, this does not refer only to such precise forms of sequencing as those produced by biological rhythms. In their analysis of peer interaction among 1-year-old toddlers, Mueller and Lucas (1975) draw attention to the influence that the "act–watch" pattern has on social behavior. Take the example of an infant's secondary circular reactions performed on objects: He will act on the object (striking it, rolling it, shaking it, etc.), and then stand back to watch the effect. What he has absorbed this effect, he may start again, repeating the same action or modifying it. Seldom will he be continuously active. Instead, his actions are punctuated by pauses during which he appears to process the feedback deriving from the act. This act–watch rhythm is just as evident in early social interaction. Mueller and Lucas describe how it contributes to the type of play seen in their first stage of peer interaction, when one rarely sees simultaneous actions performed by two children focusing on a single toy. Instead, each child in turn acts on the object. When the other one performs, he watches. Simultaneity of action on the object with attention to the partner's behavior occurs only later, having evolved out of the act–watch pattern, which thus represents one organismic factor contributing to the sequencing of social interactions.

THE PARENT'S ROLE

Rhythms and Environment

The inherent equipment that allows the infant to begin immediately to participate in social interaction is, of course, not immune to environmental influence. On the contrary, even endogenous rhythms quickly show signs of adaptation to the demands of the infant's world.

We can illustrate this process of *entrainment* by means of two examples. The first is provided by an early study by Marquis (1941), who investigated hourly changes in activity patterns in two groups of infants during the first 10 days of life. One group was fed according to a regular 3-hour schedule, the other according to a regular 4-hour schedule. After only a few days each group had already developed a peak of restlessness just before its respective feeding time—a finding that became particularly obvious when the 3-hour group was subsequently shifted to a 4-hour schedule and so had to wait an extra hour for their feeding.

The second example comes from the diurnal distribution of infants' sleeping–wakefulness patterns. In neonates, sleep tends to occur in many short periods randomly distributed throughout the day and interspersed by periods of wakefulness that are even shorter (Kleitman, 1963). Within a few weeks, however, both sleeping and waking begin to assume a different pattern. Individual periods become longer, they are less randomly distributed within each 24-hour interval, and in due course they become organized in a diurnal pattern. Parmelee, Wenner, and Schulz (1964) found a slight difference in the day–night distribution already evident in the first week of life, in that their subjects slept an average of 7.75 hours during the day and 8.30 hours at night (presumably differences in light, noise, and the activities of adults can account for this divergence). By 16 weeks, however, these figures had become 4.58 and 9.95 hours, respectively. A circadian rhythm of diurnal waking and nocturnal sleeping was thus coming into being, and although maturational changes clearly play some part in stabilizing the pattern, it is difficult to escape the conclusion that, as in Marquis's study of activity changes, we can witness here instances of acculturation whereby an endogenous pattern of behavior changes its temporal pattern as a result of environmental pressures.

These two examples only indicate that environmentally induced changes do occur; they tell us little as to how they are brought about. For this purpose a much more detailed examinaton is required, in particular of the behavior of the main agent of change, namely, that of the mother, and of her role in relation to the infant's behavior. Just what is this role?

Maternal Synchronization

We have already referred to two general features that characterize infant behavior, namely, its *selectivity* (as seen in particular in relation to the perceptual attractiveness of other human beings) and its *periodicity* (i.e., the particular kinds of temporal organization found in different responses). Let us note a third characteristic also found from the beginning, namely, the *spontaneity* of infant behavior. That the infant is by no means an inert, passive being that is stirred into action only through the impact of environmental stimulation is now widely acknowledged. It appears, on the contrary, that there are endogenous forces that regulate much of his behavior and account for changes in his ongoing activity — as illustrated, above all, by the now quite voluminous literature on state changes (cf. Korner, 1972) and as documented well by Wolff's (1966) detailed description of such spontaneously occurring responses as mouthing, smiles, and startles. The parent, that is, will never be confronted by an inert, passive being who needs to be stimulated into life. An external stimulus always impinges on an active organism — whatever its age. The task of the parent is thus not one of creating behavior out of nothing but rather of fitting in with an existing organization in such a way that some form of interpersonal synchrony can emerge. How this is achieved, the interactional techniques employed toward this end, and the way in which these are integrated with infant responses constitutes one of the major areas of present-day research in early social development (Schaffer, 1977a, 1977b).

The starting point in any attempt to understand this process must be the fact that infant behavior occurs spontaneously and that a definite temporal patterning can frequently be discerned in it. Add to that a further consideration — namely, the parent's sensitivity to this temporal patterning and her willingness to interweave her responses with those of the infant's — and the beginnings of dialogue become possible.

There are now a number of examples available that provide empirical justification for this account. We have already referred to one of these — Kaye's (1977) observations of mothers' behavior in relation to the burst-pause pattern of their infants' sucking. Interpersonal synchrony is achieved during feeding because the mother allows herself to be paced by the infant. She fits in with his natural sucking pattern, remaining quiet during bursts and generally intervening only during pauses. In this way she sets up a dialogue in which each partner takes turns in being principal actor.

The same pattern is found in another interactive situation studied by Kaye (1976), in which mothers attempted to teach their 6-month-old infants the new skill of reaching around a barrier to obtain a toy. The infants' visual attention under these circumstances was not continuous but tended to assume a regular on-off pattern, with periods of attention interspersed by periods of looking away — somewhat analogous to the burst-pause pattern found in sucking. And the same analogy was found in the mothers's behavior. During periods of infant attention, the mothers tended to be quiet, whereas the child's looking away was regarded as a cue to intervene and in some way to induce the infant to make new attempts at the task. Again we see the mother's willingness to slot her responses into the infant's sequential behavior pattern, interpreting particular aspects of his behavior as being cues for her own responses.

Just how powerful a cue an infant's gaze can be to a mother has also been shown by Collis and Schaffer (1975). When they observed mother-baby pairs in a novel environment containing a number of specific attention-compelling objects (large, brightly colored toys), two findings emerged. First, it was noted that there was a strong tendency for both partners to be attending to the same object at the same time — the phenomenon of "visual co-orientation." And second, when one determines by means of sequential analysis how such mutual attention is brought about, it emerges that almost invariably it is the baby who leads and the mother who follows. In other words, the baby's spontaneous interest in toys is closely monitored by the mother and then, almost automatically, she looks in the same direction. The mother is thus in a position not only to know of the child's present interest but also to predict his likely future action. What is more, having established a focus of mutual interest, the mother can elaborate on it by verbally commenting on it, labeling it, manipulating it, and so on. Given the rapidity of shifts of gaze, a very fine sense of timing is, of course, required on the part of the mother. Though they are unlikely to follow every one of their infants' looks, most mothers remain sufficiently attuned to be continuously aware of the direction of their babies' interest. A sharing experience is thus brought about, instigated by the infant's spontaneous attention to his environment but established by the mother who allows herself to be paced by the baby and who uses his interest as the context for further comment.

Perhaps the example *par excellence* of the sequential integration of two individuals' responses can be found in a conversation. As various studies (e.g., Duncan & Niederelie, 1974; Kendon, 1967) of adult vocal interchange have shown, an exquisite sense of timing is involved in the turn-taking pattern that generally characterizes such interchange, with definite cues regulating the way in which speaker-listener roles are exchanged and with little clashing (i.e., overlapping) of role playing under most circumstances. It appears, however, that such "smoothness" of vocal interchange is already present at preverbal levels. In a comparison of 12- and 24-month-old children (Schaffer, et al., 1977) it was established that the ability of mother and child to take vocal turns and to avoid overlapping was as characterstic of the younger as of the older group, that relatively few overlap episodes occurred at either age and that when they did occur, they tended to be brief and not to throw the interactive flow out of gear. It was also established that the overlap episodes were as likely to be brought about by the mother's interruptions as the child's, that most speaker-switch pauses were extremely brief, and that the cues for turn taking said to play a part in adult conversations were not evident here but appeared to take a different form. Turn taking, an essential prerequisite for most forms of verbal interaction, thus predates the appearance of words. "Pseudo conversations" can therefore occur before information is passed on in verbal form.

It must be stressed that turn taking is a dyadic phenomenon and that it tells us nothing per se about the "abilities" of infants to take turns. There are, in fact, at least three possible ways in which turn taking may be brought about. In the first place, each partner "knows" the rules, and the child as much as the mother is therefore responsible for ensuring a smooth interaction. Second, through the mother's initiative alone, she allows herself to be paced by the infant and merely fills in the pauses between his vocalization bursts. And third, from the beginning some mechanism is already present that makes production of vocalizations and listening to other sounds inherently incompatible. The first possibility may well apply, to some extent at least, to older children: One need only consider the frequency with which mothers warn their over-eager 4- or 5-year-olds, "Don't interrupt me, wait till I have finished talking." However, it is hardly likely to play a part at a very early age. The second possibility, on the other hand, fits in with the evidence from the various other interactive situations that we have discussed and would thus once again draw attention to the supportive role played by the mother. By behaving "as though" the infant wanted her to reply, she maintains the interaction and appears to convert it into a dialogue. Yet, however plausible such an account, it may well not be the whole story, for it seems unlikely that the infant produces his vocalizations oblivious of all external considerations. Some tentative evidence for the third alternative emerges from studies by Webster, Steinhardt, and Senter (1972), in which it was found that auditory stimulation had a marked suppressant effect on infants' vocalizations. The adult's difficulty in simultaneously speaking and listening is often commented on; it is conceivable that this is based on an even more primitive incompatibility—that between production of any form of vocal output and the simultaneous processing of auditory input in general. Such an association needs further investigation, particularly in the light of findings by Stern, Jaffe, Beebe, and Bennett (1975) and Strain and Vietze (1975) that under certain circumstances (usually connected with emotional arousal) a pattern of "co-action" (i.e., simultaneous vocalizing by mother and infant) is commonly found in the early months. Even with the alternating pattern, however, it is often difficult to tell from observations of normal mother–infant dyadic exchanges to what extent the child is himself capable of the relevant interactive skill or how far it is the mother who is maintaining the exchange. Experimental interference in the adult's behavior is one way of settling this issue; examining peer interaction, with both partners functioning at the same level, is another (Mueller & Lucas, 1975).

What can be concluded with confidence is that, in early interactive situations, it is not only the *how* but also the *when* of the mother's interventions that plays a crucial part. The infant largely sets the pace, and the mother, by virtue of great sensitivity to the temporal flow of his behavior, replies, fits in, supports, and elaborates on his activities. Of course, it is not suggested that the mother never takes the initiative. As described elsewhere (Schaffer, 1977b), maternal dyadic techniques may be classified under six main headings (i.e., phasing, adaptive, facilitative, elaborative, initiating, and control techniques), which may be roughly arranged (in the order given) along a continuum from passivity to activity. Our concern has been largely with phasing techniques, but there are naturally many situations in which mothers must assume a much more active role. Yet (as some ongoing research into maternal control techniques is beginning to show) even at the active end, mothers' directives are frequently not of the "bolts out of the blue" fashion but do take into consideration the child's ongoing activity and are often timed even then to slot in precisely with the flow of his behavior (Schaffer & Crook, 1978).   Thus, the infant's behavior becomes incorporated into a dyadic process, and it is the adult's role to ensure that this occurs.

Social Pathology

The establishment of mutuality in the infant's relationship with the parent is dependent on the behavior of both partners. When one or the other partner fails to play his expected role, the interaction may become unpredictable, and disintegrates. Either infant pathology or maternal pathology can be the initial source of such a breakdown, although in practice it is often difficult subsequently to disentangle the precise contribution of the two sets of factors.

Infant pathology in its clearest form is found among the brain injured, the autistic, and the handicapped. Take a study by Jones (1977), based on a comparison of mother–child communication patterns in infants with Down's syndrome and in normal infants. In many respects the two groups were found to be similar. Clearly this particular pathological condition, at any rate in the first year of life, did not prove to be as totally disruptive as one might expect, say, with autistic children. Yet a number of observations illustrate that the mothers' task in establishing interactive sequences was considerably harder in the case of the Down's syndrome group. For one thing, these children engaged in far less "referential" looking than did the normal infants. They looked only infrequently to and fro between toy and mother, and as a result made it very much less obvious that they wished to draw the mother into their play activity. Again, the vocalizations of the Down's syndrome infants tended to be repeated quickly on top of one another, leaving little room for the mother to "reply" and thus making vocal turn taking more difficult. And finally, there were indications that the children with Down's syndrome initiated sequences rather less frequently than did the normal children and that the mothers of the former group, therefore, had to employ rather more direction in the conduct of the relationship.

Maternal pathology is perhaps best considered in terms of lack of sensitivity to the infant's signals. Again, there are indications that this may prove disruptive to the relationship (Ainsworth, Bell, & Stayton, 1971) and make the establishment of mutuality more difficult. For an infant to connect two events into one sequence, the events must occur within certain critical limits set by his memory capacity (Millar, 1972; Watson, 1967). If a mother fails to respect these limits and thus responds in a noncontingent way, the growth of interactional sequences is likely to be considerably handicapped. We return later to the issue of temporal relationships, which clearly has considerable relevance to the understanding of social development.

THE INFANT'S INTERACTIVE ACHIEVEMENTS

Pseudo-dialogues

Face-to-face interaction assumes many intricate forms. Most of these, however, are based on an alternation of the participants' roles—an on-off pattern in which the individuals take turns in assuming the actor and spectator roles. Verbal interchanges, in particular, illustrate this pattern. Such alternation provides dialogues with their most striking formal characteristic, and it is this pattern, as we have seen, that is already evident in the earliest interactions of the infant with his mother.

However, it would be more accurate to characterize these early interactions as *pseudo-dialogues*. The precision of their temporal patterning may be every bit as exquisite as is found later on, yet the parts played by the two participants do not show the same symmetry that one finds among more mature couples. The indications are that initially it is the mother who is primarily responsible for keeping the interaction sequence in being, that it is she who ensures that the to-and-fro pattern is maintained and that the exchange of roles is conducted smoothly and without clash. She does this partly through providing sufficient time for the infant's behavior to occur and partly through then responding in an "as if" fashion, that is, by converting his responses into signals *as if* they were meant to elicit her behavior.

The infant's responses thus become incorporated into a wider entity, a dialogue, before he as yet shows any awareness that such entities exist.

Acquiring the concept of the dialogue will clearly be a continuous and long-drawn-out development, component processes of which can be found first to emerge at various points throughout the early years. The review by Glucksberg, Krauss and Higgins (1975) of communicative development in childhood makes this clear. Nevertheless, the major developmental step can be said to take place toward the end of the first year and it may be summarized most suitably in terms of two aspects — reciprocity and intentionality.

Reciprocity

The notion of reciprocity refers to the realization that a dialogue needs to be sustained by *both* partners, that *both* are equally responsible for steering its course, and that the roles they play are not only integrative but also interchangeable. Bruner's (1977) description of the development of give-and-take play routines illustrates this point well. Up to the age of 7 to 8 months, according to Bruner's observations, the infant's participation in such games is entirely limited to "take". They are one-sided affairs in which the mother offers the toy, but they tend to end with the child merely dropping it. From about 10 months, however, the child begins to initiate the sequence by showing and even offering the object and also now handing it to the mother at her request. However, although the child can be induced to take part in exchanges, he does so hesitantly, constantly checking between object and mother as though not sure of the procedure. By 12 months, on the other hand, the game has now become established as a "game". It is routinized, possession time is decreased, the number of exchanges per game is increased, it can take diverse forms (e.g., both mother and child offering simultaneously), and the whole is played with great pleasure and enjoyment. The child, that is, has learned that his behavior is part of a sequence defined by the behavior of both participants, that the sequence depends on the coordination and integration of the two sets of responses, and that he as much as his partner is responsible for maintaining it.

A somewhat similar progression becomes evident from Mueller and Lucas's (1975) account of peer interaction in children around the beginning of the second year. Mueller and Lucas order this progression into three stages. In the first stage ("object-centered contacts"), the previously mentioned act–watch rhythm underlies the kind of sequencing one sees when two children act on a common object. Their actions are seldom simultaneous; each watches as the other performs and performs as the other stops. Yet because each one's interest is invested in the object itself, neither child recognizes the effects of his own actions on the behavior of the other child. In the second stage ("simple and complex contingency interchanges") the children now begin actively to seek and receive "contingencies" from one another. Child–child circular reactions appear, such as when a child laughs at another's vocalization, thereby getting the latter to repeat his vocalization. As yet, however, the children do not know how to form a whole series of socially directed behavior in which one serves the function of attracting the other child's attention and the other defines the interchange. This skill develops in the third stage ("complementary interchanges"), when the participants now become able to do different but intercoordinated or reciprocal things instead of, as before, doing things either independently or imitating each other. Thus, they offer and receive a toy, throw and catch a ball, chase and are chased. In each case there are two different actions, and each action derives its meaning form the reciprocal act. Coordination in time also now becomes important. The child must hold out his hand at the right moment to receive a toy. Thus, the act–watch rhythm is replaced by simultaneous and synchronous activity. Both reciprocity and timing are therefore basic to behavior at this stage.

Mueller and Lucas's (1975) account illustrates well the changes in sequences that take place in early social interactions. Even in the earliest stage the infant is capable of coordinating periods in which he acts on his environment with periods of perceptual processing. However, the coordination is successive—the act–watch pattern. Only subsequently can he simultaneously produce an action and at the same time process its complement from another child. At the same time, however, he is learning about the complementary nature of the component parts of interactive patterns. He may at different times be giver and receiver, chase and be chased, vocalize and listen. Through being involved in such interactions, he then comes to comprehend, in a practical sense, the notion of reciprocity with its attendant ideas of complementarity, synchrony, and role reversal. These constituents do not appear at the same time, of course. The endless drop-and-retrieve games that infants tend to play around the end of the first year arise, like give-and-take games, when the child discovers that his action elicits a predictable response in his partner—he drops, she picks up. Thereupon, he may repeat this sequence indefinitely for the sheer sadistic pleasure of seeing the mother play the retriever again and again. Unlike give-and-take, this particular game never evolves into role reversal! Nevertheless, as Bruner (1977) points out, it is through involvement in joint action sequences that the child can find out about reciprocity, just as he learns about speaker–listener roles through being involved with the mother in vocal turn taking. And what also becomes apparent is that reciprocity is found very much earlier in the course of development than previous accounts of the young child's egocentrism would have led us to believe. A child solely concerned with his own needs and wishes is hardly likely to make the continuous readjustments in his flow of behavior that need to be made in the light of the other person's responses in an interactive situation.

Intentionality

The first sign of reciprocity can be found in the child's behavior toward the end of the first year. It is then, too, that the other component of dialogue we have referred to — intentionality — becomes evident in the infant's communicative behavior. From the beginning, of course, any responses may have communicative force as far as the mother is concerned: a cry, a smile, a shift in posture, a gaze in a particular direction — each may provide the mother with some information as to the infant's state and condition and result in approriate action. Whether such responses should be labeled as being communicative is a matter of definition (see Hinde, 1972. There are certainly those (e.g., Wiener, Devoe, Rubinov, & Geller, 1972) who consider the term appropriate only when the sender's intentionality can be included as one element of the situation. What does become apparent is that all signs of intentionality are missing in the infant's behavior in the early months of life and that it is only toward the end of the first year that these signs become evident.

Not that it is easy to arrive at a consensus as to what these signs are. Piaget (1954) suggests three criteria: (1) The infant has a goal in mind from the beginning and does not discover it accidentally; (2) if an obstacle arises in the attainment of the goal, some kind of indirect approach will be employed and; (3) the means employed to overcome the obstacle are different from those employed in the case of the goal. Unfortunately, these criteria do not yield the kind of unequivocal indexes that would help one to identify occurrences of the relevant behavior. However, there does seem to be general agreement that it is not until Piaget's sensorimotor Stages IV and V, with the advent of means–ends differentiation, that behavior assumes the kind of flavor that we associate with intentionality. In other words, secondary circular reactions, when they first emerge, are accidental acts not meant to produce interesting results, and it is only as a result of repeated contingencies that the infant learns that his actions are related to external effects. Once the infant sees the connection, he will then repeat the interesting event and use different means to accomplish the same end. An infant in the early weeks of life will cry because he has a pain. Subsequently, he will cry *for his mother* to deal with the pain. Should this response not produce its desired effect, he will employ a whole range of other help-seeking strategies toward the same end. To graduate from one point to the other he needs to be involved in lots of contingency experiences with the mother.

The link between means–ends differentiation, intentionality, and social behavior is well brought out by Bates, Camaioni, and Volterra (1975) in their study of the onset of intentional communication in the first year. Following Austin (1962), they distinguish between the performance of prelocutionary and illocutionary acts, the former referring simply to signals that affect another person (such as a neonate's hunger cry), the latter involving the intentional use of a conventional social act (not necessarily a verbal one), recognized as such by both speaker and listener. Developmentally, as Bates and her colleagues show, the former gives rise to the latter, in that at first the infant has no awareness of the control he exercises over others and only subsequently becomes capable of using signals intentionally to convey requests and to direct adults' attention to objects and events. However, this control is not possible till toward the end of the first year when the infant has achieved means–ends differentiation and can therefore use adults in order to obtain desired objects and use objects as a means of obtaining adult attention. Having previously kept object schemata and person schemata separate, the child can now combine them into sequences that are much more complex, more flexible, and of an intentional nature (see also McCall, Chapter 8, and Nelson, Chapter 13, this volume).

Let us just add to this account that these changes in the child's social competence are brought about primarily through the mother's involving the infant in dialogue-like situations. It is only through the contingent response of other people to his behavior that the child learns the communicational value of his responses. He learns, that is, that his cries, smiles, vocalizations, and so on will be attended to by others and will tend to produce particular effects on those others. In time, therefore, he will send out such signals intentionally, in the definite expectation that they will be responded to. Having learned to anticipate future effects, he can now demand, summon, request, and plead.

COGNITIVE MECHANISMS AND
SOCIAL DEVELOPMENT

A child cannot perform particular kinds of social operation until he is cognitively equipped to do so. Recognition of the mother, for example, implies some degree of ability to match perceptual input with stored representation. Using the adult to obtain a toy out of reach indicates that ends and means have become differentiated. Crying for the absent mother cannot take place unless one assumes those abilities of recall that are generally associated with object permanence. That the level of cognitive maturity exerts some sort of influence on social development is readily accepted. However, two rather more specific questions arise, namely, (1) can one identify the particular cognitive mechanisms that play a part in relation to particular social manifestations, and (2) how is one to conceptualize the linkage between the cognitive and the social spheres? We consider each of these questions in turn.

Cognitive Requisites

In a sense every cognitive achievement by a child may have implications for his social behavior. We are, after all, not confronted with an organism that operates according to two distinct sets of laws, one relating to its behavior toward inanimate objects and the other to its behavior toward other human beings (see, for example, Fagan, Chapter 4, this volume). The real problem is a more specific one: Given a particular kind of social activity, can we isolate the cognitive abilities that make its emergence possible?

Much of the research effort relevant to this question has concerned the third and fourth quarters of the first year—sensorimotor Stages IV and V. There can be no doubt that during this period, in particular, a considerable amount of cognitive restructuring occurs, with considerable implications for social development (Schaffer, 1971b). In another discussion primarily concerned with developments implicated in the onset of fear of strangers (Schaffer, 1974), it has been suggested that these may be summarized in terms of three kinds of changes:

From impulsiveness to wariness. An initial tendency toward indiscriminate motor approach to all stimuli, irrespective of perceived familiarity or strangeness, becomes replaced in the third quarter of the first year by selective approach–avoidance behavior (e.g., Schaffer & Parry, 1969, 1970; Schaffer, Greenwood, & Parry, 1972). Before this age the infant "knows" the stranger is strange, yet shows none of the wariness that develops thereafter, when visual memory comes to exert an influence on approach–avoidance responses.

From sequential to simultaneous consideration. The young infant tends to live in the here-and-now, with no apparent concern for events separated in time and space from that which happens to preoccupy him at the moment. Piaget's (1950) description of sensorimotor intelligence as "a slow motion film," in which all the pictures are seen in succession but without fusion, and so without the continuous vision necessary for understanding the whole expresses this notion well. Initially there is a deficiency in the ability to connect various events; only subsequently (and again the third quarter of the first year appears to be the main period when the relevant changes take place) will the infant show signs of being able to consider several events simultaneously and jointly instead of only sequentially and separately.

From recognition to recall. In the first half of the first year an infant's memory shows, above all, one marked deficiency: He can recognize, but as yet he cannot recall. Only after the age of about 7 to 8 months can infants spontaneously retrieve stored information and act in the absence of the corresponding object. The best known illustration of this phenomenon lies in the development of the object concept, with its demonstration that at a certain point the infant becomes capable of remaining oriented to stimuli not present in his perceptual field. The relevance of this achievement to social development has long been recognized (Anthony, 1956), primarily because of the similar circumstances under which separation upset occurs and the suggestion that it may be based on identical psychological processes (Schaffer, 1958). The mother cannot be cried for until the infant is capable of evoking her representation in her perceptual absence.

The Social Context of Cognitive Development

As to the nature of the link between social behavior and cognitive processes, Bates, Benigni, Bretherton, Camaioni and Volterra (1976) have reviewed the various forms the link may take and have argued that a simple linear association of the kind most often advocated at present, according to which social developments depend on preexisting cognitive mechanisms, may not be entirely adequate. The details of whatever etiological linkage there may be remain problematic. However, what can be asserted with much greater confidence is another kind of proposition, namely, that cognitive mechanisms do not develop in a social vacuum but, quite on the contrary, appear by virtue of the child's exposure to the kinds of environmental input that are largely provided in the context of interacting with other people.

That cognitive development needs environmental input is a statement unlikely to be questioned these days. However, the environment to which a child is exposed is not simply a static set of inanimate objects. Quite on the contrary, particularly in the case of infants, it is primarily composed of people with the following functions. First, they themselves represent highly salient sources of stimulation and become objects of interest in their own right. Second, they largely determine what parts of the inanimate environment the infant is exposed to. And finally, in whatever stimulation episodes (face to face or by means of objects) they are involved, they are capable of carefully and continuously adjusting the type of stimulation offered to the infant throughout the course of the interaction.

The first two of these functions need no elaboration. When the social context of cognitive development is taken into account at all, it is usually in relation to these two aspects. The third, on the other hand, needs some further discussion.

That adults most sensitively, yet quite unconsciously, adjust their input to a child in the light of their perception of the child's capacities has been documented by a number of writers. Take the account by Newson and Newson (1976) of the way in which an adult will tackle the task of getting a 4-week-old infant to follow a dangling ring visually. First she ensures that the child's attention is properly "hooked" on the ring. She then begins gingerly to move it across his field of vision, continually monitoring his precise focus and line of regard, ever ready to modify her movements in the light of the infant's success or failure to follow. She thus attempts to ensure that the infant's rudimentary capacities are not overtaxed and that the stimulation is offered in such a way that it matches the infant's ability to assimilate it.

This matching process can be seen in many aspects of adults' behavior toward children. The best documented aspect refers to the nature of speech: As several studies have shown (e.g., Phillips, 1973; Snow, 1972) complexity of speech varies systematically with the age of the child addressed in terms of syntax, length of utterance, range of vocabulary, and so on. The younger the child, the simpler the linguistic environment to which the mother exposes him. And similarly with the manner of her delivery: Stern (1977) has provided detailed accounts of the way in which a mother will slow down her speech to an infant, pause between phrases for considerably longer than in adult-addressed speech, greatly exaggerate her gestures and facial expressions, and provide much repetition of all she says and does. For example, her phrases are only about half as long as those in adult-to-adult discourse, whereas the pauses are almost twice as long. Thus, she acts as if the infant can take in smaller chunks of information at any one time than can an adult and as if he needs more time to process each before receiving the next. And the fact that she does this on the basis of the feedback the child provides her is suggested by one interesting exception to the age-related process of simplification: Phillips (1973) found that the speech provided to 8-month-old infants was *more* complex than that to eighteen-month-olds — presumably because the younger children could give no indication as to their comprehension of what was being said to them.

Through such capacity-appropriate behavior on the adult's part the child is provided with the opportunity to master developmental tasks. Take the mother's facial exaggerations: According to Stern (1974) their function is to enable infants in the early weeks of life, when their perceptual abilities are still limited, to perceive them more easily than would be possible with normal, quickly changing expressions, and in this way to help maintain continuity in identifying the mother's face across different instances of appearance. Perceptual constancy despite transformations is thus fostered.

Yet mothers do not provide only the sort of stimulation that the child can very easily assimilate; the input they offer is often slightly more advanced than the child's current level of functioning, thus providing him with material for further progress. The speech addressed to children may be simple but not as simple as the child's own productions (Moerk, 1975). At the age of 12 months infants are not yet capable of taking part in question–answer sequences, but this does not prevent mothers from continuously addressing them with utterances marked by rising intonation (Ryan, 1977). Or take the development of object constancy. Long before sensorimotor Stage IV mothers can already be found to play games of peek-a-boo with their infants, hiding for very brief moments in order not to lose the infant's attention but thereby already giving him experience with tasks more appropriate to a further level of functioning. And similarly with hiding-object games: One need only observe the strategies mothers use to coax their infants along (for instance, by teasingly covering the object again and again for a second or two at a time, or making it disappear very slowly to ensure the infant's visual accommodation, or leaving it half exposed) to realize that every mother must be steeped in Piagetian theory! Thus, the infant is continually challenged, and if he cannot cope and loses interest any sensitive mother will immediately alter her strategy and provide something more appropriate, just as she will when she finds that there is no joy in a task too easy or familiar to the baby. Accommodation may be brought about by the child's experimentation, exploration, and trial and error play with the environment, but this occurs most profitably in the presence of a supporting adult rather than when he is alone.

If cognitive growth is dependent on the child's interaction with the environment, social aspects of that environment are easily in the best position to play such a part. It is not too fanciful to suggest that an infant is much more likely first to obtain the idea of permanently existing objects through the mother's repeated appearances and disappearances than through the hiding and finding of those celluloid ducks and cigar cases that provided Piaget with his illustrative material. For one thing, the mother is perceptually a much more potent stimulus. For another, her presence or absence has far more personal implications for the child's well-being. And finally the mother can, if she wishes, carefully adjust the timing and manner of her departures and arrivals in a manner appropriate to the child's state at the time. No wonder that Bell (1970) found evidence for object permanence to appear earlier in relation to social than to inanimate objects.

Thus, cognitive growth occurs primarily in a social context. Without the opportunitites provided by adults, the child would stay at a primitive level of functioning. But these opportunities are not merely provided by passively putting objects in front of the child. They tend more. often to occur in the games and daily routines that bring mother and child into active contact with each other. And of course, once new cognitive achievements have been attained through social interaction, they will in turn affect the child's social abilities and thus allow these interactions themselves to occur at higher levels of functioning.

CONCLUSIONS

In asking how dialogues come to be established in the course of infancy, we have drawn attention to three kinds of prerequisites: biological, social, and cognitive, which together enable interactive development to take place. *Biological prerequisites* are implicated in that the infant's behavior has from the beginning a temporal organization that is specifically adapted for social interaction. For one thing, rhythms have a regularity that make it possible for the mother to anticipate the infant's behavior, and it seems highly likely that the split-second timing that characterizes so much of interactive behavior is a result of such anticipation. And for another, the on-off nature of sensorimotor activity enables the partners to take turns and thus ensures that each performs while the other's attention is fully on him. The most characteristic formal aspects of social interaction are thus embedded in the endogenous temporal structure of the infant's behavior.

However, through participation in interactive sequences these primitive temporal patterns soon become transformed into vastly more complex and flexible structures. Thus, their very exercise in interactive contexts brings about their transformation—provided, that is, the child's social partners are willing to sustain his behavior by responding contingently and appropriately and so incorporating it in dialogue-like exchanges. It is such activities that constitute *social prerequisites,* and they point to the very active role that the mother must assume if the transformation is to come about. Development of interactive skills cannot take place without interactive experience; it is the mother's task to ensure that such experience occurs. To focus on the child and his characteristics alone is thus not sufficient; our explanations must also encompass the nature of his social environment.

It is further apparent, however, that a considerable array of *cognitive prerequisites* is involved in social interaction. The nature of a child's cognitive structure, in the sense of the total system of his information-processing strategies, varies from age to age and thus sets limits on the kinds of social behavior that one can expect at various ages. The precise linkage between cognitive and social functions remains problematic. What is apparent, however, is that it is primarily through social interaction that the child receives those forms of stimulation that make it possible for him to attain new cognitive achievements—a conclusion that places even greater importance on the provision of appropriate interactive experiences.

On the basis of these three kinds of prerequisites, the child will in due course become capable of fully participating in interactive sequences — a participation characterized by reciprocity of roles and intentionality of communicative behavior. Together these account for what we have referred to as the child's acquisition of the concept of the dialogue. The dialogue may then come to be expressed in diverse modes through the increasing number of communication channels (verbal, gestural, visual, etc.) to which the child gains access in the course of the early years.

ACKNOWLEDGMENT

This paper was written during the author's tenure of a fellowship at the Van Leer Jerusalem Foundation, Israel. It is part of a research program into early social development financed by the United Kingdom Social Science Research Council.

REFERENCES

Ainsworth, M. D. S., Bell, S. M., & Stayton, D. J. Individual differences in strange-situation behavior of one-year-olds. In H. R. Schaffer (Ed.), *The origins of human social relations.* New York: Academic Press, 1971.

Anthony, E. J. The significance of Jean Piaget for child psychiatry. *British Journal of Medical Psychology,* 1956, *29,* 20–34.

Appleton, T., Clifton, R., & Goldberg, S. The development of behavioral competence in infancy. In F. D. Horowitz (Ed.), *Review of child development research* (Vol. 4). Chicago, Ill.: University of Chicago Press, 1975.

Austin, J. L. *How to do things with words.* London: Oxford University Press, 1962.

Bates, E., Camaioni, L., & Volterra, V. The acquisition of performatives prior to speech. *Merrill–Palmer Quarterly,* 1975, *21,* 205–226.

Bates, E., Benigni, L., Bretherton, I., Camaioni, L., & Volterra, V. From gesture to the first word: On cognitive and social prerequisites. In M. Lewis & L. Rosenblum (Eds.), *Origins of behavior: Communication and language.* New York: Wiley, 1976.

Bateson, M. C. Mother–infant exchanges: The epigenesis of conversation interaction. *Annals of New York Academy of Science,* 1975, *263,* 101–113.

Bell, S. The development of the concept of object as related to infant–mother attachment. *Child Development,* 1970, *41,* 291–313.

Brazelton, T. B., Koslowski, B., & Main, M. The origins of reciprocity: The early mother–infant interaction. In M. Lewis & L. Rosenblum (Eds.), *The effect of the infant on its caregiver.* New York: Wiley, 1974.

Bruner, J. S. The ontogenesis of speech acts. *Journal of Child Language,* 1975, *2,* 1–19.

Bruner, J. S. Early social interaction and language acquistion. In H. R. Schaffer (Ed.), *Studies in mother–infant interaction.* London: Academic Press, 1977.

Collis, G. M., & Schaffer, H. R. Synchronization of visual attention in mother-infant pairs. *Journal of Child Psychology & Psychiatry,* 1975, *16,* 315–320.

Condon, W. S. A primary phase in the organization of infant responding behavior. In H. R. Schaffer (Ed.), *Studies in mother–infant interaction.* London: Academic Press, 1977.

Condon, W. S., & Sander, L. W. Neonate movement is synchronised with adult speech: Interactional participation and language acquisition. *Science,* 1974, *183,* 99–101.

Duncan, S., & Niederelie, G. On signalling that it's your turn. *Journal of Experimental Social Psychology,* 1974, *10,* 234–247.

Glucksberg, S., Krauss, R., & Higgins, E. T. The development of referential communication skills. In F. D. Horowitz (Ed.), *Review of child development research* (Vol. 4). Chicago: University of Chicago Press, 1975.

Hinde, R. A. (Ed.), *Non-verbal communication.* New York: Cambridge University Press, 1972.

Hinde, R. A., & Hermann, J. Frequencies, durations, derived measures and their correlations in studying dyadic and triadic relationships. In H. R. Schaffer (Ed.), *Studies in mother–infant interaction.* London: Academic Press, 1977.

Hutt, S. J., Hutt, C., Lenard, H. G., Von Bernuth, H. V., & Muntjewerff, W. J. Auditory responsivity in the human neonate. *Nature,* 1968, *218,* 888–890.

Jaffe, J., & Feldstein, S. *Rhythms of dialogue.* New York: Academic Press, 1970.

Jaffe, J., Stern, D. N., & Peery, J. C. "Conversational" coupling of gaze behavior in pre-linguistic human development. *Journal of Psycholinguisitic Research,* 1973, *2,* 321–330.

Jones, O. H. M. Mother–child communication with prelinguistic Down's syndrome and normal infants. In H. R. Schaffer (Ed.), *Studies in mother–infant interaction.* London: Academic Press, 1977.

Kaye, H. Infant sucking behavior and its modification. In L. P. Lipsitt & C. C. Spiker (Eds.), *Advances in child development and behavior* (Voi. 3). New York: Academic Press, 1967.

Kaye, K. Infants' effects upon their mothers' teaching strategies. In J. C. Glifewell (Ed.), *The social context of learning and development.* New York: Gardner, 1976.

Kaye, K. Toward the origin of dialogue. In H. R. Schaffer (Ed.), *Studies in mother–infant interaction.* London: Academic Press, 1977.

Kendon, A. Some functions of gaze-direction in social interaction. *Acta Psychologica,* 1967, *26,* 22–63.

Kessen, W., Haith, M., & Salapatek, P. H. Human infancy: A bibliography and guide. In P. Mussen (Ed.), *Carmichael's manual of child psychology* (Vol. 1). New York: Wiley, 1970.

Kleitman, N. *Sleep and wakefulness.* Chicago, Ill.: University of Chicago Press, 1963.

Korner, A. F. State as a variable, as obstacle, and as mediator of stimulation in infant research. *Merrill–Palmer Quarterly,* 1972, *18,* 77–94.

Kron, R., Ipsen, J., & Goddard, K. Consistent individual differences in the nutritive sucking behaviour of the newborn. *Psychosomatic Medicine,* 1968, *30,* 151–161.

Lashley, K. The problem of serial order in behavior. In F. A. Beach, D. O. Hebb, C. T. Morgan, & H. W. Nissen (Eds.), *The neuropsychology of Lashley.* New York: McGraw-Hill, 1951.

Marquis, D. P. Learning in the neonate: The modification of behavior under three feeding schedules. *Journal of Experimental Psychology,* 1941, *29,* 263–282.

Millar, W. S. A study of operant conditioning under delayed reinforcement in early infancy. *Monographs of Society for Research in Child Development,* 1972, *37* (2, Whole No. 147).

Moerk, E. Verbal interactions between children and their mothers during the preschool years. *Developmental Psychology,* 1975, *11,* 788–794.

Mueller, E., & Lucas, T. A developmental analysis of peer interaction among toddlers. In M. Lewis & L. A. Rosenblum (Eds.), *Friendship and peer relations.* New York: Wiley, 1975.

Nelson, K. Concept, word and sentence: Interrelations in acquisition and development. *Psychological Review,* 1974, *81,* 267–285.

Newson, J. An intersubjective approach to the systematic description of mother–infant interaction. In H. R. Schaffer (Ed.), *Studies in mother–infant interaction.* London: Academic Press, 1977.

Newson, J., & Newson, E. On the social origins of symbolic functioning. In V. P. Vamva & P. Williams (Eds.), *Advances in educational psychology* (Vol. 3). London: Hodder and Stoughton, 1976.

Parmelee, A. H., Wenner, W. H., & Shulz, H. R. Infant sleep patterns from birth to 16 weeks of age. *Journal of Pediatrics,* 1964, *65,* 576–582.

Piaget, J. *The psychology of intelligence.* London: Routledge & Kegan Paul, 1950.

Piaget, J. *The child's construction of reality.* London: Routledge & Kegan Paul, 1954.

Phillips, J. R. Syntax and vocabulary of mothers' speech to young children: Age and sex comparisons. *Child Development,* 1973, *44,* 182-185.

Roffwarg, H. P., Muzio, J. N., & Dement, W. C. Ontogenetic development of the human sleep-dream cycle. *Science,* 1966, *152,* 604-619.

Ryan, M. L. *Baby talk and intonation in adult speech to preverbal infants.* Unpublished doctoral dissertation, University of Strathclyde, Scotland, 1977.

Sameroff, A. Non-nutritive sucking in newborns under visual and auditory stimulation. *Child Development,* 1967 *38,* 443-452.

Schaffer, H. R. Objective observations of personality development in early infancy. *British Journal of Medical Psychology,* 1958, *31,* 174-183.

Schaffer, H. R. *The growth of sociability.* Baltimore, MD. Penguin Books, 1971.(a)

Schaffer, H. R. Cognitive structure and early social behavior. In H. R. Schaffer (Ed.), *The origins of human social relations.* London: Academic Press, 1971. (b)

Schaffer, H. R. Cognitive components of the infant's response to strangeness. In M. Lewis & L. A. Rosenblum (Eds.), *The origins of fear.* New York: Wiley, 1974.

Schaffer, H. R. Introduction: Early interactive development. In H. R. Schaffer (Ed.), *Studies in mother-infant interaction.* London: Academic Press, 1977. (a)

Schaffer, H. R. *Mothering.* London: Fontana/Open Books; New York: Harvard University Press, 1977. (b)

Schaffer, H. R., Collis, G. M., & Parsons, G. Vocal interchange and visual regard in verbal and pre-verbal children. In H. R. Schaffer (Ed.), *Studies in mother-infant interaction.* London: Academic Press, 1977.

Schaffer, H. R., & Crook, C. K. The role of the mother in early social development. In H. McGurk (Ed.), *Issues in childhood and social development.* London: Methuen, 1978.

Schaffer, H. R., Greenwood, A., & Parry, M. H. The onset of wariness. *Child Development,* 1972, *43,* 165-175.

Schaffer, H. R., & Parry, M. H. Perceptual-motor integration in infancy as a function of age and stimulus familiarity. *British Journal of Psychology,* 1969, *60,* 1-9.

Schaffer, H. R., & Parry, M. H. The effects of short-term familiarization on infants' perceptual-motor co-ordination in a simultaneous discrimination situation. *British Journal of Psychology,* 1970, *61,* 559-569.

Snow, C. E. Mothers' speech to children learning language. *Child Development,* 1972, *43,* 549-565.

Stern, D. N. Mother and infant at play: The dyadic interaciton involving facial, vocal and gaze behavior. In M. Lewis & L. A. Rosenblum (Eds.), *The effect of the infant on its caregiver.* New York: Wiley, 1974.

Stern, D. N. The infant's stimulus world during social interaction. In H. R. Schaffer (Ed.), *Studies in mother-infant interaction.* London: Academic Press, 1977.

Stern, D. N., Jaffe, J., Beebe, B., & Bennett, S. Vocalizing in unison and in alternation: Two modes of communication within the mother-infant dyad. *Annals of New York Academy of Science,* 1975, *263,* 89-100.

Strain, B., & Vietze, P. M. Z. *Early dialogue: The structure of reciprocal infant-mother vocalization.* Paper presented to Society for Research in Child Development, Denver, 1975.

Trevarthen, C. Descriptive analyses of infant communicative behavior. In H. R. Schaffer (Ed.), *Studies in mother-infant interaction.* London: Academic Press, 1977.

Trevarthen, C., Hubley, P., & Sheeran, L. Psychological actions in early infancy. *Recherche,* 1975, *6,* 447-458.

Watson, J. S. Memory and "contingency analysis" in infant development. *Merrill-Palmer Quarterly,* 1967, *13,* 55-76.

Webster, R. L. Steinhardt, M. H., & Senter, M. G. Changes in infants' vocalizations as a function of differential acoustic stimulation. *Developmental Psychology,* 1972, *7,* 39-43.

Wiener, M., Devoe, S., Rubinov, S., & Geller, J. Non-verbal behavior and non-verbal communication. *Psychological Review,* 1972, *79,* 185-214.

Wolff, P. H. The causes, controls, and organization of behavior in the neonate. *Psychological Issues,* 1966, *5,* No. 1., Monograph No. 17.

Wolff, P. H. The role of biological rhythms in early psychological development. *Bulletin of Menninger Clinic,* 1967, *31,* 197–218.

Wolff, P. H. The serial organization of sucking in the young infant. *Pediatrics,* 1968, *42,* 943–956.

Wood, D., & Middleton, D. A study of assisted problem solving. *British Journal of Psychology,* 1975, *66,* 181–192.

13

The Role of Language
in Infant Development

Katherine Nelson
Graduate Center,
City University of New York

INTRODUCTION

Development of language by the human infant is as nearly universal as walking, and the child escapes from it only at the peril of severe physical, mental, or emotional disability. Yet, despite the enormous body of work on the development of language that has emerged in recent years, we are still far from having an answer to the basic question with which this chapter is concerned: How does the infant master language and in so doing become transformed into a child? In many ways, mastery of language is the key transition between infancy and childhood, and thus it is important to examine its basis in infant development. As we will see, however, achievement of cognitive and social prerequisites in infancy do not automatically produce a language user, and essential transition points remain unstudied and undefined. It is the purpose of this chapter to identify these gaps in our knowledge as well as to set to forth a hypothesis as to what we will find when we look at those gaps.

Recent research on language development has tended to follow one of two directions: to specify stages in the acquisition of an adult grammar, or, in a more recent turn, to emphasize the roots of linquistic competence in prelanguage development. These approaches represent efforts to understand the acquisition of language and to understand the relation of language to infant development, but the two have not yet made contact with each other. For the most part they do not even overlap. We have on the one hand the infant arriving at the end of the first year of life ready to speak a few words, equipped with cognitive and communicative skills that enable him to understand and begin to produce words. We have on the other hand the almost-child at the end of the second year, beginning now to combine a few words into two-word sentences, having arrived at last at Stage I of grammatical development (Brown, 1973). What has happened in between? According to this brief summary, and contrary to most people's assumptions, very little overt progress in language has taken place during this year. Moreover, as we shall see, this is not because dramatic progress is being made in other growth systems during this time. Indeed, much of the second year appears to be spent on a developmental plateau. This statement must be somewhat tentative because, in point of fact, surprisingly little is known about development in the second year of life.

If one examines the developmental literature for theory and data on development from 12 to 24 months, one finds an extraordinary gap and considerable confusion. Our knowledge of perceptual and cognitive capacity and development during the first 6 and even 12 months has grown prodigiously over the past 20 years, and our understanding of language development between 2 and 3 years has advanced rapidly with the detailed scrutiny of the sentences produced by 2-year-old children around the world. But our knowledge of basic processes—social, cognitive, and linquistic—remains underdeveloped with respect to the year from one to two. It is precisely because of the need to know how language emerges from the basis of the 1-year-old infant's prelinquistic social and cognitive competence that this gap is so keenly felt.

Let me briefly forecast the argument presented here. The child at the end of the first year of life is seemingly equipped cognitively and socially with the basic skills necessary to learn language. However, the first half of the second year is a period when little measurable progress is made in language or in any other domain. The last half of the second year sees a renewed progression that leads finally to a new level of functioning culminating in the acquisition of the adult language system beginning about the age of two. This chapter presents a hypothesis about development during this time within and without language, presents evidence from existing literature, and suggests ways to test the hypothesis further.

COGNITIVE PREREQUISITES

Infant cognition has been viewed primarily in terms of the child's understanding of the physical world, in particular the understanding of objects and relations between objects — for example, movement in space, causality, and temporal order. This emphasis is reflected in the tradition of research on visual and auditory perception, on learning, and on the development of sensorimotor schemata in Piagetian terms, especially those concerned with object permanence. When the attempt has been made to incorporate social knowledge, it has usually been attempted in terms of the physical mode (e.g., Bates, Camaioni & Volterra, 1975, on means–end differentiation; Bell, 1970, on person perception).

This bias obscures the fact that the child differentiates early between animate and inanimate world (according to Richards, 1974, as early as the first 2 months), and that he must develop cognitive schemas and affective attitudes toward each world. Nonetheless, for the purposes of considering cognitive prerequisites to language, we will accept the current research bias and concentrate on the infant's knowledge of the inanimate world. Relations among objects have been widely viewed as being of central importance to the infant's mastery of language, particularly of the understanding of reference and of semantic roles such as actor, action, and object.

Piaget's States of Sensorimotor Development

In attempting to identify the cognitive prerequisites of language acquisition most theorists have appealed to Piaget's (1952, 1954) description of sensorimotor development, especially development in Stage IV (8 to 12 months), Stage V (12 to 18 months), and Stage VI (18 to 24 months).

In very brief summary, at the end of Stage IV, that is by 1 year, the infant has achieved the rudiments of object permanence in that he can be observed to hunt for hidden objects, although he is still unable to consider the object independent of its location. Also at this time, the infant coordinates action schemas and applies them to new situations in goal-directed sequences, indicating a differentiation of means and ends. During Stage V the infant shows an increase in applying old as well as novel schemes to new situations and adjusting them to novel objects, that is, an increase in accommodating and experimenting behavior. He also becomes capable of following an object through visible displacements, that is, of considering the object independent of its place. Finally, during Stage VI the child is capable of the invention of new means through mental combinations, rather than being limited to overt trial and error as previously. Correlatively, he is able to represent the movement of objects internally and thus to follow objects through invisible displacements. From this theoretical standpoint the child between 1 and 2 years is an active explorer of and experimenter on objects, first overtly and in the end covertly. Development takes place in terms of accommodation to objective reality, understanding of object relations independent of self, and mental representation.

The preceding sketch, of course, conveys only the most superficial conception of development in Piaget's terms toward the end of the first and during the second year. In addition to the claim that representational thought, a fundamental prerequisite to language, develops only at the end of the second year, three major components of the theory have especially attracted those concerned with language development — namely, the development of the object concept, the differentiation of means and ends, and the understanding of object relations in terms of space, time, and causality.

Before considering specific studies that have attempted to relate object and language, an examination of the basis for the proposed relation between the development of the object concept and language development is in order. Should one expect a direct relationship between the two and, if so, of what kind? The simplest prediction is that the infant will not name objects until he has achieved a firm understanding of the substantial, independent, permanent status of the object. Something like this view is reflected in Bloom's (1973) account. However, it is clear that the child is not prevented from naming something whose existence is not understood to be permanent. For example, many children acquire a term for "cookie" among their first words at about 12 months, but cookies are not permanent in Piaget's sense, and in fact their fate is at the disposal of the child's actions. When the child eats it, the cookie ceases to exist. Food and drink in general, in fact, follow just the egocentric laws that, according to Piaget's account, the child must learn to reject in the achievement of the concept of object permanence. If the child names first objects, such as cookie, which do not follow the law of object permanence, it would appear that mastery of the concept of object permanence can have little to do with whether learning of object labels is possible.

In fact, an empirical relationship between the two has not been established. Although Bloom (1973) speculated that her daughter Allison's relative lack of lasting substantive terms prior to 18 months was related to her incomplete object concept, there was no independent measure of the concept, and other data have not shown the same object–term deficiency during this period (e.g., Greenfield & Smith, 1976; Nelson, 1973a; Rescorla, 1976). In Corrigan's (1976) study of children from 10 to 26 months, no relation between object–concept development and language development was apparent when age was partialled out, although there was a suggestion of a correlation between vocabulary acceleration and the final substage of Stage VI, that is, with the achievement of representational thought. Bates et al. (1975) found a correlation of word use with means–end relations but not with the object concept scale.

One problem with evaluating the evidence here is that language development has been measured almost exclusively in terms of production, with little attention being paid to comprehension. However, evidence for understanding reference to objects, even when those objects are not present, is evident in comprehension long before production (Benedict, 1976) — on the average 6 months earlier. Given this fact, then, the suggestion of a relation found between production of object labels and object permanence would be questionable simply on the grounds of the time lag between achievement of a given level in comprehension and in production. In brief, the suggestion of a relation between the achievement of object permanence and naming does not appear to be justified either theoretically or empirically.

A problem that continuously arises in relevant studies is the discrepancy between the ages assumed for Stages IV, V, and VI on the basis of Piaget's account and the achievement of those stages according to standard tests. A related problem is whether abilities said to belong to a single stage actually hang together in stage-like fashion for individual children. Uzgiris and Hunt (1975) suggest that they do not. Piaget himself leaned heavily on the concept of décalage in his descriptions of development at the end of the sensorimotor period, taking examples of Stage VI behaviors from a wide range of ages from 13 months to over 2 years. Recent attempts to relate language development to sensorimotor stages have found that Stage V and VI performances generally appear far earlier than the ages suggested by Piaget and Uzgiris. For example, a recent study by Corrigan (1976), which combined samples of 30 cross-sectional subjects and three longitudinally studied children, found transition Stage VI performance on the object permanence scale as early as 10 months and advanced Stage VI behaviors from 14 to 26 months.

One of the most striking aspects of Corrigan's (1976) study was the revelation of plateaus in both language and cognitive development during the second year. Table 13.1 shows the group scores for the cross-sectional sample. The language scores assign a score of 0.50 to "sensorimotor morphemes," 1.00 to single words, and above 1.00 values to word combinations, using standard Mean Length of Utterance computations. The object permanence scale was a modified form of the Uzgiris–Hunt scale, on which scores of 11 to 14 represent a transition phase from Stage V to VI of invisible hiding (hiding first in hand, then under screen) and scores of 15 to 21 are Stage VI behaviors with respect to invisible displacements. It is clear here that the major advance in object concept development takes place between 10 and 14 months, with a long period thereafter, lasting until 26 months, during which little progress is made. The plateau between 14 and 26 months is not a result of ceiling effects. Of six children in each age group, only two at 18 months, one at 22 months, and two at 26 months scored at the highest level. Furthermore, the lack of advance on this scale from 14 months to 26 months was replicated with the three children Corrigan followed longitudinally. Rather than claiming that the oldest children had not achieved Stage VI, it seems more reasonable to suggest that the most critical development had taken place prior to 14 months of age and that the later scale items were of peripheral significance.

It may be that object permanence scales as now constituted represent a poor index of the development that Piaget proposed for Stages V and VI. Still, if most of the proposed sensorimotor development is complete or even well underway by the beginning of the second year, it would seem to be a poor candidate for explaining subsequent language development. Rather, the evidence suggests that, although Stage VI development may be necessary, it does not appear to be sufficient for language to emerge.

TABLE 13.1
Mean Language Scores and Object Permanence Ranks
for each Age Group in Corrigan's (1976) Cross-Sectional Sample
(N = 6 in each age group)

Age Group (months)	Mean Language Score	Mean Object Permanence Score
10	0.51	9.83
14	0.56	18.67
18	0.56	18.67
22	1.10	19.83
26	1.57	19.67

Bates, Benigni, Bretherton, Camaioni, and Volterra (1977) have presented the most comprehensive effort to date to delineate cognitive and social prerequisites of language in terms of theoretical considerations as well as direct empirical comparisons. Bates and her colleagues studied both growing communicative competence and cognitive performance on a variety of Piagetian-derived measures of sensorimotor development during the eighth to thirteenth months. Subsequently, they recognized that the notion of a prerequisite, whether social or cognitive, was far from clear, and they described numerous possible relationships that might hold among the social, cognitive, and linguistic systems. In fact, they concluded that there were in excess of 30,000 possible logical relations among them. Originally, they expected that a particular competence (e.g., the separation of means and ends) would appear first in a "pure cognitive" (i.e., object-related) form and only later in a social or language form. However, they pointed out that this was not a necessary implication from the hypothesis. Rather, each surface form, including performance on cognitive tasks, might reflect an underlying cognitive competence that could manifest itself in a variety of performances without implying the priority of any. Despite this somewhat agnostic theoretical conclusion, the data described by Bates et al. (1977) present some of the strongest relationships between preverbal cognitive achievement and language acquisition yet found. In particular, they showed that a Stage V competence in terms of means–ends relationships appeared to be necessary to the use of language in an instrumental, in contrast to an indicative, mode.

As in Corrigan's study, however, in the Bates et al. (1977) sample of 25 Italian and American children, Stage V of sensorimotor development was achieved toward the end of the first year, and the great majority of the children had achieved Stage VI of object permanence by 13 months. Contrary to expectation, Bates and her colleagues did not find a relation between language use and performance on the object permanence scale, which lagged behind the means–ends scale. Bates et al. (1977) did not extend their observations beyond the 13-month period, but if they had done so, it seems likely that they would have found the same kind of plateau in both cognitive and linguistic functioning that Corrigan (1976) found, inasmuch as the children in their sample were equivalently advanced at the end of the first year.

This certainly presents us with an even greater puzzle than previously. If the child has accomplished so much by the beginning of the second year in both the object and social domains, and if he is able to coordinate his accomplishments in the early use of words, why then is he not launched into speech and also into representational thought? What happens to these systems over the next 12 months? (Although we do not know that, in fact, these children did not begin to talk in well-formed sentences over the next few months, our knowledge of age norms makes it a pretty good bet that they did not.)

A more general relation between the Piagetian description of sensorimotor development and language development has been suggested by Brown (1973) and in a more detailed form by Edwards (1973). According to these accounts, the first meanings expressed in the child's sentences are those reflecting the achievement of the understanding of object relations. Brown's list of the relationships found at Stage I (Table 13.2) has served well as a general summary. As noted above, Stage I grammar occurs for most children toward the end of the second year and the beginning of the third.

TABLE 13.2
The First Sentences in Child Speech[a]

I. Operations of reference.	
Nominations:	That (or it or there) + book, cat, clown, hot, big, etc.
Notice:	Hi + Mommy, cat, belt, etc.
Recurrence:	More (or 'Nother) + milk, cereal, nut, read, swing, green, etc.
Nonexistence:	Allgone (or No-more) + rattle, juice, dog, green, etc.
II. Relations	
Attributive:	Ad + N (Big train, Red book, etc.)
Possessive:	N + N (Adam checker, Mommy lunch, etc.)
Locative:	N + N (Sweater chair, Book table, etc.)
Locative:	N + V (Walk Street, Go store, etc.)
Agent–Action:	N + V (Adam put, Eve read, etc.)
Agent–Object:	N + N (Mommy sock, Mommy lunch, etc.)
Action–Object:	V + N (Put book, Hit ball, etc.)

[a]Reprinted with permission from R. Brown (1970).

Simple existence, recurrence, and disappearance are among those meanings presumably related to knowledge of object permanence per se, whereas relations of agent-action-object, locative-object, and attributive-object all reflect the elaboration of spatial and causal relations that presumably are achieved during the later stages of sensorimotor development. Thus far, the account is unproblematical but also relatively uninteresting. It would be more interesting if a developmental sequence of the acquisition of relational meanings were predicted, or if, correlatively, the child were incapable of producing some meanings prior to a certain age or stage. However, no attempt has been made to correlate the emergence of those meanings with cognitive development. Moreover, Greenfield and Smith (1976) have made a good case for the expression of most major meanings of what Brown calls Stage I speech (i.e., the first stage of combinational sequences) during the one-word period, which for the two children they studied, was the period between 12 and 18 months. Also, as noted earlier for the case of word meaning, comprehension of two and more words in these relationships precedes their production by several months (Benedict, 1976). These findings contradict the possible claim that there is a connection among (1) the final stage of sensorimotor development, (2) two-word speech, and (3) the meanings expressed in two-word sentences. Of course, if Stage VI is achieved by the beginning of the second year, then the meanings expressed and understood in the 12- to 18-month period might also be a reflection of these developments. (See also Kagan's discussion of these developments, Chapter 7, this volume.) However much understanding such object relations may be a necessary condition for their appearance in speech, it is clearly not a sufficient one. In summary, specific Piagetian developments studied thus far do not appear to shed much light on how the child develops from infancy within the language system.

The specific relationships that have been described here are not critical to the general theory advanced by Piaget and do not contradict it in any important way. In Piaget's view, language is but one realization of the semiotic function that emerges at the end of the sensorimotor period and that characterizes the subsequent period of symbolic representational thought. Bates (1976) bases her theory of a close relation between cognitive and linguistic achievements on this general claim regarding the onset of symbolic functioning and she presents, for that reason, a more convincing case. However, the research we have discussed indicates that symbolic functioning itself may begin much earlier than Piaget asserted. These studies also reaffirm Sinclair-de-Zwart's (1973) statement that one cannot directly transpose Piaget's theory into the terms of developmental psycholinguistics.

Categorizing

One of the elementary meanings in Brown's table (Table 13.2), the nominations, deserves further consideration. This meaning is among the first observed in single words as well as in word combinations. Greenfield and Smith (1976) term them *indicative objects* and found them to be among the first meanings expressed at 8 and 9 months by their two subjects. Bates et al. (1975) noted referential use of words (which is similarly defined) in one of their longitudinally studied children at 13 months and in another at 16 months. In their cross-sectional study about one-third of their sample had used words in a declarative or referential manner by 13 months. Dore (1974) reported similar findings. Although these naming behaviors appear early for most children, considerable individual variation is shown. These behaviors are thought by both Bates and Dore to be related to sensorimotor development, but they are subject to several other possible interpretations (among them the simple practice of terms).

The interpretation favored here is that object labeling represents an early use of language by the child for cognitive—specifically categorization—purposes. Halliday (1975) subsumes this function under the term *heuristic,* one type of mathetic (related to knowing) functions that he contrasts with and places subsequent to pragmatic (interactive, regulatory, and instrumental) functions in his developmental hypothesis. Naming pictures and asking "What's that?" are related activities that appear for many children in the first half of the second year but show considerable individual variation. Similarly, the overextension of early object terms (e.g., the use of "doggie" for other animals) may be best viewed as an attempt to categorize objects (see Nelson, Benedict, Gruendel, & Rescorla, 1977).

Indeed, much of the child's early language, including the first word combinations, may serve a heuristic function (i.e., a private cognitive, rather than a public communicative) function. When the child says "Mommy eat" he is making a statement that categorizes an event in terms of a particular type of action and the actor who engages in it. As Halliday (1975) has emphasized, the child is not using the language to inform. Rather, it is being used to comment on a topic in the immediately apparent and shared environment. The child's statements, in fact, are quite different from those that are made by older children and adults who know that conversational rules discourage commenting on the trite and obvious. The young talker may make such statements because he has not acquired these rules, because the relations are novel to him and not to others, because his egocentric view cannot account for the obviousness to others of the statements. Or the young talker may not intend to communicate information with such statements at all but rather to categorize the world using the new-found tool of language. The fact that children quite often talk as readily when playing alone as when they are with others (Piaget, 1926, 1962; Weir, 1962) is in accord with such an interpretation. Whether it conflicts with or complements the notion of language embedded in an early communication framework is a question for future exploration.

The suggestion put forth here is that much of the language used during the second year is used by the child as a heuristic or categorizing tool. If language serves a cognitive function of this kind, does the cognitive function precede its appearance in language, or does it derive from language? In some sense, categorizing is necessary prior to language use because language itself requires the establishment of categories — of sound, of objects and events, of word classes and grammatical forms. Moreover, much recent research on perceptual development in infancy has shown that the infant discriminates events in the world with the same categories as adults do (see Bornstein, Chapter 3, this volume). This research essentially tells us that there are natural or constructed categories in perception that divide up a physically defined continuum in psychologically meaningful ways. The question being raised here is a more complex one. Given a set of perceptual events, which can be discriminated by the infant, at what point does the infant group together discriminable events that share some similarity in order to form a concept or a category? Categorizing activity does not simply assign an event to a canonical or prototypical concept. It classifies but also recognizes dimensions that do not fit the canonical form, thus remaining open to recategorization along different dimensions. It is no small claim to suggest that the young child is capable of such behavior, given the fairly large body of evidence supporting the claim that in middle childhood the child is quite a rigid classifier (e.g., Kogan, 1974). However, it can be shown that there is evidence both within and without language use to suggest that such is the case.

That categorization takes place even before language use is supported by the studies of Ricciuti (1965) and Nelson (1973a) which found evidence for grouping objects on the basis of similarity of form, function, and color in children as young as 12 months. Subsequent studies (e.g. Ross, 1976) have shown that after repeated presentations of stimuli from categories of people, furniture, and food, dishabituation of attention in the form of preference for a member from a novel category occurred for infants at 12, 18, and 24 months of age. This experiment was carefully controlled for both stimulus preference and stimulus novelty. (See also the discussion by Kagan of concept and category development during infancy in Chapter 7, this volume.)

Evidence for recategorization after initial assignment is also available. One of the experiments reported in Nelson (1973a) showed that after discriminating balls from nonballs, children who were given the opportunity to play with the ball-like objects made new classifications of which were balls and which were not. The most cogent evidence in this respect comes from within the language-learning period itself when a child will, for instance, take his own boot, examine it closely, place it on his head, and announce, "hat" (Gruendel, 1976). Here the object retains its identity as boot for the child; it is only temporarily classified as "hat." It is not permanently assimilated to the hat schema in the sense that the child's cowboy hat is, for example.

A number of different experiments recently have confirmed the suggestion that not only does categorization according to a concept take place prior to language but that the conceptual basis for categorizing tends to be functional (Nelson, 1973a, 1974). Our unpublished experiments with infants between the ages of 8 and 12 months showed that attention was greater and memory was better for the movement, action, or function component of an object than for either shape or color (Nelson, Kessen, & Platt, 1978). What these experiments show is that infants not only are disposed to categorize novel events but that the most informative dimension along which such categorization takes place is that of the function of things. This categorization is reflected in early language in that children name objects that do interesting things (e.g., car, dog, and ball), and they also name attributes that change (e.g., broken and dirty) (Nelson, 1973a, 1976). Thus, their early language terms are a reflection of their prelinguistic biases for categorizing the world. If much of early language is in fact used heuristically, as a categorizing tool, this result is quite comprehensible, because the child will name those objects and events most useful for his purposes.

From this account, which shows the continuity of the categorizing function in preverbal and early language activity, it might be expected (and it would accord with Piaget's description of the accommodation activity of the Stage V child) that cognitive development in the second year involves increasing skill in the categorization of objects. It is something of a surprise, then, to find that in Ross's (1976) study there were no age differences among her subjects from 12 to 24 months in their dishabituation to new category members. That is, the child at one year showed the same categorical effect as the child at two years. Here is another of the striking plateaus, where the basic competence appears early and subsequently shows little change over much of the second year. Like object permanence and causal relations, category formation may be a necessary prerequisite to language but seemingly it does not explain development within the early language period.

A different proposal has been put forth by Kagan (1976) with respect to the shift in cognitive functioning at the end of the first year. In his view, the child at this time becomes capable of activating hypotheses to explain novel events, thus generating uncertainty or unpredictability about those events (Kagan, Kearsley, & Zelazo, 1975): "The second year seems to mark the first fragile appearance of the capacity to think about the future—a capacity that will grow until the person is able to think in millenia rather than moments [p. 205]." This capacity is of obvious relevance to both learning and using language. However, it must be noted without prejudice that the theory helps very little in resolving the progress—or lack of it—being made by the child during the language-learning period, inasmuch as the activation of hypotheses, like the other cognitive capacities discussed, is said to become possible by 13 months. And regrettably, Kagan's own published observations again skip over the crucial period betweeen 13 and 20 months.

What we have found at every turn in this brief survey of cognitive achievements thought to be related to language is that the necessary basic capacities are achieved by late in the first year or early in the second. We have few clues to development in the second year except for language development itself, but as we have noted, at least during the first half of that period, language itself is quite limited and shows little overt development.

There are only a few possible conclusions to draw from these various studies and proposals about the cognitive foundation of language development. First, the child may indeed be on a plateau with respect to understanding objects and their relations during the second year. He may be concentrating on other systems — for example, the motoric. Second, the child may be so consumed with elaborating figurative knowledge — that is, knowledge of particular objects — that more general cognitive skills (or operations — see Elkind, Chapter 9, this volume) do not advance. He may use those skills to learn more about the particular world he lives in, but for the time being more general abstract schemes are exercized but not advanced. A third possibility is that some cognitive development is taking place, but neither our theory nor our measurements have tapped it. This possibility is not to be discarded out of hand, considering how little knowledge we yet have about development during this period. And finally, although each system considered above appears to be at a standstill, a more fundamental reorganization may take place.

THE COMMUNICATION COMPONENT

It is striking that in social-communicative development, as in cognitive development, we know more about the 8- to 13-month-old infant than we do about the infant-becoming-child of 12 to 24 months. Attachment theory, which has had such an important influence on our thinking about early social development, makes its strongest claims with respect to development in the first year. Indeed, the period when the child has established a specific attachment to the mother, as demonstrated through approach or separation protest, and has demonstrated differentiation of strangers by showing stranger anxiety, is the last quarter of the first year. Thereafter, according to theory, the child extends attachment to include other people. It is for this reason, presumably, that studies of peer relations (e.g., Lewis & Rosenblum, 1975) typically begin in the second year. However, Lamb (1976) has shown that father attachment at least is coextensive in time with attachment to mother.

Of more direct relevance to language development, but obviously dependent on the establishment of a mother–child bond, are studies of preverbal communicative development. Before the child begins to speak or to understand what is said, he usually has the opportunity to participate in social exchanges involving gesture, touching, vocalization, smiling, and imitation. Toward the end of the first year, most mother–child pairs seem to develop a variety of such structured contexts within which each partner plays a well-understood role, thus setting up the possibility that the child will be able to interpret what is intended by the mother, linguistically or not, within this context. (See the discussion by Schaffer, Chapter 12, this volume.)

Bruner (1975a, 1975b) and his colleagues have given detailed attention to the way in which these repeated exchanges (for example, the "Give and take" game) established "the regulation of *joint* attention and *joint* activity within the mutuality between mother and infant" (Bruner, 1975b).

When the child is between 6 and 12 months old, mothers "standardize" forms of joint actions by "setting up standard action formats by which the child can be helped to interpret the mother's signals, her gestures, and her interactions" (Bruner, 1975b, p. 12). Thus, according to Bruner (1975b):

> The claim is that the child is grasping initially the requirements of joint action at a prelinguistic level, learning to differentiate these into components, learning to recognize the function of utterances placed into these socially ordered structures, until finally he comes to substitute elements of a standard lexicon in place of the non-standard ones. The process is, of course, made possible by the presence of an interpreting adult who operates not so much as a corrector or reinforcer but rather as a provider, an expander and idealizer of utterances while interacting with the child [pp. 17–18].

This is a persuasive picture, and one begins to see how the early comprehension skills of a child (Benedict, 1976) fit into the scheme. One is persuaded to expect to find children of game-setting mothers emerging effortlessly into speech. Unfortunately, Bruner's published observations do not extend beyond the last part of the first year, and there are no comparable observations to supplement them. However, if these mother–child exchanges are the nonverbal equivalent to dialogue (cf. Schaffer, Chapter 12, this volume), one clearly would expect to find very soon the linguistic equivalent taking shape, and the child taking part in it. That development, however, is many months away. Like other complex language skills, it emerges in the last half of the second year. Thus, the expected continuity is missing.

Another dimension of the social-communication component is the function of preverbal and verbal messages. By analyzing function we may be able to see how language develops within the communicative scheme. One early function — the heuristic — was described in the previous section, and it was pointed out that this was essentially a noncommunicative function. Here we are concerned with communicative functions, not private cognitive functions.

In the study referred to earlier, Bates et al. (1977) have traced the development of communicative function in *speech act* terms from early infant cries to the first functional words. Using Searle's (1969) terminology, they distinguish three stages of development during this time: the perlocutionary, during which the infant's vocalizations have an effect on the listener without true intention; an illocutionary stage when the infant uses vocalizations with intent but without lexical meaning; and finally a locutionary stage during which the infant uses words to refer as well as to encode intention. This stage was reached by the child with the first use of words in an instrumental way at about 13 months in Bates's sample. This analysis again emphasizes the continuity in development from prelinguistic to linguistic forms, but the final form that combines all three Speech Act components in the single word can serve so many specific functions that it sheds little light on linguistic development itself. In fact, Dore (1974) takes issue with Bates's analysis and claims that both the performative and the constative components of the Speech Act undergo development in the early language period.

Probably the longest lived and the most generally accepted functional theory is that which states that the child first learns words to obtain needs. Its corollary is that if all needs and wants are satisfied without language, the child will not be motivated to learn it. This popular traditional view underlies the behavioral theories of Skinner (1957) and Staats (1963). From this point of view the *conative* (i.e., need-satisfying) function should be the first to appear (equivalently in Halliday's, 1975, terms, the instrumental and regulatory functions).

It is somewhat dismaying to find that, aside from Halliday's (1975) single-subject study of his own son, there is actually very little in the way of a descriptive taxonomy of functions in early speech so that we cannot say with confidence that there is no truth to the traditional view. The position implies, however, that (1) speech is needed to express conative functions and that (2) conative functions are the first to appear in speech. Even without data on the second point we can consider the first, and it would appear to be easily falsified. The crying, vocalizing, and gesturing behaviors of young infants appear to be quite adequate to the expression of many needs and desires. Indeed Bates's (1975) perlocutionary stage in communicative development is characterized by the effectance of a message (e.g., "I'm hungry") even prior to the point where the child intends a message (the illocutionary stage). Unless it can be shown that the child's needs and desires undergo a great change in complexity, abstractness, or "distancing" between 10 and 20 months (and this does not appear to be the case), the claim that the use of language is necessary to fulfill them appears to be unwarranted. There is, of course, a limit to this proposition. One child in my longitudinal study (Nelson, 1973b) used the phrase "I want it" repetitively at 2 years to express the desire for a truck, banana, apple, peach, bottle, or record. At no time did he use any of those object labels. If the object had not been directly in his purview and available to the pointing gesture, he would not have been able to make his wants known. His perfectly correct English sentence "I want it" was in fact the equivalent of the younger infant's cry or the protolinguistic "eh-eh-eh" sometimes used by the prelinguistic child. That is, the language form was not necessary to the expression of the want, and functionally it was no more effective than prelinguistic signals.

The question remains open as to whether conative functions are among the earliest expressed by most young children; they have been identified very early by most investigators, such as Leopold (1939) and Halliday (1975). The regulatory function identified by Halliday and the similar imperative discussed by Bates, in which the child attempts to control the actions of others (e.g., "up," "no," meaning "pick me up," "stop it") are equivalent to the traditional conative. The regulatory function involves only two persons whereas Halliday's instrumental function involves, in addition, a desired object. For this reason both Halliday and Bates consider the regulatory to be more basic than the instrumental, which involves the coordination of social and object goals. Both types, however, appear to involve similar communication levels, and both appear to be expressible in nonlinguistic as well as linguistic forms.

A third type of function that is easily related to prelinguistic communication is what Halliday (1975) terms *interactive* and what others have called *expressive* (Bruner, 1975a; Nelson, 1973b, 1977a, 1977b). Such messages establish and maintain an affective bond between the communicators or sustain a social relationship. Although language is clearly used by both children and adults for these purposes, again language is not essential to their expression. Given physical proximity, nonverbal communicative signals such as smiles and other facial expressions, or physical gestures (touches, hugs, or kisses) may accomplish the same purpose equally well or even better.

The functions just described are related to social goals and relationships; they serve to regulate and maintain relations between people. In this respect, they differ from functions that communicate about states of affairs in the real world, a group of functions that fit the traditional term *referential* (Halliday, 1975, uses *mathetic*) and include those classifying and descriptive functions described in the previous section. (See Chapter 14 by Sameroff and Harris in this volume for a more detailed description of Halliday's analysis.)

From this discussion it is clear that many of the communicative functions served by language are observable in preverbal form. There are two implications here. First, the child is socially set for communication through the establishment of mother–child exchanges and the practice of basic communicative functions by the end of the first year. But second, to the extent that nonverbal communication fulfills these functions, language is not necessary to them. Once again we find a necessary but not sufficient prerequisite fulfilled by about 13 months of age.

THE MISSING LINK: DEVELOPMENT FROM 12 TO 18 MONTHS

By 12 to 13 months, as we have seen, the child has achieved a rather advanced level of sensorimotor development and is capable of categorizing and generating hypotheses about events. He has also normally experienced social interchanges that set the stage for language use and has practiced expressing communicative messages nonverbally. As Kagan (1971) noted, "the concordance of events around the first birthday may signify the gradual end of one developmental stage and the beginning of another [p. 176]." The conditions all seem right for language to explode at this point. Indeed, this seems to be the general expectation by laymen and psychologists alike.

Consider McCall's (1976) description, derived from his analysis of psychometric tests:

> ... at 6 months the child is predominantly an explorer of perceptual consequences: he studies the perceptual-cognitive information or uncertainty in his environment. An important aspect of this exploration is the contingent consequences to his physical interaction with the environment. By 12 months his "environment" is more likely to include social beings with whom he engages in reciprocal imitation of sensorimotor and rudimentary verbal behaviors. *As his ability increases to symbolize mentally, his language improves and he continues to imitate the verbal-social behavior of adults as well as to demonstrate skills in vocabulary comprehension and production.* By 24 months the dominant theme has evolved into grammatical fluency and production [p. 114, emphasis mine].

However, if we look for evidence of the promised language progress in the second year, we will be generally disappointed. The vast majority of language studies begin where McCall leaves off, that is, around the second year of life when grammatical productions have begun. Most children do not reach Brown's (1973) Stage I (Mean Length of Utterance = approximately 1.75) until around their second birthday or later, and with some exceptions this has been the earliest stage considered by most recent researchers. Furthermore, if we look at language norms we find a similar blank. Although infant tests credit the child with a few words at about 1 year, there generally follows a long plateau during which few words are added. This is reflected in both the summary based on early vocabulary studies (Table 13.3), as well as in the backward learning curves (Figure 13.1)

TABLE 13.3
Increase in Size of Vocabulary in Relation to Age[a]

Years	Age Months	N	Number of Words	Gain
	8	13	0	
	10	17	1	1
1	0	52	3	2
1	3	19	19	16
1	6	14	22	3
1	9	14	118	96
2	0	25	272	154

[a]Based on Smith (1926); vocabulary size estimated from standardized tests (see McCarthy, 1954).

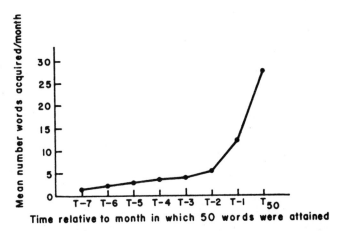

FIG. 13.1. Backward learning curves for vocabulary acquisition. T = month of attainment of first 50 words. From Nelson (1973b), reprinted with permission.

that more faithfully mirror individual progress (from Nelson, 1973b).

The import of these studies would seem to be that little language development takes place during at least the first half of the second year. That is evidenced also by Lenneberg's (1967) summary of motor and language development, taken from age norms and shown here as Table 13.4. As seen in this table, there appears to be little language progress from 12 to 18 months, and although there is more development between 18 and 24 months, it is slight compared to the dramatic developments yet to come.

If not language, what else? As we have seen, most studies of infant development stop at 1 year. Kagan's (1971) project did not assess behavior between 13 and 27 months, and most studies of early childhood begin at 3 years and at best reach down to 2 years. In a very basic sense, the second year remains unmapped.

Of course, we do have some evidence from psychometric tests as to what goes on from 12 to 24 months (e.g., in motor behavior) as shown in Table 13.4. However, as Kagan (1971) also noted, the Bayley (1969) infant tests show a rather sudden drop in the correlation between mental and motor scales at 12 months, a drop which lasts throughout the second year. Only at 15 months does the correlation arise above 0.40 and otherwise ranges from 0.23 to 0.31, whereas in the first year the correlations range from 0.42 to 0.75. Of course, as McCall (1976, and Chapter 8, this volume) has pointed out, the components of the mental test change over the second year, becoming more verbal. Nonetheless, the correlations tend to suggest that the motor component is less important or less intimately connected to cognitive functioning than it may have been earlier. McCall's stage analysis in Chapter 8 of this volume, based to a large extent on the analysis of standardized tests, is consistent with the present claim in showing discontinuities at

13 and 20 months, although his data do not shed light on development within stages, which is the source of concern here.

TABLE 13.4
Developmental Milestones in Motor and Language Development[a]

	Motor	Vocalization and Language
12 mo.	Walks when held by one hand: walks on feet and hands — knees in air; mouthing of objects almost stopped; seats self on floor.	Identical sound sequences are replicated with higher relative frequency of occurence, and words (mamma or dadda) are emerging; definite signs of understanding some words and simple commands (Show me your eyes).
18 mo.	Grasp, prehension, and release fully developed; gait stiff, propulsive, and precipitated; sits on child's chair with only fair aim; creeps downstairs backward; has difficulty building tower of 3 cubes.	Has a definite repertoire of words — more than three but less than 50; still much babbling but now of several syllables with intricate intonation pattern; no attempt at communicating information and no frustration for not being understood; words may include items such as "thank you" or "come here," but there is little ability to join any of the lexical items into spontaneous two-item phrases: understanding is progressing rapidly.
24 mo.	Runs, but falls in sudden turns; can quickly alternate between sitting and stance; walks stairs up or down, one foot forward only.	Vocabulary of more than 50 items (some children seem to be able to name everything in environment); begins spontaneously to join vocabulary items into two-word phrases; all phrases appear to be own creation; definite increase in communicative behavior and interest in language.

Adapted from Table 14.1 (pp. 129–130) in Lenneberg (1967); adapted with permission.

Using standard instruments to get an insight into social development, one turns to the Behavioral Scale of the Bayley (1969) test, where we find that, compared to 12 months, at every age from 15 to 24 months infants are rated as being "happier." At 18 and 24 months they are less responsive to persons; at 18 and 21 months they are less responsive to the examiner and more responsive to the mother; and at 18, 21, and 24 months they are less cooperative than at 12 months. Although there is no change in the scale for manipulating objects, there is, as would be expected, more imaginative play with objects from 21 months on. This presents a mixed picture of children who are less cooperative but happier, less responsive to strangers, and more responsive to their mothers during the second year than at its start. But the changes overall are slight, and the general picture is again one of stability. Furthermore, laboratory studies of social relations—in particular, peer relations—have sometimes also revealed a quite surprising lack of change over the second year (Bronson, 1975; Lewis, Young, Brooks, & Michaelson, 1975), again indicating a plateau in social development over this age range. (But see Schaffer, Chapter 12 in this volume, for the suggestion of the development of coordination in peer play during this period.)

By this point, it is apparent that wherever we look—at cognitive, social, or communicative systems — the child at about age one appears to have reached a point in development that (1) is much the equivalent of the level usually posited for a considerably later age, (2) changes little over the next 6 months, and (3) appears to be a necessary but not sufficient condition for the development of language.

What is most striking about the period from 12 to 18 months, however, is not the evidence of plateaus of development but the virtual lack of either research or theory directed to this period. Thus, drawing firm conclusions about either the true existence of what appear to be plateaus or the explanation for them is not feasible at this point. Study after study stops at 13 months, skips from 13 to 20 months, or begins at 2 years. One is driven to ask: What is going on here? If one wishes to understand how language develops within the matrix of competencies established at the end of the first year, it is necessary to dig deeper into development during this period than we yet have.

Fortunately, within the study of language development itself there are a few recent studies that have attempted to connect the earliest evidence for language use to later stages and thus have given detailed attention to this age period. Benedict (1976) has recently traced the beginnings of language understanding, which has heretofore been taken for granted but little studied (see also Huttenlocher, 1974). Benedict found that by an average age of 13 months the children in her sample understood more than 50 words, most of them object terms, and they were beginning to respond to words in combinations, that is, to more than one word in a sentence at a time. This level of comprehension is comparable to the level attained in production by the same children at about 19 months (which is similar to the findings in Nelson, 1973b). One possible way of viewing the first half of the second year, then, is as a period of growing language understanding. Some of the phenomena we traced earlier are understandable from this view. For example, comprehension of language is covert and thus less open to measurement than is production; indeed, its measurement has only recently begun to be developed, beginning with a path-breaking study by Shipley, Smith, and Gleitman in 1969. Also, infant testers have often run into problems with tapping early understanding because of the close dependence of the 1-year-old on the sometimes idiosyncratic system of meanings established with the mother.

The early comprehension system is quintessentially social. It develops within the game-playing, picture-sharing, caregiving situations shared by mother and child, which were documented by Bruner (1975a). The system may or may not involve reference to objects (or their representation in pictures). It almost always begins with simple social games and moves on to object terms (Benedict, 1976) and their relations later. At about the same age, of course, the child has usually begun to produce a few words, and he uses them to a greater or lesser degree for a number of different functions during this period. In a number of recent studies, these words have been considered from different angles: in terms of their reference (Clark, 1973; Gruendel, 1976; Nelson, 1973b, 1974; Rescorla, 1976) in terms of their grammatical function (Goldin–Meadow, Seligman, & Gelman, 1976; Nelson, 1973b) in terms of their semantic roles (Greenfield & Smith, 1976) or in terms of their pragmatic function (Dore, 1974; Halliday, 1975).

Some generalizations can be set forth from these studies. Most of the words the child learns refer to objects; most of the objects named are of interest and importance to the child because they do something interesting; some, but a minority, of the words are used to refer to a category of objects that is broader than the category referred to by the adult term. Within the time span considered, children use their words for a number of different semantic roles and pragmatic functions, and the same functions in fact that will be served by later grammatical constructions of two words or more. There are still too few children who have been studied longitudinally during this period to say whether there is a developmental progression in terms of the use of certain roles and functions, as claimed by Greenfield and Smith (1976) with two subjects and by Halliday (1975) with one subject, respectively. Their claims can be briefly summarized, however.

Greenfield and Smith (1976) see development during the holophrastic period (roughly 8 to 20 months) primarily in terms of the type of semantic roles the child expresses. They see a progression from "pure" performative utterances to more language-like ones. They found a progression from the descriptions of the child's own actions and states to the description of others' actions and states, a sequence that they saw as involving decentration. Another progression marked the move from involvement of a single entity as agent or object to two or more related entities. Of considerable interest is Greenfield and Smith's attempt to discern an explanation for the movement from one-word to two-word utterances, a clear developmental move that has thus far eluded adequate explanation. They maintain (1976) that:

The use of almost every semantic function passes through a number of stages before it is first used in two-word utterances. Most functions appeared first in isolated, one-word form. From this point, there are two directions of development. One is the use of single words in relation to verbal, as opposed to non-verbal, context. The other is the use of single words in sequences, as opposed to in isolation. Conversational sequences might be considered a combination of these two developments [p. 166].

Of course, there was also an increase in total utterances observed over the period, as well as an increase in the frequency of use of certain semantic functions.

Halliday's (1975) claim with respect to development is framed within his theory of communicative function. He viewed his son Nigel's progress as moving through Phase I, when primarily pragmatic functions (interactive, instrumental, and regulatory) were expressed, to Phase II, in which mathetic functions (heuristic and imaginative) were added. Finally in Phase III, around 19 to 20 months, the meaning potential of the adult system was achieved. Here, "the ideational, concerned with the representation of experience" and "the interpersonal, concerned with the communication process as a form and as a channel of social action" are distinguished, but according to Halliday the two are coordinated in every adult utterance. This move toward coordination of functions, according to Halliday, is integrally related to the development of grammar and to the development of dialogue. Considering the part that dialogue is felt to play in this theory, as well as in Greenfield and Smith's account of the development of the sentence and considering the apparent readiness that the child shows for participating in communicative sequences at the end of the first year leads us to a final consideration of what develops within and without language during this period.

THE COORDINATION OF THE SOCIAL
AND OBJECT WORLDS IN AND OUT OF LANGUAGE

Although the social and cognitive systems have been spoken of here and elsewhere as being independent domains, their interdependence and even inseparability are also generally recognized. *Social cognition* is a term now widely used to describe understanding that involves social relationships. Cognition is not confined to knowledge of the physical world, and the infant's caretakers are not simply alternative objects: People are different in many dimensions from inanimate objects, and the infant treats them differently from an early age (Richards, 1974). There is a primary distinction between the physical object–world and the social-communicative world in terms of their affordances; one allows primarily individual exploration, and the other allows primarily interactive communication. As we have seen, at least by the last half of the first year the infant has these domains well differentiated.

At least two investigators (Bates, 1976; Sugarman-Bell, 1976) have emphasized the coordination of social relations and object relations in the last part of the first year and the first part of the second as part of the means–ends differentiation that takes place at that time. That is, the adult comes to be used by child instrumentally to achieve an object-oriented end either by using language forms or prior to language use. The coordination of the social and objective worlds in this way is, however, only a first step along a long road.

A number of investigators have recently observed that substantial individual differences exist among young children with respect to their interest in and engagement of the social and object worlds during the first 2 years. For example, in a study contrasting the attainment of object permanence and person permanence, Bell (1970) found that most infants solved the hiding problem first for salient persons, in particular their mothers. A minority, however, solved the problem with respect to objects first. In a recent unpublished study in our laboratory at Yale, Kessen and Nelson (1978) have found that social orientation, contrasted with orientation to the physical environment, in a strange situation is a strong individual characteristic, is relatively stable across the age range from 8 to 12 months, and predicts performance on some object-focused laboratory tasks. Children clearly differ at later ages as well with respect to their social versus object orientation (cf. Jennings, 1975). To the extent, however, that the child needs to coordinate the two domains, strong prior emphasis on one or the other would be expected to have consequences for the course of development during the coordination process.

Let us hypothesize at this point that a major task of the second year of life is in fact to bring about the coordination of social and object knowledge within a general cognitive and affective framework, and that this coordination is essential to the development of language. We have seen that prior to this time the child has reached a certain cognitive level with respect to an understanding of objects and object relations and that he has certain social-communicative skills with respect to making needs and affects known to others. The last half of the first year, when attachment behaviors and anxiety about strangers come to the fore, as do also exploration of space and objects and the beginnings of classification skills, appears to be a period of the differentiation of these two primary domains from a more generalized cognitive-affective frame.

This differentiation of the two realms, however, leads to an unstable adaptation to the world in which both intra- and inter-individual differences can be expected. Some children may be consistently social oriented whereas others are consistently object or action oriented, but most children are likely to swing from one extreme to the other depending on the context of the situation. Thus, clinging to the mother or crying in distress appear in situations interpreted as posing a threat to social understanding (Ainsworth, 1974) whereas sustained exploration and manipulation appear when the social equilibrium is not upset. When the child is able to coordinate the two, he will be better able to use the mother as an interpreter of objective situations and to use exploratory and manipulative skills in mastering strange or threatening social situations. Thus, the last half of the first year is a period of the achievement of differentiation, but this very achievement leads to an instability that must be resolved through a higher level coordination, a development of the first half of the second year.

It seems obvious that acquisition of language might help the child in achieving this kind of coordination. However, there is also evidence from the earliest period of language development (i.e., between 10 and 20 months) that these different emphases are not yet integrated. This is seen in the fact that different children employ different styles and functions of speech when they first begin to talk early in the second year (Nelson, 1973b).

According to Bruner's (1975a) observations, mothers often set up situations in which objects play a central part in protocommunication games, suggesting that one of the functions of early verbal exchanges is to embed referring expressions in a social framework, thus coordinating the two. However, it appears that children are not able to take advantage of the entire framework offered in this way. Rather, some children appear to pick up the *social* message offered, and others pick up the *object* message (Nelson, 1973a, 1977b). That is, some children seem to operate with a social (or expressive) theory of the function of language, and others operate with an objective (or referential) theory. The former children translate into language forms the preverbal social messages (regulatory, instrumental, and interactive) that they have previously encoded in nonverbal signals and gestures. The latter children learn language that supplements their preverbal skills, that is, they learn words that refer to objects and actions and that can be used to stand for those objects and actions in their absence. For this reason, the referential style of language use has greater functional potential than does the expressive style, which is nearly as limited as the prelinquistic communication system. The contrast between these two styles is apparent in some examples of words used in a 20-minute play period when the children were 15 and 13 months old respectively, as shown in Table 13.5. The expressive child (Lisa) uses different words appropriate to different social situations, but her words are social stereotypes. On the other hand, the referential child (Jane) in this situation uses many more words to differentiate among different referents, but she does not differentiate between social contexts. For example, she uses the same terms whether she is giving and taking, looking at pictures, or playing with objects.

Is there anything to suggest that what we observe in terms of individual differences in early language is related importantly to the child's efforts at coordinating his understanding of the social and physical environment? If this coordination is a centrally important task during the second year as hypothesized, we might expect to see an emphasis on one or the other end of the spectrum, as observed, but we would expect also to find that this early emphasis was overridden later in language development as the child gained control of and integrated both aspects. We do, indeed, find this to be the case. Studies that have followed up early style differences (Nelson, 1973b, 1975a, 1975b; Starr, 1975) have found that the expressive-referential distinction diminishes toward the end of the second year.

Furthermore, we would expect that children who began to talk a good deal early in the second year (between 12 and 18 months) would show an emphasis on one or the other function in their early word forms and uses, whereas children who only began productive language later on (at 19 to 20 months) would show a more balanced pattern, indicating that the social and object spheres have been coordinated prior to language learning, so that early language then reflects this coordination. As shown in Table 13.6, this is precisely the pattern that is found when the sample described in Nelson (1973b) is divided according to early and later vocabulary acquisition and referential, expressive, and balanced styles of speech.

TABLE 13.5
Words Used During Play Session[a]

	Lisa	Jane
Words used in play with objects	What (3)	Bag (1)
	What's that (2)	Bottle (12)
	Dat (3)	Baby (3)
	Where (4)	Ball (4)
	Okay (2)	Block (1)
	Sit (2)	
	Baby (2)	
Words used in giving or taking	Here (3)	Bottle (4)
	Dere (2)	Block (3)
	What's that (1)	Kitty (1)
	Thank you (1)	Want (1)
Words used for pictures	Dat (3)	Ball (1)
	What (5)	Doggie (2)
	See (2)	Car (1)
	What's this (1)	Gate (1)
	Yah (2)	Mooo (3)
		Baby (1)
		Kitty (1)
		fff (doggie sound) (1)

[a]Frequency of use in parentheses. From Nelson (1973a).

Especially notable is the fact that early talkers tended to be either expressive or referential, whereas those in the middle range were more balanced, indicating that both functions were reflected in their vocabularies. If we contrast functional emphasis and balanced emphasis for these ages, the difference is significant at the 0.01 level by Fisher's Exact Test. The even distribution among the late talkers can be explained in terms of the difficulties these children encountered in mastering speech, which accounted for the delay. The two expressive children, for example, were described in Nelson (1973b) as experiencing extreme difficulties related to language during the second year. In retrospect, these difficulties may we have been related to the problems they had in coordinating social and object goals both within and outside of language. The three later-talking referential children similarly appeared to have more than the usual problems with language acquisition, including highly directive and even rejecting mothers.

TABLE 13.6

Distribution of Functional Styles by Age
of Basic Vocabulary Achievement[a]

Age at 50 Words	Expressive (≤ 40% Object Words)	Referential (≥ 60% Object Words)	Balanced (41–59% Object Words)
Young (14–18 months)	3	3	0
Middle (19–20 months)	0	1	5
Older (21–24 months)	2	2	2

[a]From Nelson (1973a).

LANGUAGE AND THE COORDINATION OF SOCIAL AND OBJECT WORLDS

We have seen that the coordination of information from the social and physical spheres appears in language relatively late in the second year, although children who talk earlier tend to talk about one or the other realm. This integration is basic to language itself, and its absence therefore may well be the deterrent to language development at an earlier point in development. Halliday (1975) stresses that adult speech coordinates the interpersonal and ideational components into a single integrated speech act, whereas earlier the functions had been separated. He also argues that the coordination of the interpersonal and ideational functions coincides in development with both the acquisition of syntax and the development of the concept of dialogue.

Halliday's claim provides the key to the relation between general cognitive and communicative development and more specific linguistic development. Prior to the point at which social (interpersonal) and object (ideational) integration takes place, language can serve only one function at a time. Expressive language, therefore, develops as a communicative instrument serving affective and pragmatic needs directly, but it is not developed as a medium through which ideas can be expressed or communicated or as a means of a communication exchange. The child can request, command, point out—as may the adult—but the direction of the communication is one way only; it does not develop into a dialogue. Similarly, referential language is used to name, to classify, and to comment on the objective world, but it is constrained to the immediately apparent and therefore obvious. Although mothers may try to sustain a referential exchange on these topics, they will generally be unsuccessful because language is used only to point out and not yet to clarify or inform.

At this point we need to consider the requirements of the language system itself and to ask: What is the relation of grammar to coordination of social and object goals, and how does it advance that coordination? Consider the implications of the Greenfield and Smith (1976) claim that the major meanings of Stage I grammatical speech are expressed in the one-word stage, together with the finding by Benedict (1976) that children understand these meanings many months before they begin producing them. According to this evidence the child does not have to learn how to form sentences or produce word combinations in order to express his relational meanings and make them clear to others. Why, then, learn grammar? Why learn to say "I want a banana' instead of simply pointing and saying "banana?" Why learn to say "Daddy has a shoe" in place of pointing to shoe and saying "Daddy"?

When the child first uses words, the word or other expression stands for only one term in the communicative relation — self, other, referential relations. Some parts of the communicative act must be inferred from the context. As table 13.5 shows, the child may make clear the reference or the interpersonal context but not both at once in a linguistic frame. To express both requires their coordination in a symbolic form and therefore an understanding of how sentence relationships are formed and understood. The primitive coordination that is possible at .the one-word stage relies on apparent social relations between speaker and listener, or it requires an apparent object relation that does not need to be designated. Only with at least two words is it possible to express a relation that does not depend on the immediately apparent context for interpretation. Therefore, although the child may use language forms early in the second year to aid in his social–object coordination, it is only after this coordination is achieved nonlinguistically that he uses language itself to express a new level of understanding. Following Slobin's (1973) dictum that new forms will be used to express old functions, the first sentences will contain primarily the relations that were previously expressed in one-word statements, as Greenfield and Smith (1976) showed, but these first sentences will coordinate in language the two forms that were coordinated in word–action relationships previously. Before long the child moves on to express coordinated statements about nonpresent (in time or space) events and thus enters the stage of informative speech. At this point he needs to learn to follow the adult system of rules encoded by the grammar that enables coordination of the two.

Greenfield and Smith's (1976) similar analysis of this development proceeds from the expression by the child of one entity in the world to the expression of an entity in language that is related to another entity in the world and to the expression of both entities symbolically in two-word combinations (see also Bates, 1976). At this point the child can achieve a coordination of social and object relations embedded in a linguistic form. However, this is still a very primitive expression. The full intercoordination

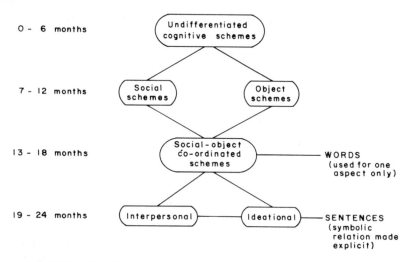

FIG. 13.2. Hypothesized course of differentiation and integration of social and object domains during first 2 years.

of social and object, interpersonal and ideational, requires a system of grammatical rules, which at this point, and only at this point, the child begins to learn. This analysis also suggests why pure interactive or expressive forms are generally absent from early word combinations, except for the stock phrases or formulas used in the one-word period. Purely interactive expressions do not coordinate the two dimensions, and therefore grammar is not necessary to their expression. For this reason the analysis of early sentences has found the concentration of actor–object relations seen in Table 13.2.

The proposed line of development is shown in schematic form in Figure 13.2, where development is seen to proceed from an undifferentiated cognitive system in the first 6 months through differentiated social and object schemes in the second half of the first year. From 13 to 18 months these schemes are coordinated, and single words are used to refer to one aspect of them. Finally, at 19 to 24 months the child makes the coordination explicit on a symbolic level and begins to develop rules for the uses of sentences and dialogue.

SUMMARY AND CONCLUSION

At the end of the first year, the child differentiates two major aspects of the environment that previously were understood as one, namely, the objective physical world whose spaces and objects he is devoted to exploring, explaining, and classifying, and the realm of social relations, represented in newly apparent strong attachments, displays of affection and fear as well as delight, and social interchanges. Coordination of the two begins to take place toward the end of the first year and the beginning of the second in the context of social games and the instrumental use of others to gain one's ends, as described by Bruner (1975b) and Bates (1976). First language forms are acquired within these contexts. Thus, language is from the beginning a tool for social–object coordination but of a limited kind. When the child first uses language early in the second year, he tends to use it either primarily as an expressive-interactive personal-social tool or as a referential, cognitive, classifying tool. The plateaus found in cognitive, social, and language development during the months from 13 to 18 are explainable in terms of the coordination of previously developed differentiated systems, a coordination that thus far we have failed to tap successfully in infant tests and have hardly tried to explore in developmental research. By the middle of the second year, coordination is sufficiently advanced so that the infant is ready to take the step from using language as one part of the relation to expressing the complete coordinated relation in language, and thus producing the first sentences. Coordination in language, moreover, permits the further step of expressing ideas about nonobvious events and carrying on a conversation, in addition to the previously established one-way speech. Not all children use language as either a cognitive or social tool during the second year. Some children manage to coordinate social and object goals before they begin to use productive language. Such children may find it possible to use sentences almost from the beginning of their productive language use, but such use will appear later than the average for beginning speech.

We are sorely in need of further research related to these questions in order to verify what are at present only a set of somewhat speculative hypotheses. What is the relation of language use to the cognitive and communicative purposes of the child? Can systematic investigation pin down the ways in which the social and object components become coordinated both within and without language? These questions are central to the more complete understanding of how the infant becomes a child and the role of language in that development.

REFERENCES

Ainsworth, M. D. S., Bell, S. M., & Stayton, D. Infant–mother attachment and social development: Socialization as a product of reciprocal responsiveness to signals. In M. P.M. Richards (Ed.), *The integration of a child into a social world.* New York: Cambridge University Press, 1974.

Bates, E. *Language and context: The acquisition of pragmatics.* New York: Academic Press, 1976.

Bates, E., Camaioni, L., & Volterra, V. The acquisition of performances prior to speech. *Merrill–Palmer Quarterly,* 1975, *21,* 205–226.

Bates, E., Benigni, L., Bretherton, I., Camaioni, L., & Volterra, V. From gesture to the first word: On cognitive and social prerequisites. In M. Lewis & L. Rosenblum (Eds.), *Interaction, conversation and the development of language.* New York: Wiley, 1977.

Bayley, N. *Bayley scales of infant development.* New York: Psychological Corporation, 1969.

Bell, S. M. The development of the concept of object as related to infant–mother attachment. *Child Development,* 1970, *41,* 291–313.

Benedict, H. *Language comprehension in 10- to 16-month-old infants.* Unpublished doctoral dissertation, Yale University, 1976.

Bloom, L. *One word at a time: The use of single word utterances before syntax.* The Hague: Mouton, 1973.

Bronson, W. C. Developments in behavior with age-mates during the second year of life. In M. Lewis & L. A. Rosenblum (Eds.), *Origins of behavior: Friendship and peer relations.* New York: Wiley, 1975.

Brown, R. *Psycholinguistics.* New York: Free Press, 1970.

Brown, R. *A first language: The early stages.* Cambridge, Mass.: Harvard University, 1973.

Bruner, J. From communication to language—a psychological perspective. *Cognition,* 1975, *3,* 255–287.(a)

Bruner, J. The ontogenesis of speech acts. *Journal of Child Language,* 1975, *2,* 1-19.(b)

Clark, E. V. What's in a word? On the child's acquisition of semantics in his first language. In T. E. Moore (Ed.), *Cognitive development and the acquisition of language.* New York: Academic Press, 1973.

Corrigan, B. L. *Individual communication and cognitive development.* Unpublished doctoral dissertation, University of Denver, 1976.

Dore, J. A pragmatic description of early language development.*Journal of Psycholinguistic Research,* 1974, *3,* 343–350.

Edwards, D. Sensory-motor intelligence and semantic relations in early child grammar. *Cognition,* 1973, *2,* 395–434.

Goldin-Meadow, S., Seligman, M. E. P., & Gelman, R. Language in the two-year old. *Cognition, 1976, 4,* 189–202.

Greenfield,. P. M., & Smith, J. H. *The structure of communication in early language development.* New York: Academic Press, 1976.

Gruendel, J. *Concepts, categories and early word use: Overextension reconsidered.* Boston University 1st Annual Child Language Conference. Boston, Mass, October, 1976.

Halliday, M. *Learning how to mean.* London: Edwin Arnold, 1975.

Huttenlocher, J. The origins of language comprehension. In R. L. Solso (Ed.), *Theories in cognitive psychology.* Hillsdale, N.J.: Lawrence Erlbaum Associates, 1974.

Jennings, K. D. People versus object orientations, social behavior, and intellectual abilities in preschool children. *Developmental Psychology, 1975, 11,* 511–519.

Kagan, J. *Change and continuity in infancy.* New York: Wiley, 1971.

Kagan, J. Emergent themes in human development. *American Scientist,* 1976, *64,* 186–196.

Kagan, J., Kearsley, R. B., & Zelazo, P. R. The emergence of initial apprehension to unfamiliar peers. In M. Lewis & L. A. Rosenblum (Eds.), *Origins of behavior: Friendship and peer relations.* New York: Wiley, 1975.

Kessen, W., & Nelson, K. What the child brings to language. In B. Z. Presseisen, D. Goldstein, & M. H. Appel (Eds.), *Topics in cognitive development* (Vol. 2). New York: Plenum, 1978.

Kogan, N. *Cognitive styles in infancy and early childhood.* Hillsdale, N.J.: Lawrence Erlbaum Associates, 1974.

Lamb, M. E. *The relationships betwen infants and their mothers and fathers.* Unpublished doctoral dissertation, Yale University, 1976.

Lenneberg, E. H. *Biological foundations of language.* New York: Wiley, 1967.

Leopold, W. K. *Speech development of a bilingual child.* Evanston, Ill.: Northwestern University Press, 1939.

Lewis, M., & Rosenblum, L. A. (Eds.), *Origins of behavior: Friendship and peer relations.* New York: Wiley, 1975.

Lewis, M., Young, G., Brooks, J., & Michaelson, L. The beginning of friendship. In M. Lewis & L. A. Rosenblum (Eds.), *Origins of behavior: Friendship and peer relations.* New York: Wiley, 1975.

McCall, R. B. Toward an epigenetic conception of mental development in the first three years of life. In M. Lewis (Ed.), *Origins of intelligence: Infancy and early childhood.* New York: Plenum, 1976.

McCarthy, D. Language development in children. In L. Carmichael (Ed.), *Manual of child psychology.* New York: Wiley, 1954.

Nelson, K. Some evidence for the cognitive primacy of categorization and its functional basis. *Merrill-Palmer Quarterly,* 1973, *19,* 21–39.(a)

Nelson, K. Structure and strategy in learning to talk. *Monograph of the Society for Research in Child Development,* 1973 *38* (1-2, Serial No. 149).(b)

Nelson, K. Concept, word and sentence: Interrelations in acquisition and development. *Psychological Review,* 1974, *81,* 267–285.

Nelson, K. Individual differences in early semantic and syntactic development. *Annals of the New York Academy of Sciences,* 1975, *263,* 132–139.(a)

Nelson, K. The nominal shift in semantic-syntactic development. *Cognitive Psychology,* 1975, *7,* 461–479.(b)

Nelson, K. Some attributes of adjectives used by young children. *Cognition,* 1976, *4,* 13–30.

Nelson, K. First steps in language acquisition. *Journal of the American Academy of Child Psychiatry,* 1977, *16,* 561–583. (a)

Nelson, K. *Learning to talk.* Unpublished manuscript, Yale University, 1977.(b)

Nelson, K., Benedict, H., Gruendel, J., & Rescorla, L. *Lessons from early lexicons.* Paper presented at the biennial meetings of the Society of Research in Child Development, New Orleans, March 1977.

Nelson, K., Kessen, W., & Platt, J. *The transition to language.* Unpublished manuscript, Yale University, 1978.

Piaget, J. *The language and thought of the child.* New York: Harcourt, 1926.

Piaget, J. *Origins of intelligence in children.* New York: Norton, 1963. (Originally published, 1952.)

Piaget, J. *Construction of reality in the child.* New York: Basic Books, 1954.

Piaget, J. *Play, dreams and imitation in childhood.* New York: Norton, 1962.

Rescorla, L. *Concept formation in word learning.* Unpublished doctoral dissertation, Yale University, 1976.

Ricciuti, H. Object grouping and selective ordering behavior in infants 12-24 months old. *Merrill-Palmer Quarterly,* 1965, *11,* 129–148.

Richards, M. P. M. *The integration of a child into a social world.* London: Cambridge University Press, 1974.

Ross, G. *Concept categories in one- to two-year-olds.* Doctoral dissertation, Harvard University, 1977.

Searle, J. R. *Speech acts.* London: Cambridge University Press, 1969.

Shipley, E., Smith, C. S., & Gleitman, L. A study in the acquisition of syntax: Free responses to verbal commands. *Language,* 1969, *45,* 322–342.

Sinclair-de-Zwart, H. Language acquisition and cognitive development. In T. E. Moore (Ed.), *Cognitive development and the acquisition of language.* New York: Academic Press, 1973.

Skinner, B. F. *Verbal behavior.* New York: Appleton-Century-Crofts, 1957.

Slobin, D. I. Cognitive prerequisites for the development of grammar. In C. A. Ferguson & D. I. Slobin (Eds.), *Studies of child language development.* New York: Holt, Rinehart and Winston, 1973.

Smith, M. E. An investigation of the development of the sentence and the extent of vocabulary in young children. *University of Iowa Studies in Child Welfare,* 1926, *3,* No. 5.

Staats, A. W. *Complex human behavior.* New York: Holt, Rinehart and Winston, 1963.

Starr, S. The relationship of single words to two-word sentences. *Child Development,* 1975, *46,* 701–708.

Sugarman–Bell, S. Some organizational aspects of preverbal communication. In I. Markova (Ed.), *The social context of language.* New York: Wiley, 1976.

Uzgiris, I. C., & Hunt, J. McV. *Assessment of infant: Ordinal scales of psychological development.* Urbana, Ill: University of Illinois Press, 1975.

Weir, R. *Language in the crib.* The Hague: Mouton, 1962.

14 Dialectical Approaches to Early Thought and Language

Arnold J. Sameroff
University of Illinois
Adrienne E. Harris
Rutgers University

INTRODUCTION

Recently there has been a fascination in psychology with the word *dialectics,* a fascination inspired by the writings of Klaus Riegel (1973, 1975, 1976a, 1976b, 1976c). The connotations of the word are broad enough to attract a variety of behavioral scientists who had despaired of working within reductionistic, specialized disciplines. Dialectics implies a unity of subject and object that transcends attempts to analyze phenomena into isolated, independent entities. Many scientists were concerned with what they saw as an artificial separation of the object of investigation from the investigator, and of science from politics. Their intuition was that behavior could be understood only in an organic context that included not only the object of study but the scientist and society as well.

The growth of developmental psychology has been accompanied by an increasing uneasiness. This discomfort is centered on the limitations of most current conceptual frameworks for dealing with change and transformation. Early psychological studies had been embedded in a speculative context made possible by a lack of empirical data. The behaviorist tradition acted as a corrective to speculations by developing an operationalism that accepted as data only consensually validated relationships between observable

This chapter is an anomaly. Rather than allow the reader to reach that conclusion after a period of discrepant feelings, we are announcing this fact in advance. After reading other chapters in this book, one might have developed a tripartite expectancy that each chapter would begin by setting a problem, continue by presenting data to demonstrate or possibly resolve a problem, and end with an attempt to find a theory to explain the data. In this chapter we begin by setting a problem, but the last two parts of the triad are reversed. We

339

phenomena. This corrective, however, included an egocentrism that argued that philosophical debates over the nature of science were irrelevant: The facts would speak for themselves. This position could be maintained as long as facts and their interrelationships could be considered to exist independently of the scientific lens through which they were viewed. However, this positivism was antithetical to a discipline that took as its subject matter development, that is, the manner in which facts and their interrelationships change over time.

Outside psychology, philosophers of science were beginning to expand their perspective from testing the truth or falsity of eclectically derived arbitrary theories (Popper, 1972) to studying the evolution of the theories themselves (Foucault, 1970; Kuhn, 1962). This perspective is now finding a place inside psychology. With the onset of the historical study of psychological issues (Aries, 1962; Buss, 1975; Riegel, 1976c) and the critique of the assumption that science is value-free, the nature of psychological explanation was seen as historically determined. It became necessary to pay simultaneous attention to paradigm shifts and the interrelation of paradigm and ideology. Two areas in which this trend is already quite developed are the clinical and normative accounts of mental illness (Braginski & Braginski, 1974; Foucault, 1973; Szasz, 1974) and studies of sex-role socialization (Hefner, Rebecca, & Oleshansky, 1975; Mitchell, 1974).

Within psychology, a historically self-conscious analysis has begun. The way in which the facts of the world were interpreted was seen to vary as a function of the individual's personality and stage of development. For example, the development of intelligence was not seen as the learning of increasing number of facts or habits but, rather, as a change in how facts and habits were organized and interpreted. The psychoanalytic model of development originated by Freud, despite its speculative foundations, had an important impact by focusing attention on the way in which the basis of the child's organization of the world changed during development. But it was left to Piaget to produce a theory sufficiently documented by empirical observations to provide a strong basis for arguing that organization of knowledge was rooted in the activity of the child and not in the surrounding world. Once the constructive role of the developing child was hypothesized, it was only a short

---

continue by presenting a theory and end with an attempt to find data to fit the theory.

Why should we be different? In part, it is in response to the courage of the editors in desiring to offer a comprehensive overview of emerging approaches to early development, even if this approach is not yet articulated. In part, it is a reflection of the foolhardiness of the authors in trying to meet the charge of the editors. What we try to do is bring a "dialectical" perspective to the data of early development. We cannot hope to be successful at our task because there is as yet no single theory of dialectics, nor may there ever be. What we do hope is that we offer an opportunity for research workers in early behavior to become aware of a recently emerging theoretical framework.

step to begin exploring the variety of psychological constructions.

Thus, one way of understanding dialectics is to see it as an application of developmental principles to theory construction and the evolution in science of particular theoretical claims. Most important, within this perspective, scientific theories are seen as being related to their social, political, and historical contexts instead of as indeterminate expressions of eclectic personalities.

The claim that explanatory models flow from particular social and historical contexts requires one to examine any theoretical construct for its role as ideology and for its connections to a particular social formation. A rough definition of ideology is a system of ideas in which particular interests are concealed and through which behaviors (whether of individuals or institutions) are legitimated. Thus, dialectics has a quite particular perspective concerning both the conscious and unconscious use of social science in the role of an ideology. This view necessitates a reflection on the source of categories in psychology and their relationship to particular interest groups. A critical and ideological analysis of the nativist tradition and the reappearance of certain forms of social Darwinism and social evolutionary theory might be of particular relevance to infancy studies. When individual differences are categorized as being immutable and biologically or genetically based, there arise the dual questions of how this claim is validated and whose interests it serves.

DIALECTICS OF DEVELOPMENT

How does one translate a theory centered in sociohistorical phenomena to a theory centered on early development? Fortunately, this task was begun by the modern father of dialectical thinking, Hegel, with some credit to Kant. The social problem is: How can one separate what originates in the thought of the individual from what originates in the sociohistorical context? The psychological problem is: How does the developing child separate himself as an entity from the other entities in his environment?

Nondialectical theories have focused on either the subject or the environment as the source of this knowledge. Piaget's (1970b) genetic epistemology, for example, is an attack on the view that knowledge is either *a priori* of the mind or copied from the environment. Knowledge is seen to be a result of a *tertium quid,* a third alternative, in which the action of the child on the environment produces knowing. Without the acting subject, nothing would be known. Without the objects to be acted upon, nothing would be known.

Philosophers since Heraclitus have engaged in various forms of dialectics, but it was Hegel who defined the contemporary characterization. The

Greeks engaged in dialectical argument in which the truth was thought to emerge through the conflict between the antagonists. Thus, a dialectical process implied a resolution that was the outcome of conflict between two entities engaged in a dialogue. The original social context of the dialectical process became objectified with the rise of empirical science. The dialectical process came to be seen as a conjunction between two separate static entities, the thesis and antithesis, to produce a new static entity, the synthesis. Kant capped the achievements of the mechanistic science of Newton and Descartes by rationalizing the separation between the knowing subject and the unknown object. Each was given its own unique independent characteristics — the mind had categories, the object had properties — and neither could influence the other. The categories of mind were innate; the real object was unknowable.

Hegel's contribution was to demonstrate that subject could not be separated from object. Whatever categories of mind did occur could only be the result of the interaction between subject and object. Hegel denied the separability of thesis, antithesis, and synthesis and argued that the trilogy was part of a unitary process. Inherent in this process was a series of internal contradictions that motivated change and development. Hegel's unique contribution was to see the dialectical process as being inherent in a unitary developing system rather than external to it.

Subsequent dialectical theoreticians, particularly in the Marxist tradition (Engels, 1939; Lukacs, 1971; Marx, 1972) criticized and altered many of the areas in which Hegel used his conception of the dialectic, but its components have remained relatively unchanged. Cornforth (1953) summarized the dialectical method of analysis in four principles:

1. Dialectics considers all things as being inseparably related and as being conditioned by their interconnections. As a consequence, no entity can be understood in isolation.

2. Dialectics considers all things to be in constant movement and change. Moreover, this change has a direction from coming into being to passing away.

3. Dialectics considers development to be not a process of simple quantitative growth but, rather, one of qualitative changes in the movement from one stage to another.

4. Dialectics considers development to be motivated by internal contradictions inherent in all things.

The first three principles are already familiar to developmental psychologists since they are part of the organismic model detailed by Reese and Overton (1970; Overton & Reese, 1973) as well as in the work of Piaget (1960, 1970a). They are relatively obvious and intrinsic to most modern biological research. The fourth principle, however, is unique to dialectics and has not been generally considered in developmental research. The principle of internal contradiction can be further elaborated as follows.

Dialectical contradiction results from and is resolved by a "unity of opposites." The opposing forces are not seen to be external and accidental but, rather, internal and necessary aspects of a single contradictory whole. As each new stage evolves, it retains part of the past from which it came as well as part of the future to which it is moving.

Dialectical movement is also characterized by a "negation of the negation." Each stage of development is negated by internal contradictions. The resulting new stage is itself eventually negated through the resolution of its own internal contradictions, but the newest stage tends to recapitulate some features of the original. A biological example (Engels, 1939) would be a population of seeds which is negated as the seeds grow into plants. As a consequence of their growth, the plants produce a new crop of seeds while passing away themselves. The new crop, the negation of the negation, represents a more advanced set of seeds than the original because the new seeds have passed through a stage of adaptive relating in transaction with the environment. At a much more formal level, Hegel used the "negation of the negation" as the prime developmental impetus for subject–object differentiation. The subject's immediate experience with the object is negated by conceptualization and categorization. An object has an infinite number of properties and relationships; the subject has a finite set of categories for those properties. Whenever the subject moves from the system of properties back to the immediate experience of the object, the previous set of conceptualizations is negated by further categorization. It is this back and forth process between the knower and the known, the negation of the negation, that propels knowledge through its various levels of organization.

Alienation

The process of subject–object differentiation is central to one of the most important concepts that derives from a dialectical approach — alienation (Lukacs, 1971). The process of abstraction leads to reification of thought for the individual and of theory for science. Concepts that originally evolved out of the activity of the subject in the objective world become abstracted and then are thought to have an existence of their own. Many theoreticians in a dialectical tradition have attempted to demonstrate that all knowledge is rooted in a real-world activity. In philosophy Hegel tried to show that Kant's *a priori* categories had to be rooted in an interactive process between subject and object and therefore could not be innate qualities of mind. Similarly, in psychology, Piaget has devoted himself to creating a genetic epistemology aimed at reconnecting abstract thought with its roots in real-world activity. From this general introduction to the dialectic approach we now relate these concepts to various areas of child development.

Interconnectedness and Inseparability

Nature and Nurture.   In developmental psychology, the principles of interconnectedness and inseparability find most common expression in the nature–nuture question. Despite the universal lip service given to the idea that the two cannot be separated, most models of development do in fact make the dichotomy. Weimer (1973) reviewed theories of cognition and argued that nothing new had been proposed in the 2500 years since Plato and Aristotle. He opted for Plato's nativism as opposed to Aristotle's empiricism. Most theories of social and personality development place major stress on the impact of environment whereas current theories of motor and intellectual capacity stress constitutional factors.

Sameroff and Chandler (1975) pointed out the differences between models of development that emphasized separateness and those that emphasized interconnectedness. They distinguished between interactional models and transactional models. Interactional models allow both constitution and environment to have roles in development but tend to treat each as a static quantity that can be added or subtracted from the mixture. In contrast, transactional models see the two as being inseparable, with both being modified as a consequence of their contact over time. The unique characteristics of children alter the unique characteristics of their environment, which then acts back on the characteristics of the children. Children's development cannot be predicted or understood removed from their relationship to their specific environment. The action of their environment cannot be predicted or understood removed from the relationship to specific children.

This example carries us to the heart of a dialectic criticism of the scientific enterprise. We see children as being physically separate from their environments, and so we draw the obvious conclusion that they are psychologically separate as well. Piaget focused on the necessary inseparability between the child and his world for the development of knowledge. The child as a figure cannot be separated from the world as ground, at least until sensorimotor activity can be internalized and organized. And even after that period the child is still enmeshed in the perceptual and affective here-and-now which continually acts to modify existing cognitive organization. Alienation results when these connections are denied or not seen at all.

Piaget, despite defining himself as a dialectician (Piaget, 1977), is still subject to attack by other dialecticians. Piaget's theory of cognitive stages is criticized for moving the individual further and further away from his connections to the real world (Buck–Morss, 1975; Lawler, 1975; Riegel, 1973). However, many of these criticisms have been based on a limited understanding of Piaget as well as a limited understanding of dialectical principles. By criticizing early Piaget as opposed to later Piaget, or the reverse, his detractors have avoided the dialectical task exposed by critical theory of understanding Piaget in terms of his own development in a specific historical and social context. Youniss (1974), after an appreciative critique of Riegel's (1973) position, proposed a need to make both dialectical and Piagetian conceptions more explicit in order to examine their compatibilities better.

Piaget's theory of cognitive development begins with an interconnectedness in which the infant, the world, and activity are all one. The child sees no differentiation among subject, action, and object. However, the rest of Piaget's theory is devoted to separating what for the dialectician is inseparable — the unity of subject and object.

For Piaget the ultimate achievement of intelligence is the ability to abstract completely one's thought from concrete reality. To all dialecticians this alienation is a conceptual anathema and a theoretical impossibility. For Marxist dialecticians (Buck–Morss, 1975), Piaget is doing for the child what Kant did for philosophy and what capitalism did for value, that is, separating the product from the means of production, separating cognition from the activity of knowing.

Piaget would not agree with this criticism. Piaget's theory of development is fully based on cognitive activity and gives little credence to preexisting or maturing categories of mind. Every cognitive achievement is based on activity with and coordination of prior cognitive achievements. Dialecticians might grant Piaget this constructivism, but they would counter that these cognitive constructions, although initially grounded in the objective world, pyramid away from the real world as they build on one another. Piaget offers plenty of fuel for this criticism by continually emphasizing the abstracted nature of mature thought.

Here the new critique of the dialecticians becomes aligned with the old critique of the empiricists. They both argue that Piaget does not give an adequate role to the environment in the child's cognitive development. The empiricists criticize Piaget for giving too much credit to the child's constructive capacities and not enough to the capacity of the environment to control these constructions. The dialecticians accept the child's constructive role, but they argue that Piaget ignores the reciprocal influence these constructions have on the environment. The child's constructions change his environment by modifying the way in which the environment is conceived (Sameroff, 1975a). The environment's response to the child is also modified by the child's improving capacities for interaction (e.g., the acquisition of language).

From the perspective of critical theory, this is an excellent example of the dialectical "negation of the negation" operating at the level of theory. Piaget negated the static environmentalism of the behaviorists and in turn was negated by the dynamic environmentalism of the dialecticians. In both views, the environment is seen as conditioning cognitive development, but whereas in the former the subject is ignored, in the latter the child is given a role in a reciprocal conditioning of the environment.

Maturation and Experience. The nature–nurture problem continually resurfaces under a variety of titles. The separation of maturation and experience is a good example of antidialectical thinking. Maturational hypotheses give a developmental twist to constitutional views by spreading the emergence of various behaviors over time. By a reductionism to principles of biology that seem to support maturation as the major factor in developmental change, a variety of psychological phenomena have been explained. Kagan's chapter in this volume (Chapter 7) presents such a perspective, explaining developmental progress as being a function of the maturation of memory capacity.

A closer look at biological phenomena shows the shortcomings of such a reductionistic view. Schneirla (1966a, 1966b) often emphasized the inseparability of maturation and experience in his criticisms of the early ethological theories of Lorenz. Gottlieb (1976) has provided a strong evidential base for this interdependence in his review of the relative roles of structure and function in embryological development. It appears that it is the early functioning of growing biological structures that plays a determining role in their outcomes. Without such functioning (e.g., experience), the ultimate form (i.e., maturation) would be quite different.

Even the ultimate biological reduction to the action of the genes emphasizes the inseparability of any entity from its environment. The earlier views that gene programs somehow unfolded to produce the finished human product have been replaced by models emphasizing the interaction of gene systems with environmental systems. Gene action is not only controlled by the action of other genes but by the biochemical environment as well. The transactions that Sameroff (1975a) described for psychological development and that Gottlieb (1976) described for embryological development occur at the genetic level as well (Waddington, 1966). The biochemical environment of the cell turns on genes that produce biochemicals that change the cell environment, which then turns on other genes that produce new chemicals, at the same time turning off the previously acting genes. The action of a particular gene structure or individual cannot be predicted in isolation but only in its unique developmental context.

Movement and Change

The movement and change that characterize a dialectical process are entirely congruent with the "active child" emphasis in current views of developmental psychology. Piaget's work has been a strong influence in this direction. Piaget's major achievement, from our perspective, has been to return to children the major role in constructing their world. Piagetian theory is quite congruent with the dialectical conception of intrinsic motion and activity. The active cognizing of the child is an expression of his biological heritage in which activity is a basic characteristic of life itself. In Piaget's (1971) view neither activity nor structure has a beginning. Later schemata are differentiated out of earlier schemata, the psychological out of the biological. Piaget (1971) states that "a schema always includes actions performed by the subject [p. 9]" and that these actions do not originate in the object or the environment. Development is a consequence of intrinsic biological activity in a constant process of restructuring.

An interesting corollary of this principle is that everything is in a process of coming into being and passing away. This view was once a political slogan used to justify revolutionary changes in the political economic system; now clear examples have emerged from modern theories of organic evolution. Population genetics has replaced mutational theories to explain biological changes. Instead of a dependence on some random event altering the adaptability of an individual within a species, evolution is seen as a probabilistic function of the adaptation of an entire population living and dying in a specific environmental niche.

An analogy in psychological development might be found in the concept of the circular reaction popularized by Piaget. The circular reaction is the outlet for the functioning of the organism and is a repetititve activity in an adaptive relation to its environment. Each repetition can be viewed as a coming into being and passing away, leaving a residue of each experience in the developing cognitive organization of the individual. It is not a single association that causes a passive connection to be made by the child but, rather, the consequence of an ongoing behavioral series that has its beginning in embryonic transactions and its end in the cultural legacy left by the mature individual.

Qualitative Change

Dialectics views change as an inseparable component of any structure. Once process is seen as the universal, one must deal with defining the forms that are changing. Kessen (1962) has seen a universal need for man to segment the course of development. If the segments are to have meaning in themselves, they must be differentiable from one another. If quantitative change were the rule, such would not be the case. Developmental change would be the result of an incremental process whereby basic units are combined *ad infinitum*.

Dialectical theories, in contrast, incorporate the notion of qualitative shifts in organization that produce unique structures at each new stage. The particular character of these structures depends on the theory considered. Hegel proposed a theory of the development of knowledge through history. Marx produced a dialectic theory defining the stages of economic development.

In our own time, the most dominant stage theory has been Piaget's model of cognitive development. Piaget's theory of stages incorporates the dialectical principle that development proceeds through qualitative rather than quantitative changes. Each new stage represents a new coordination of what had come before. The new principles of organization are not reducible to the principles of the previous stage. In each stage, there is the old as well as the new. The old structures are utilized at the new stage, but the way they are organized is through a new coordination.

Stage theories have been subjected to a variety of formal analyses in order to define meaningful utilizations of such concepts (Flavell, 1971; Kessen, 1962). Those stage theories that merely assign labels to different kinds of behavior appearing at different ages are not dialectical. To fit a dialectical perspective, the developmental changes producing qualitatively new levels of organization must be rooted in the previous level of organization. The motivating force for such changes is the system's inherent contradictions, which we discuss more fully later.

A major difficulty in our understanding of theories that focus on qualitatively different modes of functioning is between *stages* of behavior and *types* of behavior. Piaget's theory of cognitive development has traditionally emphasized the highest level of functioning—formal operations. All preceding stages are treated as milestones on the path to the final coordination. The connotations of such a theory have been that one does not operate at lower levels of organization once a higher level is reached. This interpretation is obviously wrong.

The direction of cognitive development in Piaget's theory is from here-and-now interaction with the real world to successively removed levels of abstraction. When formal operations are used, the world has lost all its reality and concreteness and is manipulated only in terms of abstract symbols that gain their meaning entirely from the relations between themselves and other abstract symbols. The highest level of abstraction achieved determines the cognitive *stage* at which an individual is capable of functioning.

The type of cognitive functioning at any given point in time does not and cannot be restricted to the highest stage. Werner's (1957) concept of multilinearity, elaborated by Langer (1970), offers a more useful perspective on how different levels of behavior are integrated in everyday behavior. Werner's central concern was in trying to understand the unity of experience. His developmental model focused on the initial undifferentiated state of man and his world. In this respect he was no different from Freud or Piaget. However, what followed offered a relatively clear basis of differentiation. Where for Piaget the past served primarily as a stepping stone for future superior achievements, and where for Freud the past served as an impediment to adult maturation, Werner respected the role of past levels and modes of functioning as being part and parcel of normal everyday living.

The continuing role of the past is especially captured in Werner's (1957) two notions of multilinearity and multiformity. Multilinearity is contrasted with the more commonly accepted view of unilinearity. Together, they represent the dialectical contradiction between an organism that maintains a single identity throughout development yet at the same time engages the world from a variety of perspectives—the sensorimotor, the perceptual, the affective, and the cognitive—each with its own developmental course. By uniformity Werner referred to the general regulative principle by which organisms moved through development toward higher levels of differentiation and integration. Yet underlying this general uniformity was a diversity or multiformity of process.

Werner (1957) captured the essence of this concept from the biologists' description of analogous processes through which different species used different organs for the same adaptive function. For example, the same function of respiration is performed by lungs in mammals but by gills in fish. In cognitive development, the analogous process concept refers to individuals who solve the same problem but through different processes, that is, a multiformity of process producing a uniformity of achievement (Farnum, 1975).

The issue of analogous processes in the performance of individuals at different developmental levels can be contrasted with the issue of analogous processes being used by the same individuals in different situations. Piaget's work has been generally interpreted as supporting a position that higher levels or stages of functioning supersede lower levels. In contrast, the work of Werner is generally interpreted as supporting a view that new levels of functioning only augment the earlier levels.

It remains a task for developmental theory to integrate domains of behavior defined by various stage theories into a unified whole. Piaget has focused on cognitive development, but there is much more to behavior than cognition. A unified theory of development must also contain an appreciation of physical grace, artistic sensitivity, and scientific insight as being parallel, integrated, and inseparable aspects of human existence.

Werner's orthogenetic principle has been appreciated for its descriptive power but depreciated for its lack of explanatory power. Dialectical principles fall into a similar category. The statement that quantitative changes in development produce qualitative changes in structure does not explain those changes. On the other hand, without a theoretical lens that focuses on qualitative differences in structures as a characteristic of life, the question of explanation would not even arise.

Internal Contradiction

Development necessarily occurs across time. Descriptions of the states of existence, be they quantitatively or qualitatively different, do not provide us with the rules for transitions. The dialectical principle that everything is in a state of change does not provide any basis for understanding the source, strength, or direction of that change. For such a rationale we must turn to the principle of internal contradiction with its corollary that there is a unity of opposites within every system.

Kessen (1971) reviewed the models of motivation in a variety of developmental theories. He characterized theories of cognitive development on a caloric continuum running from "cold" theories, typified by Piaget, in which motivation is intrinsic to cognitive structures through mechanisms of discrepancy or disequilibrium, to "hot" theories, typified by psychoanalytic or learning theories in which cognitive change is the result of aroused drive states or libidinal investments. The dialectical concept of contradiction incorporates both ends of the caloric continuum. The cold end is traditional in its location within thought, where a reflective consciousness operates to resolve contradictions at ever higher levels of organization. The hot end is less traditional because it is not rooted in drives or instincts but, rather, in the child's action in the real world. As with Piaget, action or praxis is the source of all knowledge, but this praxis is embedded not only in a cognitive context but also in an affective and social matrix in which needs, desires, intentions, and aspirations are all combined.

The apprehension of contradiction either on the individual or collective level provides both the occasion and energy for transformation and change. A focus on the disequilibrating moment in the assimilation–accommodation dyad is long overdue in Piagetian theory. It is not sufficient to provide evidence of two equilibrated structures, one preoperational, (e.g., a nonconserver blissfully sure that lemonade poured from a short, fat into a long, skinny glass has increased its quantity) and the other concrete (e.g., a conserver with principles of reversibility and compensation organized and operative). We must ask what occurs, either maturationally or in some ongoing praxis, to lead the child to apprehend anomalous data and therefore to revise preexisting schemas. In philosophical writing on dialectics, contradiction is coterminous with development. We shall see if this codetermination applies in psychology as well.

Contradiction is deeply and immediately implicated in the dialectical preoccupation with process and diachronic change. This construct has been the subject of an evolving interpretation. Although a dialectical analysis aims at identifying and ordering contradictions, more generally, however, contradiction is an inherent property of material life, or matter in motion. Contradiction arises and takes on particular forms within each system. In psychological development, it becomes an important, indeed a critical, source of the conscious experience of the growing individual as well as a source for consciousness on the collective level.

In an articulation of the laws of dialectics, Hegel identifies the movement of objects or phenomena in terms of internal contradiction. Opposing but interdependent aspects of phenomena in interaction become the locus for their own transformation and development. Objects or structures are in an unceasing flux that strains the limits of existing structures and are then reformed in altered systems. Indeed, a satisfactory treatment of the locus of change and the transformation must be the heart of any developmental theory.

Piaget's model of adaptation, involving the processes of assimilation and accommodation, has been seen as an excellent example of dialectical contradiction at work. However, this adaptive functioning has been restricted to the sensorimotor period in which there can be no separation of the processes. Indeed, there is a unity of opposites. Assimilation has represented the conservative aspect of the organism's resistance to structural change, whereas accommodation has represented the revolutionary aspect of forced modification.

At the end of the sensorimotor period, Piaget proposes that assimilation and accommodation can be separated and manipulated independently, in essence destroying their dialectic unity. This separation is most marked in formal operations, in which there is no accommodation involved in the transformation within equilibrated logical systems. Piaget's early writing on the issue does lend itself to a nondialectical interpretation. In 1956 (Tanner & Inhelder, 1971), he claimed that "equilibrium is only attained . . . with logico-mathematical structures capable of assimilating the whole universe to thought without ever being broken or shaken by the innumerable accommodations called for by experience [p. 85]." Yet a page earlier he states the "operational structures constitute a very special case, whose properties cannot be generalized for the whole of mental life, even under its cognitive aspect [p. 84]." Piaget may have been caught in a bind at that time because he saw formal logic as being the absolute highest level of cognition, just as Kant was caught two centuries before when he thought concepts of space, time, and causality had an eternal uniqueness. Categories of mind can exist only in the realm of absolutes. The advance of scientific theory undercut both Kant's categories and Piaget's logic. Piaget (1970a) implicitly recognized this advance in his book on structuralism. There he describes the new work of the Bourbaki group in mathematics which pushes toward new levels of mathematical models that could be related to potential new levels of thought. Logical models are thus forced to undergo further development.

There is no doubt that Piaget (1970a) is aware of the issue of dialectics since he devotes a section of *Structuralism* to its discussion. He maintains that his own constructivism is dialectical in that it emphasizes historical development, opposition between contraries, syntheses, and the idea of wholeness. He supports Marx's emphasis on "theoretical practice" or the activity of the subject in creating knowledge. He also agrees with Godelier's (1972) analysis of the Marxist system in which structure and function, genesis and history, individual subject and society are seen as inseparable.

Perhaps in response to a dialectical critique, Piaget gives greater emphasis to contradiction in his introduction to one of the more recent works of the Geneva school (Inhelder, Sinclair, & Bovet, 1974). He defines contradiction amorphously as a disturbance of which the subject has become aware. The source of this disturbance could be anywhere. Of greater relevance is a reference to the subject's attempt to accommodate two incompatible schemas, one to the other. Here we come closer to a dialectical contradiction that occurs within a unified whole.

In general, however, Piaget has chosen to deemphasize contradiction as the primary motivating force in favor of a far less robust equilibration notion. Many critics (Flavell, 1971; Kessen, 1962) sympathetic to the structural aspects of Piaget's theory have pointed out the problems in his theory of equilibration as the primary force that moves the child from one stage to the next.

Sensorimotor Contradiction.   Sameroff (1975b) tried to distinguish between an equilibrational and a dialectical explanation of contradiction. In Piaget's equilibration model, there is a focus on the mismatch between the cognitive structures and the aliment, or input, to that structure. The schema involved would then adapt through assimilation and accommodation to the aliment. For example, at the sensorimotor level the infant will adapt its sucking schemas to the nipple both by adjusting his mouth appropriately to the size of the nipple (accommodation) and by positioning the nipple so it will fit right into his mouth (assimilation). The contradiction is not seen within the subject, as in a Hegelian dialectic, but between the subject and object, as in a Kantian dialectic. For Piaget, transitions between stages result from coordinations of these schemas into hierarchical systems through mutual accommodations. Thus, the coordination of sucking, looking, and listening schemas produces the permanent object, or at a later stage the coordination of height and width concepts would produce conservation of mass.

In contrast, dialectical contradictions result not between the knowing subject and the unknown object but rather, between the contradictory ways in which the subject knows the object. Piaget tends to confuse these meanings of contradiction. A dialectical model would focus not on the coordination of structures at a lower level, which produces the next stage of development, but, rather, on the contradictions between the lower structures that can be resolved only by the agency of a new level of coordination.

From a dialectical perspective, any advance in cognition must be the result of contradiction within the previous stage. What contradiction would lead to object permanence? Initially, each sensory modality independently assimilates the same object. An object has a visual existence only while being looked at and a tactual existence only while being felt. At 3 and 4 months the infant will begin bringing felt objects into the visual field and also reaching for looked-at objects. While this coordinated activity is occurring, the child may look away. A contradiction is created. If the object is tied to the child's action, it exists in the tactual modality but does not exist in the visual. The developmental resolution of this contradiction is that the object exists independently of the child's activity. The visual appearance of the object is not a result of the infant's looking at it but, rather, inheres in the object itself.

From this perspective the development of object permanence is not tied to the coordination between modalities but to the conflict between them. Their coordination in time is a necessary condition for the resulting conflict but in itself should not produce the disequilibrium necessary for cognitive growth.

Another implication of this view is that the cognitive achievement of object permanence is not tied to any specific modality but to a particular relationship between any two independent sensors of a common object. Potentially, only two fingers should be necessary for this achievement. This view is in clear contrast to those who have become even more particularistic than Piaget. For example, Lewis (1975) has argued that motor activity is unnecessary for the growth of cognitive structures. He has narrowly defined sensorimotor behavior to mean movement of the limbs or head. Citing Décarie's (1969) data that thalidomide infants with severe limb deformations achieve object permanence, Lewis argues that these results are proof that the use of the sensory system alone is sufficient for cognitive growth. Décarie (1969) herself draws exactly the opposite conclusion. She states that most of her subjects were able to engage in hand-to-hand and hand-to-mouth behavior as normal children would. Another group of children could use "substitute channels" for coordination such as between toes and mouth, eyes and toes, or among shoulders, chin, and eyes. The three infants in her sample who did not achieve the last stage of the object concept had the least possibility for even substitute coordinations. Décarie (1969) concludes that her results in no way contradict Piaget because, although the normal child mostly uses hand prehension, "the schema of prehension, like intelligence itself, has many ways of reaching [sic] its goal [p. 181]."

Similarly, Kopp and Shaperman (1973) studied an infant with no limbs who, they claim, could not interact with an object and simultaneously observe what he was doing to the object but yet achieved object permanence. However, the child is described as not only looking and listening but also as batting and rolling objects with his head and trunk. Fraiberg's (1977) work with blind infants also makes it clear that the infant must have multimodal experiences in order to achieve object permanence.

Does a dialectical approach help in understanding infant development? Sensorimotor development could be a good test of the method. At the simple level, one can interpret the infant's behavior as being a passive integration of sensory input to produce concepts or representations (Kagan, 1971; Lewis, 1975). At a second level, one can argue that sensorimotor coordinations require the active involvement of the infant in making the connections by a manipulation of the objective world with a combination of schemas (Held & Hein, 1963; Piaget, 1952). At a third level one can argue that sensorimotor coordination can lead to object permanence only if the activity schemas are set in contradiction to one another. Each level of interpretation limits the kinds of questions that are asked and the analyses that are made. The dialectic level pushes us a little further in what we should look for in our analysis of early development.

In the dialectic view, it is the contradiction among various schemas in their attempts to assimilate a common object that produces the permanent object as a coordination resolution. At the operative level, it may be the contradiction between defining "more" in terms of height or in terms of width that leads to "more" being defined in terms of a unified concept of "mass" at a new level, which coordinates the previously contradictory height versus width definitions.

From the perspective of the dialectical model, the motivation for each new coordination must be tied to some internal contradiction. In each of the two preceding examples, the contradictory meaning systems did not come into arbitrary conflict but were related in their common origin in a single cognitive system. It is the unity of the organism that must be preserved in the face of its developing differentiation. Ultimately, it is a conflict between differentiation and integration in all developing systems that is at the heart of the dialectic.

The current concern with a dialectical approach to developmental psychology has been initiated and maintained in the writings of Klaus Riegel. Riegel (1973) criticized Piaget for proposing formal operations as a final stage of cognitive growth. Piaget was seen as emphasizing equilibrium and balance rather than an open-ended process of transformation and change. Riegel (1975) saw Piaget as preferring to study how problems were solved rather than generated. Dialectics emphasized the generation of problems rather than the solution.

In our discussion of sensorimotor development, we have emphasized contradiction and the unity of opposites in the achievement of object permanence. Yet object permanence is only one aspect of the infant's cognitive development, and cognitive development is only one aspect of the child's psychological universe. Uzgiris (1976, 1977) has explored the variety of cognitive domains the infant must traverse during the sensorimotor period. She has emphasized the lack of stability in rates of progress across these domains and has suggested how these rates are influenced by experiential factors.

Riegel recognized the possibility of temporary equilibria in specific domains of behavior such as cognition, but he emphasized that life consisted of many other aspects that had to be integrated into a broad totality. He hypothesized four such areas of behavior — the inner-biological, the individual-psychological, the cultural-sociological, and the outer-physical. Development to new levels of organization was a result of discordance between any two of these. As yet, these areas are ill-defined, and the developmental progression within any one of them has not been described. However, the conception that development is a result of many interacting behavioral domains is critical. Linguistic development, for example, requires an analysis that covers both individual and social contexts. The way these contexts interact in producing language behavior is dealt with in a later section.

Negation of the Negation.   Piaget's theory contains an analogue of the dialectical negation of the negation in his concept of vertical décalage. Vertical décalage is defined as being the placing of an old content into a new structure at a higher level of development. Space that is initially cognized through sensorimotor schemas is transformed into a representational space at the next stage and is even further transformed into an abstracted mapping at a later stage. Although vertical décalage does include the "negation of the negation", the restructuring of a former content at a new level, it does not emphasize the original negation. As we have already seen, from a dialectical perspective contradiction in the form of negation between unified opposites is one of the major missing features in the Piagetian model.

In our view, the inherent unity of opposites that produces the negation of the negation is rooted in the hierarchical structuring of both subject and object. In hierarchical development there are two major poles nicely captured in Werner's (1957) orthogenetic principle. These are *differentiation* and *hierarchical integration.* Piaget devotes most of his efforts toward integration and a minimum to differentiation. In the sensorimotor period, differentiation is seen primarily in the accommodation of reflex schemas to the environment rather than within the cognitive organization as a whole. For the rest, hierarchical integration holds sway. Sensorimotor schemata becoming reciprocally accommodated to produce object permanence, objects become integrated to form functions, functions become integrated to form group structures, and finally group structures become integrated into formal logics.

A simultaneous process that is given short shrift is the actual differentiation of thought relevant to the reflex and conceptual schemas. Although it is easy to view the child adultomorphically as being able to differentiate visual, auditory, tactual, and other inputs, since there are specific anatomical structures designed for these tasks, this need not be the initial situation. The generalized responses of the newborn (e.g., increased motility and eyeblink) to a variety of seemingly specific stimuli (e.g., auditory or visual) could lead one to conclude that at the same time that perceptual modalities are being integrated in response to external objects; they are also being differentiated as modalities. There is a constant simultaneous process of unitary objects being negated by modalities sensitive to particular properties and of unitary modalities being negated by objects with many properties. In these contradictions we find the beginnings of the reflective consciousness hypothesized in Hegel's *The Phenomenology of the Mind (1910).*

Piaget (1971) has argued that an entity and its negation cannot occur simultaneously within an equilibrated system. However, that argument applies only to a system suspended in time. The process of life permits no such stabilization except in abstraction. The negation of the negation represents the continuing interplay between parts and wholes, and thus between the subject and the objective world. In the hierarchical organization of thought, each entity is at one and the same time a superordinate whole and a subordinate part. It is the temporal dimension that constitutes the continuing basis for the endless oscillation between negations in a dialectical process.

DIALECTICS AND LANGUAGE DEVELOPMENT

Our dialectical treatment of child language has two foci. First, in a critique of developmental psycholinguistics, we note the consequences of certain dominant explanatory systems. Historical changes in the field from an early empiricism to Chomskian mentalism (Chomsky, 1957) and back to a more holistic empiricism are analyzed as an instance of the negation of the negation. We explore the impact of Chomskian linguistics with its emphasis on syntactic rules and individual output, as well as the ideological functions served by that perspective.

Second, alternative goals and methods are suggested by the dialectical approach. Using categories outlined earlier in this chapter, we offer suggestions for studying the child's control over the public language system. The dialectical principles of interconnectedness, qualitative change, alienation, and contradiction constitute optics through which language acquisition can be fruitfully viewed.

Critique of Developmental Psycholinguistics

A genetic view of work on child language indicates a drift toward more dialectical or at least more interactional models. However, modern psycholinguistics was created initially within the hegemony of Chomskian generative grammar (Chomsky, 1957, 1965). Early work on children's langauge stressed synchonic analyses of individual output. Langauge was identified as being a set of abstract rules and an innate capacity of a quite determinate form (McNeill, 1970). This early work claimed a dramatic discontinuity between infant experience and the onset of the child's control over a public symbol system. What children said, moreover, seemed unrelated to what they heard. There have been modifications of this view. Currently, there is a concern for semantic and not exclusively syntactic relations, an increased attention to context, and an openness to alternative linguistic models (Bowerman, 1973). Nonetheless, the chief impact of post-Chomskian linguistics on developmental psycholinguistics has been to replace the earlier crude behavioral analyses with a theoretical approach in which both nativism and mentalism are embedded.

What is the relationship between the linguist's project of a formal account of language structure and the developmentalist's project to account for the acquisition, representation, and production of language? In the interface of transformational grammarians and developmental psycholinguists, the influence and penetration of linguistics has been formidable. Perhaps in an inevitable counter-swing from the earlier dominance of behaviorism, the first modern psycholinguists, despite provisos to the contrary, initiated the practice of making a structural isomorphism between the theoretical apparatus developed to describe language structure and the state of knowledge in the child's head. Why psychologists should have been so enthralled with models developed in a discipline with a profoundly different set of goals is an intriguing question. A materialist perspective was negated with an essentially idealist one. We see, currently, the beginnings of a transformation that will negate that negation by rerouting the child into a broader material context that now encompasses a social component.

Purely formal accounts of structure generated without recourse to meaning or context have not been sustained. This failure would have been predicted from a dialectical perspective and is testimonial to the potential power of this approach. Language functions, context, and the social dimension have all crept into the standard account of language acquisition. This change is noted first in Bloom's (1970) work, which marks the initiation of what Brown (1973) has termed the "rich interpretation."

Both Bloom (1970, 1973) and Bowerman (1973) use context—defined as including ongoing activity, available objects, and the social and physical terrain—as a reference point for interpretation. Context is separate from the child and the child's language production. Its importance is only as a tool for the linguist. Greenfield and Smith's (1976) work on single word utterances departs from this use of context. They insist on a continuity between preverbal and verbal expression, between action and word. Context is thus part of utterance. This perspective noted by Greenfield and Smith lines up with that of Werner and Kaplan (1963) and Halliday (1975) in grounding language development in action and seeing the evolution of a general attentional signaling function. Halliday (1975) has proposed a developmental sequence in which learning how to say is built on learning how to make meaning, which is in turn built on learning how to do. Options for action give way to options for expression, and these may be verbal, gestural, vocal, or enactive.

Another important shift in psycholinguistic research is in the analysis of underlying relations as expressed in utterances. Increasingly, these relations take on a semantic or conceptual flavor, even when the theoretical apparatus is syntactic, as in Bloom's work. In most cases, the set of semantic relations proposed appear to have been arrived at inductively. Various taxonomies have been suggested, and a variety of semantic relations now brought into play in studies of child language converges around certain key conceptual relationships (Bloom, 1970; Chafe, 1970; Fillmore, 1968; Schlesinger, 1971). In these conceptual schemes, a set of relationships between objects and events in the world is delineated. Most of the relationships proposed conform to what Werner and Kaplan (1963) have characterized as the "human action model," a representation of construed causal relationships between acting, initiating, and responding individuals and objects. We might look, as Green-field has done, to the relations between sensorimotor schemas and early ut-terances for the point of origin for these conceptual relations. It is interesting that Piaget's work on sensorimotor development focuses on general prin-ciples of discovery and control over cause-and-effect relationships. His analysis is only very generally about the child's experiences with real-world constraints over objects and action. Piaget has never produced an exhaustive or even suggestive taxonomy of action schemas. Yet in some of the current psycholinguistic accounts of semantic relations, such taxonomies are being developed (Bloom, 1970; Greenfield & Smith, 1976).

The psycholinguists' task with regard to these underlying relations is twofold: First, one is interested in how and why the child is reduced to ex-pressing these distinct conceptual possibilities in a simple concatenation of words or word and action. Second, one must account for the steps and energy that lead the child to a more elaborated expression of these conceptions. In other words, what leads the child to modify what is manifestly a functional and perhaps even equilibrated system? It will be seen that the dialectical prin-ciple of contradiction may usefully be applied to this problem.

In all this work, there is the bedeviling problem of the psychological reality of the proposed linguistic structures, whatever the theoretical framework. Even without engaging the issue of language production, the psychologist wishing to make claims concerning the competence of children faces the considerable conceptual task of justifying the choice of constructs or explanatory systems as maps to the child's epistemology. Even Greenfield's prescription that semantic functions be operationally distinguishable, productive, and expressed with some variation in lexical items does not adequately handle the legitimation of any particular concep-tual categories for the child. Here, it would seem that linguist and parent are joined in the same heuristic activity of trying to understand the communica-tion system of the child. In that sense, the current primacy of semantic in-terpretations — the identification of cognitive schemas as being deep structures and the interpretive use of context — seems intuitively more appropriate and apt as an account of the adult's role in the language ac-quisition process. Greenfield and Bloom both worked with their own off-spring. Thus, their work is an account both of the productions of these children and the strategies for interpretation and interaction of the parents. Greenfield and Smith's (1976) introduction acknowledges that their treat-ment of one-word utterances grew directly out of the practical application of parenting. Two possibilities flow from their observations. First, current developmental psycholinguistics can be read as being an increasingly close reading of the interpretive strategies of parents faced with a signaling, active infant. Second, we would expect both strategies and signals to change historically and to come into the hands of observers situated in different social or historical matrices. This dialectical perspective on the work in psycholinguistics is, in essence, a critique of the search for universal and formal categories.

In summary, then, despite the preoccupation with semantic concerns, contextual information, and dialogue, developmental psycholinguistics have continued to be more individually than socially focused. Context, present to aid the interpreter, is not fused with social and linguistic activity.

The Dialectical View

Interconnectedness. The first step in the application of dialectics to the study of child language would establish the connections and interdependence between early social experience and later control over the language system. Lewis and his associates have been concerned with placing children's language in the nexus of their social interactions (Lewis & Freedle, 1973; Lewis & Lee–Painter, 1974).

The interactions of mother and infant establish a continuum of informational exchange, an orchestrated dance of sounds and gestures knitted by the adults in the parent–child dyad into an interpreted fabric with signal significance (Harris, 1975). When interconnectedness is assumed, the context of language use is construed differently. There can be no such thing as context-free language. Context must be construed widely to include not merely the immediate experimental situation but also the social and ideological milieu in which such data are collected. Data-collection methods for studies in child language were quickly regularized after the onset of Chomskian influences. Quasi-naturalistic protocols were collected through the use of audio- or videotaping procedures. Although the interest was exclusively on formal syntactic rules, little attention was paid or importance given to the understanding of the impact of context. More recently, however, strategies for studying language activity in young children include the exploration of varieties of contexts (e.g., home, laboratory, variability of objects in the setting, and presence of other people).

Another major contribution of a dialectical perspective is to acknowledge the intrusion of the experimenter into the experimental scheme. Experiments are interactions; subject and object are bound in a mutually influential interpenetration. Studies in child language are a domain in which to study that interaction. Rather than fine tuning the observations to make the experimenter even more unobstrusive, another strategy would be to treat the language sample as an instance of parent and child interaction as observed by psychologists. In this way, one hopes to get at the belief system of the parents with regard to the ideal parenting of the capacities of their own child. These settings would possibly allow us to observe the ambivalence of parents toward those figures symbolized by the experimenters, who appear to hold real or imagined power to legitimate and define parental and child competences of various kinds. One would expect that the experimental encounter with parent–child dyads from different social groups would reflect discrepancies, conflicts, and incompatibilities among competing ideologies.

Certainly Labov's work (1972) would suggest that one is not able to conclude out of hand that the protocols of mothers do not reflect the impact of the observer's stance vis-à-vis expertise and class-specific interests. Labov found that speakers of nonstandard English produced richer and longer protocols when observed on their own terrain rather than under alienating laboratory conditions.

The assumption that events and individuals are interconnected is not simply the addition of context to the analysis of individual output. Despite the great conceptual difficulty, one must imagine a dynamic unit of analysis in which the unit is a social and interactive event. One way of beginning to work within this perspective is to study dialogue (see Schaffer, Chapter 12, this volume). Here we are interested in the ways in which speakers link utterances in relationships that are transpersonal. An interest in dialogue already present in contemporary work in child language has produced several interesting outcomes. First, there are now convincing empirical demonstrations that sequencing and patterning of interchange are early and persistent facts of parent–child dyadic experience (Lewis & Freedle, 1973). Therefore, we must look into the interactive matrix to ask questions about how social and cognitive linguistic skills unfold. Greenfield and Smith (1976) and Bloom (1970) have provided observations on the creation of constituent structures through dialogue. It was observed that mothers build on the single utterances of their offspring.

Halliday and Hasan (1976) have developed measures of cohesion that may be used to study the creation of text and language skill through interaction and dialogue. Cohesion relations are mechanisms for binding utterances. Referencing, as a cohesion measure, allows speakers to refer to something just said or about to be said, or to refer to present or absent objects. Applied in a developmental context, such measures can be used to analyze changes in referencing capacity. Pilot work by Harris and Bauer (1975) suggests a developmental trend toward increased autonomy of mother and child away from the contextual setting. That is, with increased control over language, reference can be made wholly within the verbal interaction. Dialogues with very young children show a substantial reliance on the context for both parent and child. This reliance can be picked up and analyzed through the use of cohesion measures. Because cohesion measures can operate across speakers, one also has a measure of changes in the capacity of the child to sustain verbally his own referencing and commentary. With such measures, we have some access to the construction of text and of language through social interaction. The exclusive concern with individual output would fall away as these new analyses focus on interconnections between speakers and contexts.

Qualitative Change. Development, dialectically conceived, undergoes periodic transformations. Change is not solely linear or additive. Rather, systems of activity or information undergo internal reorganizations and alterations. Much of the work on the evolution of syntactic structures does in fact record qualitative changes in language competence. Post-Chomskian analyses certainly offer a more dialectical view of productive changes than did earlier assessments that focused on type-token ratios and additions to lexicon (McCarthy, 1954). Stages in the production of negatives or interrogatives (e.g., Bellugi–Klima, 1965) constitute synchronic slices that record the outcome of systematic transformations (e.g., inversions or embedding of elements in the utterance). Halliday's (1975) functional systemics also treats developing language competence in dialectical terms.

Halliday's treatment of child language is process-oriented, looks at the interplay of continuities and discontinuities in unfolding streams of parent–child dialogue, and charts periodic qualitative reorganizations of the child's mapping of conceptual to linguistic structure. The speech system inherently contains elaborate and rich options for the expression of meaning. The view that Halliday (1975) advances provides a grounding assumption for understanding such different theorists as Jakobsen (1971) in his exploration of metaphor and metonymy, Pavlov (1928) in the study of the second signal system, and Vygotsky (1963), who identifies the intersection of language and thinking in units of word meaning. To route intentions for action, communication, or description through the vehicle of words expands and transforms prior behavioral or concrete forms of knowledge. Halliday's analysis stresses: (1) the continuity in social, linguistic, and intellectual development, (2) the variability and multidirectionality of routes for progression in language learning, and (3) the transformations that characterize the shift from enactive understanding to representation and linguistically mediated knowledge.

The first qualitative transformation comes when the primary functions initially expressed through "options to do" are expressed through "options to mean." A new modality with novel distinctive features is used to express old and preexistent functions. At this point single expressions serve single functions. Halliday (1975) predicts a simple linear expansion of one-to-one content–expression pairs until the system essentially overloads and collapses. Another dialectical principle is implicated here. The one-to-one system collapses by virtue of an internal but developing contradiction between the elaborating materials and intentions available for expression and the limitations on memory or processing capacity.

An intermediary coding system now needs to be interpolated into the child's utterance system. The introduction of this new syntactic structure has two functions. First, the expressive system is streamlined and reorganized; from "options to mean," the child evolves "options to say." Second, the introduction of grammar permits multiple mapping and coordination of meanings with different functional origins. Halliday's (1975) claim is that lexical development allows the realization of new meanings (or the transformation of more primitive functions) and that grammar allows new combinatorial possiblities. The functional potential of language at this point is less accessible for observation because it is dumped into the heart of the language system, into the grammar. The hierarchical nature of qualitative and dialectical reorganization is observed here. The new formations embed old ones but are not reducible to these more ancient components. Functions are incorporated into the linguistic system, but in radically new ways they are particularized in syntactic structure.

Alienation.   In Werner and Kaplan's (1963) terms, elaborated by Sigel (1974), words possess a distancing capacity that permits word users to make differentiations about objects, events, and self in relation to others. This distancing is essentially what is subsumed under the construct of alienation. Words can thus be one of the primary mediations between man and nature and between men and man. They lead to objectification (Meszaros, 1970). However, words are arranged into systems, and these rules of arrangement operate within syntactic, semantic, or programmatic components of language. Moreover, these rules reflect historically and culturally specific ways of dividing the physical and social space. Hence, the mediating activity of words, although in theory offering the potential for "pure" differentiation, in practice leads to particular social relations and particular conceptions of objects. Because language serves an ideological function, word users are left in an alienated condition. The child does not merely acquire a neutral semiotic system that he tailors to express social and cognitive functions. The internalization and substitution of the public for the private reference makes the prior concept, the underlying need or function, inaccessible. This view is echoed in the work of Lacan (1965), a French psychoanalyst, who has sought to invigorate the psychoanalytic treatment of the unconscious by promoting a rapproachement between Freud and the linguistics of Jakobsen (1971).

For Lacan (1965) the unconscious is structured like a language. Need is organized and manipulated into a desire coded through the social semiotic. Once needs are communicated through the medium of language, the child's communicative efforts contain in masked forms the contradiction between the original analogic functions and their altered forms distorted through words. Language acquisition is thus one important place in which to see the onset and interaction of the necessary mediations that initiate development. The historically determined forms of mediation ensure only particular kinds of development.

The potential for representation, classification, and personalization explodes with the child's control over the human semiotic system. Yet this knowledge-bearing apple that is language comes with its own particular worm. If the bait is increased precision and increased elaborative possibilities, the hook is a prescribed role in a social system. Nelson's work (Chapter 13, this volume) can be seen as a demonstration that alternatively some children are first hooked into developing language for social functions, which in turn expands cognitive possibilities. Similarly, Halliday (1975) has suggested that entrance into language may be through mathetic (i.e., heuristic, problem-solving, and imaginative) functions or pragmatic (i.e., social and interpersonal) functions.

Another way of examining forms of alienation in language acquisition lies in examining current work on dialogue or interaction. Most investigators in this area (Bell, 1974; Jaffee & Feldstein, 1970; Lewis & Freedle, 1973) envision a more or less democratic process in which each participant signals, controls, responds, initiates, or terminates "bouts" of interaction. The impression is one of mutuality or even the infant's control over the mother (Bell, 1974). Stochastic models in particular create this impression (Jaffee & Feldstein, 1970).

We have stressed that one strategy of a dialectical analysis is to penetrate categories of analysis in order to examine underlying relationships not immediately or easily accessible. From this perspective, the democratization of dialogue is an ideologically based category that masks the substantial power differential and the conditions or structures of domination present in the parent–child dyad. The parent's control over the public meaning system is substantial and important. Although we do not underestimate the capacity of infants to terrorize their parents, it is the parents who control and operate the interpretive schemes and the ideology that produces them. Bell (1974) has written very imaginatively about the signaling capacity of the infant. Clearly, there are many subtle and important cues produced by the infant that constitute the child's contribution to the creation of a social interaction. But those products of the child are organized by the parent into a preexistant frame influenced by socially derived and historically determined systems of meaning. Belief systems about the infant, about child-rearing imperatives, and about the parent's rights and obligations create the categories through which signals of the infant are filtered and understood.

Contradiction. The dialectical principle of contradiction can provide a critical construct for many behavioral analyses with developmental interests. Qualitative change requires integration with some mechanism for effecting transformation. We have identified contradiction as such a candidate. Psycholinguists record a set of stages in the evolution of language and syntactic structures in particular (Foucault, 1970). Movement in these analyses has essentially been bracketed. Contradiction as the triggering mechanism for change may provide an important tool for refocusing psycholinguistics on the diachronic aspects of language.

Contradiction, understood as discrepancy, is implicated in a number of general models for human performance. One well-known model, that of the TOTE units developed by Miller, Galanter, and Pribram (1960), stresses the system in equilibration, that is, when act and plan match, at the expense of contradiction. The general discrepancy model is reflected in the work of Anohkin (1970), Bernstein (1970), and MacNeilage (1970).

We have argued earlier that dialectical contradiction is not the traditional discrepancy between model and input but, rather, the conflict between different organizational systems. In describing sensorimotor development, contradiction was seen in the infant's attempt to use two different schema to assimilate the same object, both schemas with the child. Language development offers an opportunity to see externalized versions of the conflicting meaning systems because they reside in different individuals. In the most general case, one is in the child and one is in the mother.

In trying to stress social interaction and not solely individual functioning, one would propose that the apprehension of contradiction and the pressures for alteration might arise in parent or in child or transpersonally with different implications. The mismatch may also reflect contradiction between the individual's behavior and his intentions or between his intentions and the impact of the behavior on others.

Applied to dialogue and language interactions of parent and child, contradiction through the detection of mismatched meaning systems offers some interesting speculations. Expansions may constitute an important nexus in which contradiction may have its transforming effect. The mother's expansion on her child's production can offer several sites for the experience of contradiction. There is the potentially comprehendable contradiction between the two surface outputs, that is, of mother and of child. In such cases, the frequently observed oscillations among the child's production, the mother's expansion, and the child's reduction would be an instance in which the feedback system does not register as error—that is, the child decodes and recodes on the basis of a preexistent schema, and mismatching although present is not yet functional. Notice that here we stress the contradictory rather than the imitative aspects of expansions in order to see in those exchanges a potential space for developmental shifts.

Expansions may also serve as the adults' technique for checking out the adequacy of their own interpretations. There is, then, potentially a contradiction between the underlying concept of relation expressed in utterance and the parent's interpretation. One would not expect approximately accurate or at least acceptable interpretations to provide much new information. Such acceptable interpretations are, after all, evidence of an equilibrated system.

However, mismatches may again be important here. Brown (1973) has suggested that a critical developmental transformation might be accessible in those moments when a breakdown in communication occurs. The mother's erroneous gloss on what the child means or her failure to make any interpretation constitutes such a gross mismatch between internal conceptual relations generated by the child and the surface utterance (the child's or the mother's) that in consequence the child is forced to alter the on-going behavior.

Here is an example of such a mismatch taken from the protocol of mother and 19-month-old daughter (Harris & Bauer, 1975). Notice that the mismatching appeared to elicit changes in the daughter's output as evidenced in the constituent structures in which the problematic word was embedded and the gestures used.

(Daughter)	Shona:	wer kuk
	Mother:	mmm?
	Shona:	wer a ba ga
	Mother:	mmm? What is that mean?
	Shona:	Guk
	Mother:	mmm.
	Shona:	gein kuk. kuk. go kuk. de da da kuk.
	Mother:	You're talking Greek to me.
	Shona:	kuk
	Mother:	mmm?
	Shona:	der oo (she pushes blocks around, appears to be searching for something on the floor)
	Mother:	You're crazy.
	Shona:	der kuk
	Mother:	mmm.
	Shona:	oo kuk, der kuk (points to cup)
	Mother:	Oh this. Oh, I'm sorry.

One might imagine that in such moments when the underlying conceptual relations are inaccessible to parents (i.e., when the surface output is uninterpretable), the child is alerted to the problem of the appropriate mapping of deep structures (semantic ones in the above example) to output and sets various heuristic strategies in motion.

Contradiction, then, at a certain stage of development and under certain conditions promotes alterations in production that move these utterances toward a better match with underlying relations. A model for detecting contradiction applied to miscommunicative exchanges between parent and child may provide important information about language development.

Werner and Kaplan's Symbol Formation.   It is surprising that if we were to seek an already articulated theory of language development that comes close to incorporating the entire set of principles associated with a dialectical perspective, we would be successful. In their brilliant book *Symbol Formation,* Werner and Kaplan (1963) have anticipated almost every current development in the study of language. Why, then, are they rarely cited or credited for concepts directly derived from their work?

The historical critique associated with a dialectical analysis can be fruitfully applied here. Werner and Kaplan's work was produced at a time when the field was in the beginning throes of its romance with the universals of transformational grammars. They suffered the isolation of a foreign tradition and a foreign paradigm. In addition, the book itself was difficult to read. Piaget's work had a similar early fate, but he lived long enough to weather the empirical and theoretical storms and to see his language become required reading. Werner did not. For students acquainted with the newest directions in the area of language development, it is a shock to read a book that not only explored these directions more than a decade ago but also defined areas that still are unstudied, (e.g., the early embedding of communication and reference in a physiognomically charged field).

One of the classic definitions of a language system is the arbitrariness of the relation between symbol and referent. The system of referents is based on the cognitive organization of the speaker, but the symbol system is not considered to share this feature. In theory, any word could have any assigned meaning. Werner and Kaplan argue the contrary, that the symbols are not arbitrary because they are organized into a dynamic system as well. For some elements in the system to have particular referents has implications for all the other elements in the system. Interconnectedness is a dominant theme in the domains of representation as well as of reference.

In contrast, onomatopoeia has been thought to represent the essence of lack of arbitrariness. The symbol used imitates the referent. Werner and Kaplan again argue the contrary. For example, the particular onomatopoetic expression for a given referent cannot be separated from the concrete speech system in which children are raised. They cite the infant's word for dog which is "wau-wau" in German, "oua-oua" in French, and "waf-waf" in Dutch. An adult example from Chamberlain (1893) contrasts his rendition of an owl's hooting "tu-whit-tu-whit-tu-whit" with a Kootenay Indian friend's "katskakitl patlke."

Werner and Kaplan argue that there are no natural systems in which the development of symbols can be understood when separated from either the concrete referential or representational organizations. Such separation and alienation occur only in laboratory studies of language (e.g., paired-associate learning of nonsense syllables).

Werner and Kaplan's model of language development includes a stage theory, which is not unusual, and a motivational theory based on contradiction, which is. At the transition point between each level of organization, conflicting systems of representation produce reorganizations and development. One of Werner and Kaplan's most interesting descriptions relates to the conflict between intonational and syntactic structures during the period when children use two-word utterances.

Should participants in the mainstream of developmental psycholinguistics be criticized for ignoring Werner and Kaplan's work? From a dialectical perspective, the answer is both "no" and "yes". The answer is "no" because each developmental progression has an organic unity that is not open to arbitrary intrusions from without. The system must already have structures capable of an approximate assimilation before adaptation can occur. Until recently such structures did not exist within American psycholinguistic theory. On the other hand, the answer is "yes" because each discipline must see itself in a diachronic as well as a synchronic structure, where each present state of organization is one aspect of a continuing development. The hierarchic integrations that we are coming to accept as reflecting the psychological development of the children we study must also be accepted as part of the historical development of ourselves and our science.

CONCLUSIONS

Throughout the history of philosophy, dialectical conceptions have been inextricably intertwined with theories of development. During the past decade American psychology has again begun to appreciate the importance of theoretical and hence philosophical issues. Developmental concerns that for the most part were embedded in the social sciences have now become intrinsic components of the natural sciences as well, as each discipline has become aware of the transformational systems that coordinate dynamic energic entities in their individual domains. General systems theories have been used to generate interdisciplinary models that attempt to incorporate developmental and hierarchical structuring.

One of the first of these general systems theories can be found in the dialectical approach identified with Hegel. The approach has been altered somewhat through its application to concrete developmental problems, but it remains a relatively coherent model. In this chapter we have defined some properties of the model and identified actual and potential applications of the model in contemporary developmental psychology.

At the most specific level, a dialectical approach offers a source of hypotheses about the structures and functions to be sought in developmental research. At a middle level, a dialectical approach would mean that empirical phenomena cannot be viewed as isolated entities (i.e., subject versus object or cognitive versus social) but must be simultaneously integrated into a multiplicity of contexts for their complete understanding. At the broadest level a dialectical approach requires that the theoretical efforts of scientists be placed into a similar multiplicity of contexts. The traditional view that society is influenced by scientists who are influenced by the facts must be augmented by the reciprocal view that society influences the ways in which scientists identify and organize their facts.

For contemporary American science this last point is the most novel aspect of dialectical thinking. There is still a predominant feeling that science must be value-free and that a fact is a fact is a fact. We have touched only briefly on this most central of issues. It is not enough to view competing scientific theories as being resolvable by the facts alone. We have seen how the facts are influenced by the theoretical paradigm that is used. Furthermore, the dominant theoretical paradigms are influenced by the dominant ideologies in the society at large. Dialectical ideology is exclusively focused on elaborating this point.

The study of the hyperactive child is a case in point. Whether hyperactivity is the result of minimal brain damage intrinsic to the child or the consequence of neurotic child rearing and an uninteresting school environment can be seen as an empirical question. At another level the practical consequences of the two etiological models are strikingly different. As long as the disorder is seen as being intrinsic to the child, the treatment of the disorder is restricted to the child. When the disorder is seen as being an environmental problem, the treatment is to change the behavior of parents and teachers. We can easily predict the scientific conclusions to be drawn from this research by assessing the relative power of the groups involved. Parents and teachers have more power than do children. As a consequence, we medicate children instead of parents and teachers. This simplistic presentation may offend many sophisticated investigators of the perceptual, attentional, motor, and physiological functioning of hyperactive children. Yet if we trace the connections between the research that is being done, the relative availability of funds to study constitutional versus environmental aspects of developmental disorders, and the political process that determines the distribution of funds, it would be difficult to deny their interconnectedness.

The seeming impossible complexity of studying and integrating the many components of a complete dialectical approach is not the problem of the model but the reality of the universe. We've come a long way since the "big bang," and it is hoped that development has a long way to go. Simplicity is a pleasant ideal, but understanding can result only from models that approximate the complexity of the real world.

REFERENCES

Anohkin, P. K. Cybernetics and the integrative activity of the brain. In M. Cole & I. Maltzman (Eds.), *The handbook of contemporary Soviet psychology*. New York: Basic Books, 1970.

Aries, P. *Centuries of childhood. A social history of family life*. New York: Knopf, 1962.

Bell, R. Q. Contributions of human infants to caregiving and social interactions. In M. Lewis & L. A. Rosenblum (Eds.), *The effect of the infant on its caregivers*. New York: Wiley-Interscience, 1974.

Bellugi–Klima, U. The development of interrogative structures in children's speech. In K. F. Riegel (Ed.), *The development of language functions*. Technical Report #8, 1965, University of Michigan Center for Human Growth and Development.

Bernstein, N. A. Methods for developing physiology as related to the problems of cybernetics. In M. Cole & I. Maltzman (Eds.), *The handbook of contemporary soviet psychology*. New York: Basic Books, 1970.

Bloom, L. *Language development: Form and function in emerging grammars*. Cambridge, Mass.: MIT Press, 1970.

Bloom, L. *One word at a time: The use of single word utterances before syntax*. The Hague: Mouton, 1973.

Bowerman, M. *Early syntactic development: A cross-linguistic study with special reference to Finnish*. London: Cambridge University Press, 1973.

Braginski, E. F., & Braginski, D. D. *Mainstream psychology: A critique*. New York: Holt, Rinehart and Winston, 1974.

Brown, R. *A first language: The early stages*. Cambridge, Mass.: Harvard University Press, 1973.

Buck–Morss, S. Socio-economic bias in Piaget's theory and its implications for cross-cultural studies. In K. F. Riegel (Ed.), *The development of dialectical operations*. Basel: S. Karger 1975.

Buss, A. The emerging field of the sociology of psychological knowledge. *American Psychologist*, 1975, *30*, 988–1002.

Chafe, W. I. *Meaning and the structure of language*. Chicago, Ill: University of Chicago Press, 1970.

Chamberlain, A. F. Some points in linguistic psychology. *American Journal of Psychology*, 1893, *5*, 116–119.

Chomsky, N. *Syntactic structures*. The Hague: Mouton, 1957.

Chomsky, N. *Aspects of a theory of syntax*. Cambridge, Mass.: MIT Press, 1965.

Cornforth, M. *Materialism and the dialectical method*. New York: International Publishers, 1953.

Décarie, T. G. A study of the mental and emotional development of the thalidomide child. In B. M. Foss (Ed.), *Determinants of infant behavior* (Vol. 4). London: Methuen, 1969.

Engles, F. *Anti-Duhring*. New York: International Publishers, 1939.

Farnum, J. E. *An investigation of analogous processes in concept attainment*. Unpublished doctoral dissertation, University of Rochester, 1975.

Flavell, J. H. Stage-related properties of cognitive development. *Cognitive Psychology*, 1971, *2*, 421–453.

Fraiberg, S. *Insights from the blind: Comparative studies of blind and sighted infants*. New York: Basic Books, 1977.

Fillmore, C. J. The case for case. In E. Bach & R. T. Harms (Eds.), *Universals in linguistic theory*. New York: Holt, Rinehart and Winston, 1968.

Foucault, M. *The order of things: An archaeology of the human sciences*. New York: Pantheon Books, 1970.

Foucault, M. *Madness and civilization: A history of insanity in the age of reason*. New York: Vintage Books, 1973.

Godelier, M. Structure and contradiction in Capital. In R. Blackburn (Ed.), *Ideology in social sciences*. London: Fontana, 1972.

Gottlieb, G. Concepts of prenatal development: Behavioral embryology. *Psychological Review*, 1976, *83*, 215–234.

Greenfield, P. M., & Smith, J. H. *The structure of communication in early language development.* New York: Academic Press, 1976.

Halliday, M. A. K. *Learning how to mean: Explorations in the development of language.* London: Arnold, 1975.

Halliday, M. A. K., & Hasan, R. *Cohesion in English.* (English Language Series) London: Longman, 1976.

Harris, A. Social dialectics and language: Mother and child construct the discourse. In K. F. Riegel (Ed.), *The development of dialectical operations.* Basel: S. Karger, 1975.

Harris, A., & Bauer, V. W. *The application of dialectics to early socialization and language development.* Paper presented at the American Psychological Association, Chicago, August, 1975.

Hefner, R., Rebecca, M., & Oleshansky, B. Development of sex-role transcendence. In K. F. Riegel (Ed.), *The development of dialectical operations.* Basel: S. Karger, 1975.

Hegel, G. W. F. *The phenomenology of mind.* London: Macmillan, 1910.

Held, R., & Hein, A. Movement-produced stimulation in the development of visually guided behavior. *Journal of Comparative and Physiological Psychology,* 1963, *56,* 872–876.

Inhelder, B., Sinclair, H., & Bovet, M. *Learning and the development of cognition.* Cambridge, Mass: Harvard University Press, 1974.

Jaffee, J., & Feldstein, S. *Rhythms of dialogue.* New York: Academic Press, 1970.

Jakobsen, R. *Selected writings* (2nd expanded ed.). The Hague: Mouton, 1971.

Kagan, J. *Change and continuity in infancy.* New York: Wiley, 1971.

Kessen, W. "Stage" and "structure" in the study of children. In W. Kessen & C. Kuhlman (Eds.), *Thought in the young child. Monographs of the Society for Research in Child Development,* 1962, *27* (2, Serial No. 83).

Kessen, W. Early cognitive development. Hot or cold? In W. Mischel (Ed.), *Cognitive development and epistemology.* New York: Academic Press, 1971.

Kopp, C. B., & Shaperman, J. Cognitive development in the absence of object manipulation during infancy. *Developmental Psychology,* 1973, *9,* 430.

Kuhn, T. *The structure of a scientific revolution.* Chicago, Ill.: University of Chicago Press, 1962.

Labov, W. *Language in the inner city: Studies in the Black English vernacular.* Philadelphia: University of Pennsylvania Press, 1972.

Lacan, J. Function et champ de parole et du language en psychonalyse. *Psychonalyse,* 1965, *1,* 81–166.

Langer, J. Werner's comparative organismic theory. In P. H. Mussen (Ed.), *Carmichael's manual of child psychology* (3rd Ed.). New York: Wiley, 1970.

Lawler, J. Dialectical philosophy and developmental psychology: Hegel and Piaget on contradiction. In K. F. Riegel (Ed.), *The development of dialectical operations.* Basel: S. Karger, 1975.

Lewis, M. The development of attention and perception in the infant and young child. In W. M. Cruickshank & D. P. Hallahan (Eds.), *Perceptual and learning disabilities* (Vol.2). Syracuse, N. Y.: Syracuse University Press, 1975.

Lewis, M., & Freedle, R. Mother–infant dyad: The cradle of meaning. In P. Pliner, L. Krames, & T. Alloway (Eds.), *Communication and affect: Language and thought.* New York: Academic Press, 1973.

Lewis, M., & Lee-Painter, S. An interactional approach to the mother–infant dyad. In M. Lewis & L. A. Rosenblum (Eds.), *The effect of the infant on its caregiver.* New York: Wiley-Interscience, 1974.

Lukacs, G. *History and class consciousness.* Cambridge, Mass.: MIT Press, 1971.

MacNeilage, P. Motor control of serial ordering. *Psychological Review,* 1970, *77,* 182–196.

Marx, K. *Capital.* New York: International Publishers, 1972.

McCarthy, D. Language development in children. In L. Carmichael (Ed.), *Manual of child psychology.* New York: Wiley, 1954.

McNeill, D. The development of language. In P. Mussen (Ed.), *Carmichael's manual of child psychology* (3rd Ed.). New York: Wiley, 1970.

Meszaros, I. *Marx's theory of alienation.* London: Merlin Press, 1970.

Miller, G. A., Galanter, E., & Pribram, K. *Plans and the structure of behavior.* New York: Holt, Rinehart and Winston, 1960.

Mitchell, J. *Psychoanalysis and feminism.* New York: Pantheon Books, 1974.

Overton, W., & Reese, H. Models of development: Methodological implications. In J. Nesselroade & H. Reese (Eds.), *Life-span developmental psychology: Methodological issues.* New York: Academic Press, 1973.

Pavlov, I. *Lectures on conditioned reflexes.* New York: International Publishers, 1928.

Piaget, J. *The origins of intelligence in children.* New York: International Universities Press, 1952.

Piaget, J. *Psychology of intelligence.* New York: Littlefield, Adams, 1960.

Piaget, J. *Structuralism.* New York: Basic Books, 1970. (a)

Piaget, J. *Genetic epistemology.* New York: Columbia University Press, 1970. (b)

Piaget, J. *Biology and knowledge.* Chicago, Ill.: University of Chicago Press, 1971.

Piaget, J. Chance and dialectic in biological epistemology: A critical analysis of Jacques Monod's theses. In W. F. Overton & J. M. Gallagher (Eds.), *Knowledge and development. Advances in research and theory.* New York: Plenum, 1977.

Popper, K. *Objective knowledge: An evolutionary approach.* London: Oxford University Press, 1972.

Reese, H., & Overton, W. Models of development and theory of development. In L. Goulet & P. Baltes (Eds.), *Life span developmental psychology: Methodological issues.* New York: Academic Press, 1970.

Riegel, K. F. Dialectic operations: The final period of cognitive development. *Human Development,* 1973, *16,* 346–370.

Riegel, K. F. (Ed.), *The Development of dialectical operations.* Basel: S. Karger, 1975.

Riegel, K. F. The dialectics of human development. *American Psychologist,* 1976, *31,* 689–700.(a)

Riegel, K. F. From traits and equilibrium towards developmental dialectics. In W. J. Arnold & J. K. Cole (Eds.), *Nebraska Symposium on Motivation* (Vol. 24). Lincoln: University of Nebraska Press, 1976. (b)

Riegel, K. F. *The psychology of development and history.* New York: Plenum, 1976. (c)

Sameroff, A. J. Early influences on development: Fact or fancy? *Merrill-Palmer Quarterly,* 1975, *21,* 267–294.(a)

Sameroff, A. J. Transactional models in early social relations. In K. F. Riegel (Ed.), *The development of dialectical operations.* Basel: S. Karger, 1975. (b)

Sameroff, A., & Chandler, M. Reproductive risk and the continuum of caretaking casualty. In F. D. Horowitz (Ed.), *Review of child development research* (Vol. 4). Chicago, Ill.: University of Chicago Press, 1975.

Schlesinger, I. M. Production of utterances and language acquisition. In D. I. Slobin (Ed.), *The ontogenesis of grammar.* New York: Academic Press, 1971.

Schneirla, T. C. *Principles of animal psychology.* New York: Dover Publications, 1966. (a)

Schneirla, T. C. Aspects of stimulation and organization in approach/withdrawal processes underlying vertebrate behavioral development. In D. S. Lehrman, R. A. Hinde, & E. Shaw (Eds.), *Advances in the study of behavior.* New York: Academic Press, 1966.(b)

Sigel, I. Language of the disadvantaged: The distancing hypothesis. In C. S. Lavatelli (Ed.), *Language training in early childhood education.* Urbana: University of Illinois Press, 1974.

Szasz, T. *The myth of mental illness: Foundations of a theory of personal conduct* (Revised ed.) New York: Harper and Row, 1974.

Tanner, J. M., & Inhelder, B. *Discussions on child development* (Vol. 4). New York:

International Universities Press, 1971.

Uzgiris, I. C. Organization of sensorimotor intelligence. In M. Lewis (Ed.), *Origins of intelligence: Infancy and early childhood.* New York: Plenum, 1976.

Uzgiris, I. C. Plasticity and structure: The role of experience in infancy. In I. C. Uzgiris & F. Weizmann (Eds.), *The structuring of experience.* New York: Plenum, 1977.

Vygotsky, L. *Thought and language.* Cambridge, Mass.: MIT Press, 1963.

Waddington, C. H. *Principles of development and differentiation.* New York: Macmillan, 1966.

Weimer, W. B. Psycholinguistics and Plato's paradoxes of the Meno. *American Psychologist,* 1973, *28,* 15–33.

Werner, H. *Comparative psychology of mental development.* (Rev. ed.). New York: International Universities Press, 1957.

Werner, H., & Kaplan, B. *Symbol formation.* New York: Wiley, 1963.

Youniss, J. Operations and everyday thinking: A commentary on "dialectical operations." *Human Development,* 1974, *17,* 386–391.

15 Commentary: A Trialogue on Dialogue

Jean M. Mandler
*University of California
at San Diego*

If in recent years there has been an overemphasis on the cognitive bases of early language acquisition, the three chapters in this section all seek to redress it. Each in its own way attempts to correct this imbalance by stressing the role of social development in learning to speak. As Sameroff and Harris (Chapter 14) would have it, this spirit represents a "negation of the negation." Whether this phrase obscures or clarifies the swings and roundabouts of scientific advances, it is clear that a new mood prevails in the study of language development.

If we look back at the temper of research in the 1960s, we find that many studies of early language tried to avoid both the cognitive and social capacities of the infant and to concentrate instead on a more neutral distributional approach. These studies asked what words go with what others in children's speech and with what frequency various combinations occur. This lofty approach avoided the messy ground of what children might mean by their simple constructions as well as the seemingly Augean task of interpreting the social context in which the constructions occurred, but it did not do justice to the richness or purposes of children's early expressions. As Bloom (1970) demonstrated with the famous example of "mommy sock," the same form could be used to express quite different meanings in different contexts.

An increasing emphasis on the semantic rather than the syntactic side of language (e.g., Fillmore, 1968; Schlesinger, 1971) led to an increasing concern with the cognitive prerequisites to language learning. At hand, of course, was the well-developed Piagetian system of cognitive growth in the first two years of life, and not unreasonably, many saw it as a promissory note for our eventual understanding of how developing cognitive categories merge into expression in language. Fillmore's case relations seemed as if they should be translatable directly into basic sensorimotor categories of understanding. However, in practice we were left with specific cognitive tasks and scales, such as those devised by Uzgiris and Hunt (1975), and these in turn need translation into simpler cognitive categories to be readily mapped onto language. Furthermore, the relation between some case relations, such as the possessive, and the Piagetian view of sensorimotor accomplishments is not obvious.

Some success has been achieved with the concepts of means–ends understanding and representational or symbolic ability (e.g., Bates, Benigni, Bretherton, Camaioni, & Volterra, 1977). As far as representational capacity is concerned, it seems reasonable to assume that language in the adult sense cannot begin until the child has developed some ability to manipulate symbols that refer to the world. Thus, it is not surprising to find positive correlations of symbolic play, recall, or deferred imitation with the child's burgeoning use of language, but this capacity, much like understanding of the permanence of objects and their features, is a necessary prerequisite, not a sufficient cause. It is hard to imagine language developing in its absence, but just how is a representational capacity translated into language, and why is it that apes, who show at least some signs of representational capacity, do not spontaneously achieve such a translation?

Similar considerations apply to the development of means-ends skills. Just because a child learns how to use an object as a tool to accomplish some end does not tell us how he learns to use language as such a tool. Here we must turn to the social-communicative underpinnings of language. As these chapters illustrate, aside from indication, one of the earliest functions of language is to communicate needs, to get others to do things for you.

The point is that the promissory note of sensorimotor development as the key to language acquisition has remained largely unpaid. We know that the connections must be there, but how are we to dig below this surface knowledge? It does seem surprising that the most elaborate and worked-over theory of early development has not proved to be more fruitful. Perhaps it is because Piaget's system was not devised with language in mind, or perhaps it is because, as the authors of the chapters in Part III of this volume stress, social developments have an even closer affinity to language acquisition than do sensorimotor conceptions of the world. If so, then we may need a reanalysis of Piagetian sensorimotor stages with language specifically in mind. The literature is plagued with discrepancies in the ages at which children attain various capabilities. These discrepancies are far too serious to be accounted for by the concept of décalage. My general impression is the same as Nelson's: Most researchers in language acquisition find children entering the apparently crucial Stages V and VI considerably earlier than Piaget indicated. It depends in part on what you are looking for. If you are charting social or language development, you will probably be acutely aware of the onset of symbolic play, whereas if you are more interested in the child's expanding notions of space of causality, such observations may be overlooked or not fit into a column on your coding sheet.

It is probably also a case of theory directing observation, as Sameroff and Harris would undoubtedly agree. Just as one finds evidence of symbolic capacity in Piaget's children considerably earlier than he admits the concept to his system (e.g., in some of the Stage IV attempts to imitate blinking by opening and closing the hand or mouth), so one also finds evidence of interesting early language use that he notes only in passing. There is a systematicity of vocalic use (e.g., Jacqueline's use of "apff" at 9 months, a sound that she made in the presence of people), that Piaget himself did not focus on because his theoretical interests lay elsewhere. What is needed now is a detailed reanalysis of sensorimotor stages in terms of social and communicative development, in which these aspects of early growth are integrated with the more physical knowledge of the world that Piaget stressed.

This is one of the primary aims of the chapters in Part III — to reemphasize an aspect of development that has been somewhat ignored by those psycholinguists whose psychological orientation has been cognitive rather than social. Schaffer's Chapter 12 is the most general in this regard. In fact, his attempt to undo the imbalance seems to send the pendulum swinging sharply back in the other direction, since he stresses that social interactions are the *primary* stimuli to cognitive growth. He provides ample documentation that cognitive growth occurs mainly in a social nexus and makes clear the inadequacy of assuming that social developments follow on already formed, independently developed, cognitive mechanisms. Such a view, which has been distressingly common, implies an unduly sharp division between cognitive and social categories, as if the child were not exercising basic cognitive understanding when waving bye-bye or when enlisting an adult's help in some endeavor.

Schaffer's view is at the far reach of the pendulum from Piaget's. Piaget observed his children as if they were abandoned in a play pen full of toys in spite of the fact that he was in continual interaction with them. Of course, children *are* frequently abandoned to play pens and *do* learn things, such as how to sit down with a judicious amount of force and to draw objects through the slats, without adult interaction or even adult observation. It would be helpful to have more detailed analyses of what is different about interacting with people and interacting with objects, since both kinds of interactions occur and are learned about with ever-increasing sophistication.

Schaffer lists three reasons for the importance of people to cognitive growth: People are salient sources of stimulation, they control the parts of the environment to which the infant is exposed, and perhaps most importantly, they continually adjust the type of stimulation the infant receives during their interactions. The last characteristic embodies still another source of cognitive change: Adults tend to be the first objects the child, even if in primitive ways, can control. Objects in the hand or in the visual field may mysteriously disappear and do not come back upon command, but crying or fussing can and frequently does make mother reappear. Thus, a sense of mastery and causality seems to have its beginnings in the social sphere, as Piaget and others have pointed out. Schaffer emphasizes the social roots of cognitive growth. We should also heed his call for attention to the temporal parameters of patterned acts, for at present we have few tools to catalogue and measure the temporal course of the highly complex interactive sequences that the young child is learning.

Nelson, (Chapter 13) attempts to strike a balance between the roles social and cognitive factors play in development. She suggests that the integration of the two realms is crucial to the emergence of language. Her argument has two parts. First, the cognitive, communicative, and social prerequisites to language, at least all those that have so far been proposed, appear to be well developed by the end of the first year. Second, although the second year remains largely unmapped, as far as syntax is concerned nothing much seems to be happening until its end when two-word speech typically begins. What is missing that prevents language, defined by the presence of syntax, from blossoming sooner from these roots? Based on her own work and Halliday's (1975) analyses of his son Nigel's early language, Nelson claims that the second year is devoted first to the coordination of social and object schemas, expressed one word at a time, followed by the acquisition of dialogue in which the interpersonal and the ideational realms are simultaneously expressed.

This account rests on the assumption that grammar, or syntactical form, is necessary for simultaneous expression of more than one meaning and that dialogue is the epitome of double-meaning speech. The limitation of one-word, or pregrammatical, speech in this view is that it is impossible to mean more than one thing at once. Children can categorize (a mathetic function) or get what they want (a pragmatic function), but they cannot put the two together on a purely verbal level. An example of Nigel on his way to adult speech was his utterance "hole," said with a plaintive quality, and the rising voice tone that he used for all his pragmatic expressions. Halliday interpreted it to mean, "There is a hole" (an ideational notion) and, "Let's do something about it" (an interpersonal notion). To put these two notions into a single purely verbal utterance requires grammar to enable Nigel both to observe and to interact with his environment at the same time. Thus, Halliday contends that the emergence of grammar (and of vocabulary as well) is not primarily due to a need to express more complex symbolic representations but to the need to combine two very general and different functions into a single utterance, namely, the ideational and the interpersonal. The child is not merely putting together more and more case relations to express increasingly complex thought, but more particularly is using grammar to combine meanings derived from two different functions of language into single, unified, structural utterances.

I believe the significance of Nelson's chapter is her emphasis on the importance and implied difficulty of integrating these two language functions. I interpret her as saying that otherwise the plateau in the second year is inexplicable, since all the important things the child must learn to pass from one- to two-word speech have already been accomplished. Of course, other things are going on during this period. As Nelson points out, children are listening, and they learn to comprehend many words, an accomplishment more difficult to document than changes in their productive use of words. Greenfield and Smith (1976) show that an increasing number of semantic functions come to be expressed in the one-word stage during the second year. This kind of learning may be crucial to the appearance of structure, and it may also be a time-consuming task. However, Nelson is saying that more than these accomplishments are needed to enter the arena of true language; what is needed is the symbolic ability to combine very difficult social and semantic functions into purely verbal form.

Dialogue, in this sense, requires grammar or structure, although grammar by itself does not produce dialogue. Halliday (1975) noted that Nigel's earliest two-word utterances were still clearly separated by intonation into pragmatic and mathetic utterances. Still, grammar must be present for dialogue to occur. Before this time, Nigel engaged in proto-dialogue, which had communicative and interactive aspects, but he could not initiate dialogue, which is one of its hallmarks, nor could he answer information-seeking questions. What he learned when he unraveled the mysteries of dialogue was not only to assume the role of addresser and assign the role of listener, which one does whenever one speaks, but the more specifically linguistic roles of asking for information and requesting a reply. It was only at this point that he began to respond to WH- questions, to respond purely verbally to other verbal statements, and to initiate dialogue.

I have gone into some detail on the notion of dialogue because this term lies at the heart of the chapters in Part III, and the reader should be aware of the diverse uses to which these and other authors put this term. Schaffer uses *dialogue* to refer to any set of synchronized interactions that takes place between infants and their social partners. The interactions he describes are not primarily linguistic ones. They undoubtedly underlie the later acquisition of linguistic dialogue, which is of course one of the reasons to emphasize them, but the fascinating problem of how this transition takes place has yet to be solved. The act–watch and turn-taking patterns Schaffer describes, for example, appear to be acquired early and to be well practiced before the child begins to engage in linguistic dialogue. Schaffer notes that the dialogue characteristics of reciprocity and intentionality have been acquired by the end of the first year, and, as Nelson comments, that is long before dialogue appears in language.

Nelson uses *dialogue* in a sense closer to that of Halliday (1975). She attributes both its onset and that of grammatical speech to a growing coordination between the child's physical and social worlds. She assumes that until that coordination is relatively complete the child will be able to express only one part of the relation at a time, relying on context and gesture to indicate the other part. Purely linguistic dialogue cannot begin until the child has achieved a synthesis of the two spheres at the symbolic level. The evidence for this assertion is still tenuous, of course, but what there is suggests important and relatively neglected areas of research.

Nelson uses as evidence for the incomplete coordination of the social and object realms during the second year the marked individual differences in the extent to which one-word speech reflects social-expressive or referential concerns. Early language users tend to opt for one or the other mode, whereas children who begin speaking at an older age tend to be more balanced in the functions they express. Nelson's observations in this regard seem to be of great importance because of the understandable tendency of workers in this field to concentrate on the language development of one or two children at a time. Nigel Halliday, for example, moved from the one- to the two-word stage extremely rapidly. Had he managed to coordinate social and object goals unusually early? Unfortunately, we have no information on this aspect of his development. As Nelson comments, we are sorely in need of research on these questions because the lack of data in the second year makes theory construction risky. But what an interesting set of speculations! It is hoped they will foster research that is directly focused on the integration of the social and object worlds.

Sameroff and Harris (Chapter 14) are also concerned with the social and interactive aspects of early language acquisition, although their chapter uses the study of language as a case history in a dialectical approach to science rather than as the main focus of their presentation. According to these authors, dialectical principles will be useful to any science, not only to place one's theoretical predilections in a wider sociopolitical context (the recent controversy over the status of IQ and IQ tests being a good case in point), but also as a foundation on which to build any particular theory. The method is fundamentally genetic; that is, all theory embodies developmental principles, and needless to say has nothing to do with child development as such. Sameroff and Harris apply four dialectical requirements to theories of language acquistion.

First, all elements in any system are interconnected. Consequently, one cannot study any single element in isolation without risk of distortion. In terms of language acquisition, Sameroff and Harris take this principle to mean that not only must social and communicative aspects of language be integrated with semantic and syntactic considerations, but more importantly, language cannot be separated from the context in which it is used. Both of these points are well illustrated in the other two chapters in Part III, and again we see the emphasis on dialogue as a unit of analysis. It is well to notice, however, that Sameroff and Harris wish to extend the meaning of *context* beyond the immediate or situational context to include the larger social and ideological milieu. Studies of this larger context presumably might shed light on individual differences in language acquisition, such as the sources of the referential or expressive modes Nelson discusses. For instance, Nelson (1973) has found differences in expressive and referential speech among firstborn and later born children, which might be explicable in terms of differences in their social milieus.

The second major principle is that development involves qualitative changes as it moves from one stage to another. This principle seems particularly obvious in language, because the shifts from preverbal to one-word to multiword speech clearly involve qualitative differences in spite of quantitative overtones. Thus, in this sense all current theories of language acquisition are dialectic.

Third, under the topic of alienation, Sameroff and Harris discuss two rather different issues. The first is that the price of learning language is alienation from preverbal conceptualizations. They do not develop this point in relation to problems of language acquisiton but instead comment that alienation typifies early dialogue. The adult and the child do not share power equally, the parents tending to dominate many aspects of the communication. It might be noted that these uses of the term *alienation* are rather far removed from its original use in dialectical theory.

Finally, and perhaps most important among the four points, Sameroff and Harris make a case for contradiction as a mechanism for effecting transformations from one stage to another, not only in language acquisition but as a general developmental principle. Much of their chapter bears on this point; the tenor of their argument is that contradiction, variously defined as discrepancy or as conflict between internal states, is the major transition rule for changes from one stage to another. The heart of this viewpoint is that development is continuous change, so that a theory which concentrates on occasional plateaus in this progress distorts the basic conception of what living organisms are about.

The implications of this view for theory are that we will need new constructs and new tools of analysis. Properly conceptualized, the phenomena are changing, interacting forms for which static structural descriptions are not suitable. Schaffer, of course, also expresses this concern, but he implies a need for supplementary tools rather than a brand new armamentarium.

However, it seems fair to ask whether it is possible to discuss transition mechanisms without first carving out of the chaos of continuous change some stable descriptions — even if only for temporary states and if only as reference points. How can we get a handle on continuous change if nothing remains stable long enough to describe? Sameroff and Harris appear to agree with Kessen (1962) that man seems to have a universal need to segment the course of development. They do not give any examples, but they say that dialectical theories are indeed concerned with the qualitative shifts in organization that produce unique structures or segments. It may be that even the most dialectical of theories must have room for structural elements, for descriptions of states, not simply change.

The problem of transition rules and how to conceive of them still remains. Sameroff and Harris point out that Piaget's theory has been bedeviled by this problem. However, potential mechanisms for change have been available to the theory from the start, in the dialectics of assimilation and accommodation and in the rough concept of equilibration and the conflict between structures that this term implies. I think, in fact, that Sameroff and Harris rather underplay Piaget's recent attempts at explicating conflict as a source of development. They say that a focus on the disequilibrating moment is long overdue. However, Inhelder, Sinclair, and Bovet (1974) have written an entire book attempting to explicate the notion of conflict between schemas and to show how restructuring occurs as a result. For example, they have pitted two schemas against each other in a task in which the schemas will be incompatible, as in the case of a well-developed number concept and an ordinal concept of length, and then studied children's attempts to resolve the conflict. Sometimes it works, and the child gains a new concept of length in terms of units of distance. At other times the child seems to go to great lengths to make the discrepant schemas compatible without doing any basic restructuring. These experiments raise many questions, but they have the advantage of being concrete explorations of the notion of conflict or contradiction. In the introduction to the Inhelder et al. work, Piaget defines contradiction as a disturbance of which the subject has become aware. Sameroff and Harris find this definition to be amorphous, but I find it considerably more amenable to test than an unexamined concept of contradiction.

A dialectical model, according to Sameroff and Harris, does not focus on the coordination of lower level structures to produce a new higher level structure. Rather, it emphasizes contradictions among the lower structures "which can only be resolved by the agency of a new level of coordination." In one sense it is not clear that these viewpoints truly differ. Take the object concept, for example. Are Sameroff and Harris saying anything practically different from Piaget when they emphasize that the sensory modalities give the child conflicting information, rather than that the child learns to coordinate disparate types of information? In another sense it is not easy to see that the various types of sensory information *are* in conflict. They should

conflict only if the child already had a concept of the object's independent existence, so that one piece of information would indicate that the object existed while the other would indicate that it did not. But the concept of the permanent object comes about only *after* the two realms are coordinated, according to Piaget, or as a result of the conflict, according to Sameroff and Harris.

It is true that undue emphasis on coordination of schemas raises the question of why, when a particular degree of coordination seems sufficient to the purposes at hand; nevertheless progress to a more advanced stage takes place. A familiar example from language acquisition was posed by Brown and Hanlon (1970) in their study of tag questions. How should we account for the increasing sophistication of the young child in using tags such as "Isn't it?" or "Did she?", since these are patently unnecessary for communicative effectiveness? Certainly conflict will not help us, but neither is it clear that coordination will do so, although the possibility of using such grammatical devices for coordinating interpersonal and ideational messages is intriguing. Sometimes, conflict *can* account for progress, as in the example of miscommunication that Sameroff and Harris discuss, although even here it is not obvious that an analysis in terms of conflict will be more fruitful than some concept of goal-corrected search.

A commitment to conflict as the only mechanism for change may suffer from its own set of restrictions. It seems to ignore a pervasive tendency toward consistency and organization at all levels of development. This tendency appears from birth. We see it in early visual-auditory coordination, which would be difficult to describe in terms of conflict or contradiction. It continues through life, from eye–hand coordination in the infant, which is a major step toward a qualitative shift in viewing the world, to learning psychology as a university student, which also sometimes results in a qualitative shift in viewing the world. In short, we should not ignore the second of Piaget's functional invariants. Adaptation does indeed involve the dialectical process of assimilation and accommodation, but the other side of the adaptive coin is the universal tendency to organize information into coherent, systematic, and sometimes even long-lasting, structures. Continuous change and continuous contradiction may be as serious an oversimplification as a structural model that provides no mechanism for change. It would seem that dialectical philosophy will need a more complex interpretation before it is successfully translated into psychological theory.

However, let us praise the clash and contradiction of new ideas. Although the negation of unified opposites may not be a scientific panacea, there are many lessons to be learned from the chapters in Part III. They tell us that we have neglected social, communicative, and contextual factors in our study of language development. We have tended to apply analytic methods more appropriate to static structures than to dynamic interactive units. We need to develop methods of handling dyadic interactions such as dialogue. Even more basically, we need to be attuned to the concept of dialogue itself.

REFERENCES

Bates, E., Benigni, L., Bretherton, I., Camaioni, L., & Volterra, V. *Cognition and communication from 9–13 months: A correlational study.* Program on Cognitive and Perceptual Factors in Human Development, Report No. 12. Institute for the Study of Intellectual Behavior. University of Colorado, Boulder, 1977.

Bloom, L. M. *Language development: Form and function in emerging grammars.* Cambridge, Mass.: MIT Press, 1970.

Brown, R., & Hanlon, C. Derivational complexity and order of acquisition in child speech. In John R. Hayes (Ed.), *Cognition and the development of language.* New York: Wiley, 1970.

Fillmore, C. J. The case for case. In E. Bach & R. T. Harms (Eds.), *Universals in linguistic theory.* New York: Holt, Rinehard and Winston, 1968.

Greenfield, P. M., & Smith, J. H. *The structure of communication in early language development.* New York: Academic Press, 1976.

Halliday, M. A. K. *Learning how to mean: Explorations in the development of language.* London: Edward Arnold, 1975.

Inhelder, B., Sinclair, H., & Bovet, M. *Learning and the development of cognition.* Cambridge, Mass.: Harvard University Press, 1974.

Kessen, W. "Stage" and "structure" in the study of children. In W. Kessen and C. Kuhlman (Eds.), Thought in the young child. *Monographs of the Society for Research in Child Development,* 1962, *27* (2, Serial No. 83).

Nelson, K. Structure and strategy in learning to talk. *Monographs of the Society for Research in Child Development,* 1973, *38* (1-2, Serial No. 149).

Schlesinger, I. M. Learning grammar: From pivot to realization rule. In R. Huxley & E. Ingram (Eds.), *Language acquisition: Models and methods.* New York: Academic Press, 1971.

Uzgiris, I. C., & Hunt, J. McV. *Assessment in infancy: Ordinal scales of psychological development.* Urbana: University of Illinois Press, 1975.

Biographical Notes

MARC H. BORNSTEIN is assistant professor of psychology at Princeton University. A Columbia College B.A. and Yale University Ph.D., Bornstein spent one post-doctoral year at the Max Planck Institute for Psychiatry in Munich and a second at Yale. Bornstein has received the C.S. Ford Cross-Cultural Research Award and the B.R. McCandless Young Scientist Award. He is editor of the *Crosscurrents in Contemporary Psychology* series and a member of societies in child development, anthropology, and visual science. Bornstein has published human experimental, methodological, comparative, developmental, and cross-cultural studies.

DAVID ELKIND is professor and chairman of the Eliot Pierson Department of Child Study, Tufts University. Elkind received his B.A. and Ph.D. at UCLA. He spent a year with David Rapaport of the Austen Riggs Center, studied clinical psychology at the Beth Israel Hospital in Boston, and worked with Jean Piaget in Geneva. Elkind was director of the Child Study Center at the University of Denver and taught at the University of Rochester. He is the author of *Children and Adolescents, A Sympathetic Understanding of the Child,* and *Child Development and Education.*

JOSEPH F. FAGAN, III is professor of psychology at Case Western Reserve University. He holds an M.A. and a Ph.D. from the University of Connecticut. His interests center on the study of infant visual perception and recognition memory, and he held a career development grant for his research in those areas. Dr. Fagan has written numerous scientific publications and contributed chapters to several books on infant development.

ELEANOR J. GIBSON is Susan Linn Sage professor of psychology at Cornell University. She graduated from Smith College and received the Ph.D. degree from Yale University. She is author of *Principles of Perceptual Learning and Development* and (with Harry Levin) *The Psychology of Reading.* Gibson holds honorary degrees from Smith College and Rutgers University and was awarded the G. Stanley Hall medal, the Wilbur Cross medal, and the Howard Crosby Warren medal. She is a member of the National Academy of Science, the National Academy of Education, and the American Academy of Arts and Sciences.

ADRIENNE E. HARRIS is associate professor in psychology at Rutgers University. She was educated at Radcliffe (B.A.) and the University of Michigan (M.A., Ph.D.), and taught at Glendon College, York University. With a group of psychologists influenced by the late Klaus Riegel, she has recently focused on the development of a dialectical psychology. Harris has written on parent-child interaction, cognitive development, and language competence and deafness.

JEROME KAGAN, professor of human development at Harvard University, received his Ph.D. from Yale University and was formerly chairman of the department of psychology at Fels Research Institute, Yellow Springs, Ohio. Professor Kagan's research has concerned long-term continuity and change in development, as well as cognitive and affective development during the first three years of life. He is the author or coauthor of *Birth to Maturity, Change and Continuity in Infancy, Understanding Children, Child Development and Personality,* and *Infancy: Its Place in Human Development.* He is a fellow of the American Academy of Arts and Sciences and consulting editor to several journals in the social sciences.

WILLIAM KESSEN has taught in the department of psychology at Yale University for 25 years; he is now Eugene Higgins professor of psychology and professor of pediatrics there. Kessen is the coauthor of *The Language of Psychology* and editor of *Childhood in China;* he has contributed a number of chapters and articles on perception and cognition in the human infant.

CLAIRE B. KOPP is associate professor in residence in the Graduate School of Education, University of California, Los Angeles. She holds a Ph.D. from Claremont Graduate School and studied previously at New York University and the University of Southern California. Dr. Kopp held a postdoctoral traineeship in the department of pediatrics/psychiatry at the Brain Research Institute, University of California, Los Angeles. Kopp has written extensively on several facets of infant development.

JEAN MATTER MANDLER is professor of psychology at the University of California, San Diego. She received her B.A. from Swarthmore College and her Ph.D. from Harvard University. Mandler has been associate editor of the *Psychological Review* and is currently on the editorial boards of *Child Development* and the *Journal of Experimental Psychology: General.* Mandler is interested in cognitive development, especially memory, perception, language, and Piagetian theory. She is coauthor of *Thinking: From Association to Gestalt* and has written extensively on the topics of memory for complex pictures and prose.

ROBERT B. McCALL is at the Boys Town Center for the Study of Youth Development. He received his doctorate at the University of Illinois and spent a postdoctoral year at Harvard. McCall taught at the University of North Carolina before becoming senior scientist and chief of the perceptual-cognitive development section at the Fels Research Institute. His scientific publications have centered on developmental transitions in mental performance — attention, memory, play and imitation in human infants, and longitudinal methodology, analysis, and statistics.

PAUL MUSSEN is professor of psychology and director of the Institute of Human Development at the University of California, Berkeley. His A.B. and M.A. degrees are from Stanford and his Ph.D. from Yale. He has been president of the Western Psychological Association and of Division 7 (Developmental Psychology) of the American Psychological Association and is currently a director of the Social Science Research Council. He is coauthor of *Child Development and Personality* and of *Roots of Caring, Sharing, and Helping.* He has been a Fulbright research fellow at the University of Florence and fellow at the Center for Advanced Study in Behavioral Sciences at Stanford.

KATHERINE NELSON is professor at the Graduate Center, City University of New York. She has a B.A. from Oberlin College and Ph.D. from UCLA. Nelson taught at Yale and was a visiting fellow at the University of Sussex and Oxford University. She is the author of monograph, *Structure and Strategy in Learning to Talk,* and has written extensively on early language as well as semantic and conceptual development.

HANUŠ PAPOUŠEK is professor of developmental psychobiology at the Max Planck Institute for Psychiatry in Munich. He was awarded an M.D. at the Masaryk's (now Purkinje's) University and a Sc.D. at the Charles University in Prague, Czechoslovakia. Papoušek was research pediatrician at the Research Institute for Mother and Child Care in Prague, a WHO Fellow, and visiting professor at the University of Denver, at Harvard University, and at the University of Munich. He is a founding member of the International Society for Developmental Psychobiology and of the International Organization for the Study of Human Development. Papoušek's research has focused on early postnatal development of learning and cognition, parent–infant interaction, and social communication.

HERBERT L. PICK, JR. is professor of child psychology at the University of Minnesota. He received both a B.A. and a Ph.D. from Cornell University and has previously taught at the University of Wisconsin. He has been a visiting professor at Makerere University, Uganda, and at Moscow State University, U.S.S.R. Professor Pick has served as Director of the Center for Research in Human Learning at Minnesota and as chairman of the Committee on Cognition of the Social Science Research Council. He is the author or coauthor of numerous articles and chapters on perception and perceptual development, which form his principal interests. He has edited two books, *Modes of Perceiving and Processing Information* and *Studies in Perception: Essays in Honor of J. J. Gibson.*

JOHN J. RIESER is assistant professor of psychology at Peabody College. He received his bachelor's degree at Harvard and his doctoral degree from the University of Minnesota. Rieser's research has focused on the mental representations children and adults have of spatial environments. He has investigated spatial representations in blind and sighted persons and has studied the ability of infants to use visual and gravitational information in coding the location of an object.

ARNOLD J. SAMEROFF is associate director of the Institute for the Study of Developmental Disabilities at the University of Illinois. Sameroff received a B.S. from the University of Michigan and a Ph.D. from Yale University, and he taught at the University of Rochester. He is the author of numerous articles and chapters on early development, and has studied learning in infancy and the developmental consequences of perinatal factors.

H. RUDOLPH SCHAFFER is professor of psychology at the University of Strathclyde, Scotland. His B.A. is from the University of London, and his

Ph.D. was awarded by the University of Glasgow. He has held professional appointments at the Tavistock Clinic, London, and at the Royal Hospital for Sick Children in Glasgow, and he has held Fellowships at the University of North Carolina and at the Van Leer Jerusalem Foundation. His research interests have centered mainly on the study of early social behavior, and the books he has written or edited are *The Growth of Sociability, The Origins of Human Social Relations, Mothering,* and *Studies in Mother–Infant Interaction.*

ALBERT YONAS is associate professor of child psychology at the University of Minnesota. He holds a bachelor's degree from the University of Michigan and a doctoral degree from Cornell University. Yonas is a consulting editor for *Developmental Psychology* and is the author or coauthor of numerous articles and several chapters on perceptual development. His primary research interests are the development of the perception of spatial layout and the development of sensitivity to pictorial information.

Author Index

Numbers in *italics* refer to pages on which the complete references are listed.

Subject Index

401